Approaching Literature

Literature and Gender

edited by Lizbeth Goodman

in association with The Open University

First published 1996
by Routledge in association with The Open University
11 New Fetter Lane, London EC4P 4EE

Simultaneously published in the USA and Canada
by Routledge
29 West 35th Street, New York, NY 10001

Reprinted 1996, 1998, 1999

Routledge is an imprint of the Taylor & Francis Group

British Library Cataloguing in Publication Data
A catalogue record for this book is available from the British Library

Library of Congress Cataloging in Publication Data
A catalog record for this book is available from the Library of Congress

ISBN 0–415–13573–7 (hbk)
ISBN 0–415–13574–5 (pbk)

Transferred to digital reprinting 2001

Printed in Great Britain by Antony Rowe Ltd, Eastbourne

Contents

Lizbeth Goodman is Lecturer in Literature at the Open University

Angus Calder is Consultant Author and former Staff Tutor at the Open University

Richard Allen is Staff Tutor and Senior Lecturer at the Open University

Preface

This book is one of a four-volume series, which has been designed to offer a range of different but current approaches to the study of literature. Each volume is free-standing and is designed as an introduction to a different aspect of literary study. This one focuses on the concept of gender as a concern relevant to the writing, reading and interpretation of literary texts, and especially those by women.

The book covers all three major literary genres: prose fiction, poetry and drama (including both play texts and performances), with reference to a wide range of themes. Among these are the conflict between 'femininity' and creativity in women's lives and writing; the construction of female characters by female and male authors of different historical periods; autobiography and fiction; the gendering of language and body language; cycles of influence between women writers; the importance of 'a room of one's own'; the theme of 'madness'; and the intersection of race, class and gender in the writing, reading and interpretation of literature. Most of the literature discussed in the book is printed in Part Two of this volume. There is a new anthology of poetry; most of it is by women, all is 'about' gender. Fiction includes a thriller by Louisa May Alcott, Virginia Woolf's short story 'The New Dress', Jamaica Kincaid's story 'Girl', Charlotte Perkins Gilman's 'The Yellow Wallpaper', Susan Glaspell's play *Trifles* and her story 'A Jury of her Peers'.

Literature and Gender has been designed to prepare readers for higher-level study, and to provide a solid understanding of the relevance and importance of gender issues. The text begins at a very accessible level and increases slightly in the level of sophistication chapter by chapter, refining the process of reading and learning throughout the book. Exercises in reading and studying literature with sample discussion are included in each chapter.

Thanks are due to Open University colleagues for contributions and feedback on the material in this book, and to the editorial, design and production teams. Particular thanks to Julie Dickens, Abigail Croydon, Janet Fennell, Nora Tomlinson, Stephen Regan, Jane de Gay, Mags Noble and Carole Brown, and to Professor Judie Newman, External Assessor.

This book is dedicated to the memory of Elizabeth Howe.

Lizbeth Goodman

Note: Many of the chapters in this book are co-authored by Lizbeth Goodman and one or more contributors. The sections and sub-sections written by contributors are marked with a separate byline; otherwise the material is written by Lizbeth Goodman.

Keynotes

... Indeed, I would venture to guess that Anon, who wrote so many poems without signing them, was often a woman.

Virginia Woolf, 1929

There I was trying to connect with all these writers who really never saw me. They were unable to see me, actually .... My experience is that it's when you're with your own people that you are most yourself; you have more of a context. So though I love the Brontës, and some of the white writers I read, still I knew that I had a tradition ... that could help me.

Alice Walker, 1986

An Obstacle

I was climbing up a mountain-path
With many things to do,
Important business of my own,
And other people's too,
When I ran against a Prejudice
That quite cut off the view.

My work was such as could not wait,
My path quite clearly showed,
My strength and time were limited,
I carried quite a load;
And there that hulking Prejudice
Sat all across the road.

So I spoke to him politely,
For he was huge and high,
And begged that he would move a bit
And let me travel by.
He smiled, but as for moving! –
He didn't even try.

And then I reasoned quietly
With that colossal mule:
My time was short – no other path –
The mountain winds were cool.
I argued like a Solomon;
He sat there like a fool.

Then I flew into a passion.
And I danced and howled and swore.
I pelted and belabored him
Till I was stiff and sore;
He got as mad as I did –
But he sat there as before.

And then I begged him on my knees;
I might be kneeling still
If so I hoped to move that mass
Of obdurate ill-will –
As well invite the monument
To vacate Bunker Hill!

So I sat before him helpless,
In an ecstasy of woe –
The mountain mists were rising fast,
The sun was sinking slow –
When a sudden inspiration came,
As sudden winds do blow.

I took my hat, I took my stick,
My load I settled fair,
I approached that awful incubus
With an absent-minded air –
And I walked directly through him,
As if he wasn't there!

Charlotte Perkins Gilman (1860–1935)
© The Feminist Press, 1992

Introduction: gender as an approach to literature

The title of this book has been carefully chosen to reflect its content, and its purpose as one of a series of books on 'Approaching Literature'. The word 'literature' has priority in the title for good reason. The emphasis in this book is on reading and analysing literature: the context and circumstances of its writing; the points of view of its authors; the processes of reading and of interpreting texts. The second term, 'gender', indicates the book's focus. Two central questions are raised throughout: What does awareness of gender contribute to a reading of literature? What does an understanding of literature say about gender in literature and society?

To consider these questions, we need to define some terms. The following definitions are challenged and qualified in this book, but they do provide useful handles.

Literature can be defined as a body of writing that aims to be creative. It includes poetry, prose fiction and drama, but usually excludes shopping lists, business letters and newspaper journalism, for instance.

'**Genre**' is a key term used to distinguish between distinct types of writing (or art, or thought). In this book, it refers to the three major forms of literature, or 'literary genres': poetry, prose fiction and drama (including play texts and performances).

So, 'literature' includes forms of writing which deliberately and creatively experiment with language in order to suggest images and ideas which engage the reader's imagination. The spacing of poetry on the page may suggest a shape; the rhyme and rhythm may create a mood. The narrators and characters of prose fiction (short stories, novellas and novels) allow readers to enter fictional worlds by identifying with other people, perspectives and ideas. The dialogue and stage directions of dramatic texts represent a three-dimensional story which readers can engage with and even 'perform'. All this work involves imagination and interpretation.

Imagination and interpretation are also central to the discussion of literature and gender in a more specific sense.

'**Gender**' refers to ways of seeing and representing people and situations based on sex difference. By contrast, 'sex' is a biological category: female or male. The term 'sexuality' refers to the realm of sexual experience and desire – sometimes it refers to a person's sexual orientation (as hetero-sexual, bisexual or homosexual). 'Gender' is a social or cultural category, influenced by stereotypes about 'female' and 'male' behaviour that exist in our attitudes and beliefs. Such beliefs are often said to be 'culturally produced' or 'constructed'.

So, when we refer to the study of literature and gender, we don't just mean literary analysis of texts with regard to the sex (female or male) or sexuality of authors, but the wider study of literary texts as they are written, read and interpreted within cultures, by women and men. We are all aware of some degree of cultural stereotyping about gender. For instance, many of us will be familiar with the Western tradition of designating colours to signify sex difference: 'pink for girls, blue for boys'. In providing visual symbols for sex difference, we allow for imaginative and interpretative associations attached to those colours: pink perhaps suggesting softness and 'girlishness' and blue suggesting 'boyishness'. While the designations 'female' and 'male' are sex categories, the imaginative ideas associated with these differences include a range of cultural and individualized ideas about gender. Preconceptions about gender might include the idea that 'women drivers' are in some way less able than 'drivers' (assumed to be male), or the notion that 'big boys don't cry'. Further examples might include giving boys bigger portions of food or giving boys trucks rather than dolls as gifts. In the world of work, there is the gendered division of labour, characterized by a striking male domination of high status, highly paid areas of work. So, gender can be read in sexual stereotypes and in power relations between individuals and groups. In the process of studying these phenomena, we engage with symbolic ideas attached to sex difference (colours, ideas, images) which involve our imaginations and interpretative skills. If we read with concern for identifying assumptions and stereotypes about gender, we learn about society as well as about literature.

This book views the study of literature as a process with a connection to you, the reader. Like the authors you will study, you too live in particular cultures, in particular places and periods, with ideas, prejudices and desires of your own. Your role as reader is active, and it is '**positioned**', or influenced, by a range of factors such as your gender, age, race and class. Just as the 'positions' of authors may influence their choice of subject-matter and styles of writing, your position as reader will affect your interpretation. So will your position as a reader of this textbook, as a student. This book acknowledges the collaborative and personalized nature of reading, and also encourages you to think critically about that process as you proceed.

In this book, we will read literature with '**gender on the agenda**'. This is a shorthand phrase for the process of reading with a concern for gender issues that affect the writing and reading of texts. For instance, it means paying attention to factors such as women's relative lack of access to higher education (particularly in previous generations), women's lower economic status, women's domestic responsibilities and the conflict between nurturing roles such as motherhood and domestic work (areas which have traditionally been undervalued) and other areas of creative work. Areas of activity which have traditionally been valued highly have also been seen – not coincidentally – primarily as 'men's work': for example, writing; thinking; making an impact in the artistic and critical domains. This book takes the view that reading with 'gender on the agenda' is a vital part of the reading and studying of literature and cultural representations.

Reading with 'gender on the agenda' offers one way of focusing on literary texts. It encourages us to see aspects of the texts and the contexts of their creation and reception which we might not otherwise notice. You may find it difficult to 'read gender' at first. It might seem awkward, or seem to obscure the other aspects of the text. But once you get used to paying attention to gender in literature, it's a bit like wearing a new pair of glasses: suddenly you notice all kinds of things you hadn't noticed before. This enhanced vision does not stop you seeing all you previously saw, but rather enlarges your scope of vision and intensifies and enriches the experience of seeing or reading.

While we'll be paying particular attention to your role as reader of this book, we won't treat the process of 'reading gender' like a personality test or measure of the 'political correctness' of you, the reader, or of the author of any text. Reading literature involves interpretation, but we are concerned with texts and their contexts, not with the reader's personality or politics in their own right. We are interested in the gender dynamics to be gleaned from a study of texts in context.

Firing the canon

The literary '**canon**' is the body of writings generally recognized as 'great' by some 'authority'. For instance, any university reading list will tend to include a body of work deemed 'great' or 'classic' or important enough to teach from generation to generation. From Greek drama to Chaucer, Shakespeare to the Realist novel to Romantic writing, different bodies of literature have been valued according to criteria of 'aesthetic worth', and according to the tastes and values of individuals in positions of authority within academic institutions. The process of choosing 'great texts' for inclusion in the literary canon involves a set of assumptions about what makes literature great. For Plato, there was one measure, for Shakespeare, another. Most literature textbooks until very recently focused primarily or exclusively on men's writing. In so doing, men's writing (and nearly always white, middle-class men's writing in English) was positioned as 'the norm', presented as if it were Literature, with a capital 'L', somehow representative of all 'great writing'. By not considering gender, such textbooks made and conveyed the assumption that the male is somehow generic or neutral, an assumption shown to be false by a focus on women's writing.

This book challenges the traditional notion of the 'canon' by considering a range of texts, mostly by women. We take the view that gender is an important area of study, and one which adds to the study of literature by offering a number of ways of evaluating 'literary worth'. For instance, a focus on gender may lead to examination of connections between literature and life, fiction and (auto)biography, characters and 'real people'. It may lead to the study of literature written by, as well as about, women. When we shift focus to these aspects of literature, we begin to choose new texts for inclusion in a possible alternative canon: perhaps including Aphra Behn alongside Shakespeare, Caryl Churchill alongside Ibsen, Alice Walker alongside William Faulkner.

In recent years, academic institutions have witnessed just this shift, which may be referred to as a 'firing of the canon': a re-evaluation of the standards by which authors and texts have been singled out and 'canonized', followed by an active search for other authors and texts for inclusion. This search may lead to previously 'hidden' texts by women, people of colour and working-class writers, and by authors working in many languages. Reading and studying literature today is, therefore, a very rich and multi-layered enterprise. It involves imagination and interpretation in the process of judging the merit of literature on artistic and also social grounds, recognizing the subjective nature of any value judgement. Today, we may find value in some stories, poems and plays which don't fit any of the previously agreed guidelines for canonization. So it should be: each generation re-evaluates its position in relation to history and the ideas of previous generations.

Like all books, this book includes some authors and texts to the exclusion of others, offering its own 'canon' of sorts. The texts discussed in these pages are all accessible to you. They are either included in this volume, or are widely available in inexpensive paperback editions and libraries. You can and should read the literature first, and then read the teaching material of this book alongside it, as a guide and companion to your reading. The book includes exercises which direct your attention to particular texts, ideas and ways of reading, as you go along. But of course, it is true that the choice of texts included in this book, like any choice of 'set texts', has involved a process of valuing and decision making – one influenced by the advancements of what has been called 'the feminist literary critical revolution'.

Feminist literary critics have been among the main opponents of the traditional male-dominated canon. Let's define our terms.

Feminism is a politics: a recognition of the historical and cultural subordination of women (the only world-wide majority to be treated as a minority), and a resolve to do something about it. Feminist thought has developed since the dramatic interventions of the Suffrage Era, when those who believed in fighting for women's rights rallied around one central cause, women's right to vote. 'Votes for women' is a phrase designating a social cause; it is also the title of a play by Elizabeth Robins, performed in England in 1907. The battle for the vote was fought in all manner of public spaces, in the theatre, the streets and political platforms. The Suffragists are often referred to as the 'first wave' of modern feminism; the 'second wave' is generally held to have begun in the late 1960s, when political upheaval in England, Europe and America began to focus particularly on women's rights.

Much has been written about the modern movement for 'Women's Liberation', about the many different schools of feminism and the divisions and allegiances between them. Feminism has always incorporated a concern for ideas and 'consciousness raising', while also acting in the public sphere to improve the situation of women's lives. In the field of literature, feminist thought has been very influential; it has pointed out the historical 'silences' of women authors not included in the 'canon'; it has 'fired the canon' in order to shake up static views about women's creative work and domestic roles, enabling women's literature to be published, read and assessed by contemporary scholars and students. It has helped to reform the gendering of social life and has influenced popular culture to the extent that Women's Studies and the associated field of Gender Studies are now accepted areas of study and research at many levels. Indeed, any general academic course on literature which did not deal at an integral level with issues of gender would now seem outdated and unbalanced.

Here, it is useful to note the distinction between Women's Studies and Gender Studies. Courses in **Women's Studies** are concerned with the representation, rights and status of women. Courses in **Gender Studies** are concerned with the representation, rights and status of women and men. This book deals with gender, but focuses primarily on women. This is partly because Gender Studies have developed in the wake of Women's Studies, and partly because readers and students of literature are overwhelmingly female, even though the position of women authors has traditionally been marginal.

There are now many books on the market about feminist literary criticism and feminist literature. (Some of these are excellent and are indeed recommended as further readings at the end of this book.) The two phrases need unpacking.

Feminist literary criticism is an academic approach to the study of literature which applies feminist thought to the analysis of literary texts and the contexts of their production and reception. It has developed in recent years into a fascinating and highly specialized field with a language, set of theories and a vocabulary all its own. Early 'European' feminist theoretical writings began with the work of Simone de Beauvoir, while 'Anglo-American' writing is often associated with Virginia Woolf.

Virginia Woolf in 1932. Hulton Deutsch Collection.

Simone de Beauvoir in 1947. Hulton Deutsch Collection.

Feminist Literature is written by contemporary women within the context of 'second wave' or even 'third wave' (that is, current) contexts of feminist awareness. 'Feminist authors' have a political agenda in the writing of their work. So, labelling literature as 'feminist' requires some knowledge of the author's *intentions*. The distinction between literature that can be read and interpreted as feminist, and literature that is intended by its authors to be feminist, is a thorny issue, and one that is addressed later in this book. Literature may have a feminist impact even if its authors do not identify themselves as feminist. For instance, some women's literature conveys feminist ideas and affects readers in a 'consciousness-raising' style. It is also important to remember that virtually all authors writing today have been influenced to some degree by the 'feminist literary critical revolution', at least to the extent that the idea of feminism is now recognized as a significant influence in our culture. Most of this book does not deal with 'feminist literature' as such. It is concerned with literature that represents gender in particular ways: it has 'gender on the agenda'.

Approaching this book: keynotes and concerns

Virginia Woolf's 'keynote' to this book reminds us that many women wrote in previous generations, but that social factors to do with gender kept many writers 'anonymous', hidden, silenced or otherwise excluded from the 'canon'. Alice Walker's 'keynote' quotation reminds us that race is also a factor keeping women writers isolated, unrecognized and even – to borrow and expand on her metaphor – invisible. When focus is shifted from the centre (the 'canon') to the margins (that which has traditionally been excluded from the 'canon' or left unattributed), a very different picture of 'what literature is' begins to form. So, although this book is concerned with literature and gender, and not exclusively with women's writing, we must consider the social and cultural conditions of writing, which are affected in important ways by gender, race and class. Here, the third and last 'keynote' of this book, the poem 'An Obstacle', by Charlotte Perkins Gilman, can be read as a poem about the 'obstacles' of gender stereotypes and prejudices which blocked the progress of women writers for so long.

These keynotes are 'tasters' of the many and varied arguments put by women writers over the years. Indeed, a great deal has been written about the obstacles faced by women authors in previous generations. Today women writers – at least in the West – have a much more constructive context in which to work; not only is writing an 'acceptable' occupation for women, but it has now been widely recognized that women contribute a great deal to the body of literature and to the body of literary criticism. When women write from a contemporary Western perspective, as do authors such as Alice Walker and Jamaica Kincaid, they work within a cultural context liberated to some extent by feminist approaches to literature. Then, of course, the author's individual position within her culture comes into play. Gender becomes visible as a factor in the writing, reading and interpreting of literature, as do factors such as race and class.

The literary texts chosen for study have been selected with two primary considerations in mind: a concern to keep the amount of reading to a reasonable level (so that your study will be challenging but not unmanageable), and a desire to provide an original and engaging range of literary styles and pieces. A combination of 'classics' or canonical works are discussed alongside a range of lesser-known works. This list includes texts which deal with race, class, gender and sexuality. They are by black and white authors, most of them women, most of them British and American. The inclusion of a body of nineteenth-century literature is meant to be

Jamaica Kincaid. Reproduced by
courtesy of Virago Press.

provocative, for it is more common to discuss gender with regard to contemporary texts, written in the context of contemporary debates about feminism and representation. But we have used a selection of nineteenth- and twentieth-century texts to show how gender is relevant in different periods, and need not be confined to the analysis of modern women's writing. This range of work from different periods allows us to illustrate the importance of feminist concerns in the contemporary work we do include: for instance, in a selection of contemporary poetry, in the novel *The Color Purple* and in Caryl Churchill's play *Top Girls*.

Each of the eight chapters takes a distinct approach, covering all three major genres. Some chapters include extracts from key critical essays in the field, in order to provide practice in engaging with literary criticism and applying it to the reading of literature.

While only one chapter has been designed specifically to deal with a 'thematic' approach to literature ('women and madness'), it might be said that approaching literature through gender is itself a thematic approach. It is certainly true that reading literature with 'gender on the agenda' brings certain aspects of literary texts to the fore. For instance, women authors tend to be included, women characters take on special significance and relationships between women and men become central to the process of understanding other relationships within texts. In addition, a few themes surface repeatedly: motherhood; domestic responsibility; conflicts in women's lives; power relationships between the sexes (including those between women and other women, men and other men); and conflicts between private and public roles and responsibilities. Domestic fiction is a category or 'subgenre' covered throughout this book, first with reference to traditional representations of women's roles in the home, and then with reference to the feminist writing which challenged and continues to challenge such traditions. A concern for appearance, dictated by norms of 'feminine attire' and internalized so that it affects women's ways of seeing themselves, is a theme which recurs with compelling frequency.

You can expect these and other themes to develop and overlap in the discussion of literature and gender. Patterns will emerge. Pieces will fall into place, though the overall 'picture' will look different to each of you.

Lizbeth Goodman

Part One

Literature and gender

by Lizbeth Goodman with Alison Smith

Jumping to conclusions: authors, readers and texts

Approaching literature through gender

In the Introduction, we argued that reading 'with gender on the agenda' involves you, the reader, in an active process of imagination and interpretation. We've also alerted you to the need to look beyond a text to consider its context and its relevance to gender issues in society as well as in literature. Let's start by reading and interpreting a literary text which you've already encountered in the 'keywords' to this book: Charlotte Perkins Gilman's poem, 'An Obstacle'.

Please read 'An Obstacle' once, and then again. Consider the following questions: **Is the narrator (speaking voice) male or female? What is the 'Prejudice' which the narrator describes?**

D i s c u s s i o n

The narrator of the poem seems to be female. In fact, it would be fair to say that the poem not only provides clues about the narrator's sex, but also that the narrator recognizes a gendered dimension to her experience of the world: she comments on herself in relation to the 'Prejudice', gendered male, which blocks her path. The poem is written in the first person voice, and the narrator is referred to as 'I'. This stylistic technique creates the impression of a bond between the narrator and the author of the poem. While such a bond may not exist, this poem implies that the narrator (and perhaps also the author) has experienced a lack of co-operation and support from the social world, characterized by 'Prejudice'. The poem may, in fact, be read as a general comment on the state of gender relations in the social world: women striving to move ahead, patriarchal attitudes standing in the way. ■

Of course, this interpretation of the poem may differ from yours, partly because you have not been provided with contextual clues to help you to decipher the text. The choice of this poem as one of the book's 'keynotes' signals a likelihood that it is a text 'to do with gender'. In fact, the poem is appropriate to this book in a number of ways. It is little known, certainly not 'canonical' in any sense. It is written by a woman whose work was respected in its day and has recently once again come to public attention, largely due to the efforts of feminist scholars. It presents as its central metaphor 'Prejudice': one of the biggest problems facing women writers in any period, and indeed facing all writers who do not conform to some 'norm' of acceptability or importance. (The same might also apply to a black writer such as Jamaica Kincaid, or a gay male writer such as Oscar Wilde.) The poem introduces many of the key themes of this book, and

1

does so in concise and eloquent form. The poem is a literary text, rather than a 'literary critical' text, yet it has a great deal to contribute to a critical discussion of literature and gender.

You may find it difficult to say much more about the poem out of context, without knowing something about Gilman, her life and the larger significance which the poem may have had to her, in her time and culture. Gilman was born in Connecticut, USA, in 1860. Largely self-educated, she became a novelist, poet, lecturer, economist, feminist and social reformer. She produced fiction and essays for many years, supporting herself as a writer when it was rare for women to do so.

Does knowing these 'facts' about Gilman affect your reading of the poem? For instance, does the concept of an obstacle which can't be moved take on a new significance?

Discussion

Of course, knowing something about an author adds a new meaning to the reading of any text. You may have found the poem less humorous, perhaps reading a certain note of urgency in the sardonic account of the intransigence of 'Prejudice'. Alternatively, you may have considered the poem more triumphant: an account of an author's recognition of the joy of moving beyond an obstacle, whether personal or general. Either reading, or a combination of both, would be valid. The more you learn about Gilman, the more meaning the poem may take on for you, even if you also found it engaging and thought-inspiring on your first reading. Knowledge of the author is not essential to appreciation of a text, though some texts benefit from contextual readings – especially those which contain some element of autobiography. (We will discuss Gilman's life and fiction in much more detail in Chapter Four.)

Later, we'll consider a range of texts, some written as semi-autobiographical accounts, and some entirely fictional. What is important here is the idea that any text, even an accessible poem such as this one, takes on a variety of different meanings depending on the knowledge brought to bear on it: the author's context, the reader's imagination and interpretation, and the status of the text itself (authors, readers, texts). ■

Gender can be seen as a pattern constructed in society, which in turn influences our views of ourselves. When we write and read, we do so as gendered individuals, not just as women and men, but as people who have been taught that there are values assigned to sex, though we may no longer believe that male = power, authority, and female = passivity, compromise. As the Women's Liberation Movement has helped us all to 'raise consciousness' about the limitations of such ways of seeing gender, so too has the growth of feminist literary criticism helped us to study gender as it is represented in literature and other art forms.

Literature is one of the many forms of cultural representation (like the visual arts, photography, television, film, advertising) in which gender relations are routinely depicted. Literary texts can both reinforce gender stereotypes and create newer, more liberating representations of gender. For instance, nineteenth-century romantic novels often depicted the social need for women to behave in a 'ladylike' manner to win a husband in an era when women were discouraged and even prevented from working outside the home to support themselves. Some novels (though not everyone would want to call them 'literature') such as Mills and Boon or Harlequin romances, still perpetuate such values today. Other forms of literature offer more liberating representations of gender relations; for example, in late nineteenth-century theatre the new female type known as the 'New Woman' was created (to be discussed in Chapter Seven), and much contemporary writing has an emphasis on re-viewing women's roles in life and literature.

Our brief reading of the poem 'An Obstacle' revealed that we may take a variety of meanings from a text. The poem stands on its own, and can also be read with reference to the poet's culture, generation, personal life and gender. Reading with gender on the agenda can effect what is known as a 'Gestalt Shift'. Look at Figure 1. **What do you see in diagram A? In diagram B? Does C look more like A or B? If you cover A and B with your hands, can you see them both at once in C?**

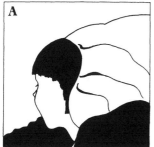 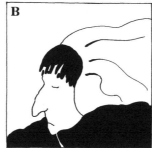 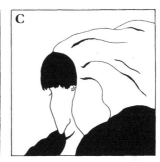

Figure 1   'Gestalt shift', three diagrams. Reproduced from John Morgan and Peter Welton, *See What I Mean? An Introduction to Visual Communication* (1986), London, E. Arnold, p.63.

Discussion

In the diagrams of Figure 1, you may at first see one image, and then another. Studies show that most people who first look at Diagram A report that C shows a young woman, while those who first look at B recognize an old woman. Whichever image you looked at first, you could probably eventually see the other as well, though you may need it pointed out to you before it takes shape in your mind's eye. This process of changing perspective, whereby deliberately ignoring some lines and details allows others to come into finer focus, is a bit like 'reading gender' in literature. Varying patterns of meaning will emerge when different issues are in focus. Here's the crucial difference, though: with the diagrams, once both images have been identified for you, you will only be able to focus on one or another at any one point in time. But reading literature allows you to see, or focus on, different images or views or ways of reading at once. ■

In German, the word *Gestalt* means 'pattern'; in English, the term is most often used in psychology, but it is particularly useful as an analogue to the study of literature and gender. A 'gestalt' view of literature and gender would analyse the patterns involved in reading and interpreting literature. We'll take the view that reading with concern for gender can also be seen as one part of the whole process or pattern of studying literature.

You can learn to appreciate the relevance of gender in the writing, reading and interpretation of texts, and also to continue to enjoy them for other reasons: for the skill of the writer, the appeal to your imagination which a story may make, the beauty of language, or the relevance of the text to various aspects of your life. None of these vital aspects of reading literature need be obscured by also learning to pay attention to gender.

The next section of this chapter is an extended exercise about gender and authorship: in it your role as reader is shown to be crucial in the relationship between author, reader and text.

Imagine you walk into a book shop or a library to choose some fiction or poetry or drama to read. You pick up a book, and the first thing you find is that the covers have been taken off it; you look around and see that the place is full of books with no covers, that none of the usual contextual information is available to you: who wrote these works, when they were written or what reviewers said about them. You don't even have that vital piece of information we all take for granted when we pick up a book – the fact of whether the writer is female or male. It's an unlikely premise, but it's the premise of the exercise which follows.

The preconception game

by Alison Smith

Would you be able to tell, just by examining the first few lines of an anonymous novel or poem or play, whether the author is female or male? How important is such information? Playing the game below should help you make your mind up about these questions. Before playing, it may help to consider two schools of thought on this issue.

First: in the first decades of this century Virginia Woolf began the early articulation of a debate which still excites and troubles critics, including the French feminist theorists Simone de Beauvoir and (later) Hélène Cixous, Luce Irigaray, Julia Kristeva and others. Woolf was weighing up whether it was possible to define a difference between men's writing and women's, since everybody, but women especially, faced the difficulty of trying to 'free their own consciousness as they wrote from the tyranny of what was expected from their sex' and also the ultimate 'tyranny of sex itself' (Woolf, 'Women Novelists', in Bowlby, *A Woman's Essays*, 1992, pp.11–14). She felt that there might exist a fundamental form or structure which could be called 'feminine'. Writing of her contemporary Dorothy Richardson's work in 1923, Woolf decided that Richardson had found:

> a sentence which we might call the psychological sentence of the
> feminine gender ... of a more elastic fibre than the old, capable of
> stretching to the extreme, of suspending the frailest particles, of
> enveloping the vaguest shapes. ... It is a woman's sentence, but only

4

in the sense that it is used to describe a woman's mind by a writer who is neither proud nor afraid of anything that she may discover in the psychology of her sex.

(Woolf, *Times Literary Supplement*, 1923)

There is a suggestion here that the psychology of the sex will influence the form and style of the work when freely allowed to do so. If Woolf's 'feminine sentence' exists, then perhaps its obverse can be found in the short, sharp style of a writer such as Ernest Hemingway. In his 'classics' (for example, *The Old Man and the Sea*, 1952 and *The Sun Also Rises*, 1926), men are active and definitively 'masculine' symbols of virility and 'humanity'. But *are* these sorts of attributes essentially 'feminine' or 'masculine'? And do such readings help us to appreciate a text?

Second: contrast Woolf's views with the opposing school of thought typified by the pragmatic approach of Scottish critic Isobel Murray, who introduced a 1980s collection of fiction by Scottish women with the following advice: 'Good fiction need not betray its author's sex' (Murray, *Original Prints*, 1985, p.5).

Armed with these thoughts, be prepared to discover, recognize and exercise your preconceptions about gender. The eight extracts which follow are all by well-known writers. They've been chosen randomly, all from twentieth-century texts. Nearly all the extracts are from the very beginning of the text in question. Each of the texts has had its 'cover removed'; all you have to go on are the words on the page. See if you can guess which of the authors is female, which male. You can play this game by yourself, noting the reasons why you think the passage is written by a woman or a man; it's also useful to play it with another or others to see what comes up in discussion. **Now read the extracts.**

EXTRACT ONE

Though I haven't ever been on the screen I was brought up in pictures. Rudolph Valentino came to my fifth birthday – or so I was told. I put this down only to indicate that even before the age of reason I was in a position to watch the wheels go round.

I was going to write my memoirs once, *The Producer's Daughter*, but at eighteen you never quite get around to anything like that. It's just as well – it would have been as flat as an old column of Lolly Parsons'. My father was in the picture business as another man might be in cotton or steel, and I took it tranquilly. At the worst I accepted Hollywood with the resignation of a ghost assigned to a haunted house. I knew what you were supposed to think about it but I was obstinately unhorrified.

This is easy to say, but harder to make people understand. When I was at Bennington some of the English teachers who pretended an indifference to Hollywood or its products, really *hated* it. Hated it way down deep as a threat to their existence. Even before that, when I was in a convent, a sweet little nun asked me to get her a script of a screen play so she could 'teach her class about movie writing' as she had taught them about the essay and the short story. I got the script for her, and I suppose she puzzled over it and puzzled over it, but it was never mentioned in class, and she gave it back to me with an air of offended surprise and not a single comment. That's what I half expect to happen to this story.

EXTRACT TWO

In the beginning there was a river. The river became a road and the road branched out to the whole world. And because the road was once a river it was always hungry.

In that land of beginnings spirits mingled with the unborn. We could assume numerous forms. Many of us were birds. We knew no boundaries. There was much feasting, playing and sorrowing. We feasted much because of the beautiful terrors of eternity. We played much because we were free. And we sorrowed much because there were always those amongst us who had just returned from the world of the Living. They had returned inconsolable for all the love they had left behind, all the suffering they hadn't redeemed, all that they hadn't understood, and for all that they had barely begun to learn before they were drawn back to the land or origins.

There was not one amongst us who looked forward to being born. We disliked the rigours of existence, the unfulfilled longings, the enshrined injustices of the world, the labyrinths of love, the ignorance of parents, the fact of dying, and the amazing indifference of the Living in the midst of the simple beauties of the universe. We feared the heartlessness of human beings, all of whom are born blind, few of whom ever learn to see.

EXTRACT THREE

The waitresses are basking in the sun like a herd of skinned seals, their pinky-brown bodies shining with oil. They have their bathing suits on because it's the afternoon. In the early dawn and the dusk they sometimes go skinny-dipping, which makes this itchy crouching in the mosquito-infested bushes across from their small private dock a great deal more worthwhile.

Donny has the binoculars, which are not his own but Monty's. Monty's dad gave them to him for bird-watching but Monty isn't interested in birds. He's found a better use for the binoculars: he rents them out to the other boys, five minutes maximum, a nickel a look or else a chocolate bar from the tuck shop, though he prefers the money. He doesn't eat the chocolate bars; he resells them, black market, for twice their original price; but the total supply on the island is limited, so he can get away with it.

Donny has already seen everything worth seeing, but he lingers on with the binoculars anyway, despite the hoarse whispers and the proddings from those next in line. He wants to get his money's worth.

'Would you look at that,' he says, in what he hopes is a tantalizing voice. 'Slobber, slobber.' There's a stick poking into his stomach, right on a fresh mosquito bite, but he can't move it without taking one hand off the binoculars. He knows about flank attacks.

'Lessee,' says Ritchie, tugging at his elbow.

EXTRACT FOUR

Lou Witt had had her own way so long, that by the age of twenty-five she didn't know where she was. Having one's own way landed one completely at sea.

To be sure for a while she had failed in her grand love affair with Rico. And then she had had something really to despair about. But even that had worked out as she wanted. Rico had come back to her, and was dutifully married to her. And now, when she was twenty-five and he was three months older, they were a charming married couple. He flirted with other women still, to be sure. He wouldn't be the handsome Rico if he didn't. But she had 'got' him. Oh yes! You had only to see the uneasy backward glance at her, from his big blue eyes: just like a horse that is edging away from its master: to know how completely he was mastered.

She, with her odd little *museau*, not exactly pretty, but very attractive; and her quaint air of playing at being well-bred, in a sort of charade game; and her queer familiarity with foreign cities and foreign languages; and the lurking sense of being an outsider everywhere, like a sort of gypsy, who is at home anywhere and nowhere: all this made up her charm and her failure. She didn't quite belong.

EXTRACT FIVE

The black bull bellowed before the sea.
The sea, till that day orderly,
Hove up against Bendylaw.

The queen in the mulberry arbour stared
Stiff as a queen on a playing card.
The king fingered his beard.

A blue sea, four horny full-feet,
A bull-snouted sea that wouldn't stay put,
Bucked at the garden gate.

Along box-lined walks in the florid sun
Towards the rowdy bellow and back again
The lords and ladies ran.

The great bronze gate began to crack,
The sea broke in at every crack,
Pellmell, blueblack.

The bull surged up, the bull surged down,
Not to be stayed by a daisy Chain
Nor by any learned man.

O the king's tidy acre is under the sea,
And the royal rose in the bull's belly,
And the bull is on the king's highway.

EXTRACT SIX

Strings in the earth and air,
Make music sweet:
Strings by the river where
The willows meet.

There's music along the river
For Love wanders there,
Pale flowers on his mantle,
Dark leaves on his hair.

All softly playing
With head to the music bent,
And fingers straying
Upon an instrument.

EXTRACT SEVEN

ACT ONE
Scene One

Robert's bedroom. The curtain goes up on almost complete darkness. Then a door opens at the back and a dim and indirect light is thrown from the corridor. MARION, in her late thirties, brisk, dark-haired, wearing a business suit, stands a moment, nervous, awed, in the doorway. She moves into the room which you can just detect is dominated by a large double bed, in which a man is lying covered with a sheet reaching up over his face. MARION stops a moment by the bed, looking down. She then turns to go back towards the door.

ISOBEL Marion?

(MARION *lets out a scream, not having realized that* ISOBEL *was sitting in a chair at the end of the bed.*)

MARION My God!

ISOBEL I'm sorry.

MARION You startled me.

ISOBEL Don't turn the main light on.

(MARION *goes to the bed and turns on a small bedside lamp.*)

I needed some peace.

(ISOBEL *is younger than* MARION *and blonder. She is in her early thirties, and casually dressed in a shirt and blue jeans. She is sitting at the end of the bed, facing us, not moving. The room is seen now to be panelled, gloomy, dark, old-fashioned. It is absolutely tidy, hairbrushes in place, the body quite still beneath the shroud.*)

I decided this would be the only place. For some quiet. There's so much screaming downstairs.

(MARION *moves gingerly towards the bed. She looks a moment.*)

MARION So you were with him?

ISOBEL There's actually a moment when you see the spirit depart from the body. I've always been told about it. And it's true. (*She is very quiet and still.*) Like a bird.

(MARION *looks across, nervous.*)

MARION Did he ...?

ISOBEL What?

MARION No, I wondered ... who dressed him?

ISOBEL Dressed him?

MARION Yes. Is he in a suit?

ISOBEL I did it. And there was a nurse.

EXTRACT EIGHT

Scene One

A restaurant. JENNIFER *and* RON, *and* TREVOR *and* ROWENA *are dancing.* YVONNE *sits at the table. Male monologue in three parts: all played by the actor who plays* CLIVE.
The sound of Concord landing. The dancers freeze. Light on the BARON.

When I was at university, my one aim in life was to go into business and get rich quick. I was extremely ambitious and not about to wait around for middle-aged spread to set in before I made it. My enterprise, enthusiasm and hard work paid off. In the last few years the tax man has gleaned over two million pounds from me. I have always kept on the right side of the law and when I was first called a purveyor of filth, it upset my mother a lot, but ours is a perfectly normal profession run by ordinary nice people, not gangsters or kinky dwarfs in soiled raincoats. That is a ludicrous myth perpetuated by the media.

We do sometimes lose stock in police raids, but we allow for the costs when building our stocks so, sadly, the consumer ends up paying more than he should.

Profit margins are high. Our trade makes more money than the film and record business put together. It will be the growth industry of the eighties. Just as betting shops were in the sixties and casinos in the seventies. I sincerely believe, had it not been for the present repressive climate, I'd have ceived the Queen's Award for Industry long ago. My mother? Well, she soon stopped crying when I brought her a luxury house in the country.

D i s c u s s i o n

Playing the preconception game can be useful if only to reveal to us our own preconceptions of how we think gender is constructed. But it's also important that we decide how much such contextualizing is necessary when we want to talk about the creation of fiction, poetry and drama. Will it change our understanding of Extract Five if the controlling hand of the writer is male rather than female, or vice versa? Will it alter the notion of voyeurism explored in Extract Three if the writer is female rather than male? Would Extract Six be a different poem altogether if it were written by a woman rather than a man? Does it matter that, in the real world where books have covers, we are usually able to consider works in the context of which gender created them? And how important is it to do so? The game ends on these questions. (The extracts are identified at the end of this chapter.) ∎

As you read these extracts, a number of factors might have influenced your view on the question of each author's gender. You might have thought, for instance, that the first extract was written by a woman, because the narrator of the extract seems to be female (judging by the reference to the narrator's memoirs, which were to have been called *The Producer's Daughter*: a gendered title). Or, you might have guessed that Extract Five was written by a man, as the subject-matter is stereotypically 'masculine', while Extract Six seems to be 'feminine' in some almost indefinable way. For instance, the subject of the poem – love and music – and the lyrical, soft language might be said to render it in some way feminine. Perhaps this suggestion recalls Woolf's idea of a 'feminine sentence' – though we have not yet defined what might distinguish such a sentence. All these guesses would have been wrong. We may have been led astray by the use of gendered pronouns and gendered narrators, making us assume, for instance, that an author is female because a character or narrator is female. But of course, women create male characters and men create female characters. Indeed, many of our preconceptions about gender are misplaced, partly because gender stereotypes are simplistic, or not sophisticated enough to account for differences in style within the work of any one writer, and partly because it is difficult to get a sense of a whole text from one short extract. So, when you checked the list of authors and sources against your own guesses, you probably found yourself 'wrong' on several counts.

Most readers guess the author's gender correctly in less than two of the eight extracts.[1] Perhaps the problem with guessing gender is complicated by the complexity of 'gender' itself. To decide the sex of the author, you need to take into account factors such as the relationship of the narrative voice to the characters, the use of language and the subject-matter. No wonder the game is so difficult to 'win'; there is no winning. But it's a fascinating game to play for what it reveals about our ways of 'reading gender'.

This game was designed to make you think about gender stereotypes and preconceptions, rather than to analyse these specific texts. The texts were chosen by Alison Smith, more or less at random, by scanning her bookshelves and choosing a selection by women and men to cover all three main literary genres. This rather arbitrary book search was a deliberate strategy, adopted in order to show that all texts have inscribed messages about gender. (Of course, Alison Smith, a fiction writer, poet and playwright as well as an academic, might have access to a range of texts which many of us wouldn't have to hand). The game shows that we do have certain preconceptions about gender, and that gender does matter in reading literature, at least in so far as it influences our expectations about authorship, which indirectly influences our perception and interpretation of texts. It also illustrates that our expectations about gender are not always supported by or supportable in our reading of literary texts, nor our views about authors and readers. A range of factors come into play in the reading of any text 'with gender on the agenda'. We may assume an author's gender based on our own individual preconceptions, formed quite unconsciously by our backgrounds, ages and experiences of reading in other contexts. We may each have a whole range of preconceptions of which we have mentioned only a few. All of these factors come into play when we try to determine the gender of an author by extrapolating from a text, out of context. Similarly, we run into problems when we try to guess other aspects of an author's position. Factors such as race, class, age, nationality, sexuality, ethnicity and language will all influence the way any text is written, possibly what is written about and certainly the way the text is read and interpreted. The preconception game does not offer any one way of thinking about 'literature and gender', but rather demonstrates just how complex and fascinating a subject it is.

Studying literature and gender

Now, let's look briefly at some examples of the representation of gender in literary texts which we may have read or heard of, and see if we can trace any patterns, themes or ideas which may help us to get a handle on literature and gender.

Gender and characterization: finding patterns

In children's fiction, characters are gendered, but gender is not often considered as a relevant factor. Children's fiction is not only found in books, but also in the media. In fact, many of us are most familiar with children's fiction in cartoons and films.

In children's cartoons on television, studies have found that, on average, the ratio of female to male characters is uniformly low. If we analyse the ratio of active, assertive, intelligent and interesting characters, as compared with secondary 'support' characters (nagging wives, passive heroines waiting to be rescued by active heroes, evil witches) the findings in favour of females are even less encouraging. The evidence suggests that representations of gender as reflected in images from television have an impact on children's perceptions of themselves and their potential roles in 'real life'. A survey conducted on the gendered images projected in children's cartoons showed that the proportion of male characters to female was overwhelming – an average of 4:1 in the popular cartoon *Fangface*, for instance (K. Durkin, *Television, Sex Roles and Children*, 1985) – and that the more active characters tended to be male. This tendency means, in practical terms, that girls *and* boys have fewer strong female characters as role models. This unbalanced representation of gender roles forms a base for making assumptions and forming preconceptions and prejudices which filter over into lived experience.

In their study 'Television and the mind of the child', Bob Hodge and David Tripp argue that 'the media's construction of reality is skewed in a number of specific ways, amongst which the dimensions of gender and class are particularly obvious' (*Children and Television*, 1986, p.93). They support their survey with a number of empirical studies and charts like the one below, which shows, by sex, which characters children identified with, or wanted to identify with, in children's cartoons:

Sex of significant TV characters by sex (percentages)

	Male Figures	Female Figures	Indeterminate
Boys	87	6	7
Girls	17	75	8

While children will tend to look for same-sex role models, the chart shows that this set of children had to choose from a quite disproportionate number of male characters to female ones. It may, therefore, be surprising that the girls still tended to identify with female characters, preferring active characters of their own sex when they were available, as boys did. But the girls had to try much harder to find female role models. ■

The search for role models is a real conundrum for children, and it gets more complicated for girls if we consider a range of representations of domesticity in popular cultural (in this case, film and ballet and pantomime) versions of 'children's classics'. There is space here only to discuss a few sample stories in brief. But let's start by 'reading' a relevant image (a picture paints a thousand words).

Look at Figure 2. Describe the image. What is depicted? Does the image have a gender?

Figure 2   Dorothy wearing the red shoes, from the Wizard of Oz, 1939, M.G.M., courtesy of the Kobal collection.

D i s c u s s i o n

The image shows a pair of shoes, which the caption tells us are red. They are clearly women's shoes, and in that sense the image has a gender. The image also evokes a certain sense of sexuality, both in the colour red and the design of these mid-heeled pumps. ■

These are not just any red shoes, but the Ruby Slippers from *The Wizard of Oz*. If you haven't read the story, you have probably heard of it, or seen the MGM film version or one of the many cartoon versions which followed. *The Wizard of Oz*, originally a popular book for children by Frank L. Baum first published in 1900, was adapted for film by Noel Langley in 1939. The heroine, Dorothy, is a young girl living in Kansas. She is troubled by the threat of a woman neighbour who wants to take away her dog. She encounters a range of people in 'real life' and when a 'twister' (tornado)

Figure 3   The Wicked Witch of the West and Dorothy, from *The Wizard of Oz*, 1939, MGM, courtesy of the Kobal collection.

roars through the town, she is knocked unconscious by a window frame. The rest of the story – her journey to the magical land of Oz – takes place as she sleeps. But when Dorothy wants to go home to Kansas, she is instructed to click together the heels of her ruby red slippers three times, chanting the magical incantation: 'there's no place like home, there's no place like home, there's no place like home'.

The slippers resonate with a power which comes from Dorothy's imagination: a force which proves stronger than that of the 'All Powerful Oz', who turns out to be a sham. Female characters within the story are depicted as either evil or angelic. Many of the characters Dorothy encounters in Oz are mirrors of people in her 'real life' back in the fictional version of Kansas. The nature of these stereotypes says a great deal about gender and power relations (and for adult readers, also about the interpretation of dreams). In Dorothy's 'real life' world, the well-meaning men are ineffectual, the mother figure of Auntie Em is cast as an overworked and under-appreciated nurturer, and the bad-tempered woman neighbour is seen as pointlessly, wickedly destructive (in Oz, she becomes the Wicked Witch of the West, see Figure 3). The Ruby Slippers are a complicated pair of shoes: functional and magical and symbolic. Like the sign which the Wicked Witch writes with smoke in the sky – 'Surrender Dorothy' – the slippers represent Dorothy's dilemma: she is instructed by the Wizard to be active and kill the bad witch, by the bad witch to surrender and by the good witch to think clean thoughts and go back home. She follows the orders of the Good Witch, as a good little girl would do.

The Ruby Slippers are a gift to Dorothy from Glinda the Good Witch. Glinda's first question to Dorothy is: 'Are you a good witch or a bad witch?' The frame of reference does not allow for Dorothy's status as an outsider. Not a witch but a girl from Kansas, Dorothy is out of context in Oz. She identifies with Glinda through the slippers, and with an ideal of femininity and benevolence through Glinda. Dorothy steps into Glinda's shoes and inherits her magical powers. But the depiction of Glinda is interesting in itself: she is powerful but not particularly active. She does not fly wildly through the air and issue threats, but appears demurely in floating clouds and gives little nods and waves of the wand. She is a 'Lady', and Dorothy follows her lead. While Dorothy was allowed the activity of adventure within her magical dream world, the shoes function as her ticket to freedom from Oz and her ticket to domesticity when she ends up back at home, in bed, promising never to leave again: lesson well learned.

Meanwhile, the Ruby Slippers are so rich in meaning for different generations, for different reasons, that they have been reproduced in many forms, including a famous postcard. Many people are familiar with the image. So, while the image 'reads' at one level as 'red shoes', at another level, it signifies a whole range of ideas and associations: imagination, magic, freedom. In the disciplines of Theatre Studies and Gay Cultural Studies, the image has been taken up in another way: *The Wizard of Oz*, and particularly the actress Judy Garland – who played Dorothy, and first wore these Ruby Slippers – is now hailed as an icon for those who seek experimentation in the theatre, who look for roads to self-expression in cross-dressing, or who otherwise search for a place to live 'over the rainbow', far from definitions of 'normalcy' (see, for instance, Brantley, 'Why Oz is a state of mind', *The New York Times*, June 28, 1994, p.C19).

14

Look again at the image of the Ruby Slippers and ask yourself why it might be chosen to symbolize the themes of this book.

D i s c u s s i o n

Here, as in considering the suitability of the poem 'An Obstacle' as a keynote, you are asked to do some detective work: to consider the arguments of the book so far and to try to relate these to a symbolic image. You may recall that we are trying, at this point at least, to leave the question of gender as open-ended as possible. If so, you may have thought about the flexibility, the many possible readings of the Ruby Slippers image. You may even have noticed that shoes are a very powerful choice of image: they represent the possibility of movement, of progress, of walking through 'obstacles'. Think of the magical transformation offered by Cinderella's slippers, or of the famous balletic red shoes, which dance out of control. The image will crop up again when we consider the importance of costume to Nora in Ibsen's play *A Doll's House* (discussed in Chapter Seven). Nora is another woman who seeks liberation from a version of normalcy; she dances the tarantella (a sexy dance, a desperate dance: the 'dance of death' of one bitten by the tarantula spider).

It might seem strange that such an image should be widely reproduced, as it has been, on its own, with no visual reference to the girl who wore the slippers. This deliberate choice of decontextualizing the 'ruby slippers' as 'red shoes' shows the familiarity of the image, not only to children, but also to adults, who 'read' in the image much more than any child might do. There are different levels at which any text 'makes sense' to any given reader, and this is true of visual images, just as it is of literature. ■

It is intriguing to compare the Wizard of Oz, a twentieth-century story about a little girl (written by a man) to earlier stories about girls by men, which also featured fantastic, active tales from which the heroines eventually awoke. Lewis Carroll's Alice (*Alice's Adventures in Wonderland*, 1865) returns from Wonderland in time for tea. E.T.A. Hoffman's Clara, in *The Nutcracker* (1816), awakens to find that her handsome prince is just a wooden doll, but because she's safe in her wealthy home, domestic harmony (rather than disappointment) is established as an end note. Sleeping Beauty and Snow White both wake to the 'magical' powers of a prince's kiss. Feminist literary critics have had a field day with analysing the gender implications of such texts and the assumptions about gender which they inscribe and reinforce.

When literature is filmed, or adapted for the stage or for television, those who do the adaptation make choices which involve interpretation; each previous interpretation affects the ones which follow. Film and other popular treatments of children's fiction allow us to see gender dynamics brought to life with visual images. *Children's Novels and the Movies* (Street, 1983) contains a detailed discussion of *Alice's Adventures in Wonderland* and such classics as *Little Women* (Louisa May Alcott, 1868), *Charlotte's Web* (E.B. White, 1952) and *The Secret Garden* (Frances Hodgson Burnett, 1909). While most 'adult' literature conveys ideas and imaginative landscapes perfectly well through the medium of language, children's literature is a field which makes the most of pictures, helping children engage in the process of reading. Looking at children's books adds to a developing understanding of the process of reading and studying literature.

Gender and children's fiction: making meaning

Children's literature is often our first encounter with written words. The stories told and the morals which unfold help to shape our views as we learn to read and take meaning from what we read.

While nearly all 'adult literature' deals with human characters, fictional though they be, even non-human characters can be assigned genders. One way of testing the 'gender-relevance' of a text – that is, deciding what relationships of power and authority are conveyed through the language and characterization of a text – is to study its gendering of non-human characters. The Forliz Study of Children's Literature, conducted in 1989 on 'easy' books in the children's catalogue produced by the American Library Association for the period 1900–1984, found:

> in the titles of books, 2.3 human males to every human female;
>
> in the titles of books, male animals outnumbered female animals by almost 6 to 1;
>
> for central characters in books, the ratio for the whole period was 3 males for every female. The leaning towards males was greater if focus was on adult characters (4.2), less if focus was on child characters (2.8) and much greater if focus was on animals (5.8);
>
> as for change, the imbalance in depicting males and females varied through the century: representations of males and females were more egalitarian in the early decades of the century and in the 1970s and 1980s, while in the male-female balance among adult characters and animal characters, males got more prominent over time.
>
> (Grauerholz and Pescosolido, 'Gender representation in children's literature', March 1989, pp.113–25)

These figures are striking and it is particularly interesting that they reveal gender balances shifting in the period 1970 to 1990, when modern 'second wave' feminism was making its biggest impact in North America and Britain. Feminist surveys of children's literature have long argued that the female role models offered to children in fairy tales and nursery rhymes are anything but liberating. See, for instance, an early study by the group Feminists on Children's Media ('A feminist look at children's books', *Radical Feminism*, 1973, pp. 94–106). *Girls Reading Gender* (Cherland, 1994) offers an anthropological perspective, with insights into the relationship between gender and reading as a social practice. In this sense, it is a good example of the way in which literature is increasingly studied outside 'English' departments: part of a general move in literary and cultural studies.

If we take a quick look at some of the most popular children's story books, we can quickly see that gender inequalities are represented there. For instance, in Kenneth Grahame's *Wind in the Willows* (first published in 1908 with illustrations by Arthur Rackham) most of the characters – and all the main characters – are male. The same holds true for the endearing but overwhelmingly male world of *Winnie the Pooh* (A.A. Milne, 1926, illustrated by Ernest H. Shephard). Gender representation in literature for older readers is not much better. For instance, in J.R.R. Tolkien's fantasy world of *The Hobbit* (1937) and *The Lord of the Rings* (1954–5), the main characters of all the species (hobbits, elves, dwarves, wargs) are male, with the exception of the wives and lovers of a few characters. Only later in the series does a female character take an active part in the story; this is Galadriel, the 'lady of light'. She is akin in many ways to Glinda the Good – and ladylike – Witch, and to Tennyson's ethereal Lady of Shallot, whom we shall consider later in this chapter, yet she is vastly outnumbered by active, assertive male characters. In recent years, some women authors have taken up the previously male-dominated field of 'sci-fi' fantasy literature, and Ursula K. Le Guin has been particularly successful in creating fantasy worlds where women are numerous, active and powerful characters. (See, for instance, Le Guin's *Earthsea Trilogy*, 1968). Women's science fiction is a burgeoning field (it is discussed from a feminist critical perspective by Frances Bonner in *Imagining Women: Cultural Representations and Gender*, 1992).

Let's consider other well-known examples of children's fiction which raise several key issues to do with gender: Lewis Carroll's *Alice's Adventures in Wonderland* and *Through the Looking-Glass*. The first Alice book was published 1865, *Through the Looking Glass* in 1871. Carroll was ahead of his time in writing fantasy stories with a female protagonist, but the scenario is strikingly similar to the story of *The Wizard of Oz*. Alice sits in the grass making daisy chains with which to decorate her cat. She drifts off to sleep and enters a fantasy world in her dreams. She imagines she sees a large white rabbit, with a waistcoat and watch, who disappears down a rabbit hole. Alice follows him and finds herself in Wonderland. This place is rather like Oz: full of fantastic creatures, mainly male, and full of magical possibilities. This world also fades when Alice wakes up. In the Alice stories, there are a few other female characters, including Alice's sister, who figures only briefly, Dinah the cat (gendered female) and the Queen of Hearts (an extreme 'evil stepmother/mad monarch' stereotype). Yet most of the fantastic creatures encountered by Alice are gendered male, from the White Rabbit to the Cheshire Cat to the Caterpillar to the Mad Hatter and even the Dormouse, to Tweedle Dum and Tweedle Dee, the Walrus and the Carpenter, the White Knight, et al. The characters are male for a reason. They serve a function to do with language and power in a male-dominated world. This is one of the few well-known children's stories written in a previous generation in which the central female character is active, inquisitive, intelligent and engaging in her own right. Yet the language of the piece and the gendering of the other characters in the story reveals that Alice is at odds in a male-dominated, male-controlled world.

Read the following passage, in which Humpty Dumpty (an a-gendered creature speaking with the authority of a man, referred to as 'he' in a specific rather than generic way) gives Alice his pronouncements on language and power:

> 'When I use a word', Humpty Dumpty said in a rather scornful tone, 'it means just what I choose it to mean – neither more nor less.'

'The question is', said Alice, 'whether you *can* make words mean so many different things.'

'The question is', said Humpty Dumpty, 'which is to be master – that's all.'

(Carroll, Complete Works, 1939 edn, p.196)

Can Humpty Dumpty's language be seen to affect Alice, in real or symbolic ways?

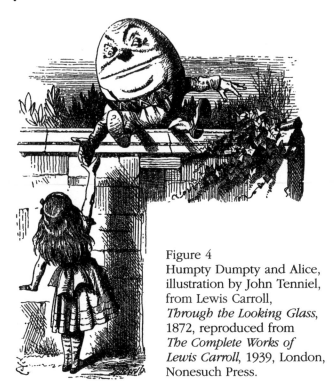

Figure 4
Humpty Dumpty and Alice,
illustration by John Tenniel,
from Lewis Carroll,
Through the Looking Glass,
1872, reproduced from
*The Complete Works of
Lewis Carroll*, 1939, London,
Nonesuch Press.

Discussion

This extract from *Through the Looking Glass* can be read for its serious message about language and power dynamics, as well as for comic effect. Alice is in the less powerful position; she asks a question of the male creature who sits on a wall, elevated above her physically (as the Wicked Witch is over Dorothy in Figure 3) and symbolically elevated as well by his over-confident style (see Figure 4). Humpty declares that he shall be master of language: he shall make it mean what he wants it to mean. He uses language to make this declaration and he asserts power through his assumption of the right to control language and thereby interpretation. Alice is cast in the role of student to Humpty's teacher, and while she is a clever student who perceives the folly of Humpty's declarations, she is in no position (either literally or figuratively) to challenge his authority. The 'wise fool', or the character who speaks wisdom in apparent nonsense, is a common device in literature and drama. The 'Fool' character in Shakespeare's *King Lear* delivers a famous speech about wisdom and inheritance to daughters, which revolves around the metaphor of the egg (symbolizing a head, a brain, an intellect and a fragile shell of human life). Similarly, Humpty Dumpty (the egg-head) is both foolish and wise, logical and illogical.

If we consider this brief extract from the story and ask the question: does gender matter, in terms of text and reader, story and interpretation, then the answer is yes, on both counts. ■

But what about the author? Well, the story behind the Alice stories is fascinating in itself, for it says a great deal about a male fascination with the female form. Charles Dodgson (pseudonym Lewis Carroll) was a respected mathematician and logician, a member of the Oxford academic community, a talented writer and keen photographer. What you may not know is that one of his favourite subjects for photography was little girls. In fact, he was a family friend of the Liddells and a great admirer of the middle Liddell sister, Alice. (Mavis Batey in *Alice's Adventures in Oxford*, 1980, offers a detailed account of the relationship between Charles Dodgson, or Lewis Carroll, and the Liddell sisters, leading to his creation of the Alice stories.) Many readers know Alice as the subject of Carroll's famous children's stories. She was also the subject of many of his photographs, often dressed in spectacular costumes, some of which portray the young girl in what might be considered 'suggestive' or 'adult' or even 'erotic' poses. Some of these portraits might be criticized as exploitative if they appeared in commercial advertisements today. Yet the poet Tennyson is said to have applauded at least one of Dodgson's photographs as 'the most beautiful of a child he had ever seen' (Batey, *Alice's Adventures in Oxford*, p.9). Cultural values change, as do social conventions about the representation of children and of women. Recent feminist critics have put some very persuasive arguments about the gender dynamics involved in the representation of women and children in art, literature and also pornography. Sarah Daniels' play *Masterpieces*, cited briefly in the preconception game, is one of many contemporary feminist texts which engage with the idea that images of women's bodies – whether in 'great art' or in pornography, in text or in the media – reflect tendencies in the cultural valuing of women. In Daniels' play, for instance, the 'masterpieces' are pornographic images, seen by and argued about by the characters on stage, but deliberately not shown to the audience.

Gender *does* matter in analysis of the close relationship between the author, Carroll, and young Alice Liddell, just as it matters in the text itself. Gender is also relevant in the sense that most of the creatures encountered by the fictional Alice are male or endowed with masculine power and authority, often expressed through their 'mastery' of, and experimentation with, language (as the exchange with Humpty Dumpty showed). But male readers can identify with the Alice stories too. There are many male characters within the story and Alice's adventures are largely a-gendered – or at least, they do not exclude boys. Therefore, gender can be said to matter in the text in a third sense as well: in that the depiction of a strong female character who is active rather than passive is a novelty, particularly for a story written in the nineteenth century. Finally, gender matters to us as readers, whether we look for positive representations of female characters, or whether we're more interested in the sociological and psychological dimension of the close relationship – however innocently construed – between a grown man, the author, and a young girl who is both his primary audience and the subject of his stories and photographs.

Another extract from *Alice's Adventures in Wonderland* raises one of the key themes in literature and gender, to be discussed in detail later: that of 'madness' as represented in literature:

> 'How do you know I'm mad?' said Alice.
> 'You must be', said the cat, 'or you wouldn't have come here.'

> (Carroll, *Complete Works*, 1939 edn, p.65)

What does the word 'mad' seem to mean? What function does it serve for the Cheshire Cat to label Alice in this way?

D i s c u s s i o n

The nonsense has a sense and also a gender. 'Madness' is a condition announced by one creature, applied to another. It is a label with all kinds of negative connotations: a powerful label, more so because it is not defined (there is no defence to an unspecified charge). So, when the Cheshire Cat uses this word, he does indeed – in Humpty Dumpty's terms –

Figure 5
The Cheshire Cat and Alice, illustration by John Tenniel, from Lewis Carroll, *Alice's Adventures in Wonderland*, 1865, reproduced from *The Complete Works of Lewis Carroll*, 1939, London, Nonesuch Press.

use it to mean what he wants it to mean. And more importantly Carroll, the author, takes control over the power of language. The characters are just pawns in his game; he is the master, 'that's all'. ■

But many real women have been called 'mad' and many of them have been creative artists and writers. This idea of 'madness' in women's lives and literature is one to which we'll be returning later, as an example of a major theme running through a good deal of women's literature and literature about women. Here, it is important to note that the labelling of women as 'mad' is one way of dismissing their creativity.

Let's look at one last example of children's fiction, this one by Virginia Woolf, whose children's story, *Nurse Lugton's Curtain* was discovered among the notes for her novel, *Mrs Dalloway* (one of Woolf's most popular and most studied novels, often set on literature courses), which was first published in 1925. *Nurse Lugton's Curtain* was actually written to Woolf's niece, Ann Stephen, in the autumn of 1924 but was not published until 1965. **Below is the first paragraph of the story. As you read it, ask yourself why Woolf might have constructed a literary text about a heroine whose 'story' happens while she sleeps.**

> Nurse Lugton was asleep. She had given one great snore. She had dropped her head; thrust her spectacles up her forehead; and there she sat by the fender with her finger sticking up and a thimble on it and her needle full of cotton hanging down; and she was snoring, snoring; and on her knees, covering the whole of her apron, was a large piece of figured blue stuff.

> (Woolf, *Nurse Lugton's Curtain*, 1991 edn, p.1)

Discussion

We have already mentioned a number of stories in which the action develops while the heroine sleeps. But this one is different. As Nurse Lugton (a woman with a useful profession) sits in her armchair one evening sewing a curtain, she drifts off to sleep and dreams. The dream is the 'fabric' of the story, which involves animals and exotic places, but which does not include any remarkable or particularly active men. Like Dorothy, like Alice, like Clara in *The Nutcracker*, we might well expect that Nurse Lugton will find her waking world much different from the romantic world of her dreams. But there are important differences between this narrative and those other children's stories. Firstly, Nurse Lugton is no little girl, nor someone with time on her hands. Instead, she is someone who works with her hands. The 'stuff' or fabric which she sews is a fantastic curtain, covered in animal figures. This is not an intricate web or loom, but a practical item she sews. But more importantly, this is not a story about what Nurse Lugton sees as she dreams, but rather about the animals on her fabric and what they see as Nurse Lugton sleeps:

> They could see her, from their windows, towering over them. She has a face like the side of a mountain with great precipices and avalanches and chasms for eyes and hair and nose and teeth.

> (Ibid., p.23)

What Woolf does in this story is offer a narrative from the animals' point of view. At the same time, she gives Nurse Lugton a tremendous power, usually reserved for men and (male) narrators in children's fiction. Nurse Lugton becomes a 'witch' of sorts: a huge and supernatural being, to be feared and respected. She becomes the landscape itself; her very movements may cause a natural disaster. So Nurse Lugton retains control over the story; her sleep allows the story to develop and her waking puts the other world back to sleep. She is a powerful figure: one who makes things and makes things happen. ■

Woolf's children's story was written at the same time as *Mrs Dalloway*, an 'adult' novel which is a stream of consciousness narrative about a woman's daily domestic routine and her thoughts and fancies as the day progresses. Mabel Waring, a character at Mrs Dalloway's party, is the main character of Woolf's story 'The New Dress'. (We will consider the narrative strategy of the story in Chapter Three). Here, suffice it to say that the three stories – *Nurse Lugton's Curtain*, 'The New Dress' and *Mrs Dalloway* – were written more or less concurrently and share common themes: a focus on women's appearance, a magnification of the importance of women's looks and, by extension, they reveal Woolf's social expectations for women. Whereas Mable Waring is highly self-conscious and concerned about the cut and fabric of her dress, Nurse Lugton is concerned with something more practical: making a curtain. And Nurse Lugton is completely unconscious as the story progresses. The fabric has a life of its own, and Woolf's narrative voice describes the Nurse as huge and grotesque. Themes which are developed subtly in 'The New Dress' are painted with much broader strokes in the story for children.

Nurse Lugton's Curtain puts a woman at the centre of the narrative. The story also contributes to a reading of gender in that it uses the central motif (repeated image or metaphor) of the curtain, an item with a practical purpose: to block out light and protect the inside of the home from the view of the outside world. You may recall that Dorothy was sent reeling into Oz by a flying window frame and that Alice entered Wonderland through a rabbit hole which functioned as the front door to the White Rabbit's home. The public and private spheres are separated by windows and doors. In children's fiction as well as in adult literature, it is useful to keep track of which spaces women (and girls) are allowed to enter and to exit. The window is also a kind of mirror, as in *Through the Looking Glass*: a mirror of self image and of imagination. Keep this in mind when we study 'The Lady of Shalott' in the next section.

Woolf's choice of sewing as an activity for Nurse Lugton is also important: it is a gendered activity and one which women do after hours, after the main business of the day is over. So, as you read the texts discussed later in the book, remember the imagery of these three children's stories: shoes and curtains, magic wands and sewing needles, private and public spaces (real and imaginary) separated by windows, doors and mirrors. Also note the frequency with which women and girls in fiction are occupied with certain kinds of creative work: making daisy chains, sewing, weaving, spinning, quilting. From the spinning done by Penelope in Greek myth, to the weaving of Tennyson's Lady of Shalott, to the seamstress's work in 'The New Dress', to Nurse Lugton's curtain-making, to quilting in Alice Walker's *The Color Purple*, to the mysterious sewing box in Susan Glaspel's play *Trifles* (which truly holds the key to a mystery), sewing is a metaphor for female creativity which operates on many levels simultaneously.

Texts and contexts

In the rest of the book, we'll be studying 'adult' literature of all three major genres and we'll be looking not only at the number of female and male characters in a story, but also at what they say and do not say, whether they are central to the story's action or marginal to it, whether they are important characters or props to other characters. We'll also be looking beyond characterization, to consider the gender of authors and readers, and to think in more sophisticated terms about the gender dynamics of writing and reading and studying literature.

As our brief study of children's fiction showed, the contexts of literature (who writes a text, when, why and for whom) are not easily read in the text itself. In some of the texts you will be asked to read in subsequent chapters, the question of authorship will be a focus of study. But for now, let's focus on identifying the genre of selected literary extracts, to point out the distinctive features of each of the three main genres and show how each is informed by gender.

The following exercise asks you to determine the genre of literary texts from reading selected extracts. Read the three extracts which follow and answer these questions:

1 **Name the genre of this extract (poetry, prose fiction or drama) and consider the probable period of its publication, judging from the style of its language.**

> It was a face
> Queenly and calm, a carved face and strong
> Nor curious, nor kindly, nor aloof,
> But self-contained and singing to itself.
> And as he met her eyes, she ceased her song
> And made a silence …

2 **Name the genre of this extract (poetry, prose fiction or drama) and consider the probable nationality and class position of its author, judging from the style of its language and its subject-matter.**

> It occurs to me, furthermore, that bantering is hardly an
> unreasonable duty for an employer to expect a professional to
> perform. I have of course already devoted much time to
> developing my bantering skills, but it is possible I have never
> previously approached the task with the commitment I might have
> done.

3   Name the genre of this extract (poetry, prose fiction or drama) and consider the probable class position and approximate age of the character who speaks in the following extract:

> BIDDY I didn't at first understand what was happening. For someone like me, who was used to being tolerated, it came as a surprise. You see, before, everything I said was passed over. Well, smiled at, but the conversation would continue elsewhere. I was like the final touches of a well decorated house. It gives pleasure, but you don't notice it.

D i s c u s s i o n

1   The first extract is taken from a long poem. The style and use of language would seem to date the poem in an earlier era of English verse, perhaps in the Romantic or Victorian period: such a response would be quite reasonable. In fact, the extract is a poetic fragment from a long poem called 'The Fairy Melusine', written by a fictional woman author within the pages of a novel by A.S. Byatt (*Possession: A Romance*, 1991, pp.296–7). The language and style suggest that the piece was written in an earlier period, but that is indeed the contemporary author's artifice. Byatt has created a fictional woman writer who is 'discovered' by a contemporary academic. This is a 'romance about romance', in which the academic begins to identify with a woman writer of the past and sets about some academic detective work in order to 're-discover' her. The novel is an example of the way in which paying attention to lost women writers from the past serves a function for women and men writing and reading today. This extract also illustrates the difficulty of identifying any text out of context.

2   The second extract is from a piece of prose fiction, as most of you will have guessed. You may also have guessed that the author was English and probably male and middle-class or even aristocratic. If you came to these conclusions, you were probably assuming, quite unconsciously, that there might be a similarity between the character and the author. The character is indeed a white Englishman: a butler and the main character of *The Remains of the Day*, by Kazuo Ishiguro (1989, p.245). (The novel was filmed by the Merchant-Ivory team in 1993, starring Antony Hopkins as Stephens, the butler and Emma Thompson as Miss Kenton, the housekeeper.) The author is Japanese, and his novel about British class prejudice and the sad introspection of one lonely man's life is an unusual and moving story, written by an author with a working knowledge of the British class system (Ishiguro studied in England). But in this as in the study of all literature, it is important to remember the distinction between authors and their characters.

3   The third extract is from a play, as the identification of the character's name printed alongside the text indicates. The character, Biddy, speaks about speaking, about the way she has been ignored in her social circle. Later in the same speech, she explains that, since her new husband got rich, people have listened to and indeed been 'riveted' by literally everything she says, no matter how trivial. While the extract does not explicitly state who that circle is, it would be reasonable to assume that the circle is upper class, white and very 'English'. All this is true of the

character, Biddy, but not of the author of the play, Timberlake Wertenbaker: an American woman, known as a contemporary feminist playwright. The play is *Three Birds Alighting on a Field* (1991, p.9), which tells the story of a woman's struggle to find a means of self-expression within the metaphorical framework of the art world. (The original Royal Court production starred Harriet Walter as Biddy, and was directed by Max Stafford Clark; Walter reads this extract and discusses the play on an Open University BBC audio-cassette on Gender and Performance designed in conjunction with this book.) Here, as in the example from Ishiguro's fiction, the particular perspective which the author takes on the class and gender dynamics of English society are taken from outside that culture. The author and the character remain separate. You might have placed the character in her late middle years, or perhaps even in retirement, because she speaks as someone who has interacted in a certain social circle for some time, and because she refers to her first marriage. But in the play, Biddy is relatively young: only in her thirties or possibly her early forties. In the short extract you read, Biddy seems to speak for all women of her social circle. (Ironically, Biddy's class background and the role which women occupy within her social circle make her seem less spirited, less young and independent than she eventually proves herself to be.)

The first two extracts send out misleading signals about periodization, while the third leads the reader to form a mental picture of Biddy as more of a character type, or stereotype, than a character in her own right. In addition, all three extracts share a common theme: language and silence. The first textual extract offers a glimpse of a woman who 'makes silence'. In this characterization, Byatt critiques the stereotype of the passive, silent woman. Ishiguro's butler, at the end of a long and disappointing day (symbolic of his life) contemplates the relative merits of learning to 'banter', to make small talk, partly as a duty to his upper class employer and partly because it might help to ease the burden of loneliness. Wertenbaker's Biddy (a 'flighty' woman, birdlike in her gestures at first and particularly in this extract from her opening speech) learns in the course of the play to use her voice, in real and symbolic terms. To use a metaphor that we will return to later, Biddy is a 'caged bird' who learns to speak, or to sing. ∎

So far we have considered particular aspects of the contexts of these three extracts: period, nationality, class. The extracts also have a great deal to say about gender. All writing is gendered in so far as all authors use language, and language is created and spoken and written in culture, where each of us has a sex and a gender, just as we have a race and class. We have been looking at contemporary writers who experiment with styles from earlier periods and with creating characters from a range of class and cultural backgrounds. Of course, authors of previous generations have done the same. The legacy of each generation of authors and readers is what gets adopted and adapted in the next. Major themes and metaphors can be traced through literature from period to period, though writing styles and cultural contexts change. For instance, the metaphor of the caged bird can be extended to include the 'cages' which block women off from public life. In this sense the walls of a house may be a cage; the rules and regulations regarding 'feminine' behaviour may be a cage. A well-known use of this metaphor occurs in Maya Angelou's *I Know Why the Caged Bird Sings* (1969), which we will return to in Chapter Five. Women authors from Jane Austen to Emily Dickinson to Louisa May Alcott to Charlotte Perkins Gilman to Virginia Woolf and Sylvia Plath have all used the metaphor of 'madness' to signal another form of 'cage' imposed on women's lives; this theme will be discussed at length in Chapter Four.

We have now considered quite a range of texts and extracts. Despite differences of genre, period and style, we have used one thread to hold all this work together. That thread is gender. Like the Gilman poem we considered at the outset, all these examples can be valued as literature in their own right, but also bear new meanings when we 'read for gender'. While a pattern may begin to emerge, it is an open pattern: reversible, readable from different angles and perspectives.

Gender in the three genres: poetry, fiction, drama

In the preconception game and in the exercise about texts in context above, extracts were chosen from all three major genres. Gender and genre are closely linked in English writing. For instance, in previous generations most women were denied access to higher education, so their 'command' of the language, and of specialized academic and professional vocabularies, was limited. But even this sentence illustrates the gendering of language: it uses a verb which implies action ('command') and uses it in a supposedly generic or neutral context, i.e. with reference to language. But I used these words deliberately, in order to make a point: such words are often assumed to be 'masculine'. In the English language, words which are assumed to be neutral are implicitly gendered. In some cases the implicit becomes explicit, as when Humpty Dumpty asserts his right to 'master' language. This gendering of the language reveals an assumption of passivity in the feminine and of activity in the 'masculine'. These linguistic assumptions may be seen to apply to some of the contexts of writing, but not necessarily to the writing itself. In fact, as we have mentioned, some have argued that there are 'feminine ways of writing' different and distinct from 'masculine writing'. For instance, it is often argued that women's writing tends to be less linear than men's – perhaps because women's lives do not always follow the structured lines of men's lives. Virginia Woolf is often said to write in a 'female' voice which challenges assumptions about the relative importance of characters and events in much fiction by men. French thinker Simone de Beauvoir argued that women have long been treated as 'the second sex'; Hélène Cixous coined the term 'écriture féminine' to refer to women's writing which derives from women's unique experience ('The laugh of the Medusa', 1976). Whatever critical position is taken on gender, the preconception game has shown that our judgements of what is 'male' and 'female', 'masculine' and 'feminine' are difficult to defend when we try to apply them to texts out of context.

Make a list of words describing writing styles and subject-matter for fiction which you think of – or you think others think of – as 'feminine' or 'masculine'.

Your list may look something like this:

Feminine Writing

soft, suggestive, non-linear, symbolic, flowing

Masculine Writing

strong, assertive, focused, clear, direct

The sample list above represents a set of conventional assumptions about writing styles. Some aspects of the conventions may now seem dated, especially as the hidden value judgements implied in them become more obvious to us. To some extent though, our assumptions about gender and writing are personal and subjective. As we have suggested, there are different feminist perspectives on this issue.

The relationship between 'gender and genre' is also complex and reveals a great deal about the culture(s) in which literary texts are written and read. Let's look at the main literary genres in detail, with relation to gender.

Reading gender in poetry: authors, readers, texts

We have already seen that 'reading with gender on the agenda' offers new insights into poetry. For instance, when we re-read the poem 'An Obstacle' in the light of the preconception game, we found that the word 'prejudice' took on new, gender-specific meaning.

In the next chapter, we'll study poetry in terms of its literary merit, its form and structure and poetic qualities. Here, we'll treat one poem in detail as a text out of context, with our focus on gender. Let's look at 'The Lady of Shalott' (reprinted in Part Two of this book) and read it 'with gender on the agenda'. The poem, by Alfred, Lord Tennyson (1809–1892), was first published in 1833 and revised for the 1842 edition of Tennyson's poems. ('The Lady of Shalott' is also read and discussed on an Open University BBC audio-cassette recording designed to accompany this book.)

Please read 'The Lady of Shalott'. Consider your answers to the following questions:

Who is the narrator of the poem?

Who are the main characters?

Which characters are active and which are passive?

Does the poem represent the Lady (and through her, 'femininity') in a particular way, as either active or passive?

The narrator of the poem is an unspecified omniscient narrator. It seems to be a male narrator, perhaps a storyteller, close in role if not in person to Tennyson himself. The main characters of this narrative poem are, in order of appearance, the Lady of Shalott and Sir Lancelot. But non-human 'characters' also feature: in Part I, the river, the sky, the fields and the island of Shalott are presented as active and alive. Here's an example:

Willows *whiten*, aspens *quiver*,
Little breezes *dusk* and *shiver*
Thro' the wave that *runs* for ever
By the island in the river
Flowing down to Camelot.
Four gray walls, and four gray towers,
Overlook a space of flowers,
And the silent isle *imbowers*
The Lady of Shalott.

The verbs in this extract are italicized to demonstrate the active function of the language pertaining to the natural world and the tower in which the Lady resides, whereas the Lady herself is passively 'imbowered'. She is 'imbowered' in two senses: she is trapped in the tower, but also she is disempowered by language itself. The passive case of the verb makes her the object of the island's action of enclosure: in most of the poem she is not the subject of active verbs. Tennyson creates the impression of an active landscape and an active man (Lancelot), contrasted with a passive Lady. The natural world is presented as if it were a 'living' character (and, of course, it is), but the most active character in the poem is Lancelot. He is introduced in the last line of the first stanza of Part III (though readers familiar with Arthurian legend will have thought of him earlier, with the first mentions of Camelot). If you re-read that line you will see that Lancelot's name is prefixed with an important adjective: 'bold'. By contrast the Lady herself is not 'bold' or even active. She watches the active world outside her window; her one choice of action, to go out into that world, is fatal. ■

You may already be familiar with the poem, as it is often taught as a 'classic' of literature. Yet it is not often viewed as a text which represents and reinforces a feminine stereotype, though this may be enlightening as one of a range of possible interpretations. Approaching *The Lady of Shalott* through a 'gendered reading' raises many of the issues and ideas which will be discussed at length in this book.

So, let's see what a 'gendered reading' of this poem might entail. We have already discussed the relationship between the Lady and the natural world. **Re-read the poem and consider other apects of a gendered reading: the private and public spheres, the role of the mirror and the window, and the significance of weaving and 'decorative' arts.**

D i s c u s s i o n

The presentation of the island and the natural world as active offers a significant contrast to the passivity of the Lady herself, introduced in the last line of the second stanza, paralleling the introduction of the island in the last line of the previous stanza. This positioning of the Lady is functional for more than the rhyme or rhythm of the poem. It compares the Lady to the island, presenting her as a part of the landscape, literally and symbolically embowered within it, locked in a tower, gazing out at the world through her mirror. In Part II, a number of minor characters appear, viewed by the Lady through her window: a damsel, an abbot and finally the lovers who provoke the Lady's lament: 'I am half sick of shadows'.

28

Once Lancelot makes his bold entrance, he becomes the active subject of the rest of the poem. The Lady's demise begins with her first view of him; her death is a reaction to Lancelot and all he represents. Her reaction propels her into the natural world outside the window and beyond her mirror. The mirror cracks from side to side, signalling the inevitable doom of the Lady. She recognizes her own 'curse' and cries out, breaking her previous silence both literally and figuratively.

The Lady is propelled from one world to another, moved by desire for the goodly knight. Here, the Lady's quaint and chaste femininity, characterized by her passivity and distance from worldly matters, is 'cursed' by the dawn of sexual desire, as Eve was cursed for 'tempting' Adam. The blaming of woman is characteristic of many narratives from Genesis to the present day. It could be argued that Tennyson participates in a narrative convention by 'blaming' his Lady in this way. In the last stanza, the activity of the Lady is negative, leading to death, not life. She boards her ship, like her coffin, and engraves it with the words 'The Lady of Shalott'. She has no first name, only a title and a designation of place, identifying her with the island and the tower. As she floats away from both, she loses her energy, becomes unreal. By the time Lancelot discovers her, she is dead. Unaware that desire for him caused her death, he remarks upon her beauty and calls for her reception in the after-world. The narrator is at great pains to describe the visual impact of the Lady in her fine white robes flowing in the breeze. The narrator seems to be male, seems to identify with Lancelot rather than with the Lady. ■

This reading, like all readings, emphasizes selected aspects of the text. By reading the text with a focus on gender, I engaged in an active process of trying to identify with the Lady. The poem took on a new meaning for me, though I can see and hear the beauty of the verse and the power of the story in 'non-gendered' terms as well, just as I can view a Gestalt Shift, or multi-layered pattern, piece by piece or layer by layer. This reading offers one interpretation, deliberately ignoring other aspects of the poem. In the next chapter you'll be offered a very different reading. Your interpretation will probably differ in some ways from others offered in this book. So it should be – interpretation is an active, creative process influenced by context.

The poem communicates through language by engaging with the imagination of the reader, by creating images in 'the mind's eye'. This poem has had many readers and much influence. Just as Tennyson modelled his Lady on sources from literature and myth, so Tennyson's poem has left a legacy of other poems and images to subsequent generations of authors and readers. Waterhouse, for example, painted three famous portraits of the Lady, captured in different moments and different phases of activity. (The Waterhouse and other images of Tennyson's Lady are reproduced and discussed in *Ladies of Shalott,* 1985. Those by Millais, Rossetti and Holman Hunt are collected in *Pre-Raphaelite Illustrations from Moxon's Tennyson,* 1978). Comparison of different images of the Lady of Shalott, by three artists, reveals very different interpretations of the narrative. The comparison also shows that any artist's rendering is at once an interpretation in itself and an influence on viewers who subsequently read or re-read the literary text which inspired it.

So, let's continue our gendered reading of the poem by looking for clues in pictorial images, which offer glimpses into the interpretations of the painters. In so doing, we'll be practising reading images, just as we did with the Gestalt Shift diagrams and with our 'reading' of the image of the Ruby Slippers.

Figure 6   John William Waterhouse (1849–1917), *The Lady of Shalott*, 1888, oil on canvas, 153 x 200 cm, Tate Gallery, London.

Look carefully at Figures 6–8, one by one and then as a set. Answer this two-part question:

1 **In each image, is the depiction of the Lady active or passive; is she active or acted upon?**
2 **What do these visual images add to our reading of the poem?**

Discussion

The painting by Waterhouse (Figure 6) depicts the Lady on her way down the river, on her way to death. More precisely, this famous image of Tennyson's Lady depicts the Fourth part of the poem. The Lady, who had previously been entrapped in a tower representing a stereotype of feminine beauty and passivity, is suddenly faced with the flowing river of sexual desire and the movement of the real world. If you re-read the poem, you may be able to find the precise passage which the painting depicts:

And down the river's dim expanse -
Like some bold seer in a trance,
Seeing all his own mischance –
With a glassy countenance

Figure 7 Dante Gabriel Rossetti (1828–1882), *The Lady of Shalott*, designed for Alfred Tennyson, *Poems*, 1857, London, Moxon. Wood engraving, proof print on India paper, 26 x 19 cm. John H. and Ernestine A. Payne Fund, Courtesy of the Museum of Fine Arts, Boston.

Figure 8 William Holman Hunt (1827–1910), designed for Alfred Tennyson, *Poems*, 1857, London, Moxon. Wood engraving, proof print on India paper, 26 x 19 cm. John H. and Ernestine A. Payne Fund, Courtesy of the Museum of Fine Arts, Boston.

For the first time, the word 'bold' is used in relation to the Lady, though only by way of analogy to a seer, gendered male (as the masculine pronoun in the next line reveals). The Lady, who previously only viewed the world from a distance, is now presented blind to it and within it. This painting may or may not correspond with your own image of the Lady (the one you formed in your mind's eye as you read). Or it may be that you saw, and perhaps remembered, the image of this painting before you read the poem, in which case the visual image may have influenced your reading. Even if you haven't seen this painting before, its similarity to other Pre-Raphaelite paintings is striking. You may notice the visual similarity to such famous work as Millais' *Ophelia*: another young woman who dies, in a sense, of unconsummated love (see Figure 9).

The presence of two other images alongside this one will have influenced your way of seeing the image. We have printed the three images on facing pages to show that context always influences reception of texts, visual or written. The painting by Dante Gabriel Rossetti (Figure 7) depicts the moment when Lancelot finds the Lady. Lancelot is very much the active figure, and his features are clearly drawn. The Lady's features are obscured, her figure and hair hidden from view. Her 'femininity' has died and with it her identity (the Victorian cum Arthurian ideal of the feminine could not encompass any other outcome). She is already part of the boat, which also functions as a coffin, moving from an identification with the natural world to another world altogether.

By contrast, William Holman Hunt (Figure 8) depicts the Lady still locked in the tower, literally tied up in the web of thread from her weaving. The mirror is prominent behind her, as her hair streams in the air and gets entangled with the threads from her loom. She is literally 'woven' into the image, the tower, the story. She is locked away from the natural world and her own sexuality. She looks powerful and strong, but is clearly restrained by bonds and ties identified with her gender.

In response to the second part of the question, we might say that the addition of visual imagery adds a new dimension to the Lady. We see her through the eyes of various artists who interpreted and defined the shadowy image suggested in Tennyson's text. We also see the images, as we read the poem, with our own eyes, from our own perspectives. In the next chapter, you'll be asked to reconsider this poem in the light of historical context. But even without that contextual knowledge to frame your reading and interpretation, there is a great deal to be gleaned from a 'gendered reading' which adds another layer to your reading of the poem. ∎

Reading gender in prose fiction: authors, readers, texts

Please read the following short extract, paying attention to both gender and genre as you read. Consider these questions and record your answers to them. **How can you tell that this is an extract from prose fiction, as opposed to poetry or drama (what is characteristic about the genre of prose fiction)? What would you guess are the genders of the author, the characters, the narrator and the assumed reader?**

Reader, I married him. A quiet wedding we had: he and I, the parson
and the clerk, were alone present. When we got back from church, I
went into the kitchen of the manor-house, where Mary was cooking
the dinner, and John cleaning the knives, and I said:
'Mary, I have been married to Mr. Rochester this morning.'

(C. Brontë, *Jane Eyre*, 1973 edn, p.454)

Discussion

Even if you had not been told that this is a piece of prose fiction (an extract
from a novel), you would probably have guessed the genre. Prose fiction is
the literary genre with which most readers have some experience, whether
from reading children's fiction, or short stories in magazines, or novels. The
use of quotation marks and the contrast between different voices, or
characters, with what appears to be a continuous narrative or story are
tell-tale signs of prose fiction. (Of course, there are exceptions, including
the first short story we'll read in full, 'Girl', discussed in Chapter Three). In
addition, you probably guessed that the author was female. The main
character (the 'I' in this extract) is female, as is the narrator (this is first
person narration; the main character, or 'I' and the narrator are one). The
assumed reader is most likely female: in this period the reading of domestic
novels was perceived as a largely female activity. The address to a reader
assumed to be interested in marriage and domestic details seems to confirm
this, though such assumptions might well be wrong.

But we can only say so much about a textual extract taken out of
context. The extract is from Charlotte Brontë's novel *Jane Eyre*, first
published under the pseudonym Currer Bell in 1847; it is the opening
paragraph of the concluding chapter, where the long-suffering heroine
makes good, with the long-suffering hero (who, unlike Jane, has brought
some of his suffering on himself). They will live happily ever after, as the
saying goes and as the rest of this chapter assures us. For those who aren't
familiar with the novel, the story of *Jane Eyre* combines elements of the
gothic and the domestic (for detailed discussion of the form, see Walder,
The Realist Novel, 1991). While the novel is often read as a romance, it can
also be read as a narrative about gender relations and class difference. For
instance, it can be interpreted as the tale of a young woman's struggles to
survive as an independent female in a conservative patriarchal culture.
Feminist critics have written about *Jane Eyre* in many different contexts,
rendering it something of a 'literature and gender' classic. This extract has
been parodied in the feminist detective thriller *Reader I Murdered Him*, the
title story of an anthology (Green, 1989). When the poor but genteel
heroine marries her beloved Mr Rochester, she rises in class status and
attains a certain power and authority. But it is not status which concerns
Jane, either as a character or as the narrator of her own tale. In the
conclusion to the novel, the narrator/character Jane is concerned with
relating the happy domestic details of the marriage and the lives of the
other main characters of the story.

Now to readdress the questions on the short passage. We can tell this
is prose fiction by its difference from poetry (it is not rhymed or metered, it
is not laid out specially on the page) and from drama (the characters' lines
are not offset, as they would probably be in a dramatic text, nor is the

name of the character printed in the margin). It would not have been so easy to make this distinction if the extract were shorter. For instance, if only the first sentence of this extract were printed, the tell-tale signs of prose fiction would not have helped you to identify the genre, and the many domestic details would not have helped you with the questions about gender. It was necessary to print the first paragraph in its entirety, to provide context clues.

Another, more subtle, means of determining genre is by focusing on the presentation of character. In this extract, for instance, there seems to be a narrator who speaks directly to you, the reader. The gender of the narrator is clearly female, as revealed in the choice of pronoun in the first sentence: 'Reader, I married him'. Unless we were dealing with a twentieth-century satire of heterosexual romance, the verb 'married' and the pronoun 'him' designate the narrator as female. Gender can also be read in the concern for domestic detail related in the mention of the wedding, kitchen, house, cookery, dinner and the cleaning of knives, all in one brief passage. ■

What is most striking about the narrative technique in *Jane Eyre* is the particular viewpoint which we, as readers, are encouraged to adopt. We identify with a narrator/character who is female, alone in the world, a descendant of impoverished gentry. The fictional form allows a sustained story line, where identification and sympathy can be manipulated and extended, to capture and hold the reader's attention. We may continue to read and enjoy *Jane Eyre* today, not only as a 'great novel', but also as a novel which touches our sympathies and fires our imaginations, at once by offering insight into the class and gender divisions of a previous era, and by showing up the continuing inequalities of society. While we might also learn about the values of past eras from, for instance, a poem such as Tennyson's 'The Lady of Shalott', the relationship between the narrator and the character is not so close, and our reading of the poem is therefore more formal and distanced. But just as importantly, the narrator of that poem is presumably male; the author is certainly male. The female perspective of *Jane Eyre* brings readers inside Jane's world and encourages us to see things from Jane's point of view.

Of course, there are poems with male narrators which bring us closer to the narrative voice than 'The Lady of Shalott' does, and there are novels and stories which take a more formal stance, distancing the narrator from the character. Twentieth-century poetry is often written from a first person voice (that of the author, or of an unspecified narrator), as in Charlotte Perkins Gilman's poem, 'An Obstacle'. Some dramatic scenes also involve direct address to the audience/readers, as in Shakespeare's soliloquies and in monologues in twentieth-century plays such as Biddy's speech in *Three Birds Alighting on a Field* and the brief extract from *Masterpieces* cited earlier. The relationship between narrator and character is something to look out for and analyse in reading literature in all genres.

We have discussed the relationship of the text to the reader and the function of both narrator and character within that dynamic. What is still to be considered is the relationship of the author to the reader: the way in which the text bridges the gap between one person, an author, and other people, the readers, who come to the text at different times, in different cultural contexts and for different reasons. If you review the discussion above, you'll see that once again, we are examining the relationship between author and reader in our discussion of the text and its context. This relationship is more complicated in the study of drama, where the text is meant to be performed, and the audience enters into the dynamic as well.

Reading gender in drama: authors, readers, texts

Read the following extract carefully, taking note of references (overt and implied) to gender, class, language and the importance of naming. What can you make of such references, reading 'with gender on the agenda'?

LIZA (*stopping her work for a moment*) Your calling me Miss Doolittle that day when I first came to Wimpole Street. That was the beginning of self-respect for me. (*She resumes her stitching.*) And there were a hundred little things you never noticed, because they came naturally to you. Things about standing and taking off your hat and opening doors –

PICKERING Oh, that was nothing.

LIZA Yes: things that showed you thought and felt about me as if I were something better than a scullery maid; though of course I know you would have been just the same to a scullery-maid if she had been let into the drawing room. You never took off your boots in the dining room when I was there.

PICKERING You mustn't mind that. Higgins takes off his boots all over the place.

LIZA I know. I am not blaming him. It is his way, isn't it? But it made such a difference to me that you didn't do it. You see, really and truly, apart from the things anyone could pick up (the dressing and the proper way of speaking, and so on), the difference between a lady and a flower girl is not how she behaves, but how she's treated. *I shall always be a flower girl to Professor Higgins, because he always treats me as a flower girl, and always will; but I know I can be a lady to you, because you always treat me as a lady, and always will.*

MRS. HIGGINS Please don't grind your teeth, Henry.

PICKERING Well, this is really very nice of you, Miss Doolittle.

LIZA I should like you to call me Eliza, now, if you would.

PICKERING Thank you, Eliza, of course.

LIZA And I should like Professor Higgins to call me Miss Doolittle.

HIGGINS I'll see you damned first.

MRS. HIGGINS Henry! Henry!

PICKERING (*laughing*) Why don't you slang back at him? Don't stand for it. It would do him a lot of good.

LIZA I can't. I could have done it once but now I can't go back to it. You told me, you know, that when a child is brought to a foreign country, it picks up the language in a few weeks and forgets its own. Well, I am a child in your country. I have forgotten my own language, and can speak nothing but yours.

(Shaw, *Pygmalion*, 1972 edn, pp.768–70)

First, let's identify the text: this is a passage from *Pygmalion*, by George Bernard Shaw. The play was first produced in German in Vienna in 1913; the first English production was in 1914 with Mrs. Patrick Campbell as Eliza Doolittle. It was first published in 1916. A film version was made in 1938, which was adapted to the stage as the popular musical *My Fair Lady* in 1956.

The textual extract is treated here as dramatic literature (or a written script for a play) rather than as a performance. At one level, we can treat this extract from a dramatic script as we would a poem or a story, looking for key themes and analysing the representation of characters. You have now practised this kind of literary analysis, so probably had no difficulty identifying the overt references to gender, class, language and the importance of naming. In some ways, Eliza's references to the way language influences her character may remind you of Alice, faced with the 'mastering' of Humpty Dumpty. But Eliza's situation is more true to life. Indeed, for Eliza Doolittle, the use of language is inextricably tied to gender and class issues. We can also imagine this text in performance by reading the lines out loud and constructing mental images to illustrate the scene. At the 'theatrical' level, Eliza's speech about language, gender and role-playing takes on a range of possibilities for interpretation.

Eliza's story is that of the working class woman 'recreated' by an upper class man, who treats her like an experiment, like an animal in a cage to be taught and rewarded for learning to act like a 'lady'. But because this is a play, there is another level at which the text can be studied: as a blueprint for performance. Indeed, it is most enlightening to view Eliza Doolittle as a character who learns, in the course of the play, to reject the class-biased values which her teacher imposes. In one interpretation, she recognizes her role as an actress playing a part, and in this scene, she rejects both the play and the director (Mr. Higgins) while embracing the knowledge she has acquired of language and social relations. We might visualize the idea that Eliza has entered a new culture, a new language, by picturing a door – she has stepped through a door and closed it behind her. Her previous ways of using language, and of seeing herself, are no longer open to her.

If you re-read the lines I placed in italics, you may see that Eliza is fully aware of her role, and of the double-standard of class prejudice. By proving herself more aware than her teacher, she 'performs' the part of the independent woman most admirably, much to Higgins' dismay (for he is only pleased with her 'progress' when it serves his own purposes). This same line introduced the voice of the author, Shaw, most powerfully. In giving such a line to his female protagonist, Shaw identifies with her (and with the general class of women and other 'underdogs') rather than with his central male character, Higgins. The author's presentation of both main characters, and his very sympathetic presentation of Pickering as a moderating character between the two, allows the reader to discern Shaw's own voice within the text, as his political and social views are expressed through the mouths of his characters.

It is, perhaps, easier to discuss an extract from a play such as *Pygmalion* than more recent plays such as *Masterpieces* or *Three*

Birds Alighting on a Field. Many of you will have seen or at least heard of *Pygmalion,* or of its musical adaptation, *My Fair Lady.* It is easier to put mental images to the words, to use our imaginations in translating dramatic literature into texts for performance, if we can put faces to the characters, or draw on images to help us in our visualization. In later chapters, we will do just that, dealing with the representation of gender in texts and performances. As we'll argue in the course of this book, drama and particularly theatre can be very useful tools for making points about gender, and vice versa (see Griffiths, *Using Gender to Get at Drama,* 1986). ■

Comparing genres

In these three extracts you have been introduced, albeit briefly and without much context, to three different literary genres and three literary characters: the Lady of Shalott, Jane Eyre and Eliza Doolittle. These characters were not made in isolation, but were, rather, the creation of an author writing in a particular historical and cultural context, in the English language and for an assumed readership. We, as readers today, were not part of the 'assumed readership' for any of these three texts. Our 'gendered readings' (informed by recent debates, ideas and cultural developments) might seem very strange indeed to the authors of those texts. You are, however, part of the 'assumed readership' of *this* textbook, which has stated its purpose as 'reading with gender on the agenda'.

Review the three textual extracts printed above and also the discussion which frames them. Then stop to consider the similarities and differences between the Lady of Shalott, Jane Eyre and Eliza Doolittle:

1 **What can you say about similarities between these three characters?**

2 **Are these characters 'feminist'?**

Discussion

1 Though they were created in and framed by different periods, all the characters were the products of British authors (two men and one woman) and all the texts were written before the term 'feminist' came into its current usage. 'The Lady of Shalott' can be read as a Victorian representation of idealized femininity by an educated man, which looks backward to a long-lost era and its chivalric code. *Jane Eyre* provides a romantic tale of one woman's struggles with learning, work and desire, in a first person narrative by an English woman. Written in roughly the same period, Tennyson's poem uses its conventional form and recreates an antique fictional age. Brontë's novel experiments with the narrative voice and sympathy of the reader. The story of Jane Eyre gives a new twist (the independent heroine) to the traditional 'Cinderella' theme of so much romantic literature, from the Arthurian romances which Tennyson recalls in his poem, to the Mills and Boon formula of today. Shaw's play offers a character, Eliza Doolittle, who is manipulated by her 'creator', Henry Higgins, as if she were a doll or a puppet. But Eliza talks back; at one level

at least, she escapes her creator and becomes a character in her own right, with more integrity and humanity than her teacher. What all these have in common is their roles as representatives of their authors' assumptions about gender. We have already discussed the cultural contexts of Tennyson's and Brontë's work. Shaw's position on gender politics was clear: he is often seen as an early pro-feminist playwright. ('Pro-feminist' is a term sometimes used for men sympathetic to feminist concerns. Feminist criticism is still debating such terminology.) The play demonstrates his awareness of gender dynamics in the theatre and in life. *Pygmalion* depicts the ultimate Cinderella story – a woman constructed, imagistically and linguistically, by a man. It contrasts being 'made over' as a woman and being created as a monster (so that Eliza becomes a version of the Frankenstein monster). Stylistically and politically, Shaw was ahead of his time in depicting strong, engaging female characters for the stage. He was influenced by another playwright whose work we'll study in Chapter Seven: Ibsen. In his earlier plays, including *Mrs. Warren's Profession* (published in *Plays Unpleasant*, 1931), as in *Pygmalion*, Shaw contributed to the new age of 'New Women' in the theatre. In this, his work was instrumental in a developing trend for strong women on the stage, which later developed in the plays of the suffrage movement – but all of this will be discussed in detail later.

2   Are the characters feminist? Well, the answer to this question depends on defining the term 'feminist': a task which could be the subject of another book. For now, if we assume that by 'feminist' in this (non-theorized) context we mean strong and independent, capable of acting without the assistance of men, then you might answer: no, maybe and yes, respectively. That is, Tennyson's Lady cannot be seen as active or strong in her own right, though this reflects more on Tennyson's intentions in creating the fictional Lady than it does on real women in the world. Jane Eyre is strong and withstands much hardship; she is bright and independent, so might be interpreted as an early 'feminist' character. On the other hand, she might be seen as a woman who would have liked a less independent life had one been on offer. Eliza Doolittle is not a character to whom a word such as 'feminist' would have meant anything: she can always be interpreted in a feminist way, but she cannot be portrayed as a feminist in her own right. Nor is it a word which Henry Higgins would have been likely to add to the list he made of useful words and phrases for a 'lady'. Yet she is wilful and able, and she acts on her own accord, however much the male creator/teacher within the play tries to confine and define her. Like Shakespeare's Kate in *The Taming of the Shrew*, Shaw's Eliza may be seen as strong, precisely because the male playwright shows the brutality of the patriarchal systems of language and power which entrap her.

Reading for gender opens up a whole new way of reading and interpreting literature, just as 'writing gender' opened up new avenues for creativity to male writers including Shaw and Ibsen, as well as to women writers. ∎

The rest of this book asks you to study texts in full, rather than extracts. Yet in reading any text, you will do well to remember that each author has been influenced by other writers and by her or his social climate, influenced in turn by the literature of previous eras. Women's writing has been influenced by the (male) canon, black writing by white writing, and vice versa. But women have also influenced women, black writers have influenced each other. As a wide range of work makes its way into alternative 'canons', the circles of influence overlap and grow. The next chapter takes you further into the genre of poetry and asks you to apply what you've learned about 'gender and genre' to the reading and interpretation of (mainly) nineteenth- and twentieth-century poems.

Before you go on to read Chapter Two, take the time to re-read Tennyson's narrative poem 'The Lady of Shalott' and also Elizabeth Bishop's poem 'The Gentleman of Shalott', both printed in Part Two of this book.

Answers to the preconception game:

Extract One: F. Scott Fitzgerald, *The Last Tycoon*, (1960 edn), p.5.

Extract Two: Ben Okri, *The Famished Road* (1991, p.3.

Extract Three: Margaret Atwood, 'True Trash' in *Wilderness Tips* (1991), p.3.

Extract Four: D.H. Lawrence, *St. Mawr* (1950 edn), p.11.

Extract Five: Sylvia Plath, 'The Bull of Bendylaw', in *Collected Poems* (1981), p.108.

Extract Six: James Joyce, 'Chamber Music' (1971 edn), p.9.

Extract Seven: David Hare, *The Secret Rapture* (1988), p.1.

Extract Eight: Sarah Daniels, *Masterpieces* (1991), pp.163–4.

Note

1   The game was originally designed by Alison Smith for her students at Strathclyde University, and was presented in this form (using a different selection of extracts) to the Open University's Post-Graduate Literature and Gender Day Conference held at Parsifal College, London, April, 1993 (chair, Lizbeth Goodman).

Gender and poetry

by Angus Calder, with Lizbeth Goodman

Gender and poetry, an introduction

In this chapter we will engage in a more extended study of gender and poetry. As the chapter involves a wide range of poems, these have been printed for you in an anthology in Part Two of this book. Please now turn to the anthology, Section II, and look first at an extract from the earliest known female poet, Sappho, then at the poem which follows it, Letitia Elizabeth Landon's 'A Suttee'. **What can you say about the imagery Sappho uses in her poetic extract? Is it unusual, or familiar? Is the imagery of the later poem in any way similar? What is the effect of situating this poem on the same page with a poem by a nineteenth-century woman writer?**

D i s c u s s i o n

The extract from Sappho is short, and meant only to provide a glimpse into the poet's ability to conjure images, to use a few well-chosen words to represent ideas which resonate in the reader's imagination. The imagery of the garland of fresh flowers in a woman's hair is evocative, 'female' in some way, and also quite familiar. This is a pleasant but not particularly remarkable extract. In fact, the most remarkable thing about the verse is the very familiarity of it – thousands of years after it was first written, Sappho's poetry seems fresh, alive. This extract from Sappho has been deliberately juxtaposed with a poem by Letitia Elizabeth Landon written some 2,500 years later. While the later poem cannot be said to be 'modelled' on the earlier verse, still it is interesting to note the similarity of the imagery of the hair and flowers: are these 'female' beauties? Perhaps such images are timeless. But the carefree tone of Sappho's poetic extract is dramatically undercut by the context of Langdon's use of similar imagery in her poem about a 'suttee': a sacrifice by fire of the bride whose husband has died. That the later event takes place in a 'modern' world is, perhaps, shocking. That the two poets from such vastly different worlds should use similar imagery, in such radically different contexts, is fascinating. ■

Sappho's legacy

The *Oxford English Dictionary* is full of interesting items, namely:

> Sapphic ... 1501 [date of first usage] ... adj. Of or pertaining to Sappho ... the poetess of Lesbos (*c.*600 B.C.); spec[ifically] epithet of the metres used by her ... Sapphism ... 1890 ... Unnatural sexual relations between women.

Encyclopaedia Britannia (1964 edition) has an entry under 'sapphic metre': the four line 'sapphic stanza' found in much of her poetry was used by the Latin poet Horace and by medieval Christian hymn writers (again, in Latin).

Chapter Two

Sappho probably came from an aristocratic family in the Greek island of Lesbos, but her poetry differs from that of other ancient Greek poets known to us in that she used what seems to be the ordinary speech of the people around her. An excursion into standard works of reference establishes several points. First, extremely skilful and highly original poetry by a woman stands very close to the beginning of Western literary tradition. Secondly, Sappho wrote about love between women – hence our twentieth-century usage 'lesbianism'. The fact that the synonym 'sapphism' dates only from the 'naughty nineties' (1890s) and had no previous equivalent indicates the extreme reluctance of Christian European society to recognize that homosexual erotic love between women existed. The Oxford English Dictionary's word 'unnatural' says it all. Thirdly – and this must be stressed very strongly – as a pioneer of written-down poetry Sappho developed techniques which were not exclusively female – male poets could and did use her metres and stanza.

To continue with this analysis, we need to define a few terms. In the next section you will find key terms capitalized so that you can relocate the definitions when you need to.

Stylistic aspects of poetry

While you will not need to memorize terminology for analysing poetry, it will help if you familiarize yourself with the basic terms and stylistic aspects of poetry before we continue. Wherever possible, we'll draw examples from the poetry anthology in Part Two of this book. In fact, you may find it a useful exercise to check the poems referred to here with the full texts in Part Two, as attaching a term to a full poem is always more illuminating than simply looking at a few lines by way of example.

In discussing Sappho above, we used the terms 'metre' and 'stanza'. METRE refers to the means by which RHYTHM in verse is measured and described, according to the pattern of stressed and unstressed syllables or units of sound. STANZAS are the form or shapes into which poetic verse or composition is organized.

A VERSE, properly speaking, refers to one line of poetry, though it is commonly used to distinguish musical or metrical writing from prose (as in *The Oxford Book of Modern Verse*). Example: the poem 'The Lady of Shalott' is divided into four parts, each subdivided in stanzas, with 9 lines (or verses) in each stanza.

A SONNET is broadly defined as a fourteen-line poem. Rhyme schemes within sonnets may differ. An unrhymed sonnet is a possible concept, but is not common. Examples: two sonnets are printed in your anthology – Shakespeare's Sonnet LXXIII, and Elizabeth Barrett Browning's Sonnet XIV from *Sonnets from the Portuguese* (pp.265–66).

A COUPLET consists of two rhyming lines. The term 'couplet' is often used in conjunction with certain forms of sonnet. Shakespeare's sonnets end with a couplet set off from what comes before, for example:

This thou perceivs't, which makes this love more strong,
To love that well which thou must leave ere long ...

To notate the pattern of rhyme in a poem, we might adopt the convention of assigning letters of the alphabet to each new end rhyme. In the Elizabeth Landon poem, 'A Suttee', the first stanza contains four lines with the rhyme scheme *abab*; the second stanza continues with the scheme *cdcd*.

The two lines forming a sentence at the end of Elizabeth Barrett Browning's sonnet do not constitute a couplet, since they rhyme with lines 11 and 12, not with each other. However, in the middle of Jackie Kay's 'The Telling Part' (p.291) the two lines set out as a stanza *might* be seen as a couplet:

> She took me when I'd nowhere to g**o**
> my mammy is the best mammy in the world **OK**

since rhyme is so strongly suggested. And assonantal 'slant' rhyme like 'bone' and 'home' at the end of Grace Nichols's 'Wherever I Hang' (p.292) is common in twentieth-century verse.

A QUATRAIN has four lines, which may be rhymed in various patterns. Other stanza forms of three, six, seven, eight and nine lines are more or less familiar in English. Examples: some of the Emily Dickinson poems in Section IV are divided into quatrains, including poems 280 and 303. 'The Lady of Shalott' is, as we've said, divided into stanzas of nine lines with quite strong rhyme schemes.

BLANK VERSE is the term used to refer to unrhymed verse, which is the usual medium of Shakespeare's plays. English 'blank verse' is invariably written, like Shakespeare's, in IAMBIC PENTAMETER – lines of five IAMBS, or sets of stressed and unstressed syllables. Example: the first line of Shakespeare's Sonnet LXXIII,

> That **time** of **year** thou **mayst** in **me** be**hold** ...

(The syllables or 'feet' in boldface are 'stressed', or pronounced more strongly than others.)

FREE VERSE obeys no consistent rules as to 'metre', line-length, rhyme or stanza form. It will, however, tend to feature patterns of ASSONANCE (repeated vowel sounds) if only because these occur 'naturally' in the language itself. Examples: free verse poems are plentiful in our anthology. Look, for instance, at the poem by Margaret Atwood (*The Reincarnation of Captain Cook*), or at the two by Sylvia Plath ('The Colossus' and 'Lady Lazarus'), and indeed most of the contemporary poetry printed in this book.

RHYME occurs only when vowel sounds match at the end of lines. If rhyme occurs on the very last syllable, we call this MASCULINE rhyme. Examples: '**sweet** ... re**peat**', or '**strong** ... **long**' (as in the Shakespeare sonnet we looked at) or 'per**haps** ... **laps**' in lines 15 and 16 of Robert Browning's poem 'My Last Duchess'. But when stressed syllables are followed by unstressed syllables, this is called FEMININE RHYME. Examples: '**eat**ing ... re**peat**ing' or '**quiv**er ... **shiv**er' in stanza 2, lines 1 and 2 of 'The Lady of Shalott' (and throughout the poem), or '**clust**er ... **lust**re' in lines 1 and 3, stanza 1, of Letitia Elizabeth Landon's poem 'A Suttee'. (We will comment on this 'gendering' of rhyme and language in a moment.)

We also speak of INTERNAL RHYME within lines, which you will find if you look again at Sonnet XIV from Elizabeth Barrett Browning's *Sonnets from the Portuguese.* Internal rhyme involving repeated vowel sounds is also called ASSONANCE. Look at Eavan Boland's poem 'Hanging Curtains with an Abstract Pattern in a Child's Room' (Section V): lines 2 and 3 have 'unicorn, half-torn' lines 9 and 10, web, sheds and lines 12 and 13, line, signs.

ALLITERATION refers to repetition of consonants. Examples: 'When weeds, in wheels, shoot long and lovely and lush.' This line by G.M. Hopkins (1844–1889) uses repeated consonants: 'w' and 'l', and also uses ASSONANCE on 'ee' (weeds, wheels) and 'uh' (lovely, lush).

Though female poets often write in 'masculine' rhyme, and male poets in 'feminine rhyme', still the labels hold. The distinction exemplifies perfectly how language creates 'gender'. It assumes that men are stronger and firmer, women lighter and weaker. Similar assumptions have influenced the use, or non-use, of certain GENRES (classifications) of poetry by women. The term EPIC, for instance, refers to very long poems describing violent action and to certain heroic and aesthetic values associated with epic poetry. Though scholars have seriously suggested that Homer was a woman, no famous Western epic is normally attributed to a female author. PASTORAL poetry, set in an imaginary, idyllic rural landscape in which feelings and ideas are conveyed via 'shepherds' and 'shepherdesses' was also a male preserve. LYRIC poetry, pioneered by Sappho, was thought more suitable for women. The term evokes songs – sung to the accompaniment of a lyre – and the expression of strong feeling in a concentrated, succinct way. But the SONNET form which was developed in the middle ages, and was handled by such male poets as Petrarch, Dante, Shakespeare, Ronsard, Milton and Wordsworth, was a versatile medium suited to 'lyric' expression of passion as well as to philosophical exploration and political statement. It was available to nineteenth-century women in Britain, as indeed the HEROIC COUPLET had been to women in the previous century, when it had been a common medium in the so-called 'Augustan' period in English literature (the eighteenth century).

Confronting poetry

Verse by present-day poets is commonly written in *free* forms, including some with 'loose' rhyme patterns, others with no element of rhyme at all. Strict stanza forms now seem rather 'old fashioned', though it can plausibly be argued that someone who can't write in traditional forms should not claim to be a 'poet' at all.

Granted that most verse is now 'free', what differentiates poetry from prose? You have already looked, on our request, at poems by Charlotte Perkins Gilman and Alfred Tennyson which are written in traditional, rhymed forms. Most of the verse which we will inspect in this chapter is likewise 'traditional'. Please now read a 'free' poem which is not – Margaret Atwood's 'Reincarnation of Captain Cook' in Section I of Part Two.

First, try to describe the poem's form as it appears on the page.

Secondly, try to explain why this is classed as 'poetry' rather than 'prose'.

Third, does the 'form' support the poem's 'meaning' in any way that you can identify and explain?

D i s c u s s i o n

1   The poem is arranged in stanzas of irregular length (4 lines, then 5, 3, 2, 4, 3, 4, 2). A basic traditional form is alluded to, the quatrain. After the first stanza, Atwood plays free variations. Yet the poem seems tightly controlled. Did you look for stresses (emphasized syllables)? My ear gives me this pattern in the first stanza:

> **ear**lier than I could **learn** [would you stress 'I'?]
> the **maps** had been **col**oured **in**.
> When I **plea**ded the **kings told** me
> **noth**ing was **left** to ex**plore** ...

2   If your reply to our second question was 'this is poetry because the lines aren't justified on the right-hand side of the page', your apparently naïve answer was pertinent. Bar 'prose poems', which are relatively rare, poetry is printed differently from prose, which always suggests – whatever its rhythmic variety when read aloud – consecutive, even flow, broken only by paragraphs, which are created at will but according to well-understood rules. (When these rules seem to be violated, we are liable to start talking about 'poetic prose', such as that used in Jamaica Kincaid's short story 'Girl', to be discussed in Chapter 3.) The way poetry is set out, whether it is 'traditional' or 'free', emphasizes pauses by the use of line-breaks.

  Pauses attract special attention to the last word in a line and normally give it extra weight (stress). Where line-breaks are unexpected, they increase the uncertainty as to where stress falls by their disruption of 'natural' flow. On the other hand they may vividly suggest the 'natural' pauses and emphases of everyday speech. The end of Atwood's second stanza does both at once. It makes our 'mind's ear' pause after 'cairns' where prose normally would carry on through the 'and'. But this means that 'tourists' comes at us with special force. (I hear a sardonic, rather disgusted North American voice rolling the 'r'.) This also emphasizes an important assonance. '**Tour**ists' echoes back to 'his**tor**ians' and now I hear the same disgust in the way that word is voiced. 'Fake' in between these two words turns out to be determining the tone here. Both the 'serious' historians and the recreational tourists are implicated in bogusness and superficiality. Do you see how the line-break at 'fake teeth/belts' is delightfully pointed? The modern-day, middle-aged historian probably has 'fake' (false) teeth but additionally she, or he in this instance, wears a 'belt' of animal teeth, pretending to be in tune with ancient or modern 'savages', along with the wreath which goes with his/her pretensions to be heir to the epic poets of ancient Greece and Rome, who were ceremonially awarded laurel wreaths (hence the modern term 'poet laureate').

3   In this poem, the 'freedom' to write verse in ways outside its mostly male 'tradition' is used to present a speaker who has been subjected to a 'traditional' geography which inhibits her or his 'freedom'. She or he claims that the atlases were always wrong and sets off, as Captain Cook set off to the unexplored Pacific, to find new places. But unlike Cook, whose ships flew the Union Jack, Atwood's speaker carries a 'blank banner'. Escaping from 'fake' history and imposed geographical ideas, the speaker disavows both nationality and preconceived 'causes'.

Since Atwood is Canada's most famous novelist, you may have known before you read this poem that she is a feminist. You may well have read the poem as a feminist statement: men ('kings') have taught us a way of looking at the world which imprisons us in bogus predestination. But apart from 'kings' no word in the poem is unequivocally 'gendered'. The 'I' of the speaker is not gender-specific. 'Historians', recently, have not always been male. If you remember that most history has been written to serve the interests of ruling élites, then 'kings' and 'historians' both evoke power and class as strongly as gender. A working-class male critic, for example, might interpret a Cook-like search in exactly Atwood's terms. Cook, after all, was a man – though his surname is the same as the noun describing one who enacts the traditional domestic role which is still conventionally assigned to women. ■

We hope this discussion has reminded you of, or introduced you to, an essential characteristic of poetry – not one which distinguishes it from all prose, but one which makes both effective verse and the prose we call 'poetic' different from utilitarian writing. You can tell a story plainly. Newspapers purport to do so. Plainly written novels give us fiction efficiently. We demand of a legal or medical textbook, a scientific paper or a car-user's manual only accuracy, and would be horrified if the utterance of any of these became 'poetic'. Poetic language is playful.

We noted 'playful' features just now in Atwood's poem. There is word-play ('Cook' carries a kind of pun and we read 'fake teeth' doubly.) There is teasing uncertainty ('how do I stress this?'). There is a kind of 'musicality' arising from assonance which helps to give the rather shapeless-looking poem form. See how the assonance of 'cleaned ... beach ... gleaming', of 'land' and 'arrows' in Atwood's last two lines gives them a sort of tightness and punch, makes them 'conclusive'.

Gender and publication

Why, since Sappho, have so few famous poets been women? Women got in 'on the ground floor' when prose fiction developed. Since Jane Austen at least, female novelists have been 'canonized'. Yet if you looked at a range of standard anthologies of verse, period by period, you would probably conclude that only Emily Dickinson has a reasonably secure place in the canon, though other women come and go according to the whims of particular editors.

No female poet had come close to 'canonization' before the Romantic period. But the omens then, around 1830, were good. Two women, Felicia Hemans and Letitia Elizabeth Landon, were at this time as famous as the most famous living male poets. Elizabeth Barrett Browning was a best-seller by the 1850s, with a boldly feminist 'novel in verse', of epic length, *Aurora Leigh*. Eliza Cook and Adelaide Anne Procter were also Victorian best-sellers, and such writers as Christina Rossetti and Emily Pfeiffer were very highly regarded by the (almost invariably male) critics of that day. Yet when Alfred H. Myles in the 1890s began to publish a comprehensive round-up of the nineteenth century's poets in English, he found just one of his ten volumes sufficient for women poets, though some female writers also featured in the volume devoted to religious verse. 'Prejudice' on Myles's part doesn't explain this, since he sought out and included some quite obscure female poets. Though he might have scoured 'provincial' public libraries for local publications, as the poet Tom Leonard has recently done (*Radical Renfrew*, 1990), this wouldn't have redressed the balance. Leonard is pro-feminist by conviction, yet of 68 'uncanonical' nineteenth-century writers anthologized by him – some anonymous – only 5 are definitely female.

Surely the women's movement of the Suffrage Era helped to set that right? No. Statistical analysis of twentieth-century anthologies undertaken by an Open University doctoral student, Christine Fitton, has established that ratios as low as Myles's 1:9 still occurred after women had 'the vote' and if representation is normally now higher than that, it has never been anywhere near equal (Fitton, 'From reactive to self-referencing poet', 1992).

Didn't the new feminist movement, from the 1960s on, at last correct this imbalance? Well, one outcome has been a sizeable number of anthologies devoted solely to poetry by women (some of them are cited in the Further Reading list at the end of this chapter). But while a very 'generous' anthology of *The New Poetry* edited by three men (M. Hulse et al.) for the specialist poetry publisher Bloodaxe in 1993 includes 55 'British Isles' poets born since 1940, only 17 – less than one in three – are female.

But that's stuffy old Britain – surely North American and Australasian women have done better? Not if we can judge from the *Oxford Companion to Twentieth-Century Poetry in English* (1994), edited by Ian Hamilton. This includes biographical entries for equal numbers of 'British Isles' and US poets, and represents Canadian, Australian and New Zealand writers fully. Out of 1500 poets, only 'about 200', Hamilton confesses, are women.

So there's no mystery, really – it's just that fewer women have written poetry, and there are still far fewer seeking print? There is some reason to doubt whether the first part of that statement was true even in the nineteenth century and much evidence from eyes and ears to suggest that the second part may be false. Poetry readings, 'writers workshops' and evening classes on writing attract lots of women. And of course, poetry is often regarded as 'a women's thing': a taste for verse is 'effeminate' in many eyes. 'Poetry' is by no means gendered male. In direct and explicit contradiction to *The New Poetry*, mentioned above, Bloodaxe in 1993 published Linda France's anthology of *Sixty Women Poets*, all but two of them living.

By the twentieth century, the independent female author – journalist, novelist, travel-writer, even poet – was commonplace. But most editors of significant magazines – those in which rising new poets are printed alongside the latest work of established writers – have been men. The same applies to publishers in prestigious firms, and to most editors of best-selling 'standard' anthologies. It is impossible not to conclude that it has been far easier for male poets to get published – first in magazines, then in 'slim volumes', finally in 'collected poems'. Female poets, like male ones, publish in a genre dominated by living and recently dead male authors who are considered 'major'.

Because the 'major' male poets have been so much anthologized, republished, studied and written about, it must (alas) be 'historically' true that their work in a sense 'defines' twentieth-century British verse. Think of Atwood's 'Captain Cook' poem in this connection; there is an influential book by John Press, anthologizing and commenting on poetry, titled *A Map of Modern English Verse* (1969) in which, of 56 poets on the 'map' only two are female! Recent women poets have faced a choice between positioning themselves within the male-dominated 'traditional' and 'canonical' construction of the genre they work in, or running the risk of marginalizing themselves within or away from the genre by finding new sites for their writing in women's groups, women's presses and feminist agitation.

Reading gender in poetry

Men and Women

Men and Women is the title of a very famous volume of poems (1855) by Robert Browning. This likeable and decent man chose to foreground 'gender' as an issue. The Victorians, arraigned by their children for 'hypocrisy', were in fact in their own way most courageous in facing up to problems and contradictions in their society. With 'gender', as with other matters at issue, there were men and women found on both sides. The philosopher John Stuart Mill was one of the male pro-feminists, but there were women, including poets, who endorsed – at the risk of self-contradiction – the subordinate role conventionally assigned to females.

Please now re-read 'A Suttee' by Letitia Elizabeth Landon. In the opening image of a woman's hair, we have already noted a similarity to that created in Sappho's poetic fragment. But we can also look for more subtle gendered meanings in the poem.

If we define ideology as a term referring to a set, or linked sets, of assumptions and notions held either by groups within a society, or by the whole society, what ideological position, if any, is represented in this poem?

D i s c u s s i o n

If you noted that the poem seems to advocate complete female submission to the male you were incontrovertibly correct, but this isn't the whole truth.

Though Landon never went to India, she used the 'oriental' subject-matter popularized by the male Romantics Thomas Moore and Lord Byron. 'A Suttee' refers to the custom whereby a widowed Hindu woman was required to burn in the funeral pyre of her late husband. It was perhaps rather daring of Landon to appear to endorse this custom, which was deplored by both church and state. But her female readers would have easily aligned the poem's sentiment with two conventional views. Firstly, the romantic lover could and should have no existence apart from her beloved. Secondly, and more prosaically, the wife must sacrifice herself for her husband. In the wholly extreme case posited by the poet, everyday wifely duty is in fact 'sublimated' – raised to glorious beauty. ■

If you look at Christina Rossetti's poem 'L.E.L.' in the anthology, you'll see a conflict expressed between opposing values in women's lives: between love of art, love of nature and romantic love. Such conflicts were often expressed in women's poetry, and in the lives of several of the female poets we'll consider. But now, let's look at a poem by a man, about a women, in the voice of a male narrator: Robert Browning's 'My Last Duchess'. Give it a first reading now, if you don't know it already. **To what extent is the poem, and the story it tells, 'gendered'?**

Discussion

Here, it helps to have some background: in so far as this is a story about a woman, told by a male narrator and written by a male poet, the 'gendering' of the poem may be seen to be similar to that of Tennyson's 'Lady of Shalott'. But this poem is quite different in its presentation of gender. 'My Last Duchess' was written by Browning in 1842, before his famous meeting with Elizabeth Barrett, who became his wife (or, to put it more positively, 'married him'). It is probably the best known of all his 'dramatic monologues.' A failed playwright, Browning developed a form which enabled him to 'dramatize' individual characters. The speakers of these monologues are in most cases self-evidently very different people from the poet himself. Here we have an imaginary Italian duke. Scholarship tells us that Browning had in mind Alfonso II, Duke of Ferrara, whose first wife, a very young woman, died after three years of marriage in 1561, after which her husband negotiated to marry a niece of the Count of Tyrol. But as the poem comes to us, its 'date' is not clear – we are somewhere between the fifteenth and the nineteenth century. The art history evoked is also vague. 'Fra' (meaning 'brother', friar) recalls two famous Italian painters in holy orders – Fra Angelico (*c.*1400–1455) and Fra Lippo Lippi (1406–1469), the subject of another famous monologue by Browning. Fra Pandolf's technique is *fresco*, involving the application of paint to damp plaster before it dries – this is why he works 'busily a day', and only a day, though we presume that he spent many hours before this sketching the Duchess. To portray a woman of distinguished rank in *fresco* was not usual, but the word itself, meaning 'fresh' in English, is important to the poem's meaning.

Formally, the poem is a wonderful success. Browning used the five-foot iambic line, which was the staple of Shakespeare's plays, where a 'weak', unstressed syllable is followed by a stressed syllable, five times. But if we look at a famous example of this, Hamlet's

To **be** or **not** to **be**, that **is** the **ques**tion …

we can see that the stress pattern is not rigidly fixed. Hamlet's next line,

whether 'tis **nob**ler **in** [or in?] the **mind** to **suff**er …

must surely begin with a stress. In fact, English writers have played infinite variation on the iambic pentameter, which remained until the twentieth century the commonest unit in English poetry. Browning's very first line exemplifies the freedom which writers could exercise within the basic pattern.

Where do we stress Browning's first line? 'That's', 'my', 'last' and 'Duchess' are all candidates. 'That's **my** last **Duch**ess' is orthodoxly iambic, but '**that's** my **last** Duchess' seems a more likely pattern in 'real-life' speech. The poem goes on like this, offering anyone reading it aloud a wide range of possible emphases, and hence of interpretations of the Duke's character. These interpretations are also alive in the mind of the silent reader. For this reason, those of us who know it well find that each re-reading suggests a new interpretation. It is in this way magnificently 'playful', refusing to settle into cut-and-dried stability, like the playfulness of the Duchess herself.

The pentameters here are ranged in couplets. However one reads individual lines, to oneself or aloud, rhyme in couplets imposes a stately pace appropriate to the Duke's dignity. The tension between anarchic 'freedom' and despotic 'order' is part of the poem's subject-matter. The very form of the poem is gendered – 'male' control (couplet-rhyme) opposes the wandering stresses of 'female' fluidity.

It is not clear what the Duke did to his wife. The painter's fate is also left obscure though 'all smiles stopped *together*' may suggest to you a common fate for the pair. We can imagine them separated, merely, or imprisoned – or murdered. This last chilling possibility would in fact serve the purpose of the Duke in making this speech. The man he addresses is the emissary of a certain Count whose daughter the Duke now wishes to marry. In return for his 'nine-hundred-years-old name' the Duke confidently expects a large dowry. But the man he addresses is warned that the Count's 'fair daughter' had better understand that she must submit completely to the Duke's will.

This would have seemed quite topical to readers in Britain *c.*1850. The 'marriage market' persisted in the upper levels of society. Conventionally a suitable 'gentleman' – an 'old' name was a great help – took another gentleman's daughter off his hands in return for a dowry in cash, kind or both. The husband then had full control of his wife's income as well as her person. Divorce was rare, and always scandalous, so that husbands might, and indeed did, resort to various cruel and coercive ways of punishing unsatisfactory partners. Browning's Duke merely takes to an extreme a patriarchal and possessive view of women common enough in Victorian Britain.

We have seen in the poem an opposition between male control and female fluidity. Other, overlapping, oppositions found in the poem might be set out like this:

Masculine	Feminine
power, pride, possessiveness	helplessness
constraint	joyousness
art	art

We are talking about matters conventionally 'gendered' but not in fact the result of biological difference: is 'joyousness' reserved only to women?

The Duchess's general fault in the Duke's eyes was that her heart was 'too soon made glad'. She related frankly and easily to everything around her – to the beauties of nature (sunset), to the fruits of nature (cherries), to creatures in nature (the mule) and to people of all ranks. The 'faint half-flush' which Fra Pandolf has captured is typical of her spontaneous expression of feeling. She experiences 'joy', the Duke mistrusts it. With the 'depth and passion' of her 'earnest glance' she further suggests profundity in her nature. She *is* life, full and quivering, and the Duke's refusal to 'stoop' denies him life.

50

Yet he is a connoisseur of art. In the last three lines he flaunts his taste. The object alluded to is a bronze. In metal, a German sculptor has 'tamed' the energy of Neptune, classic God of the Sea – himself seen 'taming a sea horse' which represents the sea's energies. This is 'masculine' and 'patriarchal' art with a vengeance! On the other hand, Fra Pandolf's *fresco*, which had to be executed swiftly, is as fresh as its subject, the Duchess. Such art, in complete contrast to the Neptune, is fluent and fluid, improvisational – and we might say, 'feminine'. However, even such art as this involves 'freezing' life and time. It can record the 'spot of joy' but neither its causes nor its outcome. And the Duchess's translation into valuable 'art' confirms her status as a possessed 'object'. ■

Browning's poem 'playfully' and obliquely raises a dilemma which many artists before and since have confronted:

> Alas! What boots it with incessant care
> To tend the homely slighted shepherd's trade,
> And strictly meditate the thankless Muse?
> Were it not better done as others use,
> To sport with Amaryllis in the shade,
> Or with the tangles of Neaera's hair?

Thus John Milton had expressed the dilemma in 'Lycidas' (1637), a pastoral work in which the poet is conventionally equated with a 'shepherd'. The artist in labouring at his craft is cut off from the pleasures of life – yet these very pleasures are part of his, or her, subject-matter. The Duchess's spontaneity cannot be conveyed spontaneously, even in *fresco*. The dichotomy or separation of two kinds of experience (art and life) is a very central theme in much women's poetry, as we shall see.

So, let's turn to Browning's 'real life' wife. Elizabeth Barrett Browning's love poetry is perhaps best captured in her *Sonnets from the Portuguese*; Sonnet XIV is printed in your anthology. In this poem, the female narrator seems to ask her lover/reader precisely *not* to do what Browning's narrator does – Elizabeth Barrett Browning's poetic voice wants to be valued for herself and her love, *not* for image or beauty (which changes and fades – and which can be mistreated, as was Browning's Duchess).

The novel in verse *Aurora Leigh* was published in 1856, ten years after the writer's marriage, aged 39, to Robert Browning, and seven after the birth of their son. The poem's narrator, Aurora, is a successful poet writing professionally. Please now turn to our second extract from it, 'The Poet, on Her Art and Its Penalties'.

Critics complained in their lifetimes about 'obscurity' in the verse of both Brownings. But the first section of this extract, down to 'book, which is a man too', despite incidental puzzles, seems to make these points pretty clearly:

1 The artist – 'he' apparently stands for artists of both sexes, as 'man' does for the human race – pays the penalty of living through ordinary experience while trying to turn it into lasting art. Such art requires passion …

2 But the passion which she or he feels and tries to express in writing does not in itself guarantee effective art. Technique is required.

The rest of the long poem shows that Aurora has won encouragement from admirers, but success does not make her feel fulfilled. Only God – certainly here the male 'Father' – knows about the special misery of the famous woman who remains 'unkissed', unmarried. She can only write out of the 'passionate womanhood' which her admirers praise because she is indeed passionate, but her passion has no physical outlet. The keenly imagined vignette of the father giving Aurora's book to his adolescent daughter could detain us for several pages with its subtle dramatization of the role of literature in patriarchal, Victorian society. The gist of it is that the poet, writing of love, sees her work caught up in the patterns of real, everyday love from which her practice of her art excludes her. 'Alas! what boots it …?' What's the use? At this stage in her story, Aurora feels that art and fame are no substitute for life itself.

Granted that 'art and life' is a subject which Elizabeth shares with Robert, are her views 'gendered' differently, and if so, how would you express the differences?

D i s c u s s i o n

Surely Elizabeth does 'gender' the 'art versus life' question differently from Robert. In 'My Last Duchess' woman is the *object* of art. She represents the delightful life which art strives to 'capture'. For Aurora Leigh, herself an artist, woman is *subject* – and subjectively her conflict is between art and marriage. In 1856 the fulfilment of having children was only open to women of her class within wedlock, and so was the sexual activity which produced children. Concentrating on her art, Aurora feels that she has denied herself a woman's true life. Of course, Elizabeth Barrett Browning's own productivity after marriage showed that the two could be combined, and at the end of her very long narrative poem, Aurora has acquired a husband on her own terms. Since he has been blinded, it is perfectly clear who will control the relationship. (This echoes, of course, the 'happy ending' reached after the blinding of Rochester in Charlotte Brontë's *Jane Eyre*, published not long before.) ■

Barrett Browning both delighted and scandalized readers with the 'masculine' worldliness of *Aurora Leigh*. She dealt with subjects – socialism, rape, prostitution, 'high society' viewed satirically – which female poets were not supposed to handle. Her assured technique, too, is 'masculine' – she employs the 'Shakespearean' iambic pentameter in blank verse with suppleness and colloquial freedom. This must have seemed especially surprising as the work of a woman who before her marriage had spent her adult years largely as a feeble invalid, and, latterly, as an almost hopeless, bookish recluse, or as a 'caged bird' (as in our first extract from *Aurora Leigh*). It was as if Tennyson's 'Lady of Shalott', to whom we now turn, had left her loom, plunged into life – and survived with aplomb and glee.

To sum up: gender differences may affect the writing and reading of poetry by women and men, even when they are of the same period, class, race and share a common stylistic approach to poetry.

From the *Lady of Shalott* to the *Gentleman of Shalott*

Tennyson's 'Lady of Shalott'

We now reconsider perhaps the most famous poem by the most successful of all Victorian poets, Alfred, Lord Tennyson. I am going to offer a markedly different reading from Lizbeth Goodman's in Chapter One, though, of course, I am not suggesting that her reading is 'wrong'. The 'playfulness' of poetic language will always permit multiple valid readings. I want to relate the poem to its time of production – to early-Victorian concerns about poetry and art in general, and the ways in which these concerns were 'gendered'.

Around 1830, when Tennyson published his first book, male Romanticism seemed exhausted. Byron, Keats and Shelley had all died young, Scott and Coleridge, both soon to die, had long been more or less silent in verse, and Wordsworth, who lived till Tennyson inherited his Laureateship in 1850, was writing only stale, conventional stuff. The young poet's chief rivals were two women – Mrs Felicia Hemans and Letitia Elizabeth Landon, who published as 'L.E.L.'. Both were professionals, living by their pens. In a recent monograph on Tennyson, Leonee Ormond has observed: 'Tennyson's preoccupation with death, desolation and frustration is characteristic of women writing at this period. He not only adopted their female persona, but in time appropriated most of their public' (Ormond, *Alfred Tennyson*, 1993, pp.24–5).

Some might argue that the choice of a 'female' persona might have been influenced by Tennyson's own ambiguous sexual identity. Though there is no evidence that he ever sought or found physical expression for it, his love for his Cambridge friend Arthur Hallam, who became engaged to Tennyson's sister, clearly went beyond the usual bounds of male friendship. Hallam's early death plunged him into gloom for years, prompting his great sequence *In Memoriam* (1850). When his second book of poems was published in 1833, one adverse critic taunted in particular a poem titled 'O Darling Room', about a bedroom which the poet had shared with Hallam (Martin, *Tennyson*, 1969, pp.169–71). What we can say for certain is that Tennyson, for whatever reason, was particularly interested in depicting female characters.

In two poems which later became especially famous, Tennyson presented lonely women as central figures. In 'Mariana', drawing on Shakespeare's *Measure for Measure*, a betrayed woman pines drearily in her 'moated grange'. The Lady of Shalott was his second such figure, comparable in her isolated yet 'beautiful' death to that sad figure, Shakespeare's Ophelia (see Figure 9).

Technically, like much of Tennyson's work, 'The Lady of Shalott' is brilliantly original. If the rhyme scheme *aaaabcccb* had ever been used before, no one remembers it; the effect is still deliciously fresh. The subject-matter, though it relates to the Arthurian cycle of legends much used in European literature, is also original. Tennyson had read a medieval Italian story about how *la Damigella di Scalot* died of love for Lancelot of the Lake. But as his modern editor points out, this old story 'has no Arthur, Queen, mirror, weaving, curse, song, river or island'; it does have a funeral

Figure 9   Sir John Everett Millais (1829–1896), *Ophelia*, 1851–2, oil on canvas, 76 x 118 cm, the Tate Gallery, London.

voyage ending on the seashore (Ricks, *The Poems of Tennyson*, 1969, pp.354–8). The mirror and loom figure largely, especially in visual representations of the Lady, as we saw in the three images of the Lady of Shalott (Figures 6–8). Two more modern images (Figures 10 and 11) also share this emphasis. **Bearing these images in mind, how would you summarize Tennyson's handling of the 'art versus life' theme in relation to gender?**

Discussion

The two modern images seem to emphasize the Lady's physical frame as a woman, as well as the frame of her loom, and mirror. So, the mirror and loom have symbolic significance. But the mirror is not free invention. It was a necessary accompaniment to the work of a weaver – set behind a tapestry as it progressed so that the worker could see the effect from the right side. The Lady is a serious working artist, though the art of weaving, like sewing, is one specially associated with women (and for this reason, perhaps, is rather lowly valued). The Lady is at work weaving representations of 'life'. But her case is more extreme than Aurora Leigh's; she is cut off not only from the joys of 'young lovers lately wed' but from the busy life of reapers and market girls. Her tapestry is a reflection of what she sees only in reflected form – 'I am half sick of shadows' refers to this. Yet she is 'cursed' to emerge into life only at the cost of her own death. Sudden love of Lancelot moves her to invite the curse. But at least, as she floats downstream, she can sing, replacing one art with another.

Figure 10   Shelah Horvitz (1960–), *'I am Half Sick of Shadows …'*, 1981, pencil on paper, 41 x 35 cm, Private Collection. Reproduced from *Ladies of Shalott: A Victorian Masterpiece and its Context* (1985), by permission of David Winton Bell Gallery, Brown University, Providence.

Figure 11   C. H. Johnson (dates unknown), *The Lady of Shalott*, 1891, half-tone process on paper. Published in *The Complete Works of Alfred, Lord Tennyson*, 1891, New York, Frederick A. Stokes and Co. Reproduced by courtesy of the Alderman Library, University of Virginia, Charlottesville.

As Lizbeth Goodman has pointed out, the voice of the poem is 'masculine' throughout in so far as we assume the first person narrator to be male – and the last word is very explicitly given to Lancelot. However, the knight's speech, in the context of the whole poem, must be read ironically. The Lady has given her life for him – all Lancelot can say is 'she has a lovely face' before uttering a conventional prayer. This prayer closes the poem in a way that pious Victorian readers probably found reassuring. But it does not resolve the tension in the poem between secret 'feminine' life charged with frustration and passion and the busy, confident 'masculine' world.

For Tennyson, it seems, the inner life of the solitary working artist is 'feminine'. We attribute the beauty achieved in the poem, in its many haunting phrases evocative of nature and medieval life, to an imagination close to the Lady's own. When Tennyson's 1830 volume of poems was attacked by critics, his friend Hallam, defending him in the *Englishman's Magazine* wrote: 'Whenever the mind of the artist suffers itself to be occupied, during its powers of creation, by any other predominant motive than the desire of beauty, the result is false in art' (Ormond, *Alfred Tennyson*, 1993, p.25). One might think of the Lady's obsessed creativity in the light of that remark. ∎

Foremothers

The idea that art was, for a woman practitioner, 'cursed' and destructive was strong during the first two thirds of the nineteenth century, greatly weakened by its end. In this section, we will examine the efforts of women who wrote poetry to clarify their role, establishing and building on the achievements of earlier writers, in prose as well as in verse.

As Barrett Browning put it in *Aurora Leigh*, reading and writing involved escape from a 'cage' – the cage in which intelligent women were placed by a combination of patriarchal authority and Evangelical propriety. Young Aurora, at first reared in Italy by her father, comes to England after his death to be under the charge of her aunt.

Please now read the first extract from *Aurora Leigh* in Section II of our anthology. **Does this text invite sympathy for Aurora's aunt?**

Discussion

Remarkably, it doesn't. Barrett Browning who, before her elopement with Robert had looked superficially like a 'caged bird' herself, is fierce, almost bilious in her satire. The church which involves Aurora's aunt in its palliative good works, the book club which preserves her 'intellectual' (her mind) from dangerous ideas, provide bars for her cage, but Aurora despises her submission to them.

Flying free, though, where did the woman poet go? The 'Muse' inspiring poets is conventionally gendered as female. For the male poet this implies an interesting dichotomy. The 'Muse' determining his own 'subjectivity' is accordingly herself 'subject', an active agent. Or so the myth of the 'muse' suggests. ∎

The poet Christina Rossetti (1830–1894) was the sister of the Pre-Raphaelite poet and painter Dante Gabriel. A second brother, William Michael, became a distinguished man of letters. In the world of the 'Pre-Raphaelite Brotherhood' sexuality was remarkably 'free' for the period – at least for the men concerned. But Christina kept out of that, and out of their combative public life. An unmarried, deeply pious Anglican, she remained devoted to their mother. This may make her sound gloomy and boring, but she wasn't. 'Goblin Market', which she published in her thirties and which brought her considerable and enduring fame, is a wonderfully original fable full of sensuous and grotesque detail in which one sister successfully defends another against the corruption offered by 'goblin' males. It permits both acceptable 'Christian' readings and highly subversive ones. (It is now often read as a Lesbian text). Christina Rossetti is technically the most brilliant of Victorian woman poets, equally at ease in conventional forms like the sonnet and in those which she devised herself.

Please now read Christina Rossetti's 'In An Artist's Studio'. **Drawing on your readings in Tennyson and both Brownings, could you summarize the relationship between 'art' and the female as Rossetti presents it?**

Discussion

'In An Artist's Studio' is a sonnet. The form, as developed by male poets had been used in many long sequences in which the lover addressed, or meditated on, his beloved; Petrarch's Laura and the 'Dark Lady' of Shakespeare's sonnets functioned like terrestrial muses. Christina Rossetti turns this inside out, examining the male painter's relationship with his female model. Her handling of the 'mirror' motif is more complex than Tennyson's in 'The Lady of Shalott'. The male artist 'mirrors' in his canvasses the beauty of a female sitter, once patient and joyful. He has tried to transform her into queen, saint, angel, 'nameless girl', but cannot alter her true 'meaning' which is contained within herself. To him we owe the preservation, up to a point, of that 'meaning'. Yet her life changed, with 'waiting' and sorrow and loss of hope. Now his 'dream', present in the paintings, stands at odds with what she actually is.

The thoughts prompted by this poem are very uncomfortable. In a sense, the male artist is justified in 'feeding' on the beauty of his sitter for the purposes of his art. But there is an awkward division not only between male artist and female 'object', but between the art which endures and the life which wanes and perishes.

The example of Sappho implied that for the woman poet the dichotomy might be fatal. Sappho had been a great poet. But the acceptable, heterosexual version of Sappho current in the nineteenth century had her hurling herself to her death in the sea at last for unrequited love of a man, Phaon. Angela Leighton comments that 'Sappho's leap gives to Victorian poetry a figure for women's creativity as penultimate and doomed – as on a cliff-edge of desire and death which is imminently self-silencing and punishing' (Leighton, *Victorian Women Poets*, 1992, pp.35–6).

As Leighton points out, the death of L.E.L. reinforced the conclusion drawn from the Sappho myth that the fruits of a successful literary career for a woman 'are, ultimately, death' (Ibid., p.57). ∎

I would like now to consider three poems in the anthology written by women about their 'foremothers'. We have already discussed Rossetti and

Barrett Browning; the third poem is by Emily Pfeiffer. Pfeiffer (1827–1890) was three years older than Christina Rossetti, but unlike her ardently embraced the movement for female emancipation which snowballed from the 1860s onward. Born Emily Davis in Montgomeryshire, the daughter of an impecunious army officer, she married Jurgen Edward Pfeiffer, a German merchant settled in Britain. Though she had no need to write for a living, she produced ten volumes of poetry and two of prose. Dying, childless, soon after her husband, she left £2,000 for the higher education of women, which was used to erect, in 1895, Aberdare Hall, the first dormitory for female students at the University of Wales.

Please now read Christina Rossetti's 'L.E.L.', Elizabeth Barrett Browning's 'To George Sand' and Emily Pfeiffer's 'The Last Light'. Note what each in turn makes of her 'foremother'.

Discussion

Barrett Browning had written a poem 'L.E.L.'s Last Question' in 1839. Christina Rossetti knew it, and misquotes or deliberately rephrases the refrain 'one thirsty for a little love' as 'Whose heart is breaking for a little love'. Her own poem is about the solitary sensibility in general rather than L.E.L. in particular. The feeling core of human experience and personality exists – like the Lady of Shalott – outside the busy world and is unable to express itself in it. Only through its title does the poem allude to art, but it evidently expresses Rossetti's own sense of the distance between the artistic self – equated with the feeling self – and the outer life. As Angela Leighton puts it, 'she embraced the pervasive myth of the woman poet as fitfully inspired, sincere and sad, and too sensitive for real life'; contemporaries who knew their Tennyson called her the 'Mariana of Albany Street' (Leighton, *Victorian Women Poets*, 1992, p.119). Formally, the poem concludes with the pious thought that after death God will solve all.

However, the poem is not dominated by piety or even by gloom. It is 'playful'. It 'plays', for instance, on conventional notions of 'dying for love.' If Sappho's heart was broken by love, this one is breaking for *lack of* love. Landon had been a lively, popular woman who had written incessantly about love. Rossetti implies that her tragedy was that she never experienced it. Her 'rustling show' of fine clothes, her 'sporting' and 'jesting' nevertheless do conceal her predicament. The poem's metres are light, not dolorous. There is a sprightliness in Rossetti's piety which implicitly belies the resignation which the poem seems to recommend.

Barrett Browning's sonnet 'To George Sand' is really much gloomier. This is another poem written by one woman to, or for, another – in this case to George Sand, the French novelist whose life and writing inspired widespread interest and respect. (Sand's masculine pen-name may also have helped in the establishment of her reputation.) The poem adds to a growing body of work about the nature of literary influence and the development of a female tradition of writing. If the last line is lame and obscure, this may be because the poet simply cannot rationalize her contradictory responses. She admires Sand's boldness, but feels squeamish about it. Sand is unable to break out of the cage into a 'manly' position without denying her 'woman's nature', which bursts out in unhappiness and is still discernible amid her 'poet-fire'. Barrett Browning is thinking of

Christians burnt for their faith; she sees Sand as a martyr. Like Rossetti, she looks to God for a solution. Sand's conflict can only be resolved by death, which will 'unsex' her.

Pfeiffer's sonnets were particularly admired. You may feel that 'The Last Light' is too smoothly resolved. It plays a feminist variation on the familiar Victorian theme of inevitable 'progress'. The 'insurgence' of womanhood which George Eliot has 'commanded' with the authority of the Greek goddess of wisdom, Pallas Athene, is on the brink of 'victory'. But is it not rather exhilarating to come across such confidence after the dubieties even of Barrett Browning? ■

The selection of poetry by Victorian Scottish and Irish women poets (Section III of the anthology) shows that the genre of poetry was popular with women writing in different languages and styles, though the situation of the female artist would remain problematic into the twentieth century But the impasses represented in the poems which we have looked at in this section were broken through with the help of such 'foremothers' as Sand and Eliot – and Barrett Browning herself. Elizabeth Bishop (1911–1979), to whom we now turn, had a far from ideal life, but neither she nor her admirers seem ever to have doubted that she had the right to use her wonderful literary gifts on exactly the same terms as any man.

'The Gentleman of Shalott'

Though Elizabeth Bishop is recognized as one of the major twentieth-century writers in English, and was a professional author throughout her adult life, she was not as prolific as the nineteenth-century women we have been looking at. She teased poems slowly into shape, finding a lucrative market for them eventually in *The New Yorker* and other magazines.

Though regarded as a United States writer, she was three-quarters Canadian by birth. Her father, from a wealthy family of New England building contractors, died when she was eight months old. Her mother had a breakdown from which she never recovered; when she died in a mental hospital Elizabeth, then 23, had not seen her for 17 years. Initially reared by grandparents in a Nova Scotia village, Elizabeth then acquired an expensive New England education which brought her into contact with several women who later became writers. She suffered acutely from depression, exacerbated by her asthma and her alcoholism, but she asked her executor to put 'Awful but cheerful' on her tombstone (Miller, *Elizabeth Bishop*, 1993, p.550).

She was lesbian, and from 1951 lived for many years in Brazil. (Bishop's correspondence from Brazil and many Bishop manuscripts are held by Olin Library Special Collections, St Louis, Missouri.) However, she did not like being praised as a woman poet and was 'deeply uncomfortable' with the notion that there might be a female tradition of poetry separate from the male (Miller, *Elizabeth Bishop*, 1993, p.33). Amongst the early influences on her were Gerard Manley Hopkins, the seventeenth-century Anglo-Welsh poet George Herbert, and such 'modernist' male contemporaries as T.S. Eliot, W.H. Auden and Wallace

Stevens. She too can be seen as a 'modernist', highly conscious of 'tradition' but also of the need, as Ezra Pound saw it, to make it new.

'The Gentleman of Shalott' is an early work, published in 1936. The influence of Herbert, a highly original metrist, is apparent in its light, quirky rhythmic patterns, but the form is 'free' in that rhyme and half-rhyme (e.g. 'slips/fix') are used in an irregular way and line length is adjusted to fit thought rather than *vice versa*. This extremely 'playful' poem has given rise to a range of rather solemn interpretations.

Please read 'The Gentleman of Shalott', then look at the interpretations quoted and note down which, if any, make sense to you.

> The hero ... a literally split personality, assumes that, because of his physical symmetry, he is half mirror image ... He has mastered the art of evading experience by inventing an absorbing game; his delusion gives him an excuse to watch himself.
>
> (Travisano, *Elizabeth Bishop*, 1989, p.29)

> The gentleman cannot believe in any full sense of his own identity. Yet ... he gets his thrill from that uncertainty ... [However] a flurry of qualifying words ... overshadow his confidence ... 'resigned' 'if ... but', 'while', 'at present' and 'enough'.
>
> (Parker, *The Poetry of Elizabeth Bishop*, 1988, pp.49–51)

> Bishop side-steps the usual sexual hierarchy and debunks myths of masculine heroism and conquest. Her Gentleman of Shalott ... supposing himself half absorbed into Tennyson's lady's mirror, is not militant but modest, not doughty but doubtful, not superhuman but silly – a long way from the legendary Sir Lancelot.
>
> (Merrin, *An Enabling Humility*, 1990, p.152)

> Bishop clearly mocks him for his narcissistic self-absorption (touted as modesty) ... [but] too many lines in the middle of the poem suggest Bishop's positive identification with the Gentleman.
>
> (Costello, *Elizabeth Bishop*, 1991, pp.28–9)

> It is perhaps [an] attempt ... to deal publicly with lesbianism ... [As] a parable about the choice of a same sex world, the poem seems only faintly tinged with melancholy about this choice.
>
> (Goldsmith, *Elizabeth Bishop*, 1992, pp.281–3)

Discussion

Seeing, perhaps, some point in all of these views, we can nevertheless pursue an interpretation which continues the discussion of 'art and life' in this section. Bishop confronts, I think, the problem raised by 'The Lady of Shalott' and *Aurora Leigh*, that the artist cannot by virtue of her or his occupation participate fully in the life which she or he reflects and reflects upon. Only the mirror holds the Gentleman together:

> If the glass slips
> he's in a fix –
> only one leg, etc.

The self-reflecting state is a fundamental condition of his being. A word which is useful here is 'solipsism'. It applies to the condition of people who relate everything in the world to themselves, whether joyously ('manic') or gloomily ('depressive'). The Gentleman, half modestly, half cockily, accepts his own solipsism: 'Half is enough.' Unlike the Lady of Shalott, 'half sick of shadows', the Gentleman is content 'at present' with a situation which cuts him off from the reality even of himself.

The poem might seem to permit extremely painful readings – as a poem about madness, by someone whose mother had gone mad. But the playfulness which dominates it – that deftly placed little 'etc.' for instance – must affect our sense of what it's 'about'. Bishop confronts the solipsism and narcissism which many, perhaps most, people have in them and appraises it wittily. We're stuck with this thing, but at least we can see what it's like, how absurd it is.

Problems which the early Victorians posed in terms of art versus life, of the lone individual bereft of society or unaccomodated within it, are wittily collapsed by Bishop into questions about individual psychology. Can we be anything but alone? If not, why should that bother us? Can art truly reflect anything, granted the self-infused vision which the artist must needs have? If it can't, can we or should we care?

However, no poem is without social context. This one was first published, in April 1936, in a magazine called *New Democracy* (Miller, *Elizabeth Bishop,* 1993, p.93). By then, in the USA, the word 'gentleman' implied an archaic, anti-democratic standard of social values. The 'new democracy' of the era of President Roosevelt's 'New Deal' – a political programme designed to favour the Common Man – was at odds with the notion of gentility. There is an element close to satire in the playfulness of Bishop's poem. The joke would not be lost on self-conscious readers of the *New Yorker,* a very influential journal to which Bishop herself later contributed, which had as a kind of logo a dandified 'gentleman' with a monocle, signifying 'half' in earnest, as well as 'half' in jest, the paper's appeal to a highly educated élite and to those who wished to imitate that élite. Bishop is playful about herself and the class to which she belonged, though it is not clear whether she would have associated herself with that *New Yorker* image. ■

In this second section we have seen how complex it can be to read with 'gender on the agenda', and how unstable are the categories of gender. We have also noticed a favourable change in the scope allowed to the female writer from the days of Landon to those of Bishop a century later. Emily Pfeiffer, as you already know, moved out of the 'cage' of domesticity in the suffrage era. **Please read her sonnet 'The Winged Soul'**.

D i s c u s s i o n

'The Winged Soul' is personal and complex. The 'cage' here could contain man as well as woman; it represents the limitations of human consciousness, unable to find rest on earth, pining for the 'infinite'. Pfeiffer affirms that this yearning is good – better to be a caged bird than a dumb ox content to 'chew the cud of knowledge'. It is characteristic of the earnestly intellectual Pfeiffer that she craves and extols *knowing*: she recognizes the power of knowledge, and of language. ■

Generations of women poets: Dickinson to the present.

Emily Dickinson

Emily Dickinson lived her outwardly quiet life as a member of a lively family. Her family provided a public stability which allowed her to develop her intensely private sense of self. (She describes herself in Poem 486 as 'the slightest in the house', though as feminist scholars have pointed out, her image of herself as 'slight' may have been more a metaphorical than a physical description.) Her grandfather helped to found Amherst College in the New England village of that name where she dwelt, her father and then her brother Austin were prominent in running the college and in many other aspects of local life, and she was evidently held in esteem by her neighbours. She did not live in obscurity, but she was a private, even 'eccentric' person. She perhaps took to an extreme traits of shyness, self-examination and profound thoughtfulness which were rooted in the remarkable culture of New England. (New England was colonized in the seventeenth century by Puritans determined to worship in their own way and was the epicentre of the Revolution which threw off British rule in 1776–83.) She rejected the Calvinism still orthodox in New England, and refused to join the church which defined and focused Amherst's spirituality, but she was not exceptional in this. Her combination (in speech and letters as well as in verse) of high seriousness and quirky humour ran in her family and was acceptable in her neighbourhood.

In the latter part of her life she would talk to callers only through the open door of her room, and even her loving sister Lavinia had no idea till Dickinson died of the sheer quantity of verse she had written: 1775 poems in the 'complete' edition we now have Towards the end of her life, her brother, who was married, had a love affair with a remarkable young woman, Mabel Loomis Todd, who edited a selection of Emily's work. When this was published in 1890, her fellow New Englanders at once recognized a great poet – she had not lived out of harmony with the world around her.

To start with let's look at a relatively well-known poem. **Please now read Poem 712. Consider the ways in which this poem is 'gendered'.**

Discussion

This poem describes a young woman's metaphorical carriage ride with Death. Though gloomy interpretations are certainly possible, the poem seems to me visionary. Both the character within the poem (the narrator) and the character of Death (Immortality) are clearly designated with gender roles. The poem plays with the notion of Death as a polite gentleman giving a lift to the speaker, a well-dressed lady. Would 'Death' be so polite to a man? One feels that the relationship would be different, though logically, and theologically, it cannot be. Emily Dickinson's highly personal style of punctuation may also be seen as 'gendered' in the sense that her use of dashes as a form of punctuation creates a sense of breathlessness as the poems are read aloud. Many feminist scholars have observed that the poems appear on the page as if they were stitched or 'pieced' together in a quilt. Indeed the manuscripts of the poems were literally stitched together by Dickinson, into what are known as the 'fascicles' (bundles of poems loosely stitched together).

Dickinson's biographer Richard Sewall believes that this poem commemorates the moment when Dickinson first sensed her own 'mission' as poet, 'her recognition of her all-encompassing theme ... the meaning of eternity in the light of which all things, from childhood to the grave, must now be seen' (Sewall, *The Life of Emily Dickinson*, 1979, p.714). The fourth stanza, according to this reading 'gives the sense of chilling awe as she contemplates the task and her own slim equipment' (Ibid.). Interesting though this suggestion is, I do not see how it is supported by the words of the poem we have. However, the point that Dickinson's great theme is 'eternity' seems valid. And a sense of lofty identity – spiritual if not poetic – is certainly there in Poem 303.

The attitude in this poem might be called 'arrogant'. The male Emperor is imagined kneeling before the solitary female soul. What acquits the poem of any charge of spiritual overbearingness is its wit. It does not present itself as the utterance of Dickinson's soul; it makes 'detached', wittily-phrased statements about the nature of the soul which would, if true, hold true for all soul-possessing humans.

Nevertheless, the sense of personality conveyed by Dickinson's poems is so strong that we cannot help relating them to her situation as a strongly

Figure 12   Emily Dickinson, Daguerrotype. Robert Frost Library, Amherst College, Massachusetts.

individualistic person within a very particular culture. Religion, philosophy and learning were important; death was a recurrent theme. In Poem 280, it assumes a nightmarish material immediacy and Reason itself cannot cope with it. ∎

Finally, I will try to tease meaning out of the most heavily 'gendered' poem by Dickinson in our selection, Poem 1737. **Please read this and summarize the 'story' which seems to lie behind it.**

Discussion

This poem evokes a secret, martyred· passion and suggests that the experience of seven years of 'troth' has been spiritually superior to what 'wifehood' would have been. The extraordinary first stanza is very hard to construe, but seems to involve indignant repudiation of the state of 'wifehood' – paradoxically the speaker could only accept it if she were unsexed, defeminized. The poem, undatable, may derive from Dickinson's complex relationship with her brother Austin's wife, a woman brilliant in her way, the queen of Amherst 'society', who made Austin miserable. But speculation about the precise origins of Dickinson's emotions is fruitless. Paradoxically (that word again!) by keeping her secrets 'bandaged', like wounds out of sight, she displays the depth and fierceness of her feelings. What the speaker asserts in the closing lines of the poem is her sense of kinship with the martyred Saviour, Jesus Christ. By day she wears, like him, a crown of thorns, but after sunset a heavenly diadem. Her poetry is both 'gendered' and transcendent, providing a vision of the timeless and the universal. ∎

Yet as we have seen, gender is relevant to the study of Dickinson's poetry, even if it is not a central theme of the poet's. Brief consideration of seven more poems illustrates the point.

Read the last seven Dickinson poems printed in your anthology. Now look at the list of phrases below, summarizing common themes and images in much women's writing and writing about women:

'"anonymous" was often a woman'

the isolated position of the female writer

writing as a creative act rarely understood or rewarded

the 'caged bird' idea (women's entrapment in a 'cage' of domesticity)

'rationality and madness' (subjective labels for women writers)

Can you see how each of the phrases or metaphors is dealt with in the Dickinson poems?

Discussion

Three of the poems – 288 ('I'm Nobody! Who are you?'), 67 ('Success') and 441 ('This is my letter to the World') – raise ideas related to the first and second themes ('"Anonymous" was often a woman', and the isolation of the female writer). The related idea that writing is a creative act rarely understood or rewarded is one of the themes which can be picked out of the web of meanings in Poem 1261 ('A Word dropped careless on a Page').

The 'caged bird' idea frames the metaphor of Poem 77 ('I never hear the word "escape"'). The 'rationality' and 'madness' theme is illustrated succinctly and comically in Dickinson's Poem 435 ('Much Madness is divinest Sense'), and more seriously in Poem 593 ('I think I was enchanted' – a poem which also chronicles Dickinson's sense of influence and inspiration by another female poet, that dark lady Elizabeth Barrett Browning).

Of course, there are many other meanings and interpretations of each of these poems. We have offered five phrases or themes alongside seven poems, to reinforce the idea that each poem may relate to several different themes. There is no one 'correct' reading of any poem, and the themes of poems may overlap in interesting ways. The themes listed here are discussed in more detail elsewhere in the book, but are mentioned in order to show that even the mysterious, hidden Emily Dickinson was in touch with the major concerns of other women writers. Dickinson's writing is heavily influenced by her personal experiences, and lack of them. But it is also influenced by her reading of literature by other writers including women such as Harriet Beecher Stowe, Charlotte Brontë, George Eliot, Elizabeth Barrett Browning, and perhaps also Louisa May Alcott. There is no direct evidence that Dickinson and Alcott knew each other, but one of the seven poems Dickinson published – anonymously – in her lifetime was 'Success', which appeared in the same volume of *The No Name Series, A Masque of Poets* as Alcott's poem 'Transfiguration', so it is likely that she read at least that poem. In addition, Dickinson's personal library held Alcott's *Little Women*, as well as Harriet Beecher Stowe's *Uncle Tom's Cabin*. There is some evidence to suggest that Dickinson and Stowe may have met in Amherst. Details of the female influences on Dickinson, and of her admiration for the Brontës, George Eliot, and others is recorded in Karl Keller, *The Only Kangaroo Among the Beauty: Emily Dickinson and America* (1979). ■

Contemporary women's poetry

The historian Eric Hobsbawm in his much-noted history of the twentieth century, *The Age of Extremes,* has deplored 'the decline of the classical genres of high art and literature' (1994, pp.510–12). These include regular verse forms as well as the symphony, the grand opera and the realist novel. Many other lovers of the arts have shared his unease. The feeling that real poetry should and must rhyme is widespread. Yet it would seem that women writers at least have profited in the last three decades from the 'freedom' of 'free verse'. It has permitted the development of new tones and themes and of quirky individual self-expression.

Please now read through all the poems in the final section of the anthology in this book. Don't pause to worry over detailed meanings. Assess 'tones' and 'themes' and 'personalities' as these first strike you and jot down answers to three questions:

1   **What contrasts emerge among these writers themselves?**
2   **How, as a group, might they be contrasted with the nineteenth-century poets you've been studying?**

1   There is surely a very great variety. Plath and Duffy are rich and thunderously resonant. Kay and Nichols make use, partly humorous, of informal 'non-Standard' English. De Souza, Adcock and Rich offer different 'conversational' voices. Truth/Stetson and, differently, Kate Rushin challenge ideas of identity linked to race as well as gender. Elfyn writes in Welsh, Ni Dhomnaill in Irish Gaelic. Though notable verse by women in Scottish Gaelic existed in earlier centuries, very few women wrote poetry in these other Celtic languages before very recent times.

2   There is a feeling of 'liberation' from old constraints here. Topics which nineteenth-century women had addressed in conventional ways ('Home and 'Family') or veiled terms ('Sex', 'Madness' and 'Racism') are now confronted with bold directness. ■

Now that you have read through the poems once, I'd like to consider them thematically, under the headings of patriarchy, sex and love, family and 'herstories'.

Patriarchy

Sylvia Plath's 'Colossus' is a powerful statement about a daughter's sense of relationship to her father, using the image of a 'colossal' head (imagine a giant sculpture) which has shattered and which she is trying to repair. The reference to the *Oresteia*, a cycle of ancient Greek tragedies by Aeschylus, relates the father to King Agamemnon (murdered by his Queen, Clytemnestra) and the daughter to Electra, mourning him and waiting for the return of her brother Orestes to avenge him. But the speaker of this poem has stopped waiting for the 'scrape of the keel' of Orestes' ship. **What does this imply?**

It suggests to me a peculiarly strong and possessive devotion to the dead father – a delight in inhabiting his ruined vastness all by herself. She has acquired power over this formidable ruin.

Plath's poem 'Lady Lazarus' stands testament to her troubled emotional state, her struggles to find a sense of identity, balancing her roles as woman, wife, daughter, mother and artist. She describes herself as a maker of art and a work of art, like the 'beautiful' dead Ophelia and the Lady of Shalott. She practices 'dying as an art' (attempted suicides), and draws on images raised in 'The Colossus', but in more disturbing terms.

Both of these poems are informed by the poet's deep sense of emotional disenfranchisement; her sense of not quite knowing who she is. In 'The Colossus' she defines herself in relation to her father, and in 'Lady Lazarus' she compares herself to the Biblical figure who rises from the dead. Here, she refers to her multiple suicide attempts; the last one, in 1963, ended in her death. These poems take on greater meaning if we recall that Plath – along with Virginia Woolf – is known as one of this century's most gifted female writers, as well as one of its most tragic figures. Plath's journals and diaries and many letters home to her mother in America (from England) testify to her troubled emotional state, which some call 'madness' and others 'chronic depression'. There is not space here to elaborate on the details of Plath's remarkable life and writing career. But what is worth noting is the very conscious metaphor of the death mask, employed in both of the poems you've read, and also in a very disturbing entry written by hand in her Journal in 1953, when she was 21 years old (ten years before her death). **Look now at Figure 13.**

Discussion

The journal entry includes a cut-out photo of Plath's own face, pasted into the text as if to illustrate her point that her face is like an 'ugly dead mask'. The young woman who would eventually write such powerful poetry had a very divided sense of herself, from an early age. She uses the image pasted into her text as if it were a mirror: showing her what she looks like, reminding her in years to come (now years passed) what she wanted *not* to look like, *not* to be. Yet the face is not ugly, and is only 'dead' when pasted on the page, when discovered by scholars years after the poet's death. That Plath thought so much about appearance, and so little of her own, is

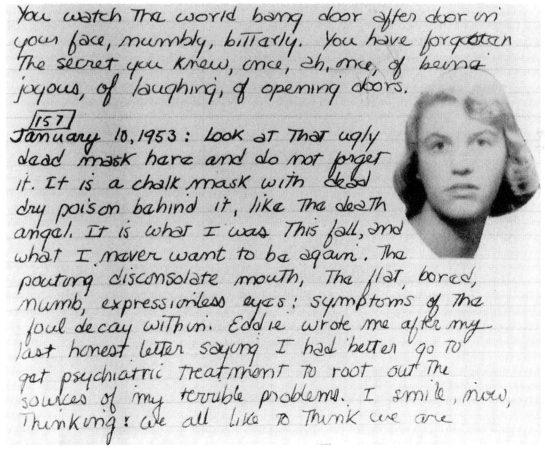

Figure 13 Sylvia Plath, diary page, entry for January 10, 1953. Mortimer Rare Book Room, Smith College Library, Northampton, Massachusetts.

informative in our study of gender. If we consider her more light-hearted 'roles' as fashion editor and 'bathing beauty' as well as her 'darker' side, the figure of Plath seems to contradict itself. She was always creating and destroying new versions of herself, in each photograph, each 'letter home', each poem, each drawing. ■

Sex and love

Please now read the poems by Adcock, Duffy, Rich and Feinstein (in Section V of the anthology). **How would you contrast the attitudes to love and sex which they project?**

Discussion

Feinstein's 'Anniversary' seems to be a 'love poem' addressed to a partner. (wedding anniversary?). But lines 8 and 9 chide this person for not being able to accept 'surprise'. The speaker exults in her own capacity to 'transfigure' herself. The tone is warm, but also challenging.

Duffy's poem is intensely erotic. It is not fully clear whether the physical contact is merely 'dreamt' or is actually made between persons, one of whom is asleep as it begins. This ambiguity in no way diminishes the poem's force. Likewise, the poet's taut control of her three-line stanzas actually strengthens the sense of explosive sexual 'release' which the poem's finale conveys.

Adcock doesn't want anything like that any more. Perhaps her poem, 'Against Coupling' and in praise of masturbation speaks for itself, but I will point out how the verses here, while 'free' (unrhymed, irregular) are elegantly controlled in six-line stanzas.

I find Rich's 'Dialogue' somewhat enigmatic. The 'old ring' on the hand of the opening speaker's interlocutor suggests a woman long married. Her own speech, in italics, indicates that she is bewildered now recalling the sexual role which she acted out in marriage. Since Rich is lesbian, the intensity of this long and sultry (August-like) dialogue presumably derives from intense sympathy, sexual attraction, or both. ■

Family

Please now re-read the poems by Boland, Elfyn and Kay in Section V of the anthology. How would you describe the parental feelings which they convey?

Discussion

Boland's 'Hanging Curtains …' plays, to recall that word which is so useful when discussing poetry, with the two-way character of windows. From the inside, the curtains, with ellipse and angle, stand in for the frost, the season's weather. But seen from the outside the speaker herself has the drabness of a winter day seen from inside when the curtains are drawn open. Hanging curtains she is, we might say, giving the child protection against the outside world, but she herself is assimilated with it. Lines 12–16, which you may have found rather difficult, suggest that 'signs' such as the shapes on the curtains help children 'come to their senses', grow to full sensual knowledge of the cold world outside, by providing the 'soul' of the weather without its harshness. The mother provides both warm protection and a sort of instruction, education. This corresponds to one role assigned to women in Victorian times, but the quizzical intellectualism expressed here is very unlike what we find in conventional Victorian verse.

In Elfyn's poem swans diving for food in a lake are compared with parents who find the 'innocence' and 'absence of arrogance' in their beloved children a 'bait for their being'. The voraciousness expressed in this image is somewhat disturbing.

Kay's poem comes from an autobiographical sequence 'The Adoption Papers'. The poet herself is the child of an African father and a Scots mother, adopted by Glaswegian parents. (The poem is voiced in 'Glaswegian'.) Different typefaces distinguish the child from the adoptive mother, whose thoughts are stated in bold print. The humour and pain of the poem arise from the lifelikeness of the 'voices'. The adoptive mother's is notably generous, thinking kindly of the girl's physical mother.

So the 'parental' attitudes displayed in the three poems are sharply different, and all 'unconventional'. But the poems have one thing in common: no fathers impinge. ■

'Herstories'

'Herstory' is a term introduced by feminist scholarship to refer to the history of women. The creation of this expression was intended to be both serious and comic. **Please now re-read the poems by De Souza, Nichols and Rushin in the anthology. How would you 'characterize' and describe their different projections of contemporary 'herstory'?**

Discussion

In 'Autobiography' De Souza's speaker puts herself down, writes of a suicide attempt and a severe nervous crisis, and ends by claiming to desire to 'rip' the world up with a 'razor blade'. But if this presents the behaviour of a neurotic 'loser', the tone of the poem – which is witty, detached, composed, not self-pitying – suggests the toughness of a 'survivor'.

Nichols's 'Wherever I Hang' expresses resilience of a less aggressive kind. The immigrant speaker still feels divided between the Caribbean and England, but seems herself to be somewhat bemused by a bewilderment which we find amusing. Her final remark in a sense provides the solution of her problem; one keeps going wherever one is.

Rushin's poem makes explicit something implicit in Atwood's 'Reincarnation of Captain Cook', which we discussed at the very start of this chapter. The individual person's banner should be blank in the terrain which women should now enter. All historically created ('engendered') categories are unsatisfactory. ■

Now re-read Ni Dhomnaill's 'The Language Issue' and recall the discussion of women's relationship to 'art' early in this chapter. Think about how the language relates to, or shapes, the poet's

'herstory'. Finally, please re-read the poem 'Ain't I a Woman!'. This is an adaptation by Erlene Stetson of the notorious speech by Soujourner Truth, delivered to the Women's Rights Convention in Akron, Ohio in 1852.

Discussion

The poem, while based on a nineteenth-century speech, is still a very contemporary literary document. The speech makes a remarkable text. Soujourner Truth, an illiterate ex-slave woman, stood up and literally bared her breast to the assembled public, showing her female form in an act of demonstration that she – and by extension, other African-American women – are as 'female' as white women, and are also strong, capable, remarkable. Her speech, captured in the poem, undermines conventional arguments against women's rights which relied on notions of female inferiority, and particularly physical and spiritual weakness. Truth points out that black women in America were never assumed to be weak. In fact, slave women were often physically, emotionally and morally strong. The speech is both a show of solidarity with women generally, and an objection to the racism which declared that white women 'counted' while black women didn't. The eloquent speech demanded that the position of black women be recognized alongside those of her white sisters. 'Ain't I a Woman!' Soujourner Truth demanded, and the poem demands that we consider the question, and the larger question 'what is a woman', as we continue to study literature and gender in historical and political context. ∎

Before moving on to the next chapter, you might find it useful to read Jamaica Kincaid's short story 'Girl'. The story reads almost like a poem in free verse, and it addresses the very question of what it means to be a girl, and a woman.

Further reading

Edmond, R. (1988) *Affairs of the Hearth: Victorian Poetry and Domestic Narrative*, Routledge.

France, L. (ed.) (1993) *Sixty Women Poets*, Bloodaxe.

Hickock, K. (1984) *Representations of Women: Nineteenth-century British Women's Poetry*, Greenwood Press.

Kelly, A.A. (ed.) (1987) *Pillars of the House: An Anthology of Verse by Irish Women from 1690 to the Present*, Wolfhound.

Kerrigan, C. (ed.) (1991) *An Anthology of Scottish Women Poets*, Edinburgh University Press.

Leighton, A. (1992) *Victorian Women Poets*, Harvester Wheatsheaf.

Morris, P. (1993) *Literature and Feminism*, Blackwell.

Prichard, R.E. (ed.) (1990) *Poetry by English Women: Elizabethan to Victorian*, Carcanet.

Rumens, C. (ed.) (1985) *Making for the Open: The Chatto Book of Post-Feminist Poetry 1964–1984*, Chatto.

Rumens, C. (ed.) (1990) *New Women Poets*, Bloodaxe.

Prose fiction, form and gender

*by Lizbeth Goodman, with Kasia Boddy and
Elaine Showalter*

Chapter Three

Gender, form and function

There are three main reasons why the gender of authors is a major concern in literary studies today:

1   because there is a considerable body of writing, much of it by women, which was 'silenced' or ignored in previous generations;

2   because looking at this body of literature challenges the canon not only by increasing the number of texts studied, but also by adding themes, images and ideas to a list of literary concerns; and

3   because there is still a freshness and mystery to approaching literary texts which we have not encountered before or which have not been widely studied.

The first point concerns the historical treatment of women and women's work: economically, socially and culturally. The second concerns the conditions of women's lives as expressed in their creative writing. The third is perhaps the most important point for readers: reading newly 'discovered' texts can be particularly thought-provoking and enjoyable. All these points inform the approach taken in this chapter, in which the focus is on prose writing by women. While gender is a concern in literature by both women and men, literary studies have traditionally focused on writing by men and, as Carolyn Heilbrun has argued, stories true to the experiences of women will emerge 'only when women no longer live their lives isolated in the houses and the stories of men' (*Writing a Woman's Life*, 1988, p.47). Heilbrun herself is a writer of detective fiction (using the pseudonym Amanda Cross) as well as a literary critic. We'll return to this idea of hers when we discuss Virginia Woolf. But first, let's consider the basic idea that stories by women may be different from those by men.

Writing as work

Let's begin by considering women's writing as a form of work. Anyone wishing to write literature in the eighteenth century would have required certain 'job prerequisites', including literacy and familiarity with at least some published literature. Writing as a form of work also had some less obvious prerequisites: access to formal education, time to read and write. If publication was desired, connections to the (male) literary establishment were also necessary. As most formal education prior to the twentieth century was reserved for men, clearly writing was not a form of work open to many women.

There is another reason why many women did not write or did not get their writing published so that little is known about it today. Many women had to undertake another form of work which occupied most of their time and energy: domestic work. When I use the term 'domestic work' I include both that performed by servants and the vast amount of often unrecognized work that women of all classes were expected to carry out in their own homes. As concepts of class status shifted from generation to generation, the restrictions on some parts of the population (women and men) have lessened to some extent. Still, the situation for women in the eighteenth and nineteenth centuries was, to varying degrees, an 'obstacle' to their writing literature.

Charlotte Perkins Gilman put the case for women's economic freedom in her ground-breaking text, *Women and Economics* (1898), where she analyses women's economic dependence on men and the reasons why it was in the interests of patriarchy to keep women so dependent. But even for those middle- and upper-class women who had access to their father's or brother's private libraries, still writing was not considered a 'feminine' pursuit, nor a proper form of work for women. If women wrote prior to the nineteenth century, it was often assumed that this was a leisure activity, not work. While there were obstacles to women's writing, however, some writers made a 'virtue of necessity' and found ways of working within the social conventions to produce writing now recognized as 'great literature'.

Research into women's writing since the turn of the century, and particularly since the 'feminist critical revolution' of the 1960s and 70s, has uncovered a fascinating range of previously ignored women's writing, including diaries by working-class women and the journals of middle- and upper-class women. Such writing, as a form, often escapes easy categorization as 'literature', for most definitions of the term do not include letters and diary entries, particularly those by relatively uneducated women. However, the autobiographies and diaries of working-class women can be read both as fascinating narratives and as valuable socio-historical documents. Interestingly, these forms of writing occupy an uneasy position between the public and the private sphere. And of course, the form of the epistolary novel – novels based on letters between characters – was greatly influenced by women writers, from (Mary) Delariviere Manley (1663–1724) to Eliza Haywood (1693–1756) to Mary Shelley (1797–1851, whose *Frankenstein* makes use of this form) to contemporary authors including Alice Walker. (Dale Spender discusses the development of women's writing and the development of the epistolary form in *Mothers of the Novel*, 1986.)

Writing as a form of work was and is clearly influenced by gender and the social construction of 'norms' for female and male activity. The limitations imposed on women of all classes influenced the themes addressed in women's writing, and the forms and genres which women chose as their means of expression. As most middle- and upper-class women spent the majority of their time in the home, their frame of reference was limited and their fiction tended to focus on the domestic, private world, even though fiction, with its assumption of a readership, is inherently a public form. It is this divided sense of the world, of public versus private, imagined ideas versus lived experience, which is Virginia Woolf's subject in *A Room of One's Own*, an essay based upon two papers read at Cambridge women's colleges in October 1928.

The relationship between form, function and gender is one which interested Woolf, and about which she often wrote in her essays and reviews, is a theme in her fiction.

Read the following extract from *A Room of One's Own*. In it Woolf discusses the theme suggested for her lecture – 'Women and fiction' – and its possible interpretations. What are Woolf's views on the relationship between fiction and gender?

> ... The title women and fiction might mean, and you may have meant it to mean, women and what they are like; or it might mean women and the fiction that they write, or it might mean women and the fiction that is written about them; or it might mean that somehow all three are inextricably mixed together and you want me to consider them in that light. But when I began to consider the subject in this last way, which seemed the most interesting, I soon saw that it had one fatal drawback. I should never be able to come to a conclusion. I should never be able to fulfill what is, I understand, the first duty of a lecturer – to hand you after an hour's discourse a nugget of pure truth to wrap up between the pages of your notebooks and keep on the mantelpiece for ever. All I could do was to offer you an opinion upon one minor point – a woman must have money and a room of her own if she is to write fiction; and that, as you will see, leaves the great problem of the true nature of woman and the true nature of fiction unsolved.
>
> (Virginia Woolf, *A Room of One's Own*, 1977 edn, pp.5–6)

Discussion

Woolf's concern in this passage is with gender and literature, and particularly with the real material conditions which long kept women from writing (see Barrett, *Virginia Woolf*, 1993). Her contention that women need money, privacy and time to write may seem like basic common sense. Woolf was not the first to express this idea, but her words have become a battle cry of sorts, cited and reformulated by many writers and literary critics, including Carolyn Heilbrun, whom I cited at the beginning of this chapter. ■

Once it was established that women needed money in order to write, it was also clear that women could benefit from writing as a form of paid work. Of course, many women had written long before Woolf laid out her argument for the material conditions for writing. But many did so secretly, publishing under male pen names, or 'anonymously', or not publishing at all. This material aspect of writing is illustrated in the work of many of the women discussed in this book, including Woolf herself and the American writer Louisa May Alcott (1832–1888). Later in the chapter, we will look closely at the interconnections between fiction, form and gender in the life and work of Alcott, an early feminist and abolitionist, who is best known as a writer of domestic fiction for children, but whose recently discovered racy tales of sex, violence and female duplicity (tales she wrote to help pay the bills) have recently come to light.

But first, it is important to consider another form of economic security more commonly offered to women: marriage.

Marriage as a trade

The following passage was written by a well-known writer in 1788. **Read the extract carefully and try to answer the following questions: Is the author a woman or a man? What is the author's view of marriage?**

> Early marriages are, in my opinion, a stop to improvement. If we were born only 'to draw nutrition, propagate and rot', the sooner the end of creation was answered, the better ...
>
> ... In a comfortable situation, a cultivated mind is necessary to render a woman contented; and in a miserable one, it is her only consolation. A sensible, delicate women, who by some strange accident, or mistake, is joined to a fool or a brute, must be wretched beyond all names of wretchedness, if her views are confined to the present scene. Of what importance then, is intellectual improvement, when our comfort here, and our happiness hereafter, depends on it.

Discussion

As you probably guessed, the author is a woman. She has had access to the education which obviously influences her use of elegant, stylish language. What is most important for our purposes is the emphasis which the author places on the need for women to be educated, at a time when they were seen as the property of their husbands. Indeed, she suggests, many women will be brighter and more creative than their husbands, and would wither without some intellectual stimulus. The opposition between marriage as a fate or 'job' for women, and the need for women to improve themselves through education, is one which informed women's writing and women's writing about writing, for many years to come.

So what is the source of the passage? It is taken from the essay 'Thoughts on the education of daughters: with reflections on female conduct', written in 1788 by Mary Wollstonecraft, the novelist who is perhaps best know as an early feminist writer on politics for her landmark work, *A Vindication of the Rights of Woman* (1792; reprinted in Jones, *Women in the Eighteenth Century*, 1990). Wollstonecraft's daughter, Mary Shelley (author of *Frankenstein*), can be seen to have considered her mother's ideas in her creation of a character, the Frankenstein Monster, who seeks – but does not attain – knowledge, companionship and acceptance on his own terms. Wollstonecraft's 'Thoughts on the education of daughters' suggests education as a palliative to marriage. Just over a century later, Cicely Hamilton saw the link between education and marriage more in terms of economics. ■

Cicely Hamilton's treatise, *Marriage as a Trade*, first published in 1909, is one of the best known and most wittily argued books to deal with this crucial theme. Cicely Mary Hammill (1872–1952), recognizing the power of names to create images, changed her own name to a stage name when she left her teaching job (her usual means of supporting herself financially) to take to the stage as a playwright and actress in 1872. Cicely Hamilton is best known as a 'suffrage playwright', but she was also an early feminist thinker, who was among the first to argue persuasively, publicly and in print that women are socially influenced and culturally trained to be domestic, to make themselves appear attractive according to generally accepted and usually male-influenced 'norms' of feminine beauty, in order to win marriage as a form of financial support. In this sense, Hamilton argues, women are far less 'romantic' than men. Women, she argued, know the real meaning of marriage in financial, practical terms. She perceived a certain obsession with romantic images of women, in fiction and in life, as largely a male construct. It is possible to support Hamilton's view with a feminist reading of just about any nineteenth-century literary text, whether by a woman or man. (For women writers were inevitably influenced by male-created ideas of romance, of 'femininity' and heterosexual romantic liaisons.)

Virginia Woolf also argued persuasively on the theme of 'marriage as a trade', though she did not use the term. Instead, she adopted the term 'the Angel in the House' from a long narrative poem by Coventry Patmore (1854–1862) and updated it. Woolf's use of the term referred to the idealized 'feminine' figure who sacrificed her creative self for domestic harmony. She wrote extensively about women's status with regard to romance, and of relationships between men and women in literature. She cites Aphra Behn (1640–1689) as the foremost literary role model for women: a writer who defied social convention, lived bravely and wrote defiantly. She also criticizes some female writers for their romantic and domestic preoccupations. Of course, Woolf's views are influenced by her own status as a middle-class English woman, and her ideas about women's economic independence are, as critics have argued, in some ways contradicted by her own standard of living, within the privileges of a class and also a marriage. (Barrett's introduction to *Virginia Woolf: On Women and Writing*, 1993, provides a very clear and persuasive analysis of Woolf's complex and sometimes contradictory views on the subject, as well as a fine selection of Woolf's own writing.)

Re-read the passage by Virginia Woolf printed earlier (p.73). In what way do Woolf's views on 'women and fiction' seem to be informed by the argument that 'marriage is a trade'?

Discussion

In this passage, Woolf argues that women need financial security and space if they are to write fiction. Woolf had both, and, in a sense, the problem was eased for her, though not for many other women. 'Marriage as a trade' would not necessarily provide the emotional and mental space for creative experimentation, nor could even the most supportive marriage make up for the larger social oppression of women as a group denied access to education in Woolf's day. Woolf's argument might imply that marriage, reliance on a husband for support, is neither a sufficient nor a necessary condition for women's creative writing. Yet Woolf's own life demonstrates that marriage could provide financial and emotional support, helpful if not necessary to the process of creative writing. So, in setting out the material conditions for writing, *A Room Of One's Own* can be seen to be influenced by the sentiments, if not the precise content, of both Wollstonecraft's and Hamilton's work. ■

In her account of the novel as *The Female Form* (1987), Rosalind Miles argues that while women have been successful in writing fiction and particularly novels, there has been and continues to be a strong tendency for women's writing to gain them the status of 'honorary men', rather than that of talented writers in their own right. Publishing under male and a-gendered pseudonyms was one way in which women writers made their work public, defied social convention, yet also became 'honorary men' in their own day. The Brontë sisters, George Eliot and even Louisa May Alcott published under pseudonyms. If, as Miles and many others have argued, women's work is valued differently from men's – if it is seen as 'silly' if it is 'feminine' or romantic or domestic – then it is not surprising that women often wrote under pseudonyms. Indeed, submitting work for publication under male or ambiguously gendered pseudonyms afforded the anonymity necessary to have work judged by its literary merit, rather than on grounds of gender difference. Alcott's most famous novel *Little Women* – and the 1994 film version of it – emphasizes a young woman's humiliation on being rejected for publication on grounds of gender. The writer in the novel – Jo – is clearly based on Alcott, as her diaries reveal. Similarly, George Eliot's expression of contempt for 'silly novels by lady novelists' (in her essay of that name) can be read as both satirical and serious. Eliot may be rejecting both a category of literature and a label generally applied to women's writing. The dilemma for women writers has been aptly described as a pull between 'gender and genius' (see, for instance, Christine Battersby, *Gender and Genius*, 1989).

Read the following passage by Virginia Woolf. How does she explain the opposition between 'gender and genius'?

> ... – it is unthinkable that any woman in Shakespeare's day should have had Shakespeare's genius. For genius like Shakespeare's is not born among labouring, uneducated, servile people. It was not born in England among the Saxons and the Britons. It is not born today among the working classes. How, then, could it have been born among women whose work began ... almost before they were out of the nursery, who were forced to it by their parents and held to it by all the power of law and custom?
>
> (*A Room of One's Own*, 1977 edn, pp.47–8)

D i s c u s s i o n

Woolf implies – whilst revealing her own middle-class position – that genius is not only a gift, but something which develops with education and the freedom to write. In the same essay, she points out that the formation of 'genius' requires the opportunity to makes oneself known, recognized and recorded as such. The passage also recalls, implicitly, the structured domesticity of women's lives, echoing Cicely Hamilton's idea that 'marriage is a trade' but expressing it indirectly, with reference to domesticity as a form of unpaid labour. ■

The passage is taken from Woolf's famous rumination about the likely fate of 'Shakespeare's sister': a female figure created by Woolf to stand for all the unrecognized and under-developed female genius of the past. Woolf names this sister Judith, and in giving her a name of her own she makes of her an individual, however fictional. This process of naming – people, ideas, lost women of the past – is now widely recognized as an important feminist strategy. Woolf's recognition of the significance of naming is illustrated in her novel *To the Lighthouse* (1927), in which the central character is called simply Mrs Ramsay: she has no first name, no 'name of her own'. Reading backwards in literary history, it is all too easy to find other female characters known only by their relations to men, or to the natural world (as in *The Lady of Shalott*). But Woolf put her ideas into practice with her creation of Judith Shakespeare: brilliant but uneducated, talented but unappreciated, buried in an unmarked grave near 'some cross-roads where the omnibuses stop outside the Elephant and Castle' (Ibid., p.47). Judith, Shakespeare's sister, was written out of history by her gender. A message that can be taken from this essay is that it is the job of all women writers and readers, and of men who are interested in gender and in the recognition and nurturing of artistic talent, to try to find the lost women writers of the past, and to give names to all those anonymous women who lie buried in unmarked graves or with only their husband's names on their headstones.

Part of the task of 'reading gender in literature' is to ask questions about issues such as the importance of women keeping names of their own, and of the relationship between 'gender and genius'. For instance, when considering the work of women writers of the past, from the Brontë sisters to George Eliot to Louisa May Alcott, we can ask what the material and cultural conditions were which influenced their decision to publish some or all of their work under male or ambiguously gendered pen names. The answers would involve a detailed study of the role of women in culture generally, with specific reference to the field of publishing and sets of expectations about what kinds of work were appropriate to women.

Another question we might usefully ask about the relationship between 'gender and genius' is how we might begin to find and give names to the many unnamed and silenced women of the past; how we might learn to hear their voices, to ask questions about them. One of the most important questions we can ask about women writers of the past is: who were they? While we engage in the act of uncovering and re-discovering women writers of the past, we also consider in more depth the idea that 'Anon, who wrote so many poems without signing them, was often a woman' (Ibid., p.48), that many 'Shakespeare's sisters' lie in unmarked graves, silenced by a culture which encouraged domesticity over more public and literary forms of creativity. Tillie Olsen, a poet, set herself the task of naming and reclaiming a number of 'lost' or 'silenced' women writers of the past in her book *Silences* (1965).

Silence, suppression and redressing the balance

Tillie Olsen's book opens with the following words:

> Literary history and the present are dark with silence; some the
> silences for years by our acknowledged great; some silences hidden;

some the ceasing to publish after one work appears; some the never coming to book form at all.

These are not natural silences, that necessary time for renewal, lying fallow, gestation, in the natural cycle of creation. The silences I speak of here are unnatural; the unnatural thwarting of what struggles to come into being, but cannot ...

(*Silences*, 1965, p.xi)

What is Olsen referring to when she writes about 'what struggles to come into being'?

D i s c u s s i o n

What 'struggles to come into being' is the expression of ideas in writing. Writing itself can be a struggle when cultural expectations and pressures are not conducive, and it can be even more difficult to write when aware of the possibility of negative criticism, even when work˙is published. So, given the cultural legacy of silencing certain (non-male, non-white, non-middle-class) voices, Olsen's idea of silences is obviously relevant to discussion of literature and gender. Women, like people of colour, have been 'silenced' as a group: treated as a minority or 'special interest group' by the publishing industry and academic institutions alike. ∎

Joanna Russ comments on the silences of women's writing in her ironically titled book, *How to Suppress Women's Writing*:

> In considering literature written by women during the last few centuries in Europe and the United States (I'm going to concentrate on literature in English ...), we don't find the absolute prohibition on women writing *qua* women that has (for example) buried black slave America, although many of the same devices are used to trivialize the latter when it does get written down ...
>
> But some white women, and black women, and black men, and other people of color too have actually acquired the nasty habit of putting the stuff on paper, and some of it gets printed, and printed material, especially books, gets into bookstores, into people's hands, into libraries, sometimes even into university curricula.
>
> What do we do then?

(*How to Suppress Women's Writing*, 1984, p.6)

'What we do then', when women's work and other marginalized work finally struggles into the public realm, depends on who we are. If we are readers sympathetic to gender issues, we may applaud this slow but steady progress. But if we think more conservatively, then we may defend the canon on 'aesthetic' grounds, constructing arguments for continuing to value what has traditionally been valued as 'classic'; we may continue to teach work by 'great authors' (i.e., by men and a few selected 'honorary men'). This is the system of 'gatekeeping' to which Virginia Woolf refers in her essays, describing the rules – official and tacit – which long barred women from the gates of Oxford and Cambridge, and against which writers from Wollstonecraft to Eliot to Hamilton to Olsen and Russ have each reacted, in their own generations and cultures, and in their own individual ways.

The role of creative writer may sometimes still come into conflict with the traditional roles of mother, lover, wife, or even teacher and friend. In earlier generations, some women were able to transcend the limitations of the domestic by writing about them, sometimes subversively and sometimes with such subtle warmth that the domestic was enlightened with a new importance, as in the fine detailed work of Jane Austen and the Brontë sisters. But writing, even about domestic themes, is not the same as living a domestic life; the writing either gets in the way of or takes the place of the domestic role to some extent, for better or worse. This opposition or conflict of forces has long been recognized in women's lives and writing, and was commented on by Cicely Hamilton and George Eliot (and many others, before and since). Such writers disdain the domestic ideal for women, while recognizing their own awkward position as female writers living and working within the framework of this conflict.

So far, we've considered three main ways of contextualizing women's writing of fiction:

1   by highlighting the importance of material considerations – 'a woman must have money and a room of her own if she is to write fiction' – in the study of literature and gender;

2   by foregrounding the significance of the conflict of the domestic and the creative in many women's lives and work;

3   by considering the silences and evidence of suppression of women's writing, and by considering the possibilities for countering such silences – perhaps by reading, studying, teaching – in order to fill the spaces where women have been erased, to hear the voices of those who have been silenced.

The practical implications of conflicts between writing as creative work and as paid work, of marriage as a trade, domesticity and creativity, femininity and form, gender and genius can be 'read' in the lives and work of many women writers, from the nineteenth century to the present. Indeed, most of the authors discussed in this book experienced and wrote about these conflicts.

Different writing styles and genres suit the talents of different writers, but fiction has long been seen as a particularly 'feminine' form (as opposed to both poetry and drama). In the rest of this chapter, we'll concentrate on comparing the ideas raised above to a number of examples of prose fiction by women. We'll consider the fictional sub-genres of short stories and novellas and will concentrate on three texts in particular: Virginia Woolf's 'The New Dress', Jamaica Kincaid's 'Girl' and Louisa May Alcott's novella 'Behind a Mask'[1]. First, we'll look at the two short stories as examples of one form or sub-genre in which gender is particularly relevant. Now read Jamaica Kincaid's story 'Girl' and Virginia Woolf's story 'The New Dress' in Part Two of this book.

Women writers and the short story

by Kasia Boddy

While critics habitually focus on an author's thematic or stylistic choices, they seldom consider the decision to use a particular genre. Instead they rely on the term 'fiction' to cover short stories of only a few thousand words, such as 'The New Dress' or 'Girl', novellas such as 'Behind a Mask' (which we will shortly be discussing), which are much more substantial in length, and novels which are long enough to be published as books on their own. When an author's work is discussed, the fact that one book is a novel and another a collection of short stories is usually not considered worthy of attention. Blurring such distinctions, however, only serves to distort an understanding of the formal choices that exist. Let's consider why many women writers choose to write short stories.

The first type of explanation that can be given as to why women write short stories is based on a consideration of the practical conditions of women's lives. In *A Room of One's Own*, Virginia Woolf suggested that women's fiction was developing into 'shorter' and 'more concentrated' forms because women do not have access to 'long hours of steady and uninterrupted work' (Woolf, *A Room of One's Own*, 1977 edn, p.74). The contemporary Canadian writer, Alice Munro says much the same thing:

> I never intended to be a short story writer ... I started writing them
> because I don't have time to write anything else – I had three children.
> And then I got used to writing stories, so I saw my material that way,
> and now I don't think I'll ever write a novel.
>
> (Rothstein, 'Interview with Alice Munro', 1986)

The sense of not having much time to themselves is certainly true of many women's lives (and, it must be said, many men's) but as an explanation of the short story form it is problematic. Even more worrying is Woolf's suggestion that women writers tend toward the short story because of 'the nerves that feed the [female] brain' (*A Room of One's Own*, 1977 edn, p.74) This type of explanation is also adopted by Claire Tomalin when she discusses the reasons why Katherine Mansfield wrote short stories. Mansfield, she claimed, 'soon realized that her gifts did not lie in the direction of a long book. As a writer, she always lacked stamina' (*Katherine Mansfield*, 1988, p.120).

The implication is that the short story is a form that requires less effort and time to write than the novel. The short story is often seen as an apprentice form, a warming-up for the mature work which will be the novel. Writers who decide to stay with the short story rather than 'progressing' on to the novel have often felt the need to justify that decision. Interestingly, no one says that writing short poems represents a lack of stamina or sustained effort.

A more fruitful way of examining the relationship between women writers and the short story would be to look at the characteristics of the genre itself and to consider what advantages the short story form holds.

The short story and the novel

Despite, or perhaps because of, the commercial and popular success of the form, the short story has been largely ignored by literary theory. One reason for this is the existence of a debate as to whether the short story does in fact constitute a separate genre at all, or whether it is the same as the novel, only shorter. Furthermore, some critics argue, what we categorize as long and what as short is to a great extent arbitrary.

But it is important to remember that brevity is always relative. The very term 'short story' suggests a relation to some other longer narrative form (see Pratt, 'The short story', 1981, pp.175–91). This longer form is the novel and it is worth noting that much critical thinking about the short story begins by looking at the novel and goes on to define the short story by contrast. Consider, for example, the way characters are presented in the novel and the short story respectively. In the classic nineteenth-century novel characters are presented as they develop through time – what we are interested in, as readers, is the process of change. In the short story, on the other hand, characters are presented in a significant, isolated moment of time. The existence of the past and the future may be suggested, but not with any certainty. All we have access to, in Woolf's phrase, are 'moments of being'.

According to the South African writer, Nadine Gordimer, the short story's presentation of such discrete moments makes it true to the lived experience of modern life,

> where contact is more like the flash of fireflies, in and out, now here, now there, in darkness. Short-story writers see by the light of the flash; theirs is the art of the only thing that one can be sure of – the present moment. Ideally, they have learned to do without explanation of what went before, and happens after this point.
>
> ('South Africa', 1968, p.460)

This is certainly how Mabel, in Virginia Woolf's story 'The New Dress', sees her life. What Mabel thinks of as 'her wretched self' lives a 'creeping, crawling life' as 'an unsatisfactory mother, a wobbly wife', while her true self only exists in tantalizing, fleeting 'divine moments'. Read the story now.

The lonely voice

The unsuitability of Mabel's new dress at a party at which everyone is 'dressed in the height of fashion, precisely like everybody else, always' (p.297) represents Mabel's fundamental alienation from the social world which she inhabits. This alienation and sense of separation is typical of the protagonists of the short story. According to Frank O'Connor, the short story expresses 'an attitude of mind that is attracted by submerged population groups, whatever these might be at any given time – tramps, artists, lonely idealists, dreamers, and spoiled priests' (*The Lonely Voice*, 1963, p.21). Another submerged population group that might be added to the list is, of course, women. Many women's short stories attempt to give voice to the submerged voices of women. The North American short story writer Grace Paley, for example, stresses that her conception of storytelling is based on 'illuminating the dark lives of women'. Paley points out the absence of women's voices in literature and the need for them to be heard:

> When I came to really thinking as a writer, it was because I began to live among women. Now the great thing is that I didn't know them, I didn't know who they were ... That, I think, is really where lots of literature, in a sense comes from. It really comes, not from knowing so much, but from not knowing ... It comes from what you want to know.

> (Paley, 'Of poetry and women and the world', 1986, p.249)

In her championing of women's stories, Paley certainly sees herself as a feminist writer, but many of her critics want to claim more. Paley, they argue, is a feminist writer, not simply because she writes *about* women, but because she writes *as* a woman – in other words, she is writing a specifically 'female' prose. We will consider what this entails more fully in a moment.

The short story and the lyric poem

The idea of the lonely voice speaking to itself is something that links the short story to the lyric poem. By the lyric poem I mean 'any fairly short, non-narrative poem presenting a single speaker who expresses a state of mind or process of thought and feeling' (Abrams, *A Glossary of Literary Terms*, 1981, p.99; Emily Dickinson's poems, for example, are lyrics). Indeed many short story writers claim an affinity between the two genres, and many write in both. The short story is seen to combine the qualities that we traditionally associate with prose – clear, everyday language which conveys facts and truths – and those associated with poetry – an emphasis on features such as rhythm, imagery and diction.

The short story's ability to merge poetry and prose was something that particularly appealed to Virginia Woolf. In *A Room of One's Own* she noted that while one could find shelves full of women novelists, women were still 'denied outlet' in poetry. The novel, she argues, was seen as a genre appropriate to women in its depiction of a private, domestic world, whilst poetry was associated with an elevated language to which only men had access. In her own work, Woolf continually sought to disrupt the boundaries between the genres available to women and men. For example, she subverts the traditionally factual forms of essay and biography with the language of poetry. The juxtaposition of prose and poetry is most explicit, however, in Woolf's short stories, and the short story is the form in which many of her experiments began.

If we look a little more closely at 'The New Dress' it will become apparent that in many ways its language works in the manner of poetry. So, for instance, nothing much happens in the story – a woman arrives at a party, talks to a few people, feels uncomfortable and leaves. What interests the reader is not the progress of Mabel's actions but the progress of her thoughts and the language in which she expresses them. The story takes the simple word 'it' and follows it through a variety of references – 'it' is negatively associated with the unfortunate dress and with Mabel's general feelings of inadequacy, but 'it' is also associated with her experience of 'divine moments', that is moments in which she recognizes that 'This is it!' (p.300). The search for a referent for 'it' parallels Mabel's search for self-identity. To the extent that the story has a narrative, it is poetic – the story progresses not through a series of publicly observable events and incidents but through the development of private understanding of the meaning of key words and the emotions they describe.

The short story collection

The creation of a pattern of repetition and variation that exists within a single story can also occur within a series of stories. 'The New Dress' originally featured in a short story sequence called *Mrs Dalloway's Party* (1922), an early version of what became the novel, *Mrs Dalloway* (1925). Woolf described her original project as creating a book in which each individual piece would be complete on its own (unlike the chapters of a novel), yet would still contribute to a larger whole. Other well-known examples of short story collections which operate in this way are James Joyce's *Dubliners* (1914) and Sherwood Anderson's *Winesberg, Ohio* (1919).

The linked short story collection offers to extend the scope of the individual piece while retaining its separate identity, and without needing to resort to the type of progressive development associated with the novel. It can explore the plurality of life, its contrasts and contradictions, without trying to resolve them into a coherent whole. Even while it puts forward one view, it suggests that there are others. Stories can be grouped around an event, as in *Mrs Dalloway's Party*, a place (Gloria Naylor's *The Women of Brewster Place*, 1987), a group of characters (Alice Munro's *Lives of Girls and Women*, 1971) or a theme (Susan Minot's *Lust*, 1990). Susan Minot describes the organization of *Lust*:

> the stories 'are grouped together to reflect that they are all basically about the same thing – each one is a different version, at a different stage, as if a different colour of wash was over it. Let's see how this looks in blue, how it looks in green ...
>
> (Boddy, 'An interview with Susan Minot', 1990)

By grouping stories around a common theme, for example that of *Wayward Girls and Wicked Women* (Carter, 1986) or what it is to have *Serious Hysterics* (Fell, 1992), anthologies work by much the same method.

Elaine Showalter identifies the linked short story collection as particularly representative of women's writing. She compares its techniques to those of quilting and piecing, arguing that features such as multiplicity and open-endedness constitute a particularly feminine way of writing (Showalter, 'Piecing and quilting', in Miller, *The Poetics of Gender*, 1986, pp.222–47). The lack of emphasis on traditional narrative in many short stories such as 'The New Dress' is also said to be an exemplary feminine strategy. If by 'narrative', we mean a chronological series of events that emphasize external action and present conflict leading to resolution, then, the argument goes, our conception of narrative is male-oriented, for only male lives (or male sexuality, which for some critics is primary), is ordered like this. (For an introduction to this school of feminist theory, see Marks and de Courtivron, *New French Feminisms*, 1981 and Jones, 'Writing the body' in Showalter, *The New Feminist Criticism*, 1985, pp.361–77. For the best general discussion of these issues see Felsi, *Beyond A Feminine Aesthetic*, 1989.) These arguments have many problems – the most fundamental being the danger that in asserting such a strong opposition between male and female writing, one ignores the very real similarities and differences between specific male and female writers. Rather than actually identifying certain forms or techniques as male or female, we must content ourselves with considerations of why some *tend* to attract male writers and others female writers. The qualities of the short story that enable women writers to deal with questions of identity, fragmentation and alienation are also available for men. Similarly, women writers are now taking up the forms of the short story that have been traditionally associated with men: the adventure story or the hard-boiled detective story (see, for instance, Paretsky, *A Woman's Eye*, 1992).

Telling stories and the oral tradition

So far we've been looking at the short story in terms of its relation to other literary forms such as the novel and the lyric poem. But the written short story also retains many connections to oral modes of storytelling such as fables, folk tales, anecdotes, parables, jokes, confessions and, in women's writing in particular, gossip. (There is a discussion of gossip in women's discourse in Meaghan Morris's 'Feminism, reading, postmodernism', in *The Pirate's Fiancé*, 1988, p.15). While some writers argue that these modes of oral storytelling are dead, many authors argue instead that oral storytelling forms are very influential in written fiction. Grace Paley stresses the continuing vitality of the oral tradition:

> I don't think it's a dead form at all. I think that women do tell a lot of stories and I think that they're probably the last of a great oral tradition, and it's called gossip ... I think that's where it's going to come from, the great oral tradition that women have of handing down stories from grandmother to granddaughter and speaking together wherever they are.
>
> (Barthelme et al., 'A symposium on fiction', 1976, p.29)

The women in Grace Paley's stories are consistently characterized by their 'listening ears' and by their desire to repeat the stories that they hear (see, for example, *Later the Same Day*, 1987, p.28). Paley strongly believes that telling stories has consequences, and listening is not only a pleasure but a duty. In one story, 'Debts', the narrator is asked by a stranger to write the story of her grandfather's life. She refuses, feeling unqualified and uninterested. The next day, however she reflects that, while she owes the stranger nothing, 'it was possible that I did owe something to my family and friends. That is, to tell their stories as simply as possible, in order, you might say, to save a few lives' ('Debts', in *Enormous Changes at the Last Minute*, 1980, p.10).

Jamaica Kincaid's 'Girl' is an example of a short story that reproduces speech – in this case a mother's instructions to her daughter on how to behave properly. While reading a story such as 'The New Dress', for example, we have no knowledge of who is telling the tale or to whom it is addressed. Reading 'Girl' on the other hand, we seem to be overhearing a specific address – both speaker and recipient are clearly represented. To say that a short story has links to an oral rather than a literary tradition is not, however, to say that it is somehow simpler and less accomplished artistically. Indeed the effects that 'Girl' creates through rhythm and the repetition of key phrases, such as 'the slut you are so bent on becoming', are every bit as poetic as those of 'The New Dress'.

The short story is an enormously diverse genre. On the one hand, it borders on poetry and can be subtle and suggestive, discrete and devious. On the other hand, it is akin to gossip, to anecdote and the throw-away line. It is almost as if the short story absorbs and transforms any genre that passes its way. The short story can, to quote Paley, again 'illuminate the dark lives of women', but it can also celebrate and mock them. Indeed, short stories are as various as the women who write them. Collections of short stories by and about women proliferate today; stories by and about women of colour are particularly relevant to the theme of oral influence on literary style.

Domestic Bliss?: Gender and fiction, from Virginia Woolf's 'New Dress' to Jamaica Kincaid's 'Girl'

Let's consider the points that have just been made. Kasia Boddy has argued that the form of the short story is suitable to the needs of many different writers. It can express great ideas, or 'small domestic' details, can open the way for huge narratives or can focus on the individual voice.

1   It has been argued that some women write short fiction due to material/practical circumstance: they do not have time to write longer work. However, the length of a story is not necessarily indicative of its quality or importance.

2   Short stories, in so far as they are a suitable form for expression of 'the lonely voice', are particularly well suited to women writers and to the creation of female characters at odds in male-dominated worlds.

3   Short stories share some characteristics with poems, especially lyric poems. As poetry has traditionally been an 'elevated' and largely male-dominated genre, and the novel has been more open to women's influence (more suitable to the representation of domestic themes), the short story may occupy a mediating position between these other forms of creative writing.

4   Short story collections linked around central themes have been and continue to be popular with women writers, editors, publishers and readers.

5   The short story can be compared to oral as well as 'literary' forms in the sense that it tells a tale or communicates a narrative that is communicable in informal settings and in short periods of time. As such, the story as a form may be particularly suitable for the expression of ideas by groups of people who do not have time to write, or do not have the material advantages which would allow them to write (women and other 'minorities').

Note your responses to these points: do you agree with them; could you provide examples from the short stories you have read?

Discussion

These points are difficult to discuss in isolation, as each informs the others. The last point links directly back to the first, so if you question one – as you well might – you are likely to question the others. These are subjective rather than objective ways of discussing the short story as a form: some of these points assume a lot about women's lives and, of course, what applies to some women in some cultures and generations does not necessarily apply to all women. We will return to this idea in a moment.

Some of these points can best be discussed by way of example. For instance, the point about the comparison of short stories to 'long stories' or novels can be illustrated with reference to the work of Virginia Woolf. Woolf, well known for her critical writing, and perhaps best known as the author of novels, also wrote short stories. Indeed, as Boddy points out, the short story 'The New Dress' which you've just read was a working draft for what would later become the novel *Mrs Dalloway*, and was originally included in a collection (with a linked theme) called *Mrs Dalloway's Party*. The story contributes to the development of the character who eventually gained considerable fame as Clarissa Dalloway, the central figure and main narrative focus of the novel. This character and the stream-of-consciousness writing style of her story were both developed by Woolf in stages. Indeed, the character of Mrs Dalloway was also developed alongside another character: the eponymous nurse in the children's story 'Nurse Lugton's Curtain'. That story, as you may remember, was found in the manuscript copy of *Mrs Dalloway*. The ideas and characters created by Woolf were not entirely separate creations, but rather took various forms in different fictions; she thought of several ideas at the same time and chose particular forms or 'sub-genres' of prose fiction most suitable to the expression of particular 'moments of being', scenarios, characters and intended audiences of readers. ■

Reading with 'gender on the agenda' can be a fairly subjective and even controversial critical exercise. Each reader will read differently, depending on the experiences brought to the reading, including such factors as books read in the past and the way in which the reader has been taught to analyse and 'value' stories and other literary texts. While 'gender-aware reading' may be subjective, however, it is not so subjective as to evade informed academic discussion. Whatever other stories you have read, we can now assume that you are familiar with at least two which we can examine in more detail: 'The New Dress' and 'Girl'.

Characters, narrators, authors

Re-read Virginia Woolf's short story 'The New Dress' and Jamaica Kincaid's 'Girl'. Consider the following questions as you read both.

1 **Who are the main characters?**
2 **Can you identify the narrators as either female or male?**
3 **Are the main characters the same as the narrators?**
4 **Do the authors seem to identify with the main characters?**

Discussion

Boddy's brief discussion of these stories may have provided some hints here. It is easiest to compare answers to these questions if they are lined up in a grid:

	The New Dress	Girl
1	Mabel	An unnamed girl (and her mother, or older women generally)
2	Probably female, third person narrator	Female voice, an internal monologue; not a narrator's voice as such
3	No: the character of Mabel is constructed by the narrator's commentary, interwoven with what she does and doesn't say about Mabel	There is no 'narrator' as such, but the main voice of the Girl; the voice of her mother, or of unspecified older female figures (perhaps a general voice of female experience), is indicated by italics.
4	Yes, to some extent. The author seems sympathetic to, if critical of Mabel. It is the narrative voice, seemingly akin to Woolf's, which gives this impression.	Yes, to some extent. The relationship between the author and character/voice is not specified, but the first person voice seems to imply (perhaps wrongly) an autobiographical element

Of course, your answers will vary, but probably not too much. I would also add further questions which could not be answered so succinctly, and which I could not presume to answer for you: Do you as a reader identify with the characters of the stories? In which story do you as a reader identify with the narrator? Are you suspicious of the narrative voice (would you have told the same story differently)? ∎

Whatever your responses, it is highly likely that your gender and perhaps also your class, race and cultural background influenced your way of reading and interpreting. Women might find these stories more interesting, or more engaging at a personal level, than men. But not necessarily so. Aside from such subjective factors, there are some readings of the stories which we all, most likely, shared. We probably all noted the difference in narrative style, the difficulty of discussing characterization in 'Girl' and the general sense that these are female (if not necessarily 'feminine' or 'feminist') narratives.

If we think of the authors as well as the narrators, we'll see that they have very different 'positions'. Woolf, as you've seen, was a white, middle-class woman living in England in the first few decades of the twentieth century. Kincaid is a black woman, born in Antigua in 1941, who has lived and written in New York. Woolf helped to clear the way for contemporary women writers; Kincaid does the same today, creating new fictional forms and characters who speak from very different perspectives. Differences in cultural values and assumptions are obviously paramount, both for the characters represented in the stories and for the writers. You may also have found that your response to the stories differed according to your gender, your age, your race and your own cultural background and views about the representation of women. No matter what you think of the two stories, though, it should be clear that they each represent women in particular ways and that gender is relevant to both the writing and the reading. Both stories also share a focus on domestic detail and physical appearance. 'Girl' offers a girl's perception of her place in a familial and cultural context. And critic Michelle Barrett, in an interview for a BBC television programme produced in association with this book, argues that 'The New Dress' presents a range of different states of consciousness experienced by the character Mabel, a woman conscious of her appearance but finally able to leave her apprehension behind as she decides to go to the library and lose herself in a good book.

Appearance over action

Finally, let's consider the gender relevance of the key theme which runs through both of these stories: the representation of the domestic.

The emphasis in each story, though expressed in very different ways, is on appearance: the public valuing of women's dress and speech and action. In looking closely at these stories, we can see that the narrative in 'The New Dress' is focused through the perspective of the main character, who is primarily concerned with the way in which she is perceived by others. In 'Girl' there are no characters as such; there are no people with names and faces and ways of being and interacting with each other, developed over the course of a narrative. Rather, this short story offers two voices: a young woman whose voice incorporates at times that of another woman, probably her mother or guardian, and possibly also the voice of some shared female experience – that framed by Girl's culture and generation. In both, as in *The Lady of Shalott*, the female characters and voices are defined by expectations of feminine attire and 'appropriate' female behaviour: appearance over action. It is easiest and most effective to show you what I mean.

Looking closely at the texts of 'The New Dress' and 'Girl', can you find one sentence or key phrase in each which seems to emphasize 'appearance over action'?

There are, of course, many different sentences and phrases which you could choose for each. In 'The New Dress', I would choose the sentence: 'If he had only said, "Mabel, you're looking charming tonight!" it would have changed her life' (p.298). This sentence refers to the story's central concern, repeated so often as to become a refrain: what Mabel looks like; what Mabel thinks other people think of her. The sentence refers to a man whose opinion is important to Mabel. It refers to the importance of external confirmation for a self-centred character who is obsessed with appearances, with 'fitting in'. The narrator's narrow focus on Mabel takes us into her consciousness. The story becomes our initiation into Mabel's way of thinking, so that we feel her agony even as we recognize her small-mindedness.

'Girl' is, of course, one long sentence: one stream-of-consciousness narrative which could almost be seen as a dramatic monologue and could easily function as one. In fact 'Girl' is reprinted as a dramatic monologue in a recent publication (Goodman, *Mythic Women/Real Women*, 1996).

In looking for one key phrase in 'Girl' which somehow encapsulates the idea of 'appearance over action', I would choose the phrase which appears roughly one third of the way into the piece, on lines 14–15:

> ... this is how to hem a dress when you see the hem coming down
> and so to prevent yourself from looking like the slut you are so bent
> on becoming; ...

(p.302)

This phrase contains the words 'slut you are so bent on becoming', which function as a kind of poetic refrain, repeated throughout the piece. But the message is anything but 'poetic', anything but romantic. This phrase – and the longer sequence of words which I've chosen – contrasts the concern with appearing to be a nice girl (as opposed to a 'slut'), with learning to perform the tasks of daily life which will give the overall appearance of niceness, of fitting in. In terms of their focus on appearance, then, the stories have a great deal in common. ∎

Though the narratives differ significantly in length and style and narrative technique, they share a concern for appearance, for the social significance of acting in particular ways, culturally approved as 'feminine' behaviour. Can you find evidence of this concern in each of the two texts?

Both of the stories represent a conflict between women's views of themselves as individuals and their awareness of the ways in which they are viewed by others. This may be seen as a 'female' concern to some extent, though this does not imply either that men are *un*concerned with appearance, or that women are *merely* concerned with appearance. But of course, as many feminist authors argue, the 'beauty myth' is one – among many – persuasive influences in many women's lives (see Wolf, *The Beauty Myth*, 1991). This was even more often the case when marriage, and the need to attract men, was still one of the most viable financial/practical 'trades' or 'forms of work' open to women. Women's writing has both expressed this concern and helped to shift emphasis away from it.

Neither 'girl' nor Mabel Waring is actually engaged in sewing, yet each story emphasizes the art of female dress; 'Girl' mentions the hem of the dress, and the 'new dress' is a fascination, almost a character in itself. You may recall the bird cage at the dressmaker's and the fact that the dress Mabel has had made is 'canary yellow' – as though it will allow her the freedom to escape from the cage of her self. In Woolf's story, the dress is an obsession. Like the Ruby Slippers we considered earlier, we might view the dress as having iconic significance for Mabel, far beyond the power of an ordinary item of clothing. For her, the dress represents an entry into society, a way of making a statement and also an embarrassment and the motivation for her desire to leave the party early. (In *The Wizard of Oz*, you will remember, the Ruby Slippers were to be clicked together with the chant: 'there's no place like home, there's no place like home'). The dress is symbolic and also functional. The focus on dressmaking, as on the hem of the skirt in 'Girl', emphasizes the 'feminine' art of sewing, of making things by hand, and at the same time stresses appearance and cultural expectations of women's sexual and social behaviour. ■

Now let's turn to the narrative style of the stories. As we argued in Chapter One, the use of quotation marks and the intrusion of a narrator's voice often indicates that an extract is 'prose' fiction. But 'Girl' is an exception to this rule. In fact, the narrative strategy of 'Girl' crosses genres: the language is poetic, the voice of the poem is so direct, so internalized that no narrator can be identified. In fact, the story could be read aloud with considerable dramatic effect.

In comparing the two stories, we give them a context and a teaching function shaped by a particular concern for the relationship between gender and literature. The stories seem to speak to each other, though of course the authors never intended them to do so. This dialogue between writers and cultures and perspectives is one of the most valuable aspects of any comparative exercise. Such a dialogue is achieved in the grouping together by theme of any collection of stories. For instance, one collection might show how different women have seen the importance of reviewing and representing the 'domestic' in subversive ways and another might provide space for experimentation with fictional sub-genres, whether feminist detective fiction, feminist science fiction or some more traditional form such as 'romance'.

Finally, it should be said that while domesticity and its subversive representation are major themes in the two stories we've looked at, there are also other themes which could have been discussed: particularly the function of veiling (referred to by Woolf in *A Room on One's Own*, 1977 edn, p.48), women's dress, costume and façade. All these are related but different forms of representing the surface appearance of women. Each is handled differently by various authors, depending on the cultural context of the writing, the class, status and politics of the authors and their intended audiences of readers. In fact, 'veiling' and 'dress' are often cited as metaphors for covering and uncovering the 'female body' of literary criticism, as well as the physical female body (see, for instance, the discussion of dress as a metaphor in Todd, *Feminist Literary History*, 1988, pp.81–3). The subject of cross-dressing is another rich vein of feminist research (in, for instance, Garber, *Vested Interests*, 1992, and Lesley Ferris, *Crossing the Stage*, 1993). Whether the emphasis on costume and dress is a central metaphor for women's status as 'objects' of men's desire, or of the related desire of women to please (in order to 'fit in', as in Woolf's story), or in order to preserve the reputation of self and family (as in Kincaid's story), the base line is the same: surface appearance is emblematic of women's social status, at odds with the desire for knowledge of the world to be acquired through study, through books.

The relationship between appearance and status is also presented in the work of Louisa May Alcott, as the following section argues. As you read Elaine Showalter's piece below, remember that she is a feminist critic who writes about a number of authors, male and female, besides Alcott. In the next section, she builds bridges between authors and ideas – and highlights the ways in which Alcott's and other authors' work can be read 'with gender on the agenda'. The section is adapted from her essay of the same title, first published as the introduction to *The Alternative Alcott* (1988).

The hidden Louisa May Alcott

Now read Elaine Showalter's account of 'Alternative Alcott' below and think about how Showalter introduces Alcott in relation to the idea that for women as well as men, 'writing is work'.

Autobiography and fiction: alternative Alcott

by Elaine Showalter

In the late years of her career, pressured by the demands of her readers and her publishers for more work from the pen that had given them the best-selling *Little Women*, Louisa May Alcott taught herself to write with her left hand. Ambidexterity allowed her to keep to her desk twice as long, to produce twice as much, in short, to become a doubly efficient writing machine. But Alcott's ambidexterity also appears as a striking physical metaphor for her creativity, the body's correlative for her 'double literary life' (Douglas, introduction to *Little Women*, 1983, p.vii). Modern critics have generally seen her enormous output (at least 270 works in every genre from poetry to tragedy) as divided between conflicting literary impulses. On the genteel, domestic and moralizing side are Alcott's famous chronicles of the March family – *Little Women* (1871) and *Jo's Boys* (1886) – as well as the seven other novels and sixteen short-story collections for young people which made her famous as the 'children's friend'. On the other hand – the left hand? – Alcott inscribed her passion, anger and satirical wit, producing a series of pseudonymous sensation stories; four novels for adults: *Moods* (1864), *Work* (1873), *A Modern Mephistopheles* (1877) and the unfinished *Diana and Persis* (1879); a comic memoir of her

Figure 14   Photograph of Louisa May Alcott,
reproduced by courtesy of Orchard House, The
Louisa May Alcott Memorial Association.

family's failed experiment in communal living, *Transcendental Wild Oats* (1872); and numerous historical and feminist essays.

Both the sensation stories she wrote from 'behind a mask' and her feminist novels for adults reveal a woman very different from her celebrated image as either the kindly 'Aunt Jo' who preached self-sacrifice, or the self-styled 'Ancient Lu' who practised it in endless support of her family. Instead we see a passionate spinner of feminist plots and counter plots, a writer drawn to 'earthquaky' (Cheney, *Louisa May Alcott,* 1889, p.129) and volcanic themes and a sharp-tongued master of a racy and unladylike American vernacular. Reading the work of this alternative Alcott also leads us back to her domestic romances with a sharper vision of their suppressed radical elements and helps us understand similar divisions, masked by domestic conventions in the writing of other nineteenth-century American women.

The double voice of women's writing has been a central topic in contemporary feminist literary criticism, where it has been analysed as the product of the daughter's psychic conflict between the cultural legacies and laws of the father and the mother. From the paternal side comes the voice of the rational, realistic and didactic, defining but also forbidding access to patriarchal cultural authority. From the maternal side comes a more imaginative, disruptive, passionate and intimate voice, seductive but culturally marginal. Alcott often wrote about such gendered cultural divisions in her fiction, casting realism as masculine, romance as feminine.

Alcott's own unusual parents mixed and challenged both sex roles and literary roles. The second of four daughters (her sisters Anna, Elizabeth and May, became the Meg, Beth and Amy of *Little Women*), Louisa was born on her father's thirty-third birthday, November 29, 1832. Amos Bronson Alcott was one of the eccentric seers of American Transcendentalism, a minor prophet, gadfly, philosopher and educational reformer admired and often subsidized by more financially successful contemporaries such as the poet and philosopher Ralph Waldo Emerson and the novelist Nathaniel Hawthorne. His inability to earn a living became proverbial even among the high-minded and unworldly Transcendentalists; he 'possesses no gift for money making,' Louisa ruefully noted in her journal (quoted in Stern, introduction to *Behind a Mask*, 1975, p.viii). She took on the roles of the surrogate son and the family breadwinner, as well as that of the dutiful daughter. To a very considerable degree, her identification and rivalry with her father would dominate her whole life.

Louisa's early years were marked by a power struggle between the two parents for psychological dominance and authority over their children and for the children's loyalty. Bronson endorsed his daughter's intelligence and imagination and served as a model of the intellectual life in what she called 'this famous land of Emerson, Hawthorne, Thoreau, Alcott, & Co.'. Her earliest memory, she recalled, was of 'playing with books in my father's study – building houses and bridges of the big dictionaries and diaries, looking at pictures, pretending to read and scribbling on blank pages whenever pen or pencil could be found' (Cheney, *Louisa May Alcott*, 1889, p.27). As a child, one of Louisa's favourite pastimes was to move her playthings back and forth between her father's study and the nursery where her mother held sway, as if unable to choose between these two powerful precursors.

For Louisa, adolescence was a difficult period. At fourteen, she despaired of ever achieving the docile little womanhood her parents and her society demanded:

> I am old for my age and don't care much for girls' things. People think
> I'm wild and queer; but Mother understands and helps me ... I've
> made so many resolutions, and written sad notes, and cried over my
> sins, and it doesn't seem to do any good.
>
> (Ibid., p.48)

The strenuous boyish activities of her childhood had to be curtailed. Without either formal education or exercise as outlets for her energies and in the face of the family's continuing poverty, the teenage Louisa lived defiantly in her imagination. She developed a sentimental passion for Emerson, writing him romantic letters she never sent and hovering outside his house in the moonlight. Many melodramatic fantasies went into writing plays that the sisters performed at home; both she and Anna dreamed of going on the stage.

Her education had always been sketchy and sporadic; among the sisters only May, the youngest, went to the public schools. After a family move to Boston, even reading had to be sacrificed; there was 'very little time to write or think' (Ibid., p.62). Her father's censorship of female self-consciousness as selfish and narcissistic conflicted with Alcott's need to explore her own feelings as a young woman and a budding writer. When she was seventeen, Bronson noted disapprovingly that while Anna's journal was 'about other people, Louisa's is about herself' (Ibid., p.60). For several years thereafter she wrote only intermittently in her journal and her struggle to deny the self shows up as well in the characteristic omission of the first person in both her diary entries and Jo's truncated speech in *Little Women*.

At one point in October 1857, Alcott was unable to find work and experienced such despair that she even thought of suicide. It was during this year that she read Elizabeth Gaskell's biography of Charlotte Brontë:

> Read Charlotte Brontë's life. A very interesting but sad one. So full of talent; and after working long, just as success, love and happiness come, she dies. Wonder if I shall ever be famous enough for people to care to read my story and struggles. I can't be a C.B., but I may do a little something yet.
>
> (Ibid., p.95)

Jane Eyre had always been one of her favourite novels and the story of the novelist's tragic life suggested many parallels to her own.

The spectacle of her mother's difficult married life – eight pregnancies in ten years, poverty and hard work – made her suspicious of marriage in general and in much of her writing she would defend the option of spinsterhood: 'I'd rather be a free spinster and paddle my own canoe' Louisa wrote (Ibid., p.69). In an 1868 essay called 'Happy Women' Alcott portrays herself as the writer A., who

> in the course of an unusually varied experience has seen so much of … 'the tragedy that is modern married life' that she is afraid to try it. Knowing that for one of a 'peculiar nature like herself such an experiment would be doubly hazardous, she has obeyed instinct and become a chronic old maid.
>
> (in Showalter, *The Alternative Alcott*, 1988, p.205)

By 'peculiar nature,' Alcott probably meant her moodiness, ambition and hot temper; nevertheless, she had passionate sexual and maternal feelings that she could never entirely repress and up until her death she would regret the seemingly necessary sacrifice of sexuality and motherhood to work. Contrasting herself to Anna and her children, she wrote, 'She is a happy woman! I sell my children, and though they feed me, they don't love me as hers do' (Cheney, *Louisa May Alcott*, 1889, p.195).

'Work and wait' became her motto. The best women artists, she tried to persuade herself, were those who were truly unselfish, and ultimately, she hoped, womanly self-denial would bring its own reward in an enriched art. In numerous short stories as well as in *Little Women*, Alcott represented suffering, dutifulness and self-sacrifice as necessary steps toward female artistic success.

In 1865–66, Alcott went to Europe for the first time, not as a journalist, but as the companion to a wealthy young invalid. The trip to Europe was

Alcott's farewell to adventure and romance. She returned home in July to her mother's welcoming arms, but also to new financial obligations and family debts. 'Behind a Mask', which she wrote in August 1866, suggests her rage at servitude and the bitterness with which she faced the prospects of eternal repression and pretence.

After several years of rising income, Alcott earned $1000 in 1867 and saw a secure future: 'I want to realize my dream of supporting the family and being perfectly independent' (Ibid., p.193).

Despite fame and prosperity, Alcott's maturity found her increasingly 'porcupiny' (Ibid., p.166), sick and embittered. Celebrity seekers invaded her privacy and she never felt pride in her work. 'When I had youth,' she wrote, 'I had no money; now I have the money, I have no time; and when I get the time, if I ever do, I shall have no health to enjoy life' (Saxton, *Louisa May*, 1978, p.359). The demands of her readers for more books like *Little Women* tied her to a particular domestic style she found maddeningly restrictive, while her family's constant needs kept her at the grindstone of literary production.

During her last years, her literary productivity finally began to decline. To the last, Alcott tried to believe that her self-sacrifice would be rewarded and that any success she had won had come because 'my ambition was not for selfish ends but for my dear family'. Yet somehow there was never time for the rest, pleasure and travel she desired. 'Shall never live my own life,' she wrote bleakly in her journal (Ibid., p.406).

Jo's Boys, which she finally managed to finish in 1886, completed the saga of the March family. The real family seemed to follow its literary destiny. After a long decline, Bronson Alcott died on March 4, 1888 and the weary Louisa wondered, 'Shall I ever find time to die?' (Ibid., p.415). Two days later, the slowly accumulating effects of mercury poisoning from treatment she received during the Civil War finally took her life. At their joint funeral, the minister suggested that Bronson had needed his dutiful daughter's help even in heaven. (For the full version of Showalter's text, see *The Alternative Alcott*, 1988.)

Following the clues: discovering Louisa May Alcott

Showalter's account of Alcott's life picks up on themes which recur in women's writing: Alcott, like many women who had to work inside and outside the home had trouble finding both emotional and physical space in which to write her fiction. But Alcott was more successful than many. Historian Sarah Elbert is an Alcott scholar known for her critical investigations of the adult fiction, including *Moods*. Elbert emphasizes that the diaries kept by Alcott reveal her keen sense of humour. This emphasis might throw a different perspective on Showalter's account of the symbolic significance of the metaphor of 'writing with two hands'. Elbert also argues that rather than focusing on the influence of Bronson Alcott, it might be more informative to think of the considerable influence between women in the family and especially the influence of Abba Alcott (the mother, 'Marmee'), who got Louisa a 'room of her own'. In Elbert's words:

Louisa thanks Marmee for her room and encouragement repeatedly in the Journals; she writes notes to Marmee, dedicates novels to her (*Work*) and inscribes the fit copy of *Little Men* 'To Marmee, From Jo'. I think Louisa May Alcott took up Marmee's role in the family and certainly took up the care-taking of Bronson, with Anna's considerable help … [illustrating] a general pattern of 'bonding' between the women of the family.

(comments on an earlier draft of this chapter, 1995)

Here, Elbert raises the theme of women's influence on women, which is also central to the two short stories we've considered: 'Girl' and 'The New Dress'. But in our study of Alcott, we must recall that there were many different patterns of female influence, both within the stories and within the society which produced them. Even the few authors we've considered so far were clearly influenced by each other in important ways: Alcott and Dickinson were contemporaries and probably knew of each other's work; Alcott admired Charlotte Brontë; Dickinson admired Elizabeth Barrett Browning; Virginia Woolf imagined the gender and genius of Shakespeare's sister, and generations later both Sylvia Plath and Alice Walker looked back to and quoted Virginia Woolf. Alcott was considered to be, first and foremost, a writer of children's and domestic fiction. Yet she has recently been discovered as an early 'feminist' whose life informed her writing. In this sense, Alcott's fiction 'holds the mirror to her life' and vice versa. The same could be said of Woolf and certainly of authors such as Sylvia Plath and Charlotte Perkins Gilman. Keep that image of the mirror in mind. Just as it helps Woolf's character Mabel to see herself as she appears to others (Figure 15, taken from *Little Women*, might equally well illustrate 'The New Dress'), so it will prove to be a key image in reading literature by women and about women, from *The Lady of Shalott* on. In 'Behind a Mask', however, the image of the mirror is used more subtly: you as the reader become the mirror, as Alcott asks you both to sympathize with and judge the appearance and actions of her central character Jean Muir.

As Showalter points out, the domestic setting was key to most of Alcott's best known work. Figure 16 is taken from the first edition of *Little Women*. It is not only about a domestic theme, but is also influenced by a domestic relationship, as it is drawn by Louisa May Alcott's youngest sister, May (the model for the character of Amy, the artistic youngest sister in *Little Women*).

And yet, the domestic role was always at odds with Alcott's more professional role as a writer. In Figure 17 we see Alcott as depicted by her sister May in an early sketch. It is not accidental that May Alcott chose to depict her sister at her desk, in the act of writing. For Louisa May Alcott, as Showalter points out, writing was a means of making ends meet; it was a creative process, but also a practical necessity. The domestic novel *Little Women* eventually earned Alcott a substantial living, but her shorter fiction was the first paying work she accomplished; the 'blood and thunder tales' were part of that. Alcott recognized the potential of these tales to suit a popular fictional market and to pay the bills. Thrillers could be serialized and sometimes adapted to other forms. They kept their readership in suspense, wanting more; they created their own audience. They were also a viable way for women to use writing as a form of paid work. But, for

Figure 15 'Vanity Fair', illustration from the first edition of *Little Women*, drawing by May Alcott. Photo: Range Bettman.

Figure 16 Frontispiece, first edition of *Little Women*, by May Alcott, reproduced by courtesy of Orchard House, The Louisa May Alcott Memorial Association.

Figure 17 Sketch by May ('Abby') Alcott of Louisa at her desk, reproduced by courtesy of Orchard House, The Louisa May Alcott Memorial Association.

Alcott and other women to use writing as a form of paid work. But, for Alcott and other women writers of the day, writing such 'blood and thunder' tales was a radical move away from the more 'feminine' domestic fictional forms. Thus Alcott wrote her thrillers under an ambiguously gendered pseudonym, A.M. Barnard. It is only very recently that Barnard has been identified as Alcott and consequently discovered as a writer of early 'feminist' thrillers.

The thrill of discovery

Before reading this section you might want to look briefly at 'Behind a Mask' in Part Two of this book, considering the possibility that Alcott might have written such a tale 'with her other hand'. It was two women academics, Madeleine B. Stern and her partner in the rare book trade Leona Rostenberg, who first discovered Alcott's pseudonym. While at work on a new biography, Stern and Rostenberg were intrigued by the details which Alcott provided of her earnings from her various stories and novels, and by the strong connection between the character of Jo, the tomboyish young writer of *Little Women*, and Louisa herself. They went to Houghton Library at Harvard and began further research into Alcott's manuscripts, journals, family papers, publishers' letters and financial accounts. In the latter, they found the key to a fascinating mystery: five letters from one of Alcott's publishers, Elliott, Thames and Talbot. The letters reveal that Alcott and the pseudonymous writer of thrillers A.M. Barnard were one and the same. Rostenberg wrote an article about the discovery ('Some anonymous and pseudonymous thrillers by L.M. Alcott', 1943), but while the article raised a minor stir in the academic community at the time, the Alcott 'revolution' did not begin in earnest for another 40 years, when the feminist critical revolution had inspired a keen interest in women writers and their 'hidden' work. It continues as more stories are discovered and re-published in Alcott's name. Sarah Elbert teaches a course including Alcott's abolitionist story 'M.L.' (first published in *The Boston Commonwealth*, January 24–February 21, 1863), and a previously unpublished novel, a romantic thriller (*A Long Fatal Love Chase*), was purchased for publication in 1994–5. The title of that novel is suggestive of the kind of writing Alcott scholars have discovered, work relying to some extent on conventional ideas of heterosexual romance – yet including twists of story and daring characterizations of women that were quite radical in Alcott's day and in the conservative community of Concord, Massachusetts (not far from Emily Dickinson's home in Amherst).

In 1862, Alcott wrote:

> I intend to illuminate the Ledger with a blood and thunder tale as they are easy to 'compoze' and are better paid than moral and elaborate works of Shakespeare so don't be shocked if I send you a paper containing a picture of Indians, pirates, wolves, bears and distressed damsels in a grand tableau over a title like this *The Maniac Bride* or *The Bath of Blood: A Thrilling Tale of Passion* (sic) …

> (letter dated 22 June, 1862)

This letter and many others are now published, as are Alcott's journals. Another fascinating subplot to the Alcott mystery is the instruction left by Louisa to destroy her journals rather than allow them to be made public. A page from her diary (Figure 18) shows Alcott's request; it sits strangely on the page as a published reminder of the author's wish for some of her work to remain private.

Look at Figure 18. Why might Alcott have wanted to destroy her journals? What is it about the nature of private writing that distinguishes it from published fiction – for Alcott as for other writers we have studied?

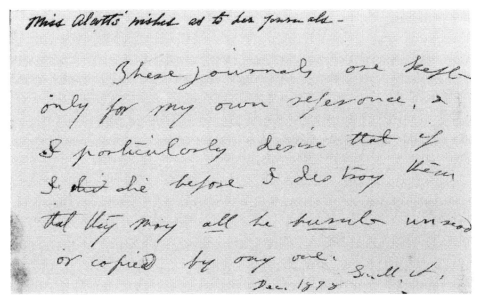

Figure 18   Louisa May Alcott's instructions for the destruction of her journals, from an entry dated December 1878. Houghton Library Manuscript 59M-509, deposited by Mrs F. Wolsey Pratt, June 1964, reproduced by permission of the Houghton Library, Harvard University.

Discussion

The page, in her own handwriting, seems somehow emblematic of the split between private and public, domestic and political, which Alcott's life and work continually reveal. Of course, many writers distinguish between the fiction which is intended for public consumption and the private letters which are not. We might feel the same about our 'public writing' and our personal correspondence. The division between public and private is often upheld by the estates of authors, whether or not that wish has been expressed. For instance, Emily Dickinson's sister Lavinia discovered a collection of letters in the same bureau where the poems were found, in the family home in Amherst. Lavinia disposed of nearly all the letters immediately. Only a few remain and these contribute to rather than detract from the academic problem of dating the poems and attempting to read the author's life in the fictional work. Another literary critical controversy of our time is posed by the estate of Sylvia Plath. Plath's husband, the poet Ted Hughes, has been criticized by feminists including Jaqueline Rose for his decision to edit some of her poems and letters before publication, as well as for the inscription of the name Hughes on Plath's gravestone (see Rose, *The Haunting of Sylvia Plath*, 1991).

The desire to destroy material is not so uncommon – and may be seen as quite understandable: writers are, after all, people with family and friends who may wish to have their own privacy respected. So Alcott's wish to destroy her journals is on one level understandable. Her 'radical' writing and views may have provided all the more impetus for her wish to distinguish between public and private writing, as between domestic fiction and 'thrillers'. ■

Of course, Alcott was not the first woman writer to break away from domestic realism and romanticism, opting instead to write 'blood and thunder' tales. As early as the seventeenth century, Aphra Behn wrote daring plays of sexual intrigue and also a well-received novel about slavery, *Oroonoko* (the influence of woman writers on Alcott may date back even further than we've suggested). In fact, the essential elements of the thriller can be traced to early experiments in Gothic novels. Thus, Mary Shelley's *Frankenstein* (1818) and Anne Radcliffe's *The Italian* (1797) – Gothic horrors and romances – are thrillers of a kind. Today, in the theatre, Agatha Christie has had more plays produced than any other contemporary woman playwright. The thriller is still a popular and lucrative form, as the work of contemporary novelist P.D. (Phyllis Dorothy) James testifies.

Alcott's longer fiction can also be studied for its autobiographical content. In addition to the domestic fiction and her many 'blood and thunder tales', she wrote poetry and two 'serious' novels, *Moods* and *Work*. Her novel *Moods* (edited and introduced by Sarah Elbert, 1991) makes a fascinating comparison to 'Behind a Mask' in its depiction of a young woman who considers suicide (by throwing herself off the Mill Dam). While Alcott signed *Moods* in her own name, she did not escape criticism of subverting feminine decorum by offering a female character with 'modern' views about marriage, who contemplates suicide as one way of dealing with her desperate lack of choices in society.

When the novel was published in 1865 it received negative reviews. Critics claimed that it was unrealistic, not true to life. Alcott defended her characterization by claiming that she actually knew women like this, real women who could be named. But she rewrote the ending: her decision to do so is highly significant, for it reveals the pressure on Alcott from the social structure in which she lived and worked to represent women's mental and emotional states more 'responsibly'. In the preface to the second edition, Alcott explained the change of ending in largely autobiographical terms, arguing that over the years she had changed her views and her way of writing. Yet the explanation tells an 'untold story' too: Alcott saw herself as a public figure ('the children's friend') by the time the second edition of *Moods* was made public and had come to accept (or to seem to accept) a new responsibility for a more positive representation of women.

The thriller as early feminist form: 'Behind a Mask'

Now read 'Behind a Mask' in full. Ask yourself what kind of 'work' the central character performs in the story.

Discussion

Jean Muir works as a governess. At another level, she works at overturning the household, at subverting the 'feminine' role. It is only in the 'unknown thrillers' that Alcott allowed her characters to get away with all manner of unfeminine, irresponsible, active, sometimes even wicked behaviour. ■

Elaine Showalter has provided one of the most accessible introductions to the character and her story. In her view, '"Behind a Mask" is the most skilful of the tales Alcott published under the pseudonym A.M. Barnard, in her first effort to disguise her gender'. She goes on to discuss the story as a 'tale of female revenge', in which Alcott can be seen to have drawn 'heavily on her childhood reading of *Jane Eyre* and on best-selling English sensation novels of the 1860s such as Mary Elizabeth Braddon's *Lady Audley's Secret* (1861) and Wilkie Collins's *Armadale* (1866)' (Introduction to *The Alternative Alcott*, p.xxix). Like the authors whose work she admired, Showalter argues, Alcott's story portrays a 'passionate governess' whose 'ambiguous position within the family' allows her the room to manoeuvre which is necessary to her scheming and initiation of romantic plots.

Alcott, like all writers, wrote with other stories and authors and styles in mind. In this case, she wrote with an awareness of the domestic constructs governing women's lives. Her own experiences of working (as a nurse and as a governess, as well as in the home and as a writer) would also have informed her representation of the difficult and 'ambiguous' position of such women. At the same time, the domestic setting is constructed as a convenient backdrop for 'unfeminine' behaviour.

When Showalter describes Alcott's effort to 'disguise' her gender with her pseudonym, the metaphor of theatrical disguise (bringing to mind the effects of costume and role-play) is clear. In Alcott's life, as in her fiction, such disguise was both necessary and dramatic: functional and symbolic. We can see how this was so by comparing our earlier reading of Alcott's life (from Showalter's Introduction) to a close reading of the novella itself.

Re-reading 'Behind a Mask'

Re-read 'Behind a Mask' and keep the following question in mind: **What is the significance of the title in relation to the subtitle, 'A Woman's Power'? It might help you to answer this question if you compare the treatment of Jean Muir to the characterization of other female literary characters we have considered, such as the Lady of Shalott, Jane Eyre, Eliza Doolittle and Mabel Waring.**

Discussion

The significance of 'a woman's power' is related to the idea of pretending to be someone – playing a role in order to gain security (financial or emotional). The story's title refers to the 'mask' of social convention, worn by women of all classes to portray themselves in the most favourable possible light in public settings. The 'mask' is that of public self: a projected image put on for the benefit of an audience. The subtitle is also significant. 'A Woman's Power' in this story seems to be the power to win her way by acting, role play and by devious means if necessary. The relationship between title and subtitle may be seen as indicative of Alcott's early 'feminist' views, since the choice of terms and the way that they are presented in the story seems to support Jean rather than criticize her. This positive framing of a negative character also gives you a hint as to Alcott's view of Jean – and of herself – as a player of roles, in public and in private, a point discussed in detail below. This is most evident in the last line of Chapter VII, when the narrative voice refers to Jean as someone who can create impressions and banish them 'by her art' – the art of acting, or gendered role play. ■

What is the central metaphor of the story, or the frame of reference within which the action of the story is most often described?

Discussion

The metaphor of performance, or role playing, is central to the story of 'Behind a Mask'. A mask may be part of a disguise, for the theatre or for carnival, or indeed for robbery or other more sinister acts. A mask hides the face, prevents others from seeing a person's true identity. Makeup, wigs and fancy dress also add to an overall effect of disguise which is both practical (in so far as it creates an image to be projected to the outside world, hiding the private self in favour of a negotiated or created public image) and 'dramatic' (it excites the imagination of viewers, who want to see beneath the mask). The mask, like the fans often used by women in Restoration drama, is also a prop (stage property) which can be used to intervene, spatially and symbolically, between people. The fluttering fan which a Lady holds gives her something to do with her hands and a symbolic way of expressing her feelings towards another person. She may use a fan as a screen, or as a means of flirtation, like a carelessly dropped glove. Here – though it may seem an unlikely parallel – we can compare the dramatic tableaux, the masks and props of 'Behind a Mask' to the well-known 'play within a play' in *Hamlet*, which functions much like a tableau vivant: 'to catch the conscience of the king'. Alcott, of course, like the characters in *Little Women* was an avid reader of Shakespeare (and Dickens). Shakespeare also 'played with gender' when designing props and disguises for his female characters: Desdemona's dropped handkerchief, for instance, becomes central to the sexual intrigue of *Othello*; cross-dressing is essential to the story of *As You Like It*. The use of theatrical scenes or tableaux within stories allows for fictional characters to step outside of themselves, to show sides of their characters we might not otherwise see and to hide sides which other characters within the fiction should not see (even if the author, via the narrator, allows us as readers to see these hidden roles). ■

The theatrical tableaux within the story of 'Behind a Mask' sets up an alternative world, where people step out of character temporarily. Alcott sets up Jean Muir as a character who reveals different parts of herself to different audiences: one role for the family, another for individual men she hopes to seduce and another for the theatrical tableaux. Jean's 'real self' is revealed only to us, the reader, when she takes off her disguise.

Can you locate the scene where Jean 'removes her mask' for you, the reader? What is the 'mask'?

D i s c u s s i o n

The scene appears in the last four paragraphs of Chapter One, when Jean removes her makeup, false hair and teeth, and her artificial expression to reveal the woman beneath: 'a haggard, worn, and moody woman of thirty at least' (p.309). The mask is Jean's pretence of being someone she is not. It symbolizes acting and role-play. This role-playing, as Alcott's own life reveals, was imposed upon women of her generation and class by a society which demanded certain kinds of 'feminine' behaviour, while also requiring at least some women to work, to earn money. Like Alcott, Jean Muir is a woman who needs paid work. There are many references within the story to her position as a servant within the Coventry household – early on the child Bella is told that it is Jean's place to move towards the family not their task to go to her (p.304). Throughout, diminutive language is used to refer to her (mainly by the men): she is call 'little Muir'. But later in the novel, when Jean's supposedly noble birth is revealed, her value seems to increase. So at one level, Alcott creates a character who is treated badly due to gender and class status. But while the author resorts to 'honest' labour, Jean manipulates men in order to gain power. Her power is the power of the actress, the performer, the woman who is able to convince her audience, or at least to help them to 'suspend disbelief' long enough for her to get her way. ■

Even in this brief discussion of the theme of power, we have moved directly to the central metaphor of the theatre. The metaphor is appropriate to the life as well as the work; Louisa May Alcott and her sisters were theatre enthusiasts, who often acted in and stage-managed productions for their local theatre, in addition to staging home theatricals (see Figure 19).

Alcott also looked to the theatre for financial support. Although she and her older sister Anna were both frustrated in their girlhood dreams of acting professionally, Alcott's story *Little Women* was adapted for the stage and produced in several major cities in the United States. The family's financial ledger notes the income from dramatic royalties and box office receipts. Houghton Library holds ledgers for performances of the play in 1914 and 1926, and, under the heading 'Receipts and Business Matters', for productions in Syracuse, New York; Providence, Rhode Island; Cambridge, Massachusetts; Oshkosh, Wisconsin; and Appleton, Wisconsin.

Like Alcott, and like many of the characters of her domestic fiction (notably the sisters in *Little Women*), Jean is an admirer of the theatre. But Jean has taken the concept of 'performing self' a major step further. She not only knows how to play the part of the feminine, but also how to

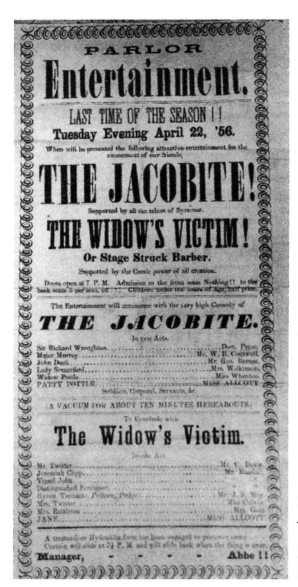

Figure 19 Playbill for *The Jacobite* and *The Widow's Victim* (1856), reproduced by courtesy of Orchard House, The Louisa May Alcott Memorial Association.

manipulate that part to suit her own needs. The extract which follows describes Jean's first entrance into the 'scene' of the household: she enters in true dramatic style. All eyes are on her as she plays her part to perfection. The emphasis which Alcott places on the active 'supporting role' played by the admiring audience of Jean's 'small domestic act' is in itself significant.

> 'Miss Muir,' announces a servant, and a little black robed figure stood in the doorway. For an instant no one stirred, and the governess had time to see and be seen before a word was uttered. All looked at her, and she cast on the household group a keen glance that impressed them seriously; then her eyes fell, and bowing slightly she walked in.

> (p.304)

Who directs the image Jean projects of herself?

Whereas in domestic stories and even in more modern women's fiction (as in 'The New Dress' and 'Girl') women are shown to see themselves as they are seen by others, in 'Behind a Mask', Jean takes on the power of actor and director: she chooses an image for herself to suit each scene, each part she must play in relation to the other characters. Her role-playing is not just a means of getting by in the world – as it is for characters such as Mabel in 'The New Dress'– but is rather a means of getting what she wants from the world. Jean's acting is schematic: planned and rehearsed. The story offers action combined with appearance: acting is the story's central metaphor. 'Behind a Mask' is the story of a woman who acts her role as a woman: who plays a part in order to get what she wants (money and power) and who succeeds. ■

Sarah Elbert argues that Alcott's creation of Jean Muir signals the literary emergence of the 'fallen woman', the sexually active woman who makes her own way in the world – a theme which was very important to Louisa May Alcott and was also a major issue for the Woman's Movement of nineteenth-century America. In Elbert's words:

> 'She's our sister', is the message, or 'there but for the Grace of God ...'
> And, just as importantly, Jean Muir is a new world jab at *Jane Eyre*.
> This Governess (Muir) marries the Lord of the manor under quite
> different circumstances. Alcott said in her adult novel *Work* that she did
> not approve of Jane's marrying to reform or to save Rochester. Jean
> Muir doesn't do that and neither does the main character, Christie, in
> *Work*, nor the main characters in Alcott's fiction for children or adults.
>
> (Elbert in correspondence with the author, 1995)

It is tempting to see Jean Muir as a 'liberated' character – one who breaks new ground for her author and for female readers. But what kind of a role model does Jean Muir provide? Perhaps the reader's attention is best directed at the contrast between the domesticated 'good little woman' and radical role-players such as Jean Muir. Somewhere between the two, or beyond the two, a more 'realistic' and complex picture of 'woman' may emerge. Indeed, Alcott's creation of both the 'good' and 'bad' female characters, and the discovery of both sides of Alcott's view of 'the female' enrich this study of literature and gender.

Jean Muir is acutely aware of appearances, but is not content to let appearances dictate her behaviour. Rather, she manipulates appearances to her own advantage. Alcott manipulates the audience/reader's expectations accordingly. Perhaps the best example is found at the close of chapter one, when Jean's 'metamorphosis' is described.

Re-read the last four paragraphs of chapter one of 'Behind a Mask'. Does the narrator of the story sympathize to any extent with the main character, Jean Muir?

Discussion

To set the scene: Jean is pleased with her first introductions to the household; she has won over her audience by playing the part of the proud but frail governess to everyone's satisfaction but Gerald's, and she is confident that she possesses the means – the beauty and 'feminine charms' – to win him over. Yet her beauty is not 'natural'. It is part of her theatrical costume removed when she goes 'backstage', as it were, to her private chamber to retire for the evening. In private, when 'the gaze' of her public is no longer upon her, she looks instead at the space around her and takes stock of her day's performance. 'Come', she says, 'the curtain is down, so I may be myself for a few hours, if actresses are ever themselves' (p.309). ■

Here, Alcott creates a character who recognizes the distinction between the public self and the private self, and who also recognizes the potential dangers of 'playing' the public part too long, or too well: it can take over and obscure any idea of who the 'real self' is underneath. By contrast, we might say that Woolf's character Mabel in 'The New Dress' is so conditioned to think of her appearance through other people's eyes that she doesn't know whether there is anything, anyone, underneath.

In 'Behind a Mask' the narrator's description of Jean – the words she chooses and the way she uses them – suggest that she identifies with Jean's sense of role-play – and perhaps with Jean's less likeable characteristics.

A traditional romantic narrative would punish Jean for her selfish ways: she might end up locked in the attic, or dead. But Alcott allows Jean to live and to thrive. The message of the story, if we should care to find one, might be that 'marriage is a trade', and women like Jean must know how to trade themselves within it: a message which Alcott could be said to have recognized at an intellectual level, though she never was able to negotiate her own position within the 'marriage business', or her own sexuality. On this level, the story might be seen as a subversive act by Alcott – though one which she never quite accomplished in life – who displays the anti-romantic sensibility about which Cicely Hamilton wrote.

Alcott's contribution to the development of feminist fiction

Elaine Showalter sums up the feminist impact of the story in this way:

> ... the story can be seen as a narrative meditation on the possibilities for feminist subversion of patriarchal culture, on the ways for women to express themselves, or at least their power, through role playing. Alcott's heroine, Jean Muir, the ex-actress Jean Muir, can never be offstage; she always acts the feminine parts that her society allows her, but acts them with a brilliance that exposes their artifice and emptiness. If women are trapped within feminine stereotypes of childishness and victimization, or duplicity and manipulation, Alcott suggests, they can unmask these roles only by deliberately overacting them. Thus Jean's well-timed and carefully staged swoons, raptures, tears, and songs reveal the secret of feminine social and literary pretence. Through this active appropriation, as the French feminist

106

theorist Luce Irigiray has argued, women can 'convert a form of sub-ordination into an affirmation, and thus ... begin to thwart it.'

(Showalter, Introduction to *Alternative Alcott*, p.xxx; she quotes Irigaray, *This Sex Which is Not One*, 1986 edn, p.76)

Discussion

It is significant that Showalter identifies the 'literary pretence' of feminine socialization. Alcott would probably not have called herself a 'feminist writer', mainly because the term was not in common currency. Alcott was known as an abolitionist and strong advocate of women's rights and her stories serve her politics well.

We know that the story was written, in part, to help pay the bills. It also allowed Alcott to release a kind of energy and feeling not expressed in the children's literature, and to do so 'safely' due to the use of the pen name. The story offers a negative female character and presents her and her situation in such a way as to elicit some support and sympathy. Because Alcott seems to identify with Jean, in direct and indirect ways, it is difficult to condemn Jean entirely, even when she is at her most manipulative. Thus, the story validates women's role-playing and suggests that, in a world governed by men and in which marriage is a trade, women might do well to play the game to their best advantage.

In writing both the blood and thunder tales – readable as early examples of 'feminist fiction' – and the domestic novels, Alcott played two roles, wrote with a 'double voice' and projected mirror images of the 'feminine' and the 'female'. She used a range of literary genres – prose fiction (adult and juvenile, 'domestic' and sensational) as well as letters and journal entries – in order to represent a diverse array of female characters, positive, negative and always fascinating. ∎

I would summarise the key points raised in a close reading of 'Behind a Mask' as follows:

1   The relationship between the story's title and subtitle is significant. 'A Woman's Power' is the power to win her way by acting, role play and by devious means if necessary; while the 'mask' is that of the public self: a projected image put on for the benefit of an audience.

2   The need to 'wear masks' (make-up, costumes, particular ways of representing self) is another way of formulating the basic idea that society imposes a range of expectations on women and men; those for women (illustrated in the stories we've read) are to do with factors such as age, beauty, class and social standing.

3   Financial considerations are both a theme of the story and a reason for its having been written. Jean's duplicity is, at least at one level, spurred by the need to make ends meet, developed into a desire to be rich – so Jean Muir can be seen as an extreme, grotesque example of a quite ordinary woman.

4   The theatrical metaphor fuels the story and helps Alcott to position herself – within the narrative convention of the story – as an observer and critic of Jean, without actually criticizing her (perhaps because some of Jean is also in Alcott, and perhaps in us all).

While these points are specific to 'Behind a Mask', they are also relevant to 'Girl' and 'The New Dress'. In fact, many key themes and ideas are contained in all three stories.

Alcott's feminist thrillers and other writers' experimental, liberating innovations have developed as part of a rich tradition of women's writing. As we have seen, the theatrical metaphor – with its focus on role playing – is a common theme in much women's fiction, whether it is expressed in terms of costume and an attention to surface appearance, or in more direct allusions to masks, veils and the drama of everyday life. This last idea is intricately related to another major theme in women's writing and writing about women: 'women and madness', a phrase popularized by the book of that title, edited by Mary Jacobus (1979). That theme is the subject of the next chapter.

Further reading

Alcott, L.M. (1991 edn) *Moods*, edited and introduced by S. Elbert, Rutgers University Press

Barrett, M. (1993) *Virginia Woolf: On Women and Writing: Her Essays, Assessments and Arguments*, The Women's Press.

Bonner, F. et al. (eds) (1992) *Imagining Women*, Polity Press.

Carter, A. (ed.) (1986) *Wayward Girls and Wicked Women*, Virago.

Olsen, T. (1965) *Silences*, Dell.

Russ, J. (1984) *How to Suppress Women's Writing*, The Women's Press.

Showalter, E. (ed.) (1988) *The Alternative Alcott*, Rutgers University Press

Stern, M.B. (ed.) (1995) *Louisa May Alcott Unmasked*, Northeastern University Press.

Woolf, V. (1975 edn) *A Room of One's Own*, Triad/Panther Books; first published in 1927.

Notes

1 The full text of the novella printed in Part Two of this book can be found in Stern (1975) *Behind a Mask and Other Thrillers by Louisa May Alcott*.

2 The author was given information and access to unpublished work in an interview with Stern and Rostenberg, 9 August, 1994 (East Hampton, Long Island, New York). Stern, Rostenberg, Elaine Showalter, Sarah Elbert and Michelle Barrett are all featured in an Open University BBC television programme produced in conjunction with this book. Stern was Alcott's most thorough biographer; she effectively re-edited the writer's life, re-introducing names and details edited out by her first biographer, Edna Dhow Cheney (*L.M. Alcott: Her Life Letters and Journals*, 1889). Interestingly, both Cheney and Stern have examined the relationship between domestic fiction and the stage in Ibsen as well as Alcott (see Cheney's *Nora's Return: A Sequel to The Doll's House of Henry Ibsen*, 1890) and Stern's discussion of it in *The Journals of Louisa May Alcott*, pp.36–37).

3 An account of the process of their discovery – which reads as a fascinating detective story in itself – is contained in the introduction to *The Hidden Louisa May Alcott* (1984).

Madwomen and attics: themes and issues in women's fiction

by Lizbeth Goodman, with Helen Small and Mary Jacobus

Themes and issues

This chapter focuses on a theme recurrent in much literature by and about women – women and madness. Our discussion will encompass a range of concerns raised earlier:

the role of the domestic in women's lives,

writing as a form of work long denied to women, and

the impact of gender-based oppression on women's views of themselves and their ways of representing themselves in writing.

While all these concerns can be discussed without reference to madness, there are intriguing and informative connections. Indeed, Elaine Showalter has used the phrase 'the female malady' to refer to both the female experience of domestic confinement and to the identification of mental and emotional disturbances in women which could be called 'female disorders'. In her book *The Female Malady: Women, Madness and English Culture* (1985), she discusses examples of this 'malady' from literature and life, including 'The Yellow Wallpaper', our case study for this chapter. Another phrase she uses in this book 'the domestication of insanity' suggests how she connects domestic confinement and oppression with 'madness'.

I'd like to begin by outlining how 'madness' has come to be discussed in connection with literature by and about women, and some of the things that have been said. To follow this discussion, you will need to have quickly read through 'The Yellow Wallpaper', which is reprinted in Part Two of this book.

The female malady

First we will be concerned with the assigning of the label 'mad', and the interpretation of that label in textual and cultural context. We have already touched on one instance of such labelling – the case of Alice and the Cheshire cat (p.20) – in our consideration of a book which has madness as one of its themes. At the same time, we considered similar issues of language, reason and power in Humpty Dumpty's assertion of his 'mastery' over language (p.18). I have returned to these two scenes because they neatly encapsulate so many ideas about the way that language both privileges the male (because he has 'mastery') and lays claim to reason – thereby disempowering the female on both counts. While the context in these cases was comic, they may still provide a useful introduction to the linked themes of madness, reason and language. You may remember, too, that these were the themes of Emily Dickinson's poem 'Much Madness is Divinest Sense'. In 'The Yellow Wallpaper' – as in all these examples – the male figures which threaten with the label 'mad' seem to present an unassailable male power which determines meaning by assuming the right to designate 'correct' uses of language and rules for female behaviour. Gilman's story provides an example where the dynamic of power is more serious than it is in in the case of Alice, not only because 'The Yellow Wallpaper' is a story for and about adults, but also because it is largely based on the autobiographical experiences of its author.

The theme of madness in literature is intrinsically gendered. At the most basic level, it is often females who are called mad and males who call them so. The conditions which make women 'mad' and the language which is used to describe madness are also gendered; they can be clarified by feminist analysis of gender and power. In 'The Yellow Wallpaper' the central female character is literally driven mad by the obstacles (symbolic and real) placed in the way of her self-expression through creative writing. For her, as for the author Charlotte Perkins Gilman, writing is more than a form of work, it is also a means of expressing identity. When this avenue for expression is blocked – like the metaphorical road in Gilman's poem 'The Obstacle' – self expression is also blocked, and some means must be found to vent that creative imagination. The question is: Can madness be a means of escape, of 'liberation for women'? Obviously, this is a contentious argument – and one we'll explore later.

Thus far, we have discussed madness in relation to fictional characters, where the label is used or implied in the text itself. More problematically, the label 'mad' is, of course, a very common and imprecise term for a variety of very real conditions. We have already encountered several authors known to have been chronically depressed: Sylvia Plath and Virginia Woolf are well-known examples. Their suicides have served to make them famous for their so-called 'madness' as well as for their literary achievements. Both also wrote about madness. Sylvia Plath's semi-autobiographical novel, *The Bell Jar* (1963), described a young woman's nervous breakdown and her experience of institutionalization. You will also remember Plath's private journal, with its description of her 'mask of a face' (Figure 13) and its disturbing revelation of the young woman's sense of hiding her self beneath surface appearances. Her poem 'Lady Lazarus', too, is very explicit about madness and suicide attempts, 'dying as an art'. Even Louisa May Alcott, in spite of her sanctified image as 'the children's friend' had struggles with what she described as 'moods'. Alcott did not kill herself, but rather projected her feelings of depression and desperation onto her characters and into her diaries and letters. In her novel *Moods*, and in her diaries, she wrote about depressions connected to the struggle to balance artistic creativity with domesticity and associated expectations of women's roles and behaviour.

Of course, 'madness' is not exclusively female terrain. While Ernest Hemingway is not routinely discussed as 'mad', his notorious suicide could be viewed alongside those of Woolf and Plath. However, it tends to be read quite differently: as a conflict between the masculine ideal created in his fiction and the life of the artist, perhaps. So his suicide is often seen as a heroic act, while Plath's and Woolf's are linked to discussion of depression, desperation, neurosis. Even suicide, it seems, is gendered; or at least, cultural readings of the act of suicide are gendered, as many feminist critics have argued. (See, for instance, Margaret Higonnet, 'Speaking silences', in Suleiman, *The Female Body in Western Culture*, 1986.) Charlotte Perkins Gilman also committed suicide. Gilman's 'madness' and eventual suicide are less well known than Woolf's or Plath's, perhaps because she has more recently been discovered and legends about her life and work have not yet had time to develop.

Of course, at one level the concept of madness needs to be discussed as a medical category requiring a specialized vocabulary – and we shall look at it in a medical context later in this chapter (this is also the subject of a BBC television programme, *Behind a Mask*, produced in association with this book). For each of the writers we'll discuss, the term means something different, depending on the psychological, physical and emotional profile of the individual and on the cultural assumptions attached to the term in her day. But as a great deal of literature depicts what are textually labelled as 'madwomen', it seems fair to take the concept of the literary madwoman for analysis first.

We have said that the madness theme in literature often relates to the conflict between artistic and domestic sensibilities. Indeed, in real life as in art, such conflict is a subtext of the lives and work of creative artists of all kinds, not only of literary women. Here I'd like to consider Elizabeth Siddal (1834–1862), a talented artist – albeit untrained – who took her own life. Perhaps it is telling that Siddal was among the first to paint the sad and mysterious Lady of Shalott (see Figure 20).

Figure 20 Elizabeth Siddal, *The Lady of Shalott*, 1853, pen, black ink, sepia ink and pencil on paper, 16.5 x 22.3 cm, Private Collection. Photograph by courtesy of the Maas Gallery, London.

What aspects of the poem are emphasized in Figure 20? Is the Lady active or passive?

Discussion

Siddal's Lady is not passive, but busy working at her loom. Weaving, like sewing and needlework, was a form of work and creative expression available to women in this period, though not one which was highly valued in the world outside the home. This type of work was seen as important to a 'lady's' grooming, and was valued not in artistic terms, but in domestic or decorative terms. Siddal emphasizes the woman and her work rather than symbols of the outside world (such as the window) or of her self-image (such as the mirror, which is not central in Siddal's image). Our attention is drawn to the concept of a woman working without outside inspiration or interaction, to her solitude and her captive imagination. Perhaps, we can surmise, Siddal felt isolated as a woman artist; perhaps she experienced something of the same conflict between creative imagination and social roles that was felt by other famous female suicides, including Woolf and Plath. ■

It may seem that the reference here to Tennyson's Lady is artificially imposed, but it is uncanny (strange and unnerving) how often the Lady crops up, in one guise or another, in discussions and images of women and madness. Let's reconsider the Siddal drawing (Figure 20) and the two more recent images of the Lady of Shalott that we considered earlier (Figures 10 and 11). Could all of these be related to images of 'madness'? Art historians have thought so (see 'Woman as sign in Pre-Raphaelite literature' by Deborah Cherry and Griselda Pollock, 1984). If we forget that the images are connected to Tennyson's poem but 'read' them instead as representations out of context, both serve discussion of 'women and madness' quite well.

A modern 'feminist' reading of the poem, too, might relate it to the theme of madness. The cracking mirror could be seen as a symbol of the cracking sanity of the Lady, who is faced with irreconcilable demands as she tries to negotiate the role she is expected to play – a role symbolized by the oppressive system of constraints to her freedom – and her own wishes and (sexual) desires. (Such a reading will not sound impractical to a woman juggling different public and private roles today.) Let's reconsider another image of the Lady: that of Rossetti (Figure 7). We can perhaps look at this differently in the knowledge of the real-life connection with Elizabeth Siddal. Siddal was Rossetti's mistress, wife and model – the model for this Lady of Shalott as well as many other Pre-Raphaelite images. She is said to have identified with the Lady and her entrapment; certainly she sketched the subject before Rossetti took it up; in fact, hers is one of the first known illustrations of the poem. Is it significant that she chose to represent the walls of the tower and the imposing solidity of the loom in her sketch rather than dwelling on the Lady's physical appearance? Her treatment of the cracked mirror and the theme of fractured identity has been commented upon in the light of her suicide. How does her version compare with the Horvitz and the Johnson? **Compare Figures 10, 11 and 20 and consider the central focus of each image: does it direct your** eye, for instance, to the Lady herself, to her surroundings, to symbols of life outside the tower or to the other characters in Tennyson's poem?

Discussion

These images focus on the woman rather than her surroundings or the other characters in the poem, yet each takes a different angle. The Horvitz image – a painting of a woman who appears to be 'mad', by a woman who identifies with the theme of madness – depicts a very real, naked woman, seated amidst clutter and embracing her own legs protectively, as if to shut out the world. (Shelah Horvitz has published an account of her approach to and identification with the Lady in an article, 'My Lady of Shalott', 1983, pp.64–8.) Behind her is the mirror and the loom, which might easily be mistaken for a bed frame. Indeed, with the same inscription – 'I am half sick of shadows' – this could be an illustration for 'The Yellow Wallpaper'. When we come to read the story in detail, we'll see just how similar the two 'ladies' and their respective stories are in some respects. Indeed, there is a striking similarity between the image of the Horvitz *Lady of Shalott* and an illustration of the narrator of Gilman's story 'The Yellow Wallpaper' in the later stages of her desperation and 'madness' (Figure 21): both show the dishevelled appearance thought to signify madness in women. ■

Figure 21   Untitled pen and ink drawing by Jo. H. Hatfield, *New England Magazine*, (new series, vol.5 no.5), January 1892.

Madness is culturally and socially defined. So, while there are certain key characteristics of 'madwomen' in images from different periods (wild hair and unkempt or discarded clothes seem to be common), there is no one all-embracing image or definition. The Johnson painting of the Lady of Shalott depicts a ghostly, incandescent woman moving away in horror from what she has seen in the broken mirror: a horror of recognition. We might contrast that image of wide-eyed terror to an image of a female 'hysteric' (Figure 22), which seems to belong to a different, more 'scientific' category.

This shows one of the women subjects of Jean Martin Charcot's (1825–1893) early studies in hypnotism which formed the origins of what would become known, after Freud, as psychoanalysis. But this more particular discussion of madness and 'hysteria' needs careful contextualization, which will be provided by Helen Small in the next section. As you read this, take note of what she says about 'reason'. If 'reason' were a person, would that person – according to the attributes and qualities attached to reason – be gendered as female or male?

Figure 22   Jean Martin Charcot demonstrating a case of hysteria at La Salpêtrière, 1882. Mary Evans Picture Library.

Madness as a theme in women's literature

by Helen Small

Madness has been an important theme in literature from Greek tragedy onwards, but in the nineteenth and twentieth centuries it has been particularly associated with women. Many of the key texts of feminist literary studies have been centrally concerned with the figure of the madwoman: Charlotte Brontë's *Jane Eyre*, Virginia Woolf's *Mrs Dalloway*, Sylvia Plath's *The Bell Jar*, Doris Lessing's *The Golden Notebook* and, more recently, Marge Piercy's *Woman on the Edge of Time* among them. And as Sandra Gilbert and Susan Gubar have shown in *The Madwoman in the Attic* (1978), even those female writers we tend to think of as far less sympathetic with feminism – Jane Austen and George Eliot, for instance – repeatedly turn to the same theme, allowing us glimpses of female insanity and rage that ruffle the calm surface their work usually presents.

The reason for women writers' interest in madness has often been immediate and personal. Indeed it is disturbing to note how many women writers have suffered from mental illness. Mary Wollstonecraft, Virginia Woolf, Charlotte Brontë, Sylvia Plath, Janet Frame and Anne Sexton are only a few of those who have written about psychological breakdown from first hand experience. Being a female writer, it seems, can involve intolerable psychological pressures on those who find that literary creativity is at odds with their expected roles as women. Elaine Showalter notes in her key study *The Female Malady* that 'Biographies and letters of gifted women who suffered mental breakdowns have suggested that madness is the price women artists have had to pay for the exercise of their creativity in a male-dominated culture' (p.4).

Some female authors and critics have, however, offered a more positive view of madness. Debilitating though mental illness is, women have occasionally found that the experience of losing and having to remake their identity gave them a hard-won independence from conventional ways of seeing the world and of using language. Janet Frame, for example, has written of her own time in a psychiatric hospital that 'There was a personal, geographical, even linguistic exclusiveness in this community of the insane':

> If the world of the mad were the world where I now officially
> belonged (lifelong disease, no cure, no hope), then I would use it to
> survive, I would excel in it. I sensed that it did not exclude my being a
> poet.
>
> (Frame, *An Angel at my Table*, 1984, p.79)

But is the sex of the author really relevant to a discussion of the theme of insanity in literature? After all, the century which produced *Jane Eyre* (1846) also produced powerful writing about madwomen by Sir Walter Scott, Charles Dickens and Wilkie Collins, among others. Indeed, what is probably the most influential piece of literary criticism to shape the current debate about women's relationship to insanity discusses a short story by a man. Shoshana Felman's 1975 article 'Women and madness: the critical phallacy' focuses on the representation of madness in Honoré Balzac's short story 'Adieu'. It is worth discussing her essay briefly, because it bears directly on the question of why women might be particularly drawn to write about madness. Felman was interested in a problem which seemed to her to link the question of femininity with that of insanity: how can we write about either women or madness in the language which society gives us, a language which privileges men and emphasizes the value of 'reason'?

Balzac's 'Adieu' tells the story of a soldier who returns from the Napoleonic Wars to find that the woman he loved has gone mad in his absence and no longer recognizes him. All she can do is repeat the word she said to him in parting: 'Adieu'. In the hope of restoring her sanity, the soldier attempts to recreate the exact conditions under which they parted. He succeeds in doing so, but at the price of her life: she recognizes him, smiles, repeats 'Adieu' and dies. Felman looked at what were then the two leading critical accounts of the short story, both of which strikingly failed to mention either the woman or her madness, and treated the story instead as an exercise in historical realism – a faithful account of conditions during the Napoleonic Wars. She argued that in producing such a reading of the text, the critics concerned edited everything out which might disrupt their own desire for a single, closed meaning and failed to recognize that the story is itself a critique of the soldier's desire for such control. Just as the soldier kills the madwoman in trying to force her to make sense for him, so the 'realistic critic' kills the play of meaning in the text by refusing to recognize the traces of violence, anguish, scandal and insanity that it bears in the figure of the madwoman.

Felman's emphasis on the madwoman's doubly subversive literary potential (subversive because she is mad and because she is a woman) proved very attractive to other feminist critics. *The Madwoman in the Attic* is the best known of the numerous books on insanity in literature which followed Felman's article. Sandra Gilbert and Susan Gubar took feminist readings of madness back to the subject of women by asking what difference the sex of the author makes: if the madwoman disturbs the meaning of men's writing, how much more significant might such disruption be in women's writing? (We shall be reading some of their comments on Charlotte Perkins Gilman later in this chapter.) For them, the frequency with which women have written about madness is to be seen as one of the most revealing symptoms of their own feelings of entrapment and oppression. Other feminist critics have taken further this appropriation of the transgressive symbolic power of madness. Some psychoanalytically-influenced writers, for example, have explicitly identified with the figure of the madwoman, claiming for themselves the same marginalized relationship to speech and writing. Hélène Cixous famously – and contentiously – welcomed what she called 'the hysterics' as her sisters, arguing in 1975 that 'the hysteric is … the typical woman in all her force' (Cixous and Clément, *The Newly Born Woman*, p.154). Juliet Mitchell similarly declared in 1984 that:

> the woman novelist must be an hysteric. Hysteria is the woman's
> simultaneous acceptance and refusal of the organisation of sexuality
> under patriarchal capitalism. It is simultaneously what a woman can do
> both to be feminine and to refuse femininity, within patriarchal
> discourse. And I think that is exactly what the novel is; I do not
> believe that there is such a thing as female writing, a 'woman's voice'.
> There is the hysteric's voice which is *the woman's masculine language*
> (one has to speak 'masculinely' in a phallocentric world) talking about
> feminine experience.
> (Mitchell, *Women: The Longest Revolution*, 1984, p.290)

The attraction of the madwoman for all these writers is obvious: as a figure of rage, without power to alleviate her suffering or to express it in terms that make sense to society, she sums up virtually everything feminism might wish to say about the suppression of women's speech. But if Gilbert and Gubar demonstrated just how dramatic the effects of liberating the madwoman from the attic could be for literary criticism, they were also in danger of romanticizing sickness and alienation. Mary Jacobus's objection to their book (which we will come to later in this chapter) is one expression of the widespread unease surrounding the celebration of madness as a theme in women's writing. Many critics have shared her view that embracing the madwoman as a symbol of the condition of all women is not the way to liberate women from structures of thought which have traditionally equated them with irrationality, silence, nature and the body (the male correlatives are reason, discourse, culture and mind).

To understand the force of that objection, it is necessary to know something about the history of women's 'madness' and about the label most commonly associated with it in the nineteenth century – hysteria. The word 'hysteria' derives from the Greek word for 'womb': *hystera*. Early medical writers believed that the uterus could move around the body, giving rise to physical and mental disturbance. Even when anatomy disproved this theory, doctors continued to believe that the womb exerted a powerful indirect influence on the mind. They represented the female body as being highly vulnerable to physical and psychological derangement because of the delicacy of the female reproductive system (see Figure 23). To some extent, this view of femininity as naturally unstable still surfaces in the way conditions like pre-menstrual syndrome are depicted in medical writing and in the media. By contrast, some feminists have represented the female body in terms of simplicity and power (see Figure 24).

Anxiety about female 'irrationality' peaked in the eighteenth and nineteenth centuries. Medical textbooks, advice manuals and novels of that period are full of images of young women mentally succumbing to the strains of their sex – fainting, giving way to uncontrollable weeping, breathlessness and phantom pains. In extreme cases, it was thought, hysteria could turn to mania, producing violent, even murderous or suicidal rages. Although a few cases of male hysteria were recorded, hysteria, as its name suggests, was first and foremost a young woman's disease and it was virtually synonymous with femininity. Many doctors recommended marriage as the cure. But they also spoke of the danger of motherhood leading to mental breakdown. A large number of the women in asylums in the nineteenth century were suffering from what we would now call post-natal depression (and this seems to be the subject of 'The Yellow Wallpaper').

Advances in medical knowledge and in women's position in society over the last hundred years have produced obvious changes for the better in the understanding and treatment of mental illness in women. The work of Jean Martin Charcot, Sigmund Freud and Joseph Breuer at the turn of the century made the link between what was known as 'hysteria' and some psychological conditions (although it was not until the massive incidence of shell-shock in the First World War that the term, with its female connotations, really lost much of its force as a label). But while use of the label 'hysteria' has dramatically declined, women are suffering more than ever from forms of psychological distress, depression and breakdown, and the statistics for women's mental breakdown in Britain and in the United States are still far higher than those for men.

One result of this ongoing history of representing madness as a 'female malady' is that there are more firmly established literary conventions for representing mad women than mad men. In literature, as in medicine, women have long been seen as more biologically predisposed

117

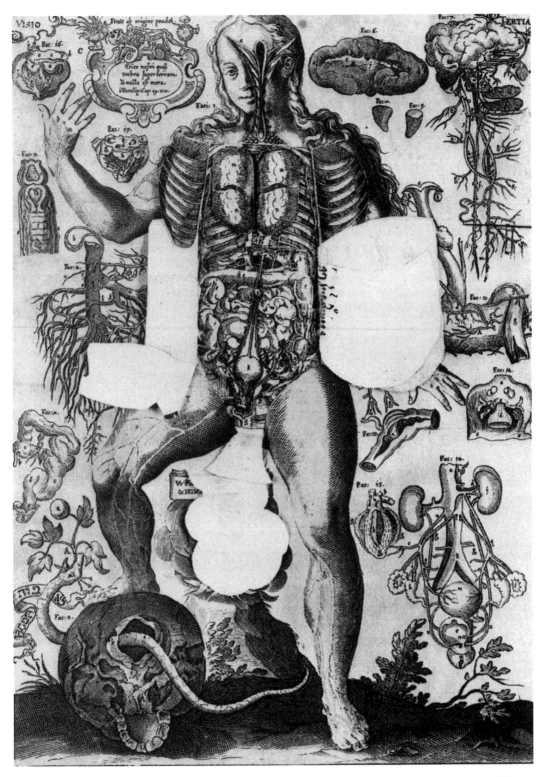

Figure 23 Plate 21 of Johann Remmelin (1583–1632), *Captoptrum Microcosmicum*, 1660, reproduced by permission of the Wellcome Centre Medical Photographic Library.

Figure 24   'The Crowning' (NP4) from *The Birth Project,* 1984, needlepoint over handpainted canvas, 100 x 153 cm, by Judy Chicago with needlepoint by Frannie Yablonsky. © 1984 Judy Chicago.

than men to madness. The subject of male insanity has often led writers (both male and female) to produce highly innovative work, probing the nature of psychological stability and our understanding of the world. *Hamlet* is the most famous example, but there are many others including Tennyson's mid-nineteenth-century poetic exploration of paranoid insanity, *Maud.* Stories about madwomen have tended, by comparison, to attract conventional treatment, typically depicting them as (in the words of one nineteenth-century sentimental novelist) 'still lovely in ruin'. Shakespeare's Ophelia, probably the most famous madwoman in literary history is usually portrayed, like Tennyson's Lady of Shalott, as beautiful, pathetic and seductive. She is decked with 'fantastic garlands', her hair loose, playing upon a lute, singing bawdy ballads and sad laments. The history of her representation is a revealing reflection of attitudes to femininity (see Showalter, 'Representing Ophelia', 1985, pp.77–94). Even now, this idea has a strong hold on our imaginations: John Evert Millais's famous Victorian painting of Ophelia (Figure 9) still sells in large numbers as a poster and print.

Taking account of the history of female insanity makes a difference to the interpretation of madness as a theme in women's writing. Recognizing the historical background may lead to a stronger recognition of the distinctively female implications of madness as a theme. Much of the conventional writing about madwomen produced in the past has, of course, been written by women, many of whom were quite as prepared as male writers to eroticize female insanity. But even when women described insanity in completely conventional ways, the fact that they were women altered the meanings of the conventions because women were taking control of their own representation with regard to madness.

And there *were* women writers who questioned the stereotype. Mary Wollstonecraft's last novel *Maria: or The Wrongs of Woman* (1798) and Jane

Austen's first novel *Sense and Sensibility* (1811) are good examples of female opposition to the late eighteenth-century sentimental vogue for madness. Both novels actively resist romanticizing mental breakdown, insisting instead on the degree to which the literary fashion for ornamental female insanity debilitated and degraded women. But the most famous single piece of women's writing about madness remains Charlotte Brontë's novel *Jane Eyre*.

Brontë's heroine, the retiring but inwardly rebellious governess Jane Eyre, falls in love with her employer Mr Rochester, only to discover on the point of marrying him that he has a mad wife, Bertha Mason, locked in the attic of Thornfield Hall. Gilbert and Gubar's reading of the grotesque, animalistic Bertha Mason as Jane Eyre's dark double is convincing and compelling. But because they treat this novel as a paradigm of female anxieties, it is ironically easy to lose sight of just how radical was Charlotte Brontë's depiction. Bertha Mason is very different indeed from the sentimental madwomen usually found in the novel before her. As critic Gayatri Spivak has pointed out in her study of race and gender in *Jane Eyre* ('Three women's texts and a critique of imperialism', 1985), Charlotte Brontë avoids confronting the implications of Bertha's origins (she is white Creole, depicted as a metaphorical 'dark other' to Jane) and manipulates her uncritically as a symbol of the heroine's anger. Still it is important to recognize how powerfully this depiction of Rochester's wife challenged the conventional representation of madwomen. *Jane Eyre,* more than any novel before it, is antithetical to Victorian ideals of femininity in a way that can be interpreted as feminist.

Writers as diverse as Virginia Woolf, Charlotte Perkins Gilman, Sylvia Plath, Doris Lessing, Janet Frame and Marge Piercy have all in various ways echoed Charlotte Brontë's determination to rethink the meaning of female insanity. However different their contexts, styles and interests, all these writers are keenly aware of the pain of insanity and the particular psychological pressures exerted on women, and they all resist the conventional depiction of madness as the product of a naturally unstable femininity. On the other hand, writing about madness is not automatically a sign of protest and disruption. We need to look carefully and closely at how individual women writers treat the theme. Do they sentimentalize it, as so many writers have done in the past, or do they try to depict it more critically? Most importantly, what reasons do they ascribe to women's madness, and what sort of language do they use to describe it? We shall return to these questions later.

Autobiography into fiction

Reasoning with the text: madness and meaning in 'The Yellow Wallpaper'

Here we will begin to apply the concept of madness as 'the female malady' to consideration of one writer, Charlotte Perkins Gilman, and her struggle with 'madness'. We now run into the key question raised earlier: how can we write about either women or madness in the language which society gives us, a language which privileges men and emphasizes the value of 'reason'?

Discussion of women's insanity is obviously influenced by the form of its expression in language, but, as we have discussed, language and even 'reason' are gendered. 'Irrational' or 'emotional' ways of seeing the world (including romance and 'intuition') have traditionally been seen as 'feminine' counterparts to male reason. Whether or not we agree with this division of personal characteristics by gender categories and assumptions, it has held sway over philosophical, religious and educational debates for centuries and still tends to influence thought on the relationship between language and power. 'Reason' may even be seen as the opposite of 'hysteria', but, of course, the meaning of both labels is highly dependent on context. We might take one powerful example: the Salem witch trials in New England in 1691–1692. The entire community of Salem was seized in a witch hunt that led to the trial and execution of tens of women and a few men. Though this was an instance of labelling women *en masse* as 'mad', we might argue in retrospect that it was a male collective hysteria that lead to these and other witchcraft deaths. (Figure 25 shows an earlier example of a witch trial.) 'Reason' and 'madness' are subjective terms, often linked.

Figure 25 'Witch' tried by ordeal, Mary Sutton, 1612, from a pamphlet *Witches Apprehended, Examined and Executed*, London, 1613. Photo courtesy of the Mansell collection.

At the end of her section, Helen Small suggested that to determine the intent of women's writing about madness, we have to consider particular authors and literary texts. We now need to do this. **Read 'The Yellow Wallpaper' carefully. As you read, look for textual clues to help you answer two questions:**

1 **What, in a nutshell, is the plot of 'The Yellow Wallpaper'?**
2 **Who tells the story (who is the narrator)?**

Discussion

1 Of course, there are many ways to summarize the plot, and each will involve a degree of interpretation. One way of answering the question while 'reading with gender on the agenda' is to consider the role of the woman at the centre of the narrative rather than that of her husband. The story is about a woman taken to live in a rented house in which she does not feel comfortable, persuaded to spend most of her time in a room she does not like (with barred windows and a peeling, faded yellow wallpaper). She is forbidden to write. As the story progresses, the woman loses her grip on the world outside her room. She is 'mad', or at least appears to be 'mad' at the story's end. The wallpaper is somehow symbolic of her madness.

2 The story is told by the woman, a nameless first person narrator. ■

Now let's return to the questions asked by Helen Small.

1 **Does the author sentimentalize madness in the story?**
2 **What kind of language does the author employ to describe madness?**

Discussion

These questions are more difficult to answer, and require a detailed discussion of several intertwined themes and issues. What can be said without hesitation is that Gilman does not in any way sentimentalize the theme of madness in the story. The author's depiction of the narrator's madness is implicitly critical, though a first reading of the text may not tell us enough to know precisely what Gilman is being critical *of.* Indeed, a first reading may not produce much more information than was contained in the short answers above: that 'The Yellow Wallpaper' is the story of a woman's increasingly tortured mental state as she tries to adjust to living in a rented home (an alien environment). The room and its decor slowly begin to mirror her mental state. But a first reading is enough to show the complexity of the use of language and narrative style: the selection of what is said and what is only readable between the lines. This is a first person narration, in which much of what the narrator thinks is not expressed directly but is rather implied. The narrator loses her grip on 'reality' as the story progresses. So, the reader is at once encouraged to question the narrator's sanity and 'authority' and is obliged to follow her, as no other version of the story is offered. The narrative reads like a Gothic novel or a mystery at times. Characters represent types, and motives are implied rather than stated. A great deal is left to the reader's imagination.

At one level the narrator's husband, Doctor John, represents (male, patriarchal) 'reason' while the unnamed narrator herself stands in for qualities such as anxiety, nervousness, uncertainty, irrationality, often ascribed to the feminine. The doctor takes his 'reasoned' position to be objective, assigning his own view centrality, positioning himself as the norm from which his 'emotional' wife deviates. Far from sentimentalizing madness, Gilman offers a disturbingly 'real' look at the conditions which may be said to 'drive women mad'. In this story, what drives the narrator mad is a confining or 'caging' of her creative imagination. She is intelligent and has ideas and aspirations to write. Yet her domestic routine, and the explicit instructions of her husband and doctor, set up considerable obstacles – remember Gilman's poem of that title – to her expressions of those ideas and of herself. The narrator is depicted as an intelligent and articulate woman who has been expressly forbidden to vent her creative energies and ideas in writing, left without the company of other educated adults for long periods of time, shut up in an unfamiliar house in a room she does not like, and generally asked to conform to a norm of 'feminine' behaviour and domesticity which stifles her. Thus, as the story progresses the narrator can be said to forget who she is as she loses strength and spirit in her efforts to conform to her husband's view (which represents that of society) of who she *should* be, and how she should behave, in her various social and domestic roles as a woman, wife and mother. She describes her feelings of frustration at being told not to write, and implicit in that frustration is a desire to be the one who writes her own story, who uses language to represent herself. All the while, what she wants to be is a writer: the one role which is denied her.

We understand that Gilman is critical of her character Doctor John – and by extension, other like-minded (male) characters and real people – but her criticism is not expressed in any direct terms within the text. Rather her views are communicated by the narrator, not in words (for she is never forthrightly critical of him) but through our sympathy with the confined woman. The reader's identification with her isolation and desperation precludes any doubt that her suffering is real, is a 'reasonable' response to an unreasonable situation. For instance, when you read the story, you might have been struck by the husband's instruction to his wife to put away her writing. While such a recommendation seems strange today, it was of course once considered to be sound advice for women, and was indeed the instruction given to both Louisa May Alcott and Virginia Woolf when they were feeling, to use Alcott's euphemism, 'moody'. In the story, this instruction not to write is precisely what the narrator writes about: she refers to it early on in the story, and, in a sense, the entire narrative becomes the expression of a stifled creative voice in the form of a secret journal. (By the story's end, we have to ask ourselves how a 'madwoman' found the clarity to write the story: who is the author, after all?) ■

Looking back over the text quickly, do you get the impression that Gilman identifies with one character more than others? Who and why?

123

Gilman sits fairly unambiguously on the side of the narrator. Even the most cursory reading reveals that Gilman, the author, has created a narrator who faces an opposition between one kind of reason and another – labelled madness. So far, it seems fair to say that the story chronicles a woman's emotional journey toward 'madness', when her creativity and intelligence have been stifled by a husband (and the male-dominated world of reason which he symbolizes) who tells her to put away her writing. It is the story of a woman's nervous breakdown. It is also part of the autobiography of its author, for while the narrator of the story has no name, she is very clearly drawn on Gilman, as the author freely admits. (In a 1992 BBC television production, the woman is named 'Charlotte': an obvious interpretation made explicit for viewers.) ■

Consider the biographical information about Gilman which follows, and ask yourself whether your reading of 'The Yellow Wallpaper' would have been different had you had this information before you read the story:

Gilman, Charlotte (Perkins) Stetson [see Figure 26], 1860–1935, novelist, poet, lecturer, artist, economist, feminist theorist, editor, reformer. b. at Hartford, Connecticut. Her parents, Mary (Westcott) and Frederick Beecher Perkins separated shortly after her birth. Related to Harriet Beecher Stowe: her Beecher aunts provided role models. She was largely self-educated, with her father's help. Spirited and intellectually lively, she espoused dress reform, fresh air, cold baths, weight-lifting, gymnastics, running, lecture clubs, language classes and history-science reading programmes ... In 1882 she married Charles Walter Stetson; severe depression followed the birth of her daughter in 1885; the rest cure prescribed for 'inappropriate' ambition by Dr S. Weir Mitchell resulted in her well-known tale, 'The Yellow Wallpaper', 1892. In 1898 she moved to California, supporting Nationalist (Utopian socialist) views and feminism; divorced in 1894; she spent five years in the 1890s on the national lecture circuit speaking on labour and women's place. In 1900 she married her cousin George Houghton Gilman. Her political poems on the women's movement, *In This Our World*, appeared in 1903. Other works include *Women and Economics*, 1898, in which she stresses the androcentric nature of the socio-economic world and the need for both sexes to have 'world work'. She accused men of weakening the race by preferring small feeble creatures. In 1909 she founded *Forerunner*, a literary periodical written entirely by her and devoted to contemporary social issues; it published all her novels ... (including) *Herland*, a masterpiece of feminist Utopian fiction, which celebrates the strength and vigour of a community of women without men. In many of her stories, traditional sex roles are reversed ... After George died (1934) she returned to California, joined by her daughter and her first husband's second wife. Contracting cancer, she committed suicide, leaving her autobiography, *The Living of Charlotte Perkins Gilman*, 1935.

(Blain et al., *The Feminist Companion to Literature in English*, 1990, pp.427–8)

Figure 26   Charlotte Perkins Gilman writing at a desk. Schlesinger Library, Radcliffe College 177-326-5.

Discussion

Knowing these facts about Gilman adds considerably to our ability to contextualize the story we've read. But being able to place it in context is not the same as understanding it. Perhaps the most important 'contextual' information contained above is that which relates directly to Gilman's own mental state. 'The Yellow Wallpaper' was written between the years 1890 and 1892. This period was one of the most difficult of Gilman's life. Following her own nervous breakdown, she embarked on a series of major changes in her life, including her courageous – and for its time scandalous – choice of separation from her husband, a move across America, and a struggle to support herself through lecturing and occasional writing. This is the context for the writing of 'The Yellow Wallpaper': a story which may have helped Gilman to heal, even as she put her narrator through the agonizing process of breaking down. All this says a lot about Gilman's valuing of creative freedom and intellectual stimulation over the domestic. But more importantly, it demonstrates what is, effectively, a central theme of the story and shows it to be a central theme in the author's life: that is, her writing was a process of catharsis (of emotional release), of healing, of coming to terms with herself and using that knowledge creatively. She not only wrote this story, but also a short essay about the process of writing the story: what led her to it, why she wanted the autobiographical material to inform the literary, to what real purpose and 'reasonable' end. ■

Gilman's own account

Read now Charlotte Perkins Gilman's account of the writing of her novella, reprinted below. As you read, ask yourself whether the author, or the advice she was given, seems 'mad'.

Why I wrote 'The Yellow Wallpaper'

Many and many a reader has asked that. When the story first came out, in the *New England Magazine* about 1891, a Boston physician made protest in *The Transcript*. Such a story ought not to be written, he said; it was enough to drive anyone mad to read it.

Another physician, in Kansas I think, wrote to say that it was the best description of incipient insanity he had ever seen, and – begging my pardon – had I been there?

Now the story of the story is this:

For many years I suffered from a severe and continuous nervous breakdown tending to melancholia – and beyond. During about the third year of this trouble I went, in devout faith and some faint stir of hope, to a noted specialist in nervous diseases, the best known in the country. This wise man put me to bed and applied the rest cure, to which a still good physique responded so promptly that he concluded there was nothing much the matter with me, and sent me home with solemn advice to 'live as domestic a life as far as possible', to 'have but two hours' intellectual life a day', and 'never to touch pen, brush or pencil again as long as I lived'. This was in 1887.

I went home and obeyed those directions for some three months, and came so near the border line of utter mental ruin that I could see over.

Then, using the remnants of intelligence that remained, and helped by a wise friend, I cast the noted specialist's advice to the winds and went to work again – work, the normal life of every human being; work, in which is joy and growth and service, without which one is a pauper and a parasite; ultimately recovering some measure of power.

Being naturally moved to rejoicing by this narrow escape, I wrote 'The Yellow Wallpaper', with its embellishments and additions to carry out the ideal (I never had hallucinations or objections to my mural decorations) and sent a copy to the physician who so nearly drove me mad. He never acknowledged it.

The little book is valued by alienists and as a good specimen of one kind of literature. It has to my knowledge saved one woman from a similar fate – so terrifying her family that they let her out into normal activity and she recovered.

But the best result is this. Many years later I was told that the great specialist had admitted to friends of his that he had altered his treatment of neurasthenia since reading 'The Yellow Wallpaper'.

It was not intended to drive people crazy, but to save people from being driven crazy, and it worked.

(Gilman, 'Why I wrote "The Yellow Wallpaper"', 1913)

This essay first appeared in *Forerunner* (the journal edited by Gilman) in 1913. (For full details see Chapter 8 of the autobiography, *The Living of Charlotte Perkins Gilman,* 1935; the chapter section is entitled 'The Breakdown'). In this piece, Gilman puts forward her reasons for writing and publishing 'The Yellow Wallpaper'. She saw writing this essay and getting it out into the public domain as a way of making the personal political, a way of making sure that lessons were learnt from her experiences. In fact, this same view about the importance of publishing even the most controversial and personal 'truths' if they have political significance is what inspired Gilman to found *Forerunner* in 1909. For Gilman, writing was a way of interacting directly in the world: of communicating ideas drawn from the most personal and painful of life circumstances, in the hope that others might benefit from them. This kind of expository writing about creative writing (whether in a short essay like this one, or the one by Alice Walker to be discussed in Chapter Five, or in a more traditional author's preface, apology, explanatory note or afterword) is a familiar form of literature in itself, though not one which is often examined as literature.

As we know from the discussion of Louisa May Alcott's instruction that her diaries should be burned (though, thankfully for literary critics and students, they were not), not all authors – even feminist political authors – wanted too much of their personal lives to be represented unfictionalized (or 'straight') in the public realm. But Gilman did make some of her most private experiences known to the public, through her publication of 'The Yellow Wallpaper' and her autobiographical and essay writing. Thus, we can study the autobiographical element of Gilman's life in her depiction of the narrator of 'The Yellow Wallpaper' and find a very strategic, careful and critical use of language in fiction, to define and represent women's madness. At one level, then, Gilman uses language to create a picture of reality: to show what is presented as 'reason' by men (the men in her life; the men in her story). Here we might well recall the voice of male reason which Gilman personified in the character of 'Prejudice' in her poem 'The Obstacle'. This version of reason, quite clearly gendered male, is neither reasonable nor healthy for the women to whom it was applied. In this sense, we might well call the Doctor 'mad', rather than the patient. ■

Now the question is: who are the women affected by this voice of reason? Or, if we look back to Gilman's poem, as well as the story, we might ask whose way in life is blocked by male prejudice; who is stifled by certain gendered ways of defining reason?

The answer seems, in both cases, to be plural: to include Gilman herself as the creative writer, and her female (autobiographical) narrators, and also readers (women and men). Here, it is interesting to note that the personified Prejudice of the poem appears in other guises in Gilman's fiction, not only in 'The Yellow Wallpaper' (most notably, though not exclusively, in the ever-reasonable figure of the husband/doctor), but also in Gilman's later Utopian novel, *Moving the Mountain*, in which women and men work and live together as true equals. Gilman allows the women in her Utopian novel the power to 'walk through Prejudice' which she describes in her poem, but which neither she nor her heroine/narrator in 'The Yellow Wallpaper' seem to have achieved.

In this sense, the literature becomes a mirror for women's position in society. But if the position of women in society is confined and restricted as both the poem and the story suggest, why should Gilman wish her readers to see themselves reflected within it? Does this not trap the reader, with the narrator, within a limiting and perhaps even 'maddening' narrative/social framework? To some extent, perhaps, we as readers do become 'trapped' in the cage of the yellow-papered room, or irritated along with the poem's narrator when her way is blocked. But we also finish reading and take a step back from the story or poem (the 'mirror') in order to evaluate our own positions. In reading the poem with its optimistic ending – wherein the narrator/poet 'walks through' Prejudice, as if it wasn't there – we can choose to study the position of women within literary texts as one measure or reflection of their social position within a given period. We can then take a crucial further step by breaking through the isolation of individual lives to find strength in numbers, and by resolving to 'move mountains' of prejudice out of the way, not only for ourselves but also for the readers and writers who will follow.

But 'The Yellow Wallpaper' is hardly so optimistic. The narrator of that story sees herself reflected in a symbolic mirror (for the figures she sees moving behind the wallpaper are all versions of herself, of other trapped women). This narrator does not, within the story at least, 'walk through' her problems. Nor does she, like the male-created Lady of Shalott, die when confronted with the natural world. Rather, the narrator/heroine of 'The Yellow Wallpaper' is left in quite an ambiguous position at the story's end. She sees herself, in her delusion, as having escaped from behind the wallpaper: she imagines that she has set free her 'other self', which we may deduce represents her creative imagination. But she is still trapped physically and emotionally in a world ruled by one man, her husband, in collusion, as it were, with a social structure valuing his view of reason as objective. So, like Alice facing Humpty Dumpty and the Cheshire Cat in the two scenarios we discussed earlier, Gilman's narrator both wins and loses: she sees the complexity of her situation, but is in no position to do anything about it (except escape it by retreating into herself, by going mad). This reading of the story's end is neither positive nor negative, but ambivalent. 'Madness' is an escape from one kind of cage into another. ■

Some feminist readings and critical perspectives

Critic Elaine Hedges wrote an afterword to the newly republished 'Yellow Wallpaper' in 1973:

> ... The story is narrated with clinical precision and aesthetic tact. The curt, chopped sentences, the brevity of the paragraphs, which often

consist of only one or two sentences, convey the taut, distraught mental state of the narrator. The style creates a controlled tension: everything is low key and understated. The stance of the narrator is all, and it is a very complex stance indeed, since she is ultimately mad and yet, throughout her descent into madness, in many ways more sensible than the people who surround and cripple her. As she tells her story the reader has confidence in the reasonableness of her arguments and explanations.

... Here is a woman who, as she tries to explain to anyone who will listen, wants very much to *work*. Specifically, she wants to write (and the story she is narrating is her desperate and secret attempt both to engage in work that is meaningful to her and to retain her sanity). [...] While she craves intellectual stimulation and activity, and at one point poignantly expresses her wish for 'advice and companionship' (one can read today respect and equality) in her work, what she receives is the standard treatment meted out to women in a patriarchal society. Thus her husband sees her as a 'blessed little goose'. She is his 'little girl' and she must take care of herself for his sake. Her role is to be 'a rest and comfort to him'. That he often laughs at her is, she notes forlornly and almost casually at one point, only what one expects in marriage.

Despite her pleas he will not take her away from this house in the country which she hates. What he does, in fact, is choose for her a room in the house that was formerly a nursery. It is a room with barred windows originally intended to prevent small children from falling out. It is the room with the fateful yellow wallpaper. The narrator herself had preferred a room downstairs; but this is 1890 and, to use Virginia Woolf's phrase, there is no choice for this wife of 'a room of one's own'.

Without such choice, however, the woman has been emotionally and intellectually violated. In fact, her husband instils guilt in her. They have come to the country, he says 'solely on [her] account'. Yet this means that he must be away all day, and many nights, dealing with his patients.

The result in the woman is subterfuge. With her husband she cannot be her true self but must pose; and this, as she says, 'makes me very tired'. [...] Finally, the fatigue and the subterfuge are unbearable. Gilman works out the symbolism of the wallpaper beautifully, without ostentation. For, despite all the elaborate descriptive detail devoted to it, the wallpaper remains mysteriously, hauntingly undefined and only vaguely visuable. But such, of course, is the situation of this wife, who identifies herself with the paper. The paper symbolizes her situation as seen by the men who control her and hence her situation as seen by herself. How can she define herself? ...

... Earlier in the story the heroine gnawed with her teeth at the nailed-down bed in her room: excruciating proof of her sense of imprisonment. Woman as prisoner; woman as child or cripple; woman, even, as a fungus growth, when at one point in her narrative the heroine describes the women whom she envisions behind the wallpaper as 'strangled heads and bulbous eyes and waddling fungus growths'. These images permeate Gilman's story. If they are the images men had of women, and hence that women had of themselves, it is not surprising that madness and suicide bulk large in the work of late nineteenth-century women writers. 'Much madness is Divinest sense ...

Much sense the starkest madness', Emily Dickinson had written some decades earlier; and she had chosen spinsterhood as one way of rejecting society's 'requirements' regarding woman's role as wife ...
The heroine in 'The Yellow Wallpaper' is destroyed. She has fought her best against husband, brother, doctor, and even against women friends (her husband's sister, for example, is 'a perfect and enthusiastic housekeeper, and hopes for no better profession'). She has tried, in defiance of all the social and medical codes of her time, to retain her sanity and her individuality. But the odds are against her and she fails.

Charlotte Perkins Stetson Gilman did not fail. She had been blighted, damaged, like the heroine in her story, by society's attitudes toward women. But having written the story she transcended the heroine's fate – although at what inner cost we shall never know. [...]

Women's ineffectual domestic status was the target of some of Gilman's strongest attacks. As she said elsewhere in *Women and Economics*, the same world exists for women as for men, the same human energies and human desires and ambitions within. But all that she may wish to have, all that she may wish to do, must come through a single channel and a single choice. Wealth, power, social distinction, fame, – not only these, but home and happiness, reputation, ease and pleasure, her bread and butter, – all, must come to her through a small gold ring.

The damaging effects on women of being manacled to that small gold ring she explored in detail. Women are bred for marriage, yet they cannot actively pursue it but must sit passively and wait to be chosen. The result is strain and hypocrisy, and an overemphasis on sex or 'femininity'. 'For, in her position of economic dependence in the sex-relation, sex-distinction is with her not only a means of attracting a mate, as with all creatures, but a means of getting her livelihood, as is the case with no other creature under heaven'.

Gilman was not opposed to the home nor to domestic work. She believed indeed that the home tended to produce such qualities, necessary for the development of the human race, as kindness and caring. But her evolutionary approach to social change enabled her to see that the institution of the home had not developed consonant to the development of other institutions in society. Women, and children, were imprisoned within individual homes, where the women had no recognized economic independence and the children often suffocated, 'noticed, studied, commented on, and incessantly interfered with ... How can they grow up without injury?' For, she argued, in the home as presently established there can be neither freedom nor equality. Rather, there is 'ownership': a dominant father, a more or less subservient mother, and an utterly dependent child. Injustice, rather than justice, was the result.

In her attack on the nuclear family Gilman thus anticipated many current complaints. Or, one should rather say, that more than half a century after she began her campaign against women's subservient status we are still struggling with the problems she diagnosed and described.

Work must be respected: this was one of Gilman's basic tenets, but women must be admitted into the human world of work on equal terms with men. The domestic work they do must be respected, and they must be free to do other kinds of work as well. Gilman believed in continuing human progress [...], and she saw the situation of women in the nineteenth century as thwarting this progress as well as thwarting their own development. For some human beings to be classified as horses, or cows, or sexual objects, was to impoverish not only themselves but human society as a whole.

She herself refused to be so thwarted. In 1900 she married her cousin, George Houghton Gilman and she continued to work until the day when she chose her own death. [...] It was her final willed choice.

(Hedges, Afterword to Gilman, *The Yellow Wallpaper*, 1973 edn, pp.37–60)

Hedges' reading of Gilman's life and work echoes many of the themes of this book besides 'women and madness'. She mentions the relationship between writing as creative expression and as a way of earning a living (for the author Gilman, not her fictional counterpart). She also refers to Gilman's ground-breaking ideas about 'women and economics', domestic work and the economic preconditions for women's writing. Lastly, in her account Hedges refers repeatedly to the gold ring, the wedding band, as visual signifier for a whole range of obligations and expectations of women: the theme of marriage as a trade. Hedges analyses 'The Yellow Wallpaper' as a text in context, with reference to the living and views of its author. She accepts Gilman's merging of fiction and a personal and political history. Is Gilman's incorporation of elements of her own life experience within her fiction in any way subversive of the traditional distinction between fact and fiction?

Many critics have asked this question, and not only about Gilman but about feminist autobiographical fiction in general. It all goes back to the basic feminist slogan: the personal is political. In the sense that Gilman saw her experiences as relevant to other women, her fiction writing was a political, interventionist activity. In this sense, we could say that she was being deliberately subversive in writing 'The Yellow Wallpaper', and also in writing about the story and publicizing the autobiographical (personal) influences on the story and its social (political) import.

The idea that literature can subvert expectations (literary and social) has been raised in several different contexts already. But in essence, the entire feminist literary critical revolution has been a deliberate process of subverting traditional values and assumptions about what makes literature valuable, what makes an author or a text 'great'. Thus, as we have argued, when women writers were disadvantaged and ignored, it became necessary to initiate social and artistic initiatives to re-value their work: to subvert the norm. Elaine Hedges has offered an account of the language and context of the writing of 'The Yellow Wallpaper' and also an effective 'plot summary' and interpretation of the story. Her reading discusses Gilman's fiction alongside her political work in order to show that the two are both connected and significantly different.

Having read and considered Hedges' reading of the story, list some similarities and differences between the author (Gilman) and her fictional character/narrator in 'The Yellow Wallpaper', in terms of the outcome of their stories and also in terms of factors such as period, gender, race and class.

Gilman and her narrator are both white (this is implied, though never stated) middle-class nineteenth-century American women. Both are reasonably well educated, intelligent and articulate. Both are creative writers (Gilman wrote a body of poetry, as well as prose). Indeed, both felt a need to write, and part of the story's 'chilling' power results from the knowledge that the narrator's desperation when instructed not to write must have been felt by Gilman as well. But what differs is the end of the stories. In one sense this is predictable. Gilman must have recovered her 'sanity' in order to be lucid enough to write the story; indeed, she must have been feeling quite strong as she put herself through the process of reliving horrific experiences in her fiction. But the end of the story is ambiguous: the narrator is 'mad', but we as readers have no handy sequel to tell us what happens next. In this sense, it may seem convenient to treat Gilman's own life as the sequel, reading the author's healing into the fate of her character. But within the story, we can read no such happy ending. It is easy to lose sight of the overall differences, to wander too far down the road of comparing the life story of the author with the story of a fictional character. In this case for instance, Gilman's eventual suicide might seem to reflect back on her fiction, yet such a reading would be unhelpfully morbid; while the suicide is important, so too does the fiction – each story and poem, and their respective endings – have an integrity of its own, quite separate the life of the author. ■

In the temptation to read too much into the autobiography/fiction connection, we engage in a common critical problem which is often associated with certain kinds of Anglo-American feminist literary criticism. In the example above, as in much critical writing about women's literature, it is tempting to construct a narrative or overall story about the history of women's writing, choosing texts and authors who illustrate that critical story rather than allowing the texts to speak for themselves. The critical balancing act of considering the context of the writing and the circumstances of the author's life, while allowing for the integrity of each literary text in and of itself, may be one of the most difficult aspects of 'reading with gender on the agenda'. French critic Roland Barthes analysed this dilemma in detail in his theoretical writing about 'the death of the author'. Each time we read we interpret, and each time we interpret we engage in a three way dynamic between authors, readers and texts.

Critics and academics engaged in the process of revising literary canons struggle with this dilemma at every turn. Gilbert and Gubar's book *The Madwoman in the Attic*, a feminist literary critical source book of considerable influence, discusses the traditional polarization of women's roles as angels and whores, domestic wives and 'madwomen in attics', in the context of nineteenth-century women's writing. It is time that the two leading voices on the topic of 'madness' were allowed to speak for themselves.

'The madwoman in the attic': a reading of 'The Yellow Wallpaper'

The extract which follows is taken from Gilbert and Gubar's discussion of Gilman and 'The Yellow Wallpaper'. **As you read, ask yourself whether the authors are simply describing the story, or are analysing and interpreting it in a particular way.**

As if to comment on [...] the anxiety-inducing connections between what women writers tend to see as their parallel confinements in texts, houses, and maternal female bodies – Charlotte Perkins Gilman brought them all together in 1890 in a striking story of female confinement and escape, a paradigmatic tale which (like *Jane Eyre*) seems to tell the *story* that all literary women would tell if they could speak their 'speechless woe'. 'The Yellow Wallpaper', which Gilman herself called 'a description of a case of nervous breakdown', recounts in the first person the experiences of a woman who is evidently suffering from a severe postpartum psychosis. Her husband, a censorious and paternalistic physician, is treating her according to methods prescribed by S. Weir Mitchell, a famous 'nerve specialist', who treated Gilman herself for a similar problem. He has confined her to a large garret room in an 'ancestral hall' he has rented, and he has forbidden her to touch pen to paper until she is well again, for he feels, says the narrator, 'that with my imaginative power and habit of story-making, a nervous weakness like mine is sure to lead to all manner of excited fancies, and that I ought to use my will and good sense to check the tendency'.

The cure, of course, is worse than the disease, for the sick woman's mental condition deteriorates rapidly. 'I think sometimes that if I were only well enough to write a little it would relieve the press of ideas and rest me', she remarks, but literally confined in a room she thinks is a one-time nursery because it has 'rings and things' in the walls, she is literally locked away from creativity. The 'rings and things', although reminiscent of children's gymnastic equipment, are really the paraphernalia of confinement, like the gate at the head of the stairs, instruments that definitively indicate her imprisonment. Even more tormenting, however, is the room's wallpaper: a sulphurous yellow paper, torn off in spots, and patterned with 'lame uncertain curves' that 'plunge off at outrageous angles' and 'destroy themselves in unheard of contradictions'. Ancient, smouldering, 'unclean' as the oppressive structures of the society in which she finds herself, this paper surrounds the narrator like an inexplicable text, censorious and overwhelming as her physician husband, haunting as the 'hereditary estate' in which she is trying to survive. Inevitably she studies its suicidal implications – and inevitably, because of her 'imaginative power and habit of story-making', she revises it, projecting her own passion for escape into its otherwise incomprehensible hieroglyphics. 'This wallpaper', she decides, at a key point in her story,

> has a kind of sub-pattern in a different shade, a particularly irritating one, for you can only see it in certain lights, and not clearly then. [...] But in the places where it isn't faded and where the sun is just so – I see a strange, provoking, formless sort of figure, that seems to skulk about behind that silly and conspicuous front design.

As time passes, this figure concealed behind what corresponds (in terms of what we have been discussing) to the facade of the patriarchal text becomes clearer and clearer. By moonlight the pattern of the wallpaper *is* 'behind bars! The outside pattern I mean, and the woman behind it is as plain as can be'. And eventually, as the narrator sinks more deeply into what the world calls madness, the terrifying implications of both the paper and the figure imprisoned behind the paper begin to permeate – that is, to *haunt* – the rented ancestral mansion in which she and her husband are immured. The 'yellow smell' of the paper 'creeps all over the house', drenching every room in its subtle aroma of decay. And the woman creeps too – through the house, in the house, and out of the house, in the garden and 'on that long road under the trees'. Sometimes, indeed, the narrator confesses, 'I think there are a great many women' both behind the paper and creeping in the garden,

> and sometimes only one, and she crawls around fast, and her crawling shakes [the paper] all over... And she is all the time trying to climb through. But nobody could climb through that pattern – it strangles so; I think that is why it has so many heads.

Eventually it becomes obvious to both reader and narrator that the figure creeping through and behind the wallpaper is both the narrator and the narrator's double. By the end of the story, moreover, the narrator has enabled this double to escape from her textual/ architectural confinement: 'I pulled and she shook, I shook and she pulled, and before morning we had peeled off yards of that paper.' Is the message of the tale's conclusion mere madness? Certainly the righteous Doctor John – whose name links him to the anti-hero of Charlotte Bronte's *Villette* – has been temporarily defeated, or at least momentarily stunned. 'Now why should that man have fainted?' the narrator ironically asks as she creeps around her attic. But John's unmasculine swoop of surprise is the least of the triumphs Gilman imagines for her mad woman. More significant are the madwoman's own imaginings and creations, mirages of health and freedom with which her author endows her like a fairy godmother showering gold on a sleeping heroine. The woman from behind the wallpaper creeps away, for instance, creeps fast and far on the long road, in broad daylight. 'I have watched her sometimes away off in the open country', says the narrator, 'creeping as fast as a cloud shadow in a high wind'.

Indistinct and yet rapid, barely perceptible but inexorable, the progress of that cloud shadow is not unlike the progress of nineteenth-century literary women out of the texts defined by patriarchal poetics into the open spaces of their own authority. That such an escape from the numb world behind the patterned walls of the text was a flight from dis-ease into health was quite clear to Gilman herself. When 'The Yellow Wallpaper' was published she sent it to Weir Mitchell, whose strictures had kept her from attempting the pen during her own breakdown, thereby aggravating her illness, and she was delighted to learn, years later, that 'he had changed his treatment of nervous prostration since reading' her story. 'If that is a fact', she declared, 'I have not lived in vain'. Because she was a rebellious feminist besides being a medical iconoclast, we can be sure that Gilman did not think of this triumph of hers in narrowly therapeutic terms. Because she knew, with Emily Dickinson, that 'Infection in the sentence breeds', she knew that the cure for female despair must be spiritual as well as physical, aesthetic as well as social. What 'The Yellow Wallpaper' shows she knew, too, is that even when a supposedly 'mad' woman has been sentenced to imprisonment in the 'infected' house of her own body, she may discover that, as Sylvia Plath was to put it seventy years later, she has 'a self to recover, a queen'.

(Gilbert and Gubar, *The Madwoman in the Attic*, 1978, pp.89–92)

Discussion

Gilbert and Gubar's book is a feminist literary text. It takes a feminist perspective and applies it to the reading of many texts, 'The Yellow Wallpaper' included. They have read the story as an exemplar of women's subversive strategies in fiction writing. You may have noticed that they see the author as imagining triumphs for the narrator in her madness, that they see the author as 'showering gold' on her heroine in her 'escape' from confinement. ■

While Gilbert and Gubar's book is very well known and highly respected, it does not summarize the entire 'feminist literary approach' to literature. There are many different positions within the broad area of feminist literary criticism, and there are as many readings of any text as there are critics. We will now go on to consider what others have argued.

Alternative critical perspectives

We have compared only a very few of the many different published perspectives on the story. Some critics have taken issue with the general trend of these accounts, arguing not that the approach is in itself 'wrong' or misleading, but rather that it tends to interpret the literary text in such a way as to fit it into a larger pattern. In this case, both the extract from Gilbert and Gubar and their book generally can be seen to offer a particular pattern, or a particular way of seeing women's writing in terms of the strategies adopted by writers to overcome obstacles to the expression of their creativity. Having read the extract, you may see that its status as an authoritative interpretation carries a certain weight which would probably have influenced your own reading of the story, had it been the first thing you read (which is the reason for leaving this material to this point in the chapter).

Feminist critic Mary Jacobus is one who has noted the way in which the treatment of women authors in *The Madwoman in the Attic* tends to mythologize them. She argues that comparing thematic similarities is very useful, but that it may also run the risk of erasing differences in the effort to construct a coherent narrative about the collective nature of women's circumstances and struggles.

In Jacobus's words, *The Madwoman in the Attic* 'is the Story of the Woman Writer. A story told and retold by an ample work of narrative interpretation which is itself an interpretative narrative' (Jacobus, in *Signs*, 1981, p.517). While Jacobus does not dismiss the book, she does warn against the dangers of reading literary texts with too narrowly focused a view of their implications. In defining what they think is 'The Story of the Woman Writer', Jacobus argues, Gilbert and Gubar then set out and tell the same story over and over, with each new author and literary text. But Jacobus's criticisms are not directed at Gilbert and Gubar so much as at literary criticism itself. A similar argument might as well be applied to this textbook, or any textbook with an agenda or critical angle (such as a focus on gender). Jacobus argues elsewhere that all literary criticism lays patterns over texts, to the point that it becomes very difficult to differentiate between a given text and the critical perspectives commonly applied to it (Jacobus, 'An unnecessary maze of sign-reading', 1992, p.277).

Below, you will find an edited version of Mary Jacobus's responses to a set of questions put to her in interview with Lizbeth Goodman. Unlike most of the other critical extracts in this book, Jacobus's material was written specially for this context – it addresses you, the reader of this book, as its primary audience in the sense that the questions were asked on your behalf, in order to clarify key issues about the reading and interpretation of 'The Yellow Wallpaper'.

Reading 'The Yellow Wallpaper'

by Mary Jacobus

One reading of 'The Yellow Wallpaper' takes the heroine's madness as a perverse triumph over the imprisoning domesticity in which she is trapped by patriarchy – embodied by her commonsensical doctor husband. But this reading makes a contradictory claim:

1   that she's driven mad by patriarchy; and

2   that it's patriarchy that's mad, not her.

In other words: women are simultaneously not mad, and their madness isn't their fault. In a way, this is what you might call a rationalist reading; that is, it tries to make sense out of the literary text. I'd want, myself, to stress instead the uncanniness of the text, the way in which the 'madness' of the text can be read as an irreducible madness in reading signs and meanings in a literary text; it's this madness to which the heroine could be thought of as succumbing – the madness of becoming a figure *for* madness.

I think it's also worth remembering that for Gilman, madness was anything but liberating. Her breakdown in 1887 led to her treatment by the infamous Weir Mitchell cure which she herself said nearly made her lose her mind. The tendency to romanticize madness, particularly hysteria, as a sort of feminist spanner in the social works, peaked in the 1970s/1980s (i.e. in recent feminist criticism) in the critical attention given to Freud's hysteric, Dora, whom some feminists viewed as heroic in her refusal to participate in Freud's attempt to analyse her (instead of her dysfunctional family). Although this reading of madness – of hysteria – has been strategically important for feminist psychoanalytic criticism, it's also open to the objection that hysteria and madness haven't provided women with much political purchase or agency and should certainly be regarded as tragic and painful for women themselves, even if their hysteria is read as a form of resistance or non-cooperation. I think myself that Gilman meant her heroine's madness to be seen as profoundly shocking – not only to her doctor husband, confronted by her 'creeping', but to her readers; that the story is intended to be 'creepy', drawing on Gothic traditions of the madwoman that go back to Bertha Mason in *Jane Eyre*. You'll recall that the setting for Gilman's story is 'a colonial mansion, a hereditary estate, I would say a haunted house …'. Gilman deliberately invokes the uncanny sense of repetition, that woman's state is an inherited one, that the house is haunted by repetition. The signs of this repetition are the traces of restraint and incarceration in her attic bedroom – and the repetition of the hideous yellow wallpaper that gives Gilman's story its title.

I don't want to resurrect 'The Yellow Wallpaper' as a late flowering of Gothic so much as point to the cultural phenomenon of Gilman's own time, which is that the tale of a woman's supernatural haunting or the mad woman's confinement in the attic had by the 1890s been turned by an age of doctors into the case-history of hysteria and its various cures, including Freud's 'talking cure' and the Weir Mitchell 'rest cure'. You could say that medical knowledge straitjackets Gilman's text as well as her heroine. But the straitjacket is loosened by what remains unaccountable in it, and that is the symptom and scene of repetition figured by the wallpaper of her title. The irrational haunts her story as its ghostly other, just as the figure of the madwoman is hidden in the wallpaper. One effect of the medicalization and domestication of women was to separate them from their political past, so that – like Gilman's heroine – their dissent appears isolated and ineffectual; it goes underground, or exists behind bars. (This replacement or repression of politics by pathology may have as one of its effects the tendency to read 'The Yellow Wallpaper' as an autobiographical reflection of Gilman's personal history.) I mentioned the word creepy earlier, and that word has a tendency to proliferate in Gilman's story – indicating both abjection (the heroine's abject posture), stealth, and something 'creepy' or blood-chilling – like the figure of the woman in the wallpaper.

The writing on the wall

The process of being driven mad by conflicting patterns and signs in studying texts may strike a chord with some of you: reading and analysing literature and literary criticism can often feel like this. 'The Yellow Wallpaper', for instance, is open to a very wide range of readings and interpretations. It leaves a lot to our imaginations as readers, partly because the story engages our sympathies with a character who by the story's end is not a comfortable point of identification, partly because the implications of the story are indeed so 'chilling' for what they say about the treatment of women, and also because there are so many different ways of interpreting the text. As we read and re-read we may get a bit lost in the maze of possible meanings. The end of the story brings the feeling of loss home, as the narrator/heroine loses all senses of herself in madness, and as we realize that in context, this loss of self may be the closest the narrator comes to being 'herself'. The image of finding self in madness, in recognizing a pattern of madness which is within ourselves, is disturbing and uncomfortable.

Figure 27 'She didn't know I was in the room', pen and ink drawing by Jo. H. Hatfield, *New England Magazine* (new series) vol. 5 no 5, January 1892.

Look at Figure 27. The illustration depicts Jennie discovering the narrator's strange attraction to the wallpaper. But in the context of the story, the same image has other possible 'readings'. As the narrator sees herself in another's eyes, Jennie becomes an image of her double (indeed, the two female figures are depicted as strikingly similar in appearance). When we know the story, we recognize the dark undertone of the image: that the sight of her double signals the narrator's breakdown, her breaking through the pattern of the wallpaper to lose herself in madness. But we have to read this sense of loss into the narrative, for the story is told by the 'madwoman' herself, and a great deal is left to the imagination of the reader.

Given the many different meanings of the story, and the narrative strategy of leaving out information (so that as readers, we become detectives filling in missing clues), we might forgive ourselves for not noticing all that we might have found between the lines of the story. Many of us will have followed the arguments put forward by Gilbert and Gubar and by Hedges, and would be surprised by a feminist critic who argues against those readings. Yet another critic, Susan Lanser, has done so and makes a convincing case. Putting aside the maze of meanings and interpretations to which Jacobus refers, Lanser argues that many feminist critics (and she includes Elaine Hedges and Gilbert and Gubar in her list) have missed a very important part of the story by focusing on certain themes and issues to the exclusion of others. Again, this is not to devalue the work of these and other feminist critics, but rather to add another perspective to the debate. In Lanser's words:

> Fully acknowledging the necessity of the feminist reading of 'The Yellow Wallpaper' which I too have produced and perpetuated for many years, I now wonder whether many of us have repeated the gesture of the narrator who 'will follow that pointless pattern to some sort of conclusion' – who will read until she finds what she is looking for – no less and no more. Although – or because – we have read 'The Yellow Wallpaper' over and over, we may have stopped short, and our readings, like the narrator's, may have reduced the text's complexity to what we need most: our own image reflected back to us. ...
> ... Yet none of us seems to have noticed that virtually all feminist discourse on 'The Yellow Wallpaper' has come from white academics and that it has failed to question the story's status as a universal woman's text.
>
> ('Feminist Criticism, "The Yellow Wallpaper" and the politics of color in America', 1989, pp.420, 422)

Lanser pinpoints what is missing in many feminist readings of the story – consideration of race as an issue which (like class) will have affected:

1   the circumstances of its writing – insofar as Gilman was herself a white middle-class woman with money and time and education enough to write; and

2   the choice of the text for the newly developing feminist alternative canon of literature, insofar as white middle-class academics have done most of the choosing of new texts, and have tended to choose texts reflecting their own concerns.

Lanser goes on to urge a re-reading of the text and its context, to show that the study of literary texts, like the study of culture and contexts, is 'more complex, shifting, and polyvalent than any of the ideas we can abstract from it'. This challenge is taken up in the next chapter on race and gender.

But before we move on, let's return to the question posed at the outset. **To what extent might 'madness' be an alternative 'role' for women to play? That is, when all the practical options for women are bleak or oppressive (stifling creativity, individuality, sexuality), might 'madness' be one way to escape? And if so, at what cost?**

Discussion

This question, raised by Helen Small and carried through the other sections of the chapter, is one of the most important issues raised by consideration of the 'women and madness' theme. There are no easy answers. The theme branches out beyond the representation of madness in literature, to the reality of 'madness' (variously defined) in the world. While it may be tempting to discard the idea of anyone adopting madness as a choice, it is also very difficult indeed to determine when any state of mind is chosen, or imposed, or adopted by default. And of course, considering the possibility of deliberate subterfuge may seem to sit too comfortably alongside a traditional paternalistic view of 'women's wiles', or women's emotional irrationality and weakness. This is a way of thinking which feminist critics would tend to avoid, both because it is dangerously essentialist – that is, based on reductive or simplistic assumptions and stereotypes about sex difference and gender roles – and because such essentialist thinking has long been an obstacle to women's development. Yet some feminists argue that role-playing in real life is an inevitable part of living in the social world, a necessary strategy for dealing with unworkable stereotypes and expectations. Elaine Showalter has analysed this position in her consideration of madness as 'the female malady'. ■

In *The Female Malady*, Showalter discusses the idea that 'madness' can itself be a form of dissent, but is also a label applied to those who deviate from a norm. For instance, she argues, the term was applied to the suffragists, who were called 'mad' when they fought publicly for the rights of women. Yet when they continued to fight, and as a number of articulate and persuasive speakers – including Gilman, Alcott and Susan Glaspell (whose work is discussed in Chapter Six) – all joined in the chorus of dissent, slowly but surely the vote was won. This process of social change was gained gradually, at great cost to the women and men involved. It was not a radical overthrow but rather a measured and powerful exposure of the flaws in the reasoning of the fundamental ideas most commonly used to restrict the rights of women. The treatment of the suffragists as 'mad' was one convenient and effective way of silencing them. And while in the end the strategy did not work and the vote was won, we must not forget that many individual women were literally institutionalized, labelled 'mad' because they did not comply.

Consider, for instance, a 'real life' image of a suffragist being forcibly fed in Holloway Gaol, in 1912 (Figure 28).

Discussion

The image is startling in itself, and even more so if we consider the equation of political activity for women (in the suffrage movement) as criminal, and punishable by real assaults on women's bodies, wills and human rights. ■

Elaine Hedges points out that Gilman did not label herself a feminist, not because she lacked sympathy for feminism but because she found 'its objectives too limited for her own more radical views on the need for social change'. In this sense, application of Showalter's analysis of the social

140

FORCIBLE FEEDING THROUGH THE NOSE OF WOMEN SUFFRAGIST PRISONERS.

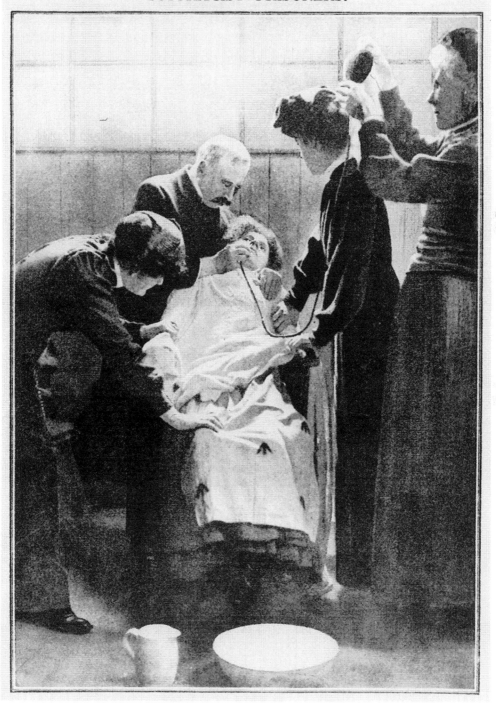

Figure 28   Forcible feeding of a suffragette, *Illustrated London News*, April 27, 1912.
Mary Evans Picture Library

construction of women's madness is particularly fitting to the project of studying Gilman's writing. If we step outside the story and look at the larger body of work, Gilman can be seen to be engaged in a project which is feminist in effect if not in intent: that of highlighting and attempting to shift some of the obstacles to women's self-expression. She wrote about gender inequalities and depicted characters who were negatively affected by the social norms of their day.

Conclusion

It has been argued in this chapter that where the treatment of women is concerned, the label 'mad' was often applied to women who were wilful, strong, determined, creative or inquisitive (from Lewis Carroll's Alice to Gilman's nameless narrator). The label 'mad' was, Showalter points out, also routinely applied to women who refused to conform to 'norms' of femininity which were physically unhealthy: the wearing of corsets, particular eating habits, and – crucially in terms of this book – the suppression of creative energy and artistic expression in favour of the domestic. As we consider the woman in Figure 27 being forcibly fed by her jailers, we may think of the many references to food in 'The Yellow Wallpaper'. Each time the narrator tells us when she is meant to eat, what she is meant to eat, how much she is meant to eat, and how it is important that her husband thinks she has behaved well with her eating (and sleeping), we may be reminded of that image of force-feeding: an image which is violent and also reminiscent of other ways of controlling women's appearances, behaviours, appetites and views of themselves. Figure 29, a cartoon that appeared in Gilman's magazine *Forerunner*, shows a woman literally 'harnessed' into her corset and dress. It comments on the pressures, literal and social, that constitute 'feminine' appearance. Similarly, eating disorders are now recognized as just one of many 'female maladies' linked to 'the beauty myth' which presses on women's lives. The role of the domestic and the emphasis on outward appearance – which we have discussed in terms of costume and surface appearance in short stories such as Woolf's 'The New Dress' – take on much darker implications when the insistence on maintaining 'feminine' standards is associated with a risk of physical or mental/emotional violence. This is the case with 'The Yellow Wallpaper'.

Gilman ends her story ambiguously, with an uncertain future for the narrator. The implication is that the narrator is 'mad' (that she has been driven mad by patriarchal authority and power structures, to put it crudely), and will be incarcerated, most probably never to recover, shut up in an asylum like the proverbial 'madwoman in the attic'. Or, she might possibly be sedated and shocked (literally and emotionally) into submission. She may become a happy housewife, or a reasonable facsimile thereof (the idea recalls the 1970s film, *The Stepford Wives*, in which the women of a small town are replaced by automatons which perform the duties expected of wives). Most of the texts discussed in this book deal with this subplot of role-play. Women in literature, it seems, are often cast in one of two roles: either the perfect wife and domestic heroine – Jane Eyre – or the madwoman in the attic, the Bertha Mason.

HARNESSING

Figure 29 'Harnessing', detail of cartoon 'Woman is man's horse' by
Maurice Ketten, *World Daily Magazine*. Reproduced from the
Charlotte Perkins Gilman scrapbook, 177·V·8° Schlesinger Library,
Radcliffe College, Cambridge Massachusetts.

Although the theme of 'women and madness' is just one of many themes
which might be explored in women's literature, it is one that is inextricably
tied to other themes which might be discussed, such as domesticity,
sexuality (its repression and the consequences of its expression), the issue
of women's physical appearance and the associated theatrical metaphor of
social role-play. We have said that, as Showalter and other critics have
argued, some degree of madness may be a subversive strategy for
intelligent, creative women with ideas and minds of their own. The second
of the two role models has been reclaimed: Bertha Mason's history (or
herstory) has been created by another of this century's most renowned and
radical feminist writers: Jean Rhys. *Wide Sargasso Sea* (first published in

1966) is a novel which tells of the life and loves of Antoinette Bertha Cosway, a young beauty who grew up to become the first Mrs Rochester, and was later incarcerated as the archetypal 'madwoman in the attic'. But if madness may be a strategy, it may also have dangerous consequences, when the voices of reason (the ones which label) are male, and seem to 'speak a different language'. To be labelled 'mad' is to be designated as incapable of conforming, to be made disposable, to be hidden away where surface appearance no longer matters. In the language of literary criticism, 'The Yellow Wallpaper' offers a text and a case-study for discussion, though the critics are by no means agreed on its merits, either as a literary text or as a 'feminist' text offering a critical depiction of a woman's madness.

Further Reading

Chesler, P. (1979) *Women and Madness*, Penguin Books.

Felman, S. (1985) *Writing and Madness: Literature/Philosophy/Psychoanalysis*, Cornell University Press; translated by M.N. Evans and the author with Brian Massumi.

Gilbert, S. and Gubar, S. (1978) *The Madwoman in the Attic: The Woman Writer and the Nineteenth-Century Literary Imagination*, Yale University Press.

Golden, C. (ed.) (1992) *The Casebook on 'The Yellow Wallpaper'*, The Feminist Press.

Jacobus, M. (ed.) (1986) *Reading Woman: Essays in Feminist Criticism*, Methuen.

Martin, P.W. (1987) *Mad Women in Romantic Writing*, Harvester.

Mitchell, J. (1984) *Women: The Longest Revolution: On Feminism, Literature and Psychoanalysis*, Pantheon Books.

Oppenheim, J. (1991) *'Shattered Nerves': Doctors, Patients, and Depression in Victorian England*, Oxford University Press.

Showalter, E. (1987) *The Female Malady: Women, Madness, and English Culture, 1830–1980*, Virago.

Showalter, E. (1990) *Sexual Anarchy: Gender and Culture at the Fin de Siècle*, Viking Penguin.

Veith, I. (1965) *Hysteria: The History of a Disease*, University of Chicago Press (this is the classic history of hysteria).

Gender, race, class and fiction

by Lizbeth Goodman, with Joan Digby

Gender, race, class and fiction

Situating The Color Purple

The subject of this chapter is the intersection of gender and race in the writing, reading and interpretation of literary texts. The chapter focuses on the study of a full-length novel by a contemporary African-American woman: Alice Walker. While 'madness' as such is not a central theme in *The Color Purple*, the novel deals with related themes, such as the emotional suffering inflicted upon women, both by individual men and by a range of legal and social impediments to women's freedom of expression. Like the novella 'The Yellow Wallpaper', *The Color Purple* (1983) centres on a strong woman with a need to write and a love of creative work; a woman who comes to know herself better as she learns to use language to her own advantage. But *The Color Purple*, as a contemporary text, situates its heroine in a world wherein it is possible – though extremely difficult – for the heroine to learn about sexuality and self-expression. As you read the novel, you'll find it helpful to think back to the key themes covered in previous chapters: the importance of work, the conflict between domesticity and creativity, 'silences' or obstacles to women's self-expression and the development of subversive strategies for breaking free of restrictive and damaging relationships and situations. As you read, ask yourself how far Alice Walker's story goes toward breaking with preceding patterns in the representation of women, and what new patterns or possibilities for women's creative expression are offered for the future. In this chapter, we'll also consider writing by and about women of colour more generally, asking the following questions about authors, readers and texts:

> what relationships do race and class bear to gender in the study of literary texts;
>
> what is the history of writing by women of colour;
>
> what authors and ideas have been influential in the development of a 'black literary imagination'; and
>
> what kinds of problems may we expect to encounter in reading and interpreting black women's writing?

Let's begin by considering a short statement made by Alice Walker. In an interview in 1986, Walker spoke about the white literary canon and her perception of her relationship to it as an African-American woman writer:

> There I was trying to connect with all these writers who really never
> saw me. They were unable to see me, actually ... My experience is
> that it's when you're with your own people that you are most yourself;
> you have more of a context. So though I love the Brontës, and some

of the white writers I read, still I knew that I had a tradition ... that could help me.

(Alice Walker in interview, *Omnibus*, BBC TV, 1986)

This statement extends the views expressed by a number of white female authors, from Virginia Woolf with her assertions that 'gender and genius' often went unrecognized in the past, through to the contemporary critic Carolyn Heilbrun's declaration that 'there will be narratives of female lives only when women no longer live their lives isolated in the houses and the stories of men' (*Writing a Woman's Life*, 1988, p.47). We might extend that argument and say that there will be narratives of black women's lives only when black women no longer live their lives in cultures dominated by a white, male 'norm', and when black women *are free* to write their own stories. In fact, this argument has been made many times, and the body of black women's writing has grown dramatically over the years. Alice Walker has acknowledged her debt to other women writers, black and white, mentioning Woolf specifically, along with a range of others, including African-American writer Zora Neale Hurston and (white) American poet and critic Tillie Olsen ('Saving the life that is your own', 1984, p.14; the essay was written in 1976, before Walker wrote *The Color Purple*).

We have been speaking of 'black women's writing'; a more precise term for the writing of Walker (and that of Toni Morrison and Maya Angelou) might be 'African-American women's writing'. There is also a distinction to be made between these two terms and writing by women and 'people of colour' – a more general term that includes First Nations people (Native Americans), as well as Aboriginal people and Asian, Hispanic, Caribbean and many other people. We'll consider the beginnings of a black literary tradition, alongside a women's literary tradition, looking for points of similarity and difference. But we'll also read critically, looking for points at which Walker – like many other authors, including Woolf – may be seen to be falsely representative of a group, when in fact she – like any single author – can only truly 'represent' herself.

It is crucial in reading literature that we are truly critical, that we look for potential problems and points of contention as well as considering the most successful aspects of any text, or simply celebrating an author's reputation. The criticism of black women's writing is, in this respect, difficult and controversial. While we may want on the one hand to highlight the tremendous advances of black women authors (African-American, African, Asian, Caribbean ...) in recent literary history, we should also try to take a critical distance and examine any text or author's contribution in relation to the wider field of literature. But in so doing, we run the risk of applying inappropriate sets of criteria: just as male critics long condemned women's writing for not being, in essence, 'male', so white critics have long castigated black authors for writing in ways which defy white critics' expectations about what is important. Balancing all these conflicting demands is not easy, but we shall try to do so in our study of black women's writing generally, and *The Color Purple* in particular.

Toni Morrison, another of the best-known African-American women writers, has also considered the complex question of the definition of a creative imagination, alongside the conflicting demands of developing an individual identity and group or race identity. She describes the balance in terms of the 'literary imagination'. I'd like to consider, now, her position.

Playing in the dark: whiteness and the literary imagination

> For reasons that should not need explanation here, until very recently, and regardless of the race of the author, the readers of virtually all of American fiction have been positioned as white. I am interested to know what that assumption has meant to the literary imagination. When does racial 'unconsciousness' or awareness of race enrich interpretative language, and when does it impoverish it? What does positing one's writerly self, in the wholly racialized society that is the United States, as unraced and all others as raced entail? What happens to the writerly imagination of a black author who is at some level *always* conscious of representing one's own race to, or in spite of, a race of readers that understands itself to be 'universal' or race-free? In other words, how is 'literary whiteness' and 'literary blackness' made, and what is the consequence of that construction?
>
> (Morrison, preface to *Playing in the Dark*, 1992, p.v)

When Morrison refers to the 'positioning' of readers, she means the assumptions or preconceptions about the reader which are found in literature. Until very recently, most readers were assumed to be or were 'positioned' as white, and probably also as male and middle class. Each of the issues raised by Morrison is also addressed in this chapter, which takes the concept of 'the captive imagination' discussed in our study of madness in women's writing, and refocuses on the concept of the literary imagination limited not solely by gender and power dynamics, but also by the impact of racial oppression.

Morrison argues not that readers are all white, but that they have traditionally been 'positioned' as white: assumed to be white, or to be interested in what interests white readers, just as many readers, until recently, were assumed to be male, or at least interested in what interests men. Now, we might want to argue that since women and men, black and white, might well share the same interests, we should not assume that either gender or race inherently cause us to read or think differently. Yet even if we subscribe to such an argument, it is still important to recognize the power dynamics involved in assuming a 'generic' position for any reader, either as male or as white or as middle class.

Morrison's achievements as a writer and reader can be analysed in terms of gender, race and class. She was awarded the Nobel Prize for Literature in 1993. The prize was richly deserved for the tremendous contribution Morrison made with her fiction, and significant in its effect of adding an African-American woman's name to the long list of mainly white male Nobel winners of the past (though Nigerian playwright Wole Soyinka and Caribbean poet Derek Walcott are also Nobel Laureates). Yet Morrison, like Alice Walker, can be seen as a 'middle-class' writer with a considerable academic training. Her construction of fictional worlds incorporating working-class black characters as well as middle-class (black and white) characters contributes significantly to the project of 'breaking the silences' of under-represented groups.

The same could be said of Alice Walker, for though she is descended from farmers, she earned a college education which undoubtedly helped her to develop her skill as a writer. She went on to win many accolades for her writing, notably the Pulitzer Prize for Fiction for *The Color Purple* in 1984. (See Shockley, *Afro-American Women Writers*, 1988, p.xxiv, for a list of black writers winning awards and recognition.) But these two women, frequently invited to speak as if they 'represent their race', to paraphrase Morrison, are also often written about as if they represent 'Black Women Writers' in general: as if that were a category which could be easily defined and the 'members' of which could be listed. But of course, many black women writers who write of working-class experiences, or from 'outside' the English language, are marginalized within the already marginal category of black women. Both Morrison and Walker are known for depicting strong working-class black women in their stories, as black American critic Susan Willis has argued. Willis analyses 'Walker's women' and the relationship between education and literacy in fiction, arguing that black women are doubly marginalized or oppressed in American culture, by virtue of being black and being women. She links status to all three positions: race, class and gender. Barbara Christian, Professor of African–American Studies at the University of California (Berkeley) has argued that Walker's novels address different class perspectives in turn, and all pay attention to gender (interview with Lizbeth Goodman, 1994, for a BBC television programme designed in conjunction with this book).

Alice Walker, like Morrison, is a particularly successful writer in an emergent tradition of 'black women writers', but so are a host of women from many cultures, with oral as well as written story telling traditions, writing and telling stories in many languages and dialects. To consider Morrison's questions about the construction and consequences of 'literary whiteness' and 'literary blackness', then, it is helpful to consider the history of black writers, male and female, first of all within the context of the United States.

The history of black writing in the United States

The first major African-American authors in the United States lived and wrote in the period of slavery. Robert Haydon, for instance, wrote important poems about former slaves and freedom fighters Harriet Tubman and Frederick Douglas. Frederick Douglas was himself a writer, whose most important and moving contribution may have been his accounts of his experience of learning to read and write as the key to his empowerment, and another kind of freedom. In Chapter Two, we also discussed Sojourner Truth, whose landmark speech 'Ain't I a Woman?' was all the more powerful given that its author was illiterate – a former slave whose words were recorded by others, and finally adapted to poetry late in the twentieth century. Another former slave who wrote about her experiences was

Harriet Jacobs, whose body of narrative writing was crucial in beginning to establish a literary tradition for women of colour. Yet, it was a white woman, Harriet Beecher Stowe, whose novel *Uncle Tom's Cabin* (1852) brought the experience of slaves and former slaves to wide public attention, in and through literature. The novel was a best seller, and the politics of the abolitionist author (Stowe) influenced many white American writers, including Bronson and Louisa Alcott.

Years later, African-American writing began to be recognized as a major literary development. The First Black Renaissance (formerly called the Harlem Renaissance or the Negro Renaissance) can be identified as beginning in the mid-1920s. It was 'a brief but powerful explosion of black culture which placed the Negro, for a time, at the heart of a national myth and dramatized a self-image at odds with that offered by American society as an adequate account of black life' (Bigsby, Introduction to *The Second Black Renaissance*, 1980, p.3). (For a brief introductory guide to the subject, see Kiernan, *American Writing Since 1945*, 1983, which includes chapters on black drama and black fiction. A more theoretically sophisticated discussion of race and gender in poetry and literary style is developed in Baker, *Workings of the Spirit*, 1991.) In other words, this was a time of rapid cultural change and literary development, much as the 1970s were for women writers. 'The Second Black Renaissance' is a term used to describe a later flowering of work by African-American writers, and other people of colour in North America. It began with the writing of Richard Wright, author of many key works including *Uncle Tom's Children* (1938) and *Native Son* (1940), and lead to a rapidly growing body of literature by people of colour, including many women writers.

Nella Larsen, a writer from the first 'Harlem' Renaissance, is an important figure in the history of black women's writing. Her work was largely ignored until the feminist literary revolution of the 1970s, but in her own time (the 1920s) she had been hailed by black and white critics, female and male, as a talented writer. Larsen was the first African-American woman to win the prestigious award of a Guggenheim Fellowship, in 1930, on the strength of her first two novels, *Quicksand* and *Passing*. But after writing her third major story, Larsen was publicly accused of plagiarism: a charge she vehemently denied and of which she was eventually acquitted in print. Yet she was stunned by the accusation and her writing career never recovered. Larsen died in relative obscurity in hospital in Brooklyn, New York, in 1963. (A detailed account of Larsen's career, and her story *Passing*, is contained in an essay by Deborah E. McDowell, 'It's not safe. Not safe at all' in Halperin, *The Lesbian and Gay Studies Reader*, 1993, pp.616–27.)

But the vast majority of writing by people of colour has developed in the late twentieth century. The civil rights and feminist movements of the late 1960s and 1970s led to the inclusion of previously 'silenced' and marginalized groups into the traditional white male literary canon, and history books in much of the English-speaking world, and first of all in North America. Early efforts to include women's writing in the curriculum tended to focus on white women such as Charlotte Perkins Gilman, Emily

Dickinson and Louisa May Alcott. But black women writers such as Harriet Jacobs, and later Phyllis Wheatley, Nella Larsen, Zora Neale Hurston, and then Maya Angelou, Paule Marshall, Jamaica Kincaid, Gloria Naylor, Toni Kade Bambara, June Jordan, bell hooks (*sic*), Ntozake Shange, Adrienne Kennedy, Toni Morrison, Gwendolyn Brooks and Alice Walker have all been introduced into the newly developing canon. The impact of these black women writers was largely made by black women themselves, while black male authors tended to 'deny a connection to those who came before them' (Introduction to *Afro-American Women Writers*, 1988, p.xxiv). So, we might argue, black women writers felt the need to challenge even the developing black male voices, as they did not adequately represent the wide range of experiences and ideas of black women. The problem of 'representation' of any group by any individual is complex and connected to gender as well as race. For instance, it is easy to see that Virginia Woolf wrote important essays and stories, which expressed ideas and experiences common to many women. But of course, Woolf's relatively privileged position as a middle-class white woman was not representative of many women of her day, and left her open to criticism for 'élitism', even though she endeavoured to represent what she knew. Similarly, Harriet Beecher Stowe made an undeniably major contribution to the development of a black literary history with her novel *Uncle Tom's Cabin*. In its first year of publication, over 300,000 copies were sold. But Stowe was a white middle-class author who moved in some of the same social circles as Emily Dickinson's family; and her contribution has been criticized as in part an appropriation of black people's experiences, reinvented and perhaps misinterpreted by a white author.

But it is not only white authors who may stand accused of 'appropriation' of the experience of others. No one black woman author can be seen to 'represent' all black women. It is often tempting to assume this kind of 'representation': for instance, we might assume that the characters in Walker's *Color Purple* are 'representative' of black people in a more general sense. But of course, the characters are fictional, not real, and they are no more 'representative' of black people generally than Woolf's character Mabel Waring in 'The New Dress' is representative of women generally. In fact, Walker's depiction of black women in *The Color Purple* is not one of the working class; by her own admission, Walker wanted in this novel to depict more prosperous black women than were usually represented in fiction. (In previous novels, Walker had looked at the experiences of working-class African-Americans.) Diversity must be recognized in any discussion of the literary representation of gender or race or class and 'literary representation' when the work of individual authors is seen as somehow 'representing' groups of people. (For further reading, see Shockley, *Afro-American Women Writers*, 1988, or one of the most frequently cited references: Richard Wright's essay 'The literature of the Negro in the United States', in *White Man Listen*, 1964.) This is precisely Kate Rushin's argument in 'The Bridge Poem' (p.292 of this book). Rushin laments the need of some white feminists to use individual black women as a bridge to black experience. (A recording of the poem, read by the poet at the Memorial Service for Audre Lorde at the National Organization of Women Conference (Boston, July 1993) is included in the poetry audio-cassette produced by the BBC in conjunction with this book.) It is just this 'representative' role which Rushin rejects in no uncertain terms, claiming instead her right to be the bridge only to her 'own true self' (p.293).

Until recently, only a handful of 'role models' for contemporary black women writers in America were recognized in any literary genre. Black female playwrights were, perhaps, least in evidence until well into the twentieth century, when playwrights Zora Neale Hurston and Lorraine Hansberry brought generations of black women and men to the stage and screen (see Figure 30).

Figure 30   Sidney Poitier in *Raisin in the Sun*, 1961, Columbia, directed by Lorraine Hansberry, courtesy of the Kobal Collection.

Today, due to the efforts of scholarship, it is possible and indeed relatively easy to trace a host of black women writers working in all three main genres. (See, for instance, Wisker, *Black Women's Writing*, 1993; Lorde, *Sister Outsider*, 1984; Smith, *Home Girl*, 1983; Grewal, *Charting the Journey*, 1988.) The publication of plays by women has slowly increased over the years: the *Black Drama Anthology* (King and Milner, 1972) contained only one short play by a black woman (Elaine Jackson's *Toe Jam*), whereas, for instance, there are many plays by women included in the three volume *Black Plays* (Brewster, 1987) and in Ahmad and George, *Six Plays by Black and Asian Women Writers* (1993). That many of these writers are engaged in a critical process of searching out their own foremothers and establishing their work as part of a tradition is important, but not surprising. Nor is it surprising that some of the most powerful and influential black writing from America has not been fictional, but autobiographical.

Autobiography, identity and teaching the caged bird to sing

Maya Angelou is the poet who gave the Inaugural Poetry Reading to mark the return of the Democratic Party to the White House with the election of Bill Clinton. She is also a respected essayist and activist, who first became famous for her autobiographical writing. The first volume of her life story, *I Know Why the Caged Bird Sings* (1969), made Angelou in 1970 the first African-American woman to make the Best Seller List. (The other volumes of the series are *Gather Together in My Name, Singin' and Swingin' and Gettin' Merry Like Christmas, The Heart of a Woman*, and *All God's Children Need Travelling Shoes.*) The story tells of Angelou's childhood rape by her mother's lover and subsequent struggles to survive an impoverished youth in the racist, sexist Southern America of the 1930s. It is now hailed as a classic of feminist and black women's writing, and as an authoritative text about learning to communicate, to educate yourself out of poverty and oppression. It was a clear influence on Alice Walker's fictional story, *The Color Purple*, and also one source of the image of the caged bird which is familiar in much feminist literature. Angelou has written and delivered many speeches about the importance of establishing a 'Black History' and a 'Black Literary History'.

In 1993, Angelou wrote about the current situation of African-American youth, looking back to the legacy of slavery and referring in particular to its impact on language and self-identity.

Read the following extract: What is it that Angelou sees as 'outrageous'?

> African-Americans as slaves could not even claim to have won the names given to them in haste and given without care, but they pridefully possessed a quality which modified the barbarism of their lives ... They employed formally familiar terms when addressing each other. Neither the slaveowner nor the slave overseer was likely to speak to a servant in anything but the cruellest language. But in the slave society Mariah became Aunt Mariah and Joe became Uncle Joe. Young girls were called Sister, Sis or Tutta. Boy became brother, Bubba, and Bro and Buddy. It is true that those terms used throughout the slave communities had their roots in the African world from which the slaves had been torn, but under bondage they began to have greater meaning and a more powerful impact ... We have used these terms to help us survive slavery, its aftermath, and today's crisis of revived racism. However, now, when too many children run mad in the land, and now, when we need courtesy as much as or more than ever, and when a little tenderness between people could make life more bearable, we are losing even the appearance of courtesy ...
>
> If our children are to approve of themselves, they must see that we approve of ourselves. If we persist in self-disrespect and then ask our children to respect themselves, it is as if we break all their bones and then insist that they win Olympic gold medals for the hundred-yard dash.
>
> Outrageous.

(Maya Angelou, 'Voices of respect', 1993, pp.101–3)

Angelou argues that it is, or would be, 'outrageous' to insist that those we oppress and injure should overcome their 'obstacles' in order to win awards or otherwise please us. Here, Gilman's poem 'The Obstacle' resonates loudly. Gilman advocated women's 'walking through' the invisible but real impediments placed in their paths by patriarchy: heavy obstacles enough. Angelou refers to the tremendous addition to the burden of black Americans, with the legacy of slavery and its impact on the self-esteem of a race, and with associated reverberations of repeated and continuing oppressions of a racist society, language and educational system. With this huge set of obstacles piled in her path, perhaps Gilman's narrator could not have been quite so comically optimistic about the ability of women to 'walk through' obstacles. In order to emphasize her point, Angelou uses the example of children to call on a collective sense of responsibility for future generations, all the more powerful coming from a woman abused as a child. She employs a metaphor of broken bones, associated with physical violence and abuse, recalling not only the treatment of the slaves but also the outbreak of race riots in Crown Heights, New York and Los Angeles in the 1990s. Finally, Angelou argues that it would be 'outrageous' to expect black youth to impress their elders under these conditions, unless they had been set a good example of courage and resilience and optimism. While the argument is polemical, it is written in the calculated yet elegant language of an essayist. ∎

As the body of black women's writing grows, the importance of teaching it as part of the academic curriculum, part of the newly developing 'alternative canon', also grows. But problems of race and representation, appropriation and interpretation persist. In teaching about and studying African–American women's fiction, it is important that we remember the dynamics of race and class, as well as gender in the classroom (where most university lecturers are white, and many are male). (Catherine Stimpson puts this argument eloquently in an essay written in 1970, 'Black culture/white teacher', in *Where The Meanings Are*, 1988, p.7.) We also do well to recognize the position of women of colour in relation to the white, male 'norm' of the university systems. Socialist feminist Cora Kaplan has written, for instance, about the 'triple oppression of black women' as expressed in the 'axis of race, class and gender, through which their subordination and struggle is lived' (Kaplan, 'Keeping the color in *The Color Purple*', in *Sea Changes*, 1986, p.181). Let's explore this idea of 'triple marginalization' further.

Multiple jeopardy: marginalization by gender, race and class

Women of colour were long excluded from higher education, from learning and teaching about creative writing, by a double or even triple oppression: race, class and gender. Angela Davis has written what is perhaps the best-known modern work on the subject of *Women, Race and Class* (1981). (Also see her *Women, Culture and Politics*, 1984.) Since then, the field has opened up considerably, to the point where it is not only quite common to consider these factors together, but difficult *not* to, when thinking or writing about the history or literature of black women, particularly in the United States, with its legacy of slavery. Davis, along with June Jordan, Toni Morrison and others, is among the still small but growing number of women who teach about black culture, passing on some of the more 'personal' versions of recent racial/cultural history in their lectures and essays. Some recent academic writing has focused on differences between black feminists and white feminists, arguing that white academics have inadvertently engaged in a process of 'assuming a white readership'. (Here we may recall the accusation put by Susan Lanser in discussion of 'The Yellow Wallpaper' and its critics in the previous chapter.) It can be illuminating, too, to assess critically the assumptions we bring to the writing of academic articles (assumptions about the race, class and gender of readers, for instance), and to the reading of them. But at the same time, it is interesting and important to recognize the differences in perspective and privilege between black and white academics and authors, even among feminists, even in textbooks such as this one. (See the reasoned and warm account of these tensions and some civilized approaches to them in 'Mary Childers and bell hooks: a conversation about race and class' in Hirsch and Fox Keller, *Conflicts in Feminism,* 1990, pp.60–81. Also see Joseph and Lewis, *Common Differences,* 1981). The various readings of *The Color Purple* which follow are all 'positioned', and each asks you to consider the idea of 'multiple jeopardy' or the marginalization of black women writers generally, with attention to the writing of Alice Walker in particular.

Reading and writing The Color Purple

In considering the intersecting factors of gender, race and class in reading *The Color Purple*, we'll focus on three different approaches to the novel: through authors, readers and texts. We'll consider the process of reading and interpreting *The Color Purple*; then we'll look at Alice Walker's own authorial statement about the novel, and finally we'll consider the status of the text as a novel which conveys different meanings in different contexts, and which has also been interpreted visually on film. Let's concern ourselves first with the author and one particular reader: you.

Reading The Color Purple

If you have not already done so, read *The Color Purple* now. As you read, look for an example of the 'multiple jeopardy' experienced by Celie in the novel.

D i s c u s s i o n

There are many examples of Celie's 'multiple jeopardy' – indeed, the novel is composed of them. One example of 'multiple jeopardy' appears very early in the novel, on page seven. Just a few lines from this passage are enough:

Dear God,
He beat me today cause he say I winked at a boy in church. I
may have got something in my eye but I didn't wink. I don't even look
at mens. That's the truth. I look at women, tho, cause I'm not scared of
them.

In this extract, Celie writes to God, for lack of any living person with whom
to share her troubles. She tells of a pointless beating by 'Pa' ironically
imposed on this passive woman because of alleged sexual forwardness on
her part. But we as readers can 'read between the lines' to see that Celie is
not forward with men, and is indeed terrified of them. Reading further into
the social context of the novel, we might well guess that the beating is
imposed on Celie not because of anything she has done, but rather to
remind her that she is her 'father's property'. In this sense, Celie is punished
for being a woman; she is punished by a black man (who perhaps feels a
sense of injustice at the hands of a racist and class-conscious society), who
takes out his rage on a woman who does not defend herself, nor
understand her 'multiple jeopardy'.

The last line of the passage printed above leads interestingly to a
significant subplot of *The Color Purple*. At this early stage in the novel, we
find a woman, Celie, taught to fear men and to devalue herself. Later, Shug
Avery teaches her to value herself as a woman, and as a black woman with
creative talents and the ability to earn her own keep. Shug helps to educate
Celie out of her 'triple oppression', step by step.

Yet many critics have questioned the extent to which Walker's
characters are truly representative of women in the world, or rather, of
black women in the world. Our views on the 'realism' of characters such
as Celie will be influenced by our positions with regard to race, class and
gender, and possibly also by our personal experiences of domestic and
social life. ■

When we consider our individual positions, we might also think about the
positions of readers from other cultures, including women in Africa. Now
that Walker is a celebrity author and *The Color Purple*, as novel and film, is
known around the world, we should consider the question of whether
some of the readers and viewers of Walker's work may feel inappropriately
'represented' by Walker. The continent of Africa, the great diversity of its
people, and the complexity of its culture are very briefly summarized and
encapsulated in the novel: in a few descriptive letters from Nettie, and in
the selection of colours and fabrics which the African missionaries wear
when they return in the novel's grand family reunion of an ending. Any
'appropriation' of African culture in the novel is clearly not intended by
Walker to be invasive. She seems to want to celebrate African culture, but
can only do so by offering brief fragments of text and a few iconic symbols
to stand in for an entire history and way of life. Whether we see the
inclusion of the African scenes as a positive contribution to the novel or as
reductive appropriation will depend largely on our own positions and
critical perspectives. As always with such complex matters, there is no one
right or wrong answer. But one issue raised by the African material is the
novel's form.

What allows Walker to introduce Africa into her small Georgia town is the use of letters sent from culture to culture, character to character. It is important to note the form of *The Color Purple*: it is an epistolary novel, composed of letters or 'epistles' exchanged between characters. The epistolary novel as form is probably most familiar from eighteenth-century literature: Samuel Richardson's novels *Pamela* (1740–41) and *Clarissa* (1747–48), for example, and Choderlos de Laclos's *Liasons Dangereuses* (1782). Women's epistolary writing also came to the fore in the eighteenth century, with Fanny Burney's *Evelina* (1778), for instance. In the nineteenth century, writers didn't often adopt the form for entire novels, but many did tend to include letters within novels, allowing facts and certain characters' views to be expressed even in their physical absence, as in Emily Brontë's *Wuthering Heights* and Jane Austen's *Pride and Prejudice*. Alternatively, some authors opted for direct first-person narration, which functions very like a letter from the narrator to the reader (as in the famous example from *Jane Eyre*: 'Reader, I married him'; and in Mary Shelley's *Frankenstein*).

The Color Purple is a contemporary epistolary novel, and the form fits the central concerns of both the author and the text very well. Walker was concerned to bring her characters to life and to allow them to speak to each other directly, as she argues in an essay about the writing of the novel which we will consider shortly. At the same time, the novel has a life and voice of its own, and the use of the epistolary form allows the text's style to be interrupted by another rhythm, another voice, introducing African culture and all the facts necessary for the piecing together of the mystery of the disappearance of Celie's sister Nettie. Thematically, the exchange of letters between the sisters emphasizes the importance of communication between them, and offers an insight into the role of writing for women more generally. In fact, the importance of words, of written and spoken language, as the medium for empowerment is a central concern in the novel. The theme is especially relevant to the female characters, denied access to education and other forms of learning and communication.

Writing to our sisters: literacy and the power of words

Earlier, we analysed the connections between gender, race and class with regard to the concept of black women as marginalized or oppressed on several different levels. **Now let's consider an extension of that argument, which develops basic ideas about multiple oppression in terms of women's writing.**

> Black is the colour of the underclass. And all Walker's women are peasants ... Bound to the land and their husbands (or fathers), worn by toil in the fields and the demands of childbearing, these women are the underclass of the underclass. This is why literacy and education are so crucial to the way Walker depicts the process of liberation ...
> Clearly, the ability to raise questions, to objectify contradictions, is only possible when Celie [in *The Color Purple*] begins writing her letters.
>
> (Willis, 'Alice Walker's women', 1990, p.126)

D i s c u s s i o n

Critic Susan Willis here argues that it is through education and the process of acquiring written language that Celie begins to raise herself from the position of the 'underclass' to a more powerful position. So, while the characters speak in an informal colloquial vocabulary (and while Walker's irregular spelling emphasizes the characters' unique speech patterns), still it can be argued that the characters in *The Color Purple* are *not* working class: Walker herself has asserted that she wanted to depict female characters who weren't so burdened and unglamorous as most depictions of black women. Thus Shug is quite a glamorous figure, and even Celie works her way into a reasonable style of living by the story's end. Indeed, Celie's embracing of the capitalist 'American Dream' is wholehearted.

The educational system may be class-based, racist and élitist, but it also offers a means of escape from these multiple oppressions both for Walker and for her female character within the novel. Writing is a means of finding freedom for Celie in *The Color Purple*, as we shall see when we discuss the novel in more detail. But it is not only a means to self-expression and freeing of the 'captive imagination' as it was for the white middle-class American writers Charlotte Perkins Gilman and Louisa May Alcott, or for the white middle-class English writer Virginia Woolf. For the black female character Celie, created by black female writer Alice Walker, the process of writing is more than that. For 'Walker's women', as for the Girl depicted by Jamaica Kincaid, the telling of stories is a way of presenting self in opposition to a language which is not your own, not part of your people's tradition. Walker's characters Celie and Nettie write their own stories. They insist on using language, learning about language. But for all these characters, and for the black woman who created them, the use of language is to do with a breaking out from the 'underclass' imposed by racism and the imperial imposition of the English language, as well as an expression of self in opposition to gender oppression. (See Margaret Busby's Introduction to *Daughters of Africa*, 1992, pp.xxxv) for a detailed analysis of the deliberate and indeed political choice of writing in dialect and 'heard English' by black American writers such as Edward Kamau Braithwaite – who introduced the concept of 'Nation Language' – and by women such as playwright and poet Ntozake Shange and poet and essayist June Jordan.) ■

For Celie, the writing of letters is not only a form of communication, for after all, most of her letters are not sent. But rather, writing for Celie is a way of thinking out loud, quietly and safely. It is a means of exploring her thoughts by expressing them on paper, and of convincing herself that she is not alone, by imagining a reader. In the early letters, the reader Celie imagines is God, and later, as she learns more about herself and the world, the intended reader is her sister Nettie. In the third part of the novel, the letters from Nettie to Celie progress the narrative and serve to reroot Celie in relation to her sister, her past. For Celie, letter writing is a creative act: something she does, consciously, deliberately, in order to reach beyond her immediate domestic life towards other lives, and other connections. In this sense, for Celie writing is a means of escape (like that which Emily Dickinson found in writing), and also a means of crossing an imaginary

157

border between the real and the imagined. And of course, for Celie, the imagined is the dream of reconnecting with her most loved, her sister. We might argue that in loving Nettie, Celie finds a way to see and love herself, for Nettie is the one person who always loved Celie for who she was, who always saw the best in her. Through Nettie's eyes, Celie sees herself differently; believing that Nettie is alive and reading her letters keeps Celie alive by helping her to believe in herself, and in the future.

The importance of the letters is closely connected to the developing knowledge of reading which Celie acquires from her sister Nettie. As Nettie teaches Celie to read, and then to write, Celie also learns about love and respect for her sister, and for herself. The ability to 'master' language is symbolic of and intricately related to Celie's dawning understanding of herself, who she is, what she can do and what she wants to be.

As Celie's journey towards self-discovery is begun by Nettie's education into language, so her understanding of herself is enhanced by the lesson which Shug Avery teaches, a lesson in sexuality. Nettie's gift to Celie is power over language, and also the power to maintain communication across distance, time and space, so that she can maintain a sense of herself even in her sister's and children's absence. Shug Avery teaches Celie to enjoy sex. The sensuality of sex is described and enjoyed in the language of the novel, so that the sex scenes are relished, like the sensuality of language. Celie learns to enjoy words and sex, to take pleasure from communication between ideas and bodies. This kind of communication is essential to Celie while she is denied access to the people she loves and the material means she needs to support herself. But as the story progresses, Celie learns just that: to earn what she needs, to see the best side of herself, overturning her previous image of herself as unworthy.

In this novel, there is a major thread running through the story which explores the importance of 'blood' and 'family' in and through the relationship between sisters. Sisters are related through blood, and also through marriage. And in the black community of Walker's novel, all the women – except one white woman, Sophia's 'oppressor' – seem to be sisters, or collaborators in a joint project of making it through life in one piece in the face of an amazing array of demanding, abusive and occasionally well-meaning men. In this novel, though, it is important to remember that Albert, the 'Mr —' of early scenes, also undergoes a process of development and transformation – unlike the immovable Dr John in Gilman's 'Yellow Wallpaper' (so Walker's story offers some sense of progress for male characters too).

Here we might recall Maya Angelou's description of the importance of naming. Albert takes on more humanity when he has a first name which the women are empowered to use. And at the collective level, to call a woman your 'sister' is an expression of a formal relationship and a familial one too: a symbolic and a real connection between individuals making up a community. So, while it is always dangerous and potentially misleading to discuss 'black characters' as if they were all the same, still it seems safe to say that within the context of the novel 'Walker's women' affirm the family by making family of the community, and community of the family.

Now read Alice Walker's account of the process of writing the novel, and consider the question: how would you describe Walker's relationship with her created characters?

Alice Walker: How I wrote The Color Purple

I don't always know where the germ of a story comes from, but with *The Color Purple* I knew right away. I was hiking through the woods with my sister, Ruth, talking about a lovers' triangle of which we both knew. She said: 'And you know, one day The Wife asked The Other Woman for a pair of her drawers.' Instantly the missing piece of the story I was mentally writing – about two women who felt married to the same man – fell into place. And for months – through illnesses, divorce, several moves, travel abroad, all kinds of heartaches and revelations – I carried my sister's comment delicately balanced in the center of the novel's construction I was building in my head.

I also knew *The Color Purple* would be a historical novel, and thinking on this made me chuckle. In an interview, discussing my work, a black male critic said he'd heard I might write a historical novel someday, and went on to say, in effect: Heaven protect us from it. The chuckle was because, womanlike (he would say), my 'history' starts not with the taking of lands, or the births, battles, and deaths of Great Men, but with one woman asking another for her underwear. Oh, well, I thought, one function of critics is to be appalled by such behavior. But what woman (or sensuous man) could avoid being intrigued? As for me I thought of little else for a year.

When I was sure the characters of my new novel were trying to form (or, as I invariably though of it, trying to contact me, to speak *through* me), I began to make plans to leave New York. Three months earlier I had bought a tiny house on a quiet Brooklyn street, assuming – because my desk overlooked the street and a maple tree in the yard, representing garden and view – I would be able to write. I was not.

New York, whose people I love for their grace under almost continual unpredictable adversity, was a place the people in *The Color Purple* refused even to visit. The moment any of them started to form – on the subway, a dark street, and especially in the shadow of very tall buildings – they would start to complain.

'What is all this tall shit anyway?' they would say.

I disposed of the house, stored my furniture, packed my suitcases, and flew alone to San Francisco (it was my daughter's year to be with her father), where all the people in the novel promptly fell silent – I think, in awe. Not merely of the city's beauty, but of what they picked up about earthquakes.

'It's pretty,' they muttered, 'but us ain't lost nothing in no place that has earthquakes.'

They also didn't like seeing buses, cars, or other people whenever they attempted to look out. 'Us don't want to be seeing none of this,' they said. 'It make us can't think.'

That was when I knew for sure these were country people. So my lover and I started driving around the state looking for a country house to rent. Luckily I had found (with the help of friends) a fairly inexpensive place in the city. This too had been a decision forced by my characters. As long as there was any question about whether I

159

could support them in the fashion they desired (basically in undisturbed silence) they declined to come out. Eventually we found a place in northern California we could afford and that my characters liked. And no wonder: it looked a lot like the town in Georgia most of them were from, only it was more beautiful and the local swimming hole was not segregated. It also bore a slight resemblance to the African village in which one of them, Nettie, was a missionary.

Seeing the sheep, the cattle, and the goats, smelling the apples and the hay, one of my characters, Celie, began, haltingly, to speak.

But there was still a problem.

Since I quit my editing job at *Ms.* and my Guggenheim Fellowship was running out, and my royalties did not quite cover expenses, and – let's face it – because it gives me a charge to see people who appreciate my work, historical novels or not, I was accepting invitations to speak. Sometimes on the long plane rides Celie or Shug would break through with a wonderful line or two (for instance, Celie said once that a self-pitying sick person she went to visit was 'laying up in the bed trying to look dead'). But even these vanished – if I didn't jot them down – by the time my contact with the audience was done.

What to do?

Celie and Shug answered without hesitation: Give up all this travel. Give up all this talk. What is all this travel and talk shit anyway? So, I gave it up for a year. Whenever I was invited to speak I explained I was taking a year off for Silence. (I also wore an imaginary bracelet on my left arm that spelled the word.) Everyone said, Sure, they understood.

I was terrified.

Where was the money for our support coming from? My only steady income was a three-hundred-dollar-a-month retainer from *Ms.* for being a long-distance editor. But even that was too much distraction for my characters.

Tell them you can't do anything for the magazine, said Celie and Shug. (You guessed it, the women of the drawers.) Tell them you'll have to think about them later. So, I did. *Ms.* was unperturbed. Supportive as ever (they continued the retainer). Which was nice.

Then I sold a book of stories. After taxes, inflation, and my agent's fee of ten percent, I would still have enough for a frugal, no-frills year. And so, I bought some beautiful blue-and-red-and-purple fabric, and some funky old secondhand furniture (and accepted donations of old odds and ends from friends), and a quilt pattern my mama swore was easy, and I headed for the hills.

There were days and weeks and even months when nothing happened. Nothing whatsoever. I worked on my quilt, took long walks with my lover, lay on an island we discovered in the middle of the river and dabbled my fingers in the water. I swam, explored the redwood forests all around us, lay out in the meadow, picked apples, talked (yes, of course) to trees. My quilt began to grow. And, of course, everything was happening. Celie and Shug and Albert were getting to know each other, coming to trust my determination to serve their entry (sometimes I felt *re-*entry) into the world to the best of my ability, and what is more – and felt so wonderful – we began to love one another. And, what is even more, to feel immense thankfulness for our mutual good luck.

Just as summer was ending, one or more of my characters – Celie, Shug, Albert, Sofia, or Harpo – would come for a visit. We would sit wherever I was sitting, and talk. They were very obliging, engaging, and jolly. They were, of course, at the end of their story but were telling it to me from the beginning. Things that made me sad often made them laugh. Oh, we got through that; don't pull such a long face, they'd say. Or, You think Reagan's bad, you ought've seen some of the rednecks us come up under. The days passed in a blaze of happiness.

Then school started, and it was time for my daughter to stay with me – for two years.

Could I handle it?

Shug said, right out, that she didn't know. (Well, her mother raised *her* children.) Nobody else said anything. (At this point in the novel, Celie didn't even know where *her* children were.) They just quieted down, didn't visit as much, and took a firm Well, let's us wait and see attitude.

My daughter arrived. Smart, sensitive, cheerful, at school most of the day, but quick with tea and sympathy on her return. My characters adored her. They saw she spoke her mind in no uncertain terms and would fight back when attacked. When she came home from school one day with bruises but said, You should see the other guy, Celie (raped by her stepfather as a child and somewhat fearful of life) began to reappraise her own condition. Rebecca gave her courage (which she *always* gives me) – and Celie grew to like her so much she would wait until three-thirty to visit me. So, just when Rebecca would arrive home needing her mother and a hug, there'd be Celie, trying to give her both. Fortunately I was able to bring Celie's own children back to her (a unique power of novelists), though it took thirty years and a good bit of foreign travel. But this proved to be the largest single problem in writing the exact novel I wanted to write between about ten-thirty and three.

I had planned to give myself five years to write *The Color Purple* (teaching, speaking, or selling apples, as I ran out of money). But, on the very day my daughter left for camp, less than a year after I started writing, I wrote the last page.

And what did I do that for?

It was like losing everybody I loved at once. First Rebecca (to whom everyone surged forth on the last page to say good-bye), then Celie, Shug, Nettie, and Albert. Mary Agnes, Harpo, and Sofia, Eleanor Jane. Adam and Tashi Omatangu. Olivia. Mercifully, my quilt and my lover remained.

I threw myself in his arms and cried.

(*In Search of Our Mother's Gardens*, pp.355–60)

Reading between the lines

Walker's account of the process of writing *The Color Purple*, above, is clear, eloquent and accessible, comparable in some ways to the short piece by Charlotte Perkins Gilman printed in Chapter Four. Gilman's account focused on the unpleasant conditions of writing autobiographical details into her disturbing fiction, and on its negative reception by male critics.

Walker's account in this essay, though not in an interview discussed below, is much more positive and comic. Walker does not concern herself in this essay with the reception of the novel, but rather with its origins in her creative imagination. In Toni Morrison's terms, this is an example of 'the black literary imagination' making itself accessible to a white and general, generic readership.

Were you surprised by the account of the characters' creation? It is likely that many of you were. The spiritual element of Walker's forays into the imagination may have surprised you most. Walker describes her characters as if they are real people, and she misses them when she has written the last words. Celie, Nettie, Sophia and Shug became 'like sisters' to both Alice Walker and her daughter, Rebecca. Perhaps the idea of missing characters or stories, which is, in effect, tantamount to missing imaginative worlds, is not alien to us as readers; we have probably all experienced a certain sense of sadness at closing a book in which we've engaged at some deep imaginative level. Yet while we may all know the feeling of not wanting a good story to end, it is not so common to think of characters as 'alive' in a spiritual sense, as Walker suggests that Celie and Shug were, or are, for her.

The subtitle to Alice Walker's book of prose essays *In Search of Our Mother's Gardens* is 'Womanist Prose'. Walker defines her terms in this way:

> **Womanist**: 1. From *womanish* (opp. of 'girlish', i.e., frivolous, irresponsible, not serious.) A black feminist or feminist of color. From the black folk expression of mothers to female children, 'You acting womanish', i.e., like a woman. Usually referring to outrageous, audacious, courageous or *willful* behavior. Wanting to know more and in greater depth than is considered 'good' for one. Interested in grown-up doings. Acting grown up. Being grown up. Interchangeable with another black folk expression: 'You trying to be grown.' Responsible. In charge. *Serious.*
>
> 2. *Also:* A woman who loves other women, sexually and/or nonsexually. Appreciates and prefers women's culture, women's emotional flexibility (values tears as natural counter-balance of laughter), and women's strength. Sometimes loves individual men, sexually and/or nonsexually. Committed to survival and wholeness of entire people, male *and* female. Not a separatist, except periodically, for health. Traditionally universalist, as in: 'Mama, why are we brown, pink, and yellow, and our cousins are white, beige, and black?' Ans.: 'Well, you know the colored race is just like a flower garden, with every color flower represented.' Traditionally capable, as in: 'Mama, I'm walking to Canada and I'm taking you and a bunch of other slaves with me.' Reply: 'It wouldn't be the first time.'
>
> 3. Loves music, Loves dance. Loves the moon. *Loves* the Spirit. Loves love and food and roundness. Loves struggle. *Loves* the Folk. Loves herself. Regardless.
>
> 4. Womanist is to feminist as purple to lavender.
>
> (pp.xi–xii)

With these definitions before us, we can say that the novel *The Color Purple* is a 'womanist' novel: a serious investigation into the representation and oppression and possibilities for liberation of black women and men, in and through the medium of fiction.

The survival of the characters Celie and Shug within the world of the novel serves Walker's 'womanist' project, as well as her more spiritual framework for the novel. In this view, the idea of a 'sin against the spirit' of a character or person becomes another way of framing the idea that identity is constructed in part by our view of ourselves, shaped in turn by the views of others, projected upon us. 'Sin', and especially violence against spirit and identity in *The Color Purple,* is seen as perpetrated primarily by men against women, and as set right by the love between women (sisterly and sexual), and by the larger philosophical or religious framework of the novel. (This theme is developed in Byrd, 'Spirituality in the novels of Alice Walker', in Braxton and McLaughlin, *Wild Women in the Whirlwind,* 1990, pp.363 ff.). This interpretation is supported by Walker herself, not only in her essay about the writing of the novel but also in a statement she made in interview: 'I am preoccupied with the spiritual survival, the survival *whole* of my people' ('From an interview', in *In Search of Our Mother's Gardens,* 1984, p.250). In referring to 'her people', Walker includes African-Americans, black people and people of colour more generally. She includes both women and men, and also those who – like the characters in her novel – have worked the land, and those who, generations later, may write and read and teach about black culture. In fact, the novel is dedicated:

> To the Spirit:
> Without whose assistance
> Neither this book
> Nor I
> Would have been
> Written

Walker positions herself with the characters of her novel and the novel itself as a creative work inspired by a spiritual force from outside (or inside), which fuels her sense of community and her belief that reading and writing can transform lives, like hers and like Celie's. Indeed, there seems to be quite a close link between Walker and her character Celie – one which can be traced through autobiographical writing, but which also manifests itself in Walker's account of the origins of the novel.

Now, reread the first two paragraphs of Walker's essay and answer the question: how does the central image which fired Walker's imagination function in the novel?

Discussion

The idea of a 'love triangle' is common enough in fiction (and in life) but the attachment of that abstract relationship to a concrete, quite specific detail – in fact, an undergarment – gets beneath the surface, right to the heart of Walker's imaginative starting point. The underwear functions as a symbol; the words of the text create a visual image of this garment with all its rich associations. We might call this kind of symbolic layering semiotics; this is the term used for the study of sign systems, or to refer to visual images which recur in relation to literary texts (the first example we encountered was the red shoes or ruby slippers of *The Wizard of Oz*). Walker goes on to say that she knows (male) critics will find her choice of image strange, or silly (not important enough to begin a novel). Yet she has a sense of confidence that women readers will understand the choice. Indeed, it is not only in *The Color Purple* but in many of our texts by women – including the play *Trifles* discussed in the next chapter – that a certain intimacy and understanding develops between women (within stories, and between female authors and readers) – a shared sense of the intimacy of everyday items and events, the clues to 'the meaning of life' to be gleaned from small things: words, gestures, silences, aprons, quilts, birds and other 'trifles', including underwear. ∎

Let's look at the example of the quilt in *The Color Purple*. In the end, Celie decides to give the Sister's Choice quilt to Sophia, though she might have liked to keep it: '… I want it for myself just for the little yellow pieces, look like stars, but not' (1983 edn, p.53). Walker also wanted to keep her story, *The Color Purple*, for herself: to keep the characters alive by continuing writing, rather than passing the story over to readers. The links between writing and quilting as creative arts are drawn very clearly by Walker:

Figure 31   Alice Walker in a rocking chair. Photo: Lynda Koolish.

The quilt in the community that I grew up in represented a lot of women working together. It was really an expression of *expressed* creativity, in that it was something that they could use all of their scraps in, their scraps of material; women who otherwise might have been writers or painters who could not because they had to work in the fields, turned to quilting because it was something utilitarian, that was not suppressed; so something that they could do to show their creativity, it's just that the creativity came out in the form of a quilt rather than in the form of a novel.

Walker continues by referring to the creative quality of music, and particularly singing, to give expression to 'silenced people', including the women in her novel:

How was the creativity of the black woman kept alive, year after year, and century after century, when for most of the years black people have been in America, it was a punishable crime for black people to read or write? Consider, if you can bear to imagine it, what might have been the result if singing too had been forbidden by law. Listen to the voices of Bessie Smith, Billie Holiday, Nina Simone, Roberta Flack and Aretha Franklin, among others, and imagine these voices muzzled for life.

(In Search of Our Mother's Gardens, 1984, p.234)

Walker requests that we imagine these voices 'muzzled', marginalized. The massive success of *The Color Purple* shows that at least a few black women writers have now been 'imagined' more than sufficiently into place in the mainstream.

To sum up, then: our reading of *The Color Purple* has considered the novel as a text about communication, education, the process of becoming one's self, learning to look at one's self without apology, and making connections with other women, through language and other forms of

Figure 32   Freedom Quilt, left, by Jessie Telfair Parrott, Georgia 1980 (Private Collection) and Patriotic Quilt, right, by Elizabeth Holmes, United States 1869 (Private Collection). Photographed in the Museum of American Folk Art, New York. Photograph: BBC/OU.

creativity, including sexual expression. The film version reinterprets the story in 'mainstream' format. With no wars on which to focus, the film still managed to bring a certain Hollywood 'epic sweep' to the story, as Joan Digby argues in the next section.

Part Three: Interpreting **The Color Purple**

The next section is extracted from a longer piece by the critic Joan Digby, in which she discusses the 'transformation' of Walker's novel as it was developed for the cinema. ('Transformations of *The Color Purple*', in Reynolds, *Novel Images*, 1993). Whether or not you've seen the 1985 film version (directed by Steven Spielberg), Digby's article will raise some interesting issues for your study of the novel in its cultural context. In the extract which follows, Digby summarizes the story of the novel, and also engages in her own interpretation of the significance of the women's relationship within the story. As you read this piece, consider the relationships between the female characters as they might be expressed through visual images in the film: through colour and shape, as well as through creative arts like sewing and quilting and writing letters.

Figure 33   Six women quilt, prepared by Stella Hobby for a BBC TV programme made in association with this book. BBC/OU photograph.

Transformations of The Color Purple

by Joan Digby

Transformation was an idea central to Alice Walker. At the end of the novel she thanked 'everybody in this book for coming'; and in a descriptive essay, 'Writing *The Color Purple*', she commented at length on the early visitations paid to her by her characters as they were 'trying to form', and the later ones in which 'Celie and Shug and Albert were getting to know each other'.

Clearly, she thought of these three characters as the emotional centre of her novel, although they are enmeshed in complex, multiple subplots.

Celie is the book's heroine. At the opening she is fourteen years old, terrified and confused by her Pa's sexual use of her as a replacement for her sick mother. 'You better not never tell nobody but God. It'll kill your mammy,' he threatens. And so she writes letters to God to relieve the agony of rape, childbirth and her mother's death, which follows despite her silence. Written as she would have spoken, the letters tell her life-story with an ingenuous simplicity that the reader responds to as the poetic voice of betrayed innocence. Pa sells the two children she has by him, then passes her off, 'spoiled' as she is, to a widower she only knows as Mr — who has actually come to court her pretty sister, Nettie. Mr — and his vicious children continue to enslave and abuse her. Having run away from Pa's threatening advances, Nettie comes to Celie for protection. She intends to become a teacher and tries to teach Celie a way out of her lamentable marriage, but she does not get too far because Mr — turns her out of the house when she refuses his sexual overtures. Their parting establishes Nettie as the author of a second set of letters:

> I say, Write.
>   She say, Nothing but death can keep me from it.
>   She never write.

Half-way through the novel it becomes clear that Nettie has been replying for nearly thirty years, but Mr — has hidden Nettie's mail from Celie. These letters are written in schooled English, by contrast with Celie's dialect, and contain several of the book's important subplots. They tell how she came to live with Corinne and Samuel, missionaries who took her to Africa to work among the Olinka. By coincidence, Corinne and Samuel are the childless couple who bought Celie's two children, and so Aunt Nettie, their protector, also becomes the biographer of Olivia and Adam. She recounts their growing-up and how Adam falls in love with and marries Olivia's African friend, Tashi. Her expository comparison of African with African-American lives contains many digressions into theories of education, traditional rites of passage and the destruction of African tribal life by colonial greed. Nettie's work in Africa comes to an end when the Olinka village is sacrificed to build a commercial road. By then Corinne has died in an epidemic, but not before revealing that she has been jealous of Nettie, believing her to be Samuel's mistress and the mother of Adam and Olivia. This provokes Samuel to unravel his own guilt-ridden history (eliminated from the film), which coincidentally proves that Nettie's real father was lynched and the man the sisters called 'Pa' was actually their stepfather. In the light of this truth – which would absolve Celie from the most profound curse of incest if she only knew about it – Nettie marries Samuel, who is the model of a loving husband. The children, having learned of their true mother, are anxious to go to America.

What brings these two halves of the novel together is the character of Shug Avery. She is the jazz singer who has been Mr —'s passion for years. She is the Fairy Godmother and Prince Charming fused into a single transforming catalyst who turns Cinderella/Celie's ashes into gold. The physical contrast between the two women is summarized by Shug's unforgettable greeting: 'You sure *is* ugly.' Celie, who shares this self-image, which has taunted her from childhood, has already fallen in love with Shug's beauty from a photograph. When Mr — (called 'Albert' by Shug) brings his ailing mistress home, Celie cares for her. In the process she grows to love Shug's sensuous femininity in a way that opens her to sexual exploration and self-discovery. The women become intimate, not only as lovers, but also as conspirators in protecting Celie from Mr —'s beating and bringing to light the hidden letters that give Celie the power to become her beautiful self.

Shug invests Celie with power. She teaches her figuratively how to wear the pants and literally how to make them. Sewing pants with Shug as they read Nettie's letters, Celie gains control of her rage and begins on the road to her economic freedom.

In their developing female friendship, Shug acts the role of the confidante, a stock character of the epistolary novel who links the traditional marriage-plot to the etiquette-book tradition. From the confidante the wife traditionally learns the conduct of marriage and management of the household. In this role, Shug teaches Celie by 'didactic example', a method [which can be traced] back to the eighteenth-century epistolary novels of Samuel Richardson which teach the rewards of virtue. By contrast, Walker's confidante teaches the rewards of feminine strength and the cultural bonding that makes women powerful allies in subverting male control. Shug's examples validate Walker's 'Womanist' philosophy and coax Celie to find her voice. She teaches Celie that washing her body feels like praying, that blues is 'something you help scratch out my head', and that sewing is a form of thought. Shug's particular examples of women's work demonstrate how Walker appropriated the epistolary novel invented by European men to educate women and grafted it to an oral, African-American folk expression of women who were otherwise denied voice.

Walker's favorite icon of folk expression is the quilt, with its repeat-pattern symmetries and patchwork of old fabric that makes something for the future out of scraps of the past. To use this metaphor, the subplots told in Celie's letters are a patchwork of love and marriage in Mr —'s extended family. Like quilting, these plots carry the didactic messages 'Work together' and 'Learn from each other'.

As Sofia puts it, 'Everybody learn something in life.' She is Celie's daughter-in-law, married to Harpo, who is a wife-beater like his father. But Sofia is Celie's opposite and fights back at Harpo, teaching Celie in the process not to side with the abuser. After a fist-fight with the white mayor in defence of her right not to become his wife's maid, she is beaten, jailed and separated from her children, although her tribulations never save her from becoming the maid. Since Sofia's story makes a critical connection between gender and racial dignity, all but her relationship with the white child she raises is developed as the most important subplot in the film. Despite her affliction, she is a comic character, and with Shug she is a model of a woman who can hold her own. Sofia's marriage is much tempered by her suffering, and in the end Harpo becomes a doting husband who bows to her authority.

This marriage, like Celie's, is a triangle that includes a jazz-singer mistress. Walker's vision of marriage conduct 'not only redefines male and female roles', but suggests a new paradigm, 'The eternal triangle in which women complement rather than compete with each other'.

Framing The Color Purple: *interpreting the novel through the film*

In her summary of the story, Digby interprets the relationships between women in the novel as crucial, arguing that they form a triangle of support for each other. In her argument, Digby conjures a visual image (the triangle) which is repeated like a pattern in the story. One triangle of female characters interacts with another; the traditional 'love triangle' plays itself out in a positive way for the community of women within the novel. The quilt is also a pattern which relies on piecing together shapes and fabric and the stories of different women's lives. The quilt is a limited metaphor, however. It offers a range of possibilities for women's support networks – which might reach out into the future in any number of positive and liberating ways; but it is also a form of art or creativity that is on the margins of material worth. For instance, in the novel the men don't make quilts, nor have much use for them except as blankets: quilting is women's work. And in the world outside the novel many critics argue that the quilting metaphor is too simplistically optimistic for sustained use in developing theories of literary influence.

If we think back to 'The Yellow Wallpaper', we'll recall that it was a text by a woman representing a woman, influenced by a man/men. The same could be said about the short stories and novella discussed in Chapter Three. But in *The Color Purple*, the man becomes a real threat rather than a background influence or comic participant in a woman's narrative. Here, the male is a threat to the female, and the heroine's journey is two-fold: not just a journey away from the 'cage' of restrictions on women's lives, but also a much more positive journey towards self-understanding, self-esteem and self-discovery.

Digby's article also highlights the visual element of colour within the novel and the film version. In *The Color Purple*, the colour describes, not a feeling generated by entrapment and enclosure within a domestic world – as did the colour yellow in 'The Yellow Wallpaper' – but its opposite: the freedom of the open air and the flowers in the field beyond the house, outside the window. The colour is a shorthand for a range of emotions and spiritual associations and ties to the country of Africa (through the descriptions of Africa written in Nettie's letters); the colour is a visual form of communication. Joan Digby has described the iconic significance of the colour in the film version:

> In the novel, Shug's arresting observation, 'I think it pisses God off if you walk by the colour purple in a field somewhere and don't notice it' is part of a long philosophical argument on the nature of God that leads to an embracing (and, some critics believe, an embarrassing) pantheism. The argument is replaced in the film by the visual symbol of the purple flowers.
>
> ('Transformations of *The Color Purple*', in Reynolds, *Novel Images*, 1993, p.165)

One shade of the colour purple, lavender, also symbolizes lesbianism. This last point needs drawing out by way of contrast to the film version. It is specifically the lesbian love depicted in the novel, in the sex scenes between Celie and Shug Avery ('the women of the underwear'), which is underplayed in the film. The absence is a 'significant silence', as it is these scenes that depict an emotional bond as well as physical desire between the women. In fact, these are teaching scenes; Shug initiates Celie into her first satisfying sex, teaches her to take pleasure from her own body. The scenes depict a love and respect between the two women which far surpasses any love between women and men in the novel; for even Shug's love for her new husband and Sophie's – and later Squeak's – love for Harpo are tinged with violence, episodes of verbal and physical abuse.

Celie and Shug love each other physically and emotionally. They understand each other, as each thinks of herself as in some sense married

Figure 34   Girls in the field of purple flowers, still from *The Color Purple*, directed by Steven Spielberg, 1985 Columbia EMI, courtesy of the Kobal Collection.

to the same man; each shares the most intimate relationship with him, and each learns to respect the other as a person in her own right, as the novel develops. So the purple flowers in the field also stand in for the lesbian love between Celie and Shug which is all but erased in the film version. The flowers come into full view at the end of the film (see Figure 34), when the sisters are reunited, and all the female characters have learned to see beyond the mirrors of their own images, beyond the obstacles of their domestic lives. At one level, this image is quite positive, indeed almost manically so: suddenly Nettie and Celie's children and family all appear, majestically draped in flowing robes symbolizing Africa, against the backdrop of the dazzling purple flowers. But while the image and the music of the film are calculated to engage a feeling of upbeat satisfaction at this grand reunion, the scene is also highly problematic, and one of the prime sites for criticism of the story and the film.

But colour is an issue in *The Color Purple* in a real, as well as a metaphorical sense. *The Color Purple* is a novel by a black woman, about black women and their lives, which are lived with and in relation to other black women and men, in the context of a racist society. But the representation of African experience, simplified and encapsulated in a colour and a set of costumes and described in letters, creates an unhelpfully 'foreign' sense of Africa. It runs the risk of positioning African women as 'other' to African-American women, rather then embracing them in a cross-cultural narrative.

In a televized interview, Alice Walker discussed the interpretive process of making the film, and the decisions which went into the directing of the story in visual terms, for a mainstream audience. In her account, it is interesting that Walker also notes the deliberate choice of underemphasizing the lesbian love scenes, and the choice of focus on certain key images, including the purple flowers and the African scenes. The televised interview is probably the most wide-reaching account available of Walker's own intervention in the process of interpreting the novel for adaptation to film. So, a brief consideration of the 'framing' of Walker, the author, within the narrative of the television programme is informative.

> Alice Walker is the first black woman to win the Pulitzer Prize for
> fiction. Her novel, *The Color Purple*, is set in her home town of
> Eatonton, Georgia, in the segregated South of the 20s and 30s. The
> story is told entirely in the form of letters, written by a young black girl
> called Celie. Celie has been sexually abused by her stepfather, and in
> her confusion and loneliness she has no one to talk to but God.
>
> (*Omnibus*, BBC TV, 1986)

This is the introduction to the voiceover narrative of the *Omnibus* TV programme: 'Alice Walker and *The Color Purple*'. The programme is quite successful in capturing the complexity of the writing process as one of sifting through history and stereotype. It also raises the issue of unconscious racism, which may have influenced the project of translating the story from Walker's imagination to text, through the reading public, and then through the imagination of the white, male Jewish film director, Steven

Spielberg, before the story was re-produced on screen. The introduction is 'true': it contains the barest outline of the story. But it also includes information to which we, as readers, do not have access at the beginning of the novel. We only learn with Celie, quite late in the novel, that the 'father' who rapes her is not her natural father, but rather her adoptive stepfather. The timing of that discovery is crucial, as part of Celie's confusion of identity and sense of low self-worth is informed by her belief that she is a victim of, and her two 'little lost babies' the products of, incest. Of course, it makes a tremendous difference to Celie when she eventually discovers the truth. Celie begins to see herself and her relationship to her children differently when she learns of their actual 'blood' relationship, the missing clue to her own identity, her own story.

The discovery is remarkable. For as in many women's narratives, self discovery is pieced together bit by bit as new facts come to light. In this sense *The Color Purple*, like 'Behind a Mask' and also 'The Yellow Wallpaper', is a kind of detective story. As we read, we find out who the main character is and what her relationship is to the other characters. If we go on to study a text in context, as we've done with *The Color Purple* in this chapter, then we may read the words of various critics and scholars, piecing together a sense of the story's importance and historical/critical context. We may read the words of the author as well, if she has written about her work, as did Gilman, or if she is alive and writing and adding to the body of material which forms the context of literary analysis, as is Walker.

The discovery of Nettie's letters is another revelation for Celie – a major step in her path to self-discovery. Spielberg grabs hold of this discovery, and positions the mailbox as a central image in the film. (If you have seen the 1994 film version of Louisa May Alcott's *Little Women*, directed by Gillian Armstrong, you will recognize the mailbox as a potent symbol for women's writing and creativity in that context as well).

Celie waits for her letters, willing them to come, and is finally overcome with joy and an almost sensual enjoyment of the reading of them when they're found. So, Celie's relationship to the potent symbol of the mailbox is poignant; her desperation for a letter is a sign of her need for affirmation of her very existence, her worth as a human being.

Another instance in which the film version frames key ideas from the novel in visual images is the scene in which Celie and Nettie write out words and hang them on each others' clothing and on objects around the house. This visualization of the process of learning to read also suggests a bond of communication into which 'Mr —' cannot enter, into which the young children cannot enter: a language of their own and a project shared between them (see Figure 35). Similarly music and song, which are key motifs in the novel, are made integral to the film – from the church song which Shug is refused by her pious father, to the song of little Squeak, who expresses herself in music. In all this, the dead mother who might have helped Celie to find herself is a missing piece in the puzzle. It is as though the mother's absence makes bonding between other women necessary, and their ultimate growth possible. And here again, Walker is herself framed within the dynamic she creates in her novel, perhaps literally (a good deal has been written about Walker's important but problematic relationships with her mother and grandmother), and also figuratively, in that the missing mother is the role model Celie lacks. The character Celie, like her creator Walker, is very much aware of the importance of role models – of a sense of family and community of black women (writers).

Figure 35   Reading lesson – two girls on a swing, still from *The Color Purple*, directed by Steven Spielberg, 1985 Columbia EMI, courtesy of the Kobal Collection.

Walker's words about the author Phyllis Wheatley are apposite here. In the *Omnibus* programme Walker discusses her sense of debt to Phyllis Wheatley, who served as a role model for her and other black women writers. Walker identifies Wheatley not only as a writer, but also as 'Negro Servant to Mr John Wheatley, of Boston, New England':

> Phyllis Wheatley, who wrote in the seventeenth century, had a very difficult time, because she was first of all *owned* by white people, and she was treated differently than most slaves of that time, because she was very sickly, and very bright, and she lived with these people who in some ways made her into a kind of pet, and they published her poetry, for instance, and they took her around to various gatherings and had her read. So her view in a way was distorted, her view of what slavery itself was I think to some extent distorted. But still she managed to give us poems in which there is a lot of power and a lot of understanding, and a lot of record keeping, which I think literature often, for us, has to be.

Wheatley has been criticized for embracing white values in her work, especially since the literary and feminist critical revolutions of the 1960s. But, Walker argues, what else did she have as a source for her literature? What other life experience did she know, what else could she draw on? The symbols we choose, the stories we tell, are not restrained by, but *are* influenced by, our own experiences. Similarly, Walker defends Zora Neale Hurston, the novelist, anthropologist and dramatist who wrote in the 1930s and 40s, and who was dismissed by many reformers and activists in the Civil Rights Movement of the 1960s. Due to Walker's efforts, her work has been reclaimed and republished; she is now an important figure in the literature of black writers. But in the 1960s, her work was criticized for its failure to reflect the contemporary values of many African-American people. Again, Walker argues, Hurston's value is that she recorded what she knew, what she learned, contributing a history to form part of a tradition for new writers.

So, though we may want to criticize Walker's glorification and over-simplification of the African scenes in *The Color Purple*, we may also want to contextualize them, to consider the novel as a first major attempt to bring together the experiences of black women from different cultures. If Walker's partial African heritage and very cursory knowledge of life in Africa is not enough to make her in any sense a 'representative' of African women, perhaps this can be acknowledged – but then put aside so that the next attempt to bridge cultures and cross boundaries may be made.

Influence and autobiography: contextualizing The Color Purple

We can build a bridge between Walker's work and that of other authors we've studied. The bridge has two parts: influence and autobiography.

Walker attended Spelman College, the 'black college' in Atlanta, on a special scholarship (due to her blinding in one eye at the age of eight, by an accidental gun shot, fired by her brother). She then went on to study literature at Sarah Lawrence College, a 'white women's college' in New York. There, she was asked to read 'the canon': mainly literature by white male authors, in which women, let alone black women, had a very marginal place. She felt, she says, embarrassed when trying to identify with Faulkner's character Dilsey, in *The Sound and the Fury*, as the full version of our 'keynote' quotation reveals:

> There I was trying to connect with all these writers who really never saw me. They were unable to see me, actually. So for instance, at Spelman, the black school, and at Sarah Lawrence, the white school, I studied Faulkner, as representative of the south and of the southern writer. Well, it's very difficult for any bright black person to read Faulkner, and read his creation of Dilsey ... and feel anything but embarrassed. She's the maid in this white family. She doesn't really have a context; you don't know who she is when she is not with these white people. Of course, my experience is that it's when you're with your own people that you are most yourself; you have more of a context. So though I love the Brontës, and some of the white writers I read, still I knew that I had a tradition, that I had people who had been writing who had things to tell me, that could help me.
>
> (Alice Walker in interview, *Omnibus*, BBC TV, 1986)

This passage suggests that each of us learns about ourselves (or may feel 'more like ourselves') when in a context reflecting our own history and values. The same idea is resonant for the study of women's literature, black and white, and also in looking at white female characters who are closed off from their histories, their more comfortable contexts, by being placed in social situations where they feel they should appear in certain ways, rather than focusing on figuring out who they are. (The focus on appearance over action will be familar to you, from our discussions of 'The Lady of Shalott', 'The New Dress', 'Behind a Mask' and 'The Yellow Wallpaper'). In the text that we'll study in the next chapter, you'll discover how the attempt to read texts and everyday actions in their social context becomes central to the mystery of *Trifles*.

In terms of autobiography influencing fiction, we argued earlier in this book that an overemphasis on the author may be misleading or distracting to the study of texts, but it can also be informative if the author herself offers insights and connections between her life and her fiction. Walker has done just that in the collection of essays from which her statement about 'Writing *The Color Purple*' was taken. In the same volume, she includes an interview which describes her discovery in her first year of college that she was pregnant (having just returned from her first trip to Africa). Unable to find information about abortion, she considered suicide, indeed very nearly killed herself. A friend saved her by taking her for an abortion. Shortly afterwards she began her career as a professional creative writer. The writing of poetry, she says, comes from deep sadness and a sense of her ugliness, disability, unimportance, while the writing of essays and fiction have a more positive source in ideas and images (like the image of the underwear which inspired *The Color Purple*). But in her description of herself as deformed, ugly and unlovable, we may find the beginnings of the character Celie. And in the descriptions of the female characters' struggles to find means of support for themselves, and ways of expressing themselves (often in song and sewing and other creative acts), we may detect the outlines of Shug Avery, Sophia and Squeak as well.

Like Woolf, Alcott, Gilman and Plath, Alice Walker's life has involved a number of bouts with depression and contemplated suicide. In her own words, 'writing poems is my way of celebrating with the world that I have not committed suicide the night before' (quoted in Reynolds, *Novel Images*, 1993, p.249). So when she says that she is concerned with the survival '*whole* of my people', it is useful to take a wider look at who 'her people' are. Most obviously the phrase refers to people of colour, and African-Americans in particular. But Walker's work also focuses on communities of women, and her treatment of her characters as friends whom she is 'sad to see go' suggests that 'her people' also include her characters, the people she creates under the influence of her own imagination. So, if there is some truth to the idea that Celie loves Nettie partly because Nettie allows Celie to love herself, then perhaps there is also some truth to the idea that Walker loves her characters because they help her to love herself. Perhaps this is not unique to Walker, but part of the creative process of writing, and one reason why the creative acts of writing and childbearing are so often contrasted in the work of women writers: they are two forms of creativity and self-representation which take up large amounts of time, and sometimes compete with each other for the author/ mother's attention.

The contrast is embraced as a positive force in Walker's poem about literary influence and her daughter Rebecca, which follows. Walker wrote this poem and hung it above her desk as a personal motto and reminder of why she writes, and for whom:

Dear Alice,
Virginia Woolf had madness,
George Eliot had ostracism
somebody else's husband,
and did not dare to use
her own name.
Jane Austen had no privacy and no love life.
The Brontë sisters never went anywhere
and died young and dependent on their father.
Zora Hurston (ah!) had no money
and poor health.

You have Rebecca – who is
much more delightful
and less distracting
than any of the calamities
above.

(In Search of Our Mother's Gardens, 1984, pp.382–3)

The poem, like the novel *The Color Purple*, takes the form of a letter. But this time, the letter is from Alice Walker to herself. The poem is a form of work, and also a statement about writing as work, and the legacy of other women writers, mostly white, all more 'burdened' than Walker. This is progress. Walker positions herself, uncomfortably but manageably, as a black woman writer in the twentieth century.

So, finally, we may consider Walker's idea that work is just love made visible. In this statement, we may review the gift of the quilt from Celie to Sophia, as a gift of love. The letters which Celie so laboriously writes to Nettie are also gifts of love, as are the trousers Celie makes. Shug's gift of sexual pleasure to Celie may be seen as another gift – not quite work, but a form of recognition of the needs of other women, and a true sign of love and respect. But some of this work is also practical; it is intended to earn money and freedom, to free the women in the novel, and Walker herself, from the 'calamities' which oppressed the women before her. However much the novel *The Color Purple* may be criticized for certain aspects of its representations, it stands as a valuable testament to the writing of women, real and fictional, black and white.

Further Reading

Baker, H. A., *Workings of the Spirit: The Poetics of Afro-American Women's Writing*, The University of Chicago Press, 1991.

Braxton, J.M. and McLaughlin, A.N. (eds) *Wild Women in the Whirlwind: Afro-American Culture and the Contemporary Literary Renaissance*, Rutgers University Press, 1990.

Davis, A., *Women, Culture and Politics*, Random House, 1984 and The Women's Press, 1990.

Kaplan, C., 'Keeping the color in *The Color Purple*', in *Sea Changes: Essays on Culture and Feminism*, Verso, 1986.

Morrison, T., *Playing in the Dark: Whiteness and the Literary Imagination*, Harvard University Press, 1992.

Shockley, A.A., *Afro-American Women Writers 1746–1933: An Anthology and Critical Guide*, G.K. Hall and Co., 1988.

Walker, A., *In Search of our Mother's Gardens: Womanist Prose*, The Women's Press, 1984.

Wisker, G., *Black Women's Writing*, Macmillan, 1993.

Gender and drama, text and performance

by Lizbeth Goodman, with J. Ellen Gainor

Gender and drama

Different stages: suffrage drama and women's rights

The struggle for the vote for women was fought for many years in the United States alongside the Civil Rights Movement. Soujourner Truth's words were often cited as a parallel between the situations of women and African-Americans in their disfranchized status: 'if colored men get their rights and not colored women theirs, you see the colored men will be masters over the women and it will be just as bad as it was before' (quoted in Tuttle, *The Encyclopaedia of Feminism*, 1987, p.369).

The women's suffrage period produced a number of plays both in the United States and in England. The American suffrage movement is generally considered to have begun in 1848, when a movement was passed at the first women's rights convention at Seneca Falls: 'That it is the duty of the women of this country to secure to themselves their sacred right to the elected franchise'. Lobbying of many kinds – including a significant number of 'suffrage plays' staged in public forums – was conducted from 1848 until 1878, when the Anthony Amendment to the US Constitution was first brought to Congress. This was named after its main advocate, the suffrage crusader Susan B. Anthony (1820–1906). She and Elizabeth Cady Stanton co-founded the National Woman Suffrage Association (NWSA), which later became the League of Women Voters, an association that still exists. In 1878 however, the Anthony amendment was blocked and at every subsequent Congressional Session right up until the 26 August 1920, when the Amendment was finally ratified.

In England, the suffrage movement began later, on 7 June 1876, when Emily Davies and Elizabeth Garrett, on behalf of the Kensington Society and 1,499 women, wrote a petition for women's enfranchizement. The English philosopher and social reformer John Stuart Mill agreed to present it to Parliament. Many more petitions followed and various women's suffrage societies formed across the country; amongst the movement's leaders were Millicent Fawcett and later Emmeline Pankhurst. Many political demonstrations were held and suffrage plays staged, including Elizabeth Robin's *How The Vote Was Won*. The Electoral Reform Bill was not passed until January 1918 and that granted the right to vote only to women aged thirty and over. It was not until 1928 that women gained equality in voting rights.

The different dates and durations of the suffrage eras in the United States and England suggest that the intersection of 'multiple jeopardy', or the prejudices against both women and black people, influenced the slower rate of acceptance of suffrage in the United States.

Figure 36   Suffragettes parading in front of the House of Commons, London, 1912. Hulton Deutsch Collection.

The plays of the two separate suffrage movements (in England and the United States) together comprise a remarkable body of drama. (See, for instance, Barlow, *Plays by American Women,* 1985; Stowell, *A Stage of Their Own* 1992; and Spender and Hayman, *How the Vote Was Won and Other Suffragette Plays,* 1985.) Suffrage era drama, taken as a whole, was a precursor or 'first wave' of modern feminist drama, followed in the 1960s and 1970s by the 'second wave', when the modern Women's Liberation Movement influenced the production of 'issue' plays and political consciousness-raising. Here we will consider the impact of the suffrage era on plays and performances by women.

The play we'll study in this chapter, *Trifles,* was written by the American author Susan Glaspell. First produced in 1916, *Trifles* was written at the end of the American suffrage movement, but is not itself a 'suffrage play', in that it is not overtly concerned with women's right to vote. The play and Glaspell's choice of themes, issues and style can, however, be seen to have been influenced in part by the dramatic developments of the suffrage era. The play deals with the major theme of communication between the sexes; it asks the audience to recognize women's and men's different expectations, different rights and different ways of supporting each other, both within and outside the law.

Before we can make sense of this or any given play, we need to acquire a basic vocabulary of terms for discussing plays, as texts and as performances.

Drama, theatre and performance

Drama is the form of literature written for performance. The standard drama text is the play and the standard form of literary critical analysis of play texts is called 'dramatic criticism'. Of course, the term 'drama' is also used in a more general way, to refer to one of the three major literary genres (along with prose fiction and poetry). Because the term 'drama' has a generic and a precise meaning, it is most useful to use more specific terms such as 'theatre' and 'performance' when referring to various aspects of the staging of plays. Dramaturgy is the process of interpreting play texts for their conceptual, visual and performance possibilities.

Theatre is the forum where plays are performed; it is a broad term which includes the physical space for performance: the venue, composed of the stage, the area reserved for the audience and the backstage area. The word 'theatre' is often used to refer to plays in performance, largely because play texts are most often performed on stages, in theatres. Theatre studies – as opposed to dramatic criticism – tends to pay particular attention to considerations such as the space in which a drama text is performed, the cultural context and economics of production, the role of the audience interpreting that text and the effects of lights, costumes, sets and props on the reception and interpretation of any play or performance.

Performance is an even broader term. A 'performance' differs from a 'play'. The play is the text, which may be performed. The 'performance' is the new entity that is created when the words of the play text are directed, acted and interpreted in three dimensions on stage, or for audio (sound only) productions. Each time a play is performed, the resulting 'performance' is unique – influenced by the size and constitution of the audience, the actors' success or failure in delivering their lines and realizing their parts on any given night and many other factors.

A **production** is the set of performances comprising one 'run' of a play: one director's choice of casting and interpretation, enhanced by the chosen designer's setting and the input which the selected group of actors – the cast – make to the interpretative process of performing.

Of course, these three terms – drama, theatre, performance – and the fourth term 'production', overlap and inform each other to a great extent. But it is helpful to remember the basic distinction when considering the development of women's plays and plays by women. In all three of the plays discussed in this book – two by women and one by a man – the performance of gender roles is highlighted within the play texts as being of special significance to the characters. Women in all three plays are aware of their roles in society, of their actions and reactions as 'performances' within certain sets of social norms and gender stereotypes.

It is easier to analyse words on a page without reference to the complicating factors of performance. To analyse a speech from a play out of context is to engage in literary criticism (as we did with the brief extracts cited in Chapter One from plays by Sarah Daniels, David Hare and Timberlake Wertenbaker). But we could engage in that 'literary critical' process only with brief extracts and even then our sample discussion began very quickly to look outward towards the context of the scenes and the audience – we were moving towards consideration of theatre studies and performance, as well as drama. But in this and the following two chapters, we'll engage in a study of plays and their performance contexts: that is, we'll reach beyond treatment of plays as 'literature' and even 'drama', to consider the social and performance impact of each.

So, we'll engage instead in an imaginative game of visualizing the play in performance, trying as we read to 'see' the play in a possible theatre space. We'll also consider the uses of space and body language readable between the lines of any play. Such alternative forms of communication are often indicated by a particular form of written language within the play's script: the 'stage direction', or indication provided by the author of the movement of actors, the setting, the mood or tone in which lines are delivered.

As readers of the text, we'll need to think carefully about how characters move and don't move. In particular, we'll be considering the different ways in which female and male characters in *Trifles* feel free to move in the domestic spaces of the house and in relation to each other. Relationships between characters and their ways of moving often reveal hidden relationships of gender and power. If we read stage directions carefully and imagine the play as performed, we can read between the lines and begin to see the whole play, in an approximation of what a performance might provide. Later, we'll consider the significance of movement across space in the play as a whole. First, let's consider one piece of information that the author of this play provides.

Look at the opening of *Trifles*. You'll notice that even before the description of the scene, the author provides a list of characters (the 'dramatis personae'). What do you notice about the names provided?

Figure 37   Susan Glaspell. Harvard Theatre
Collection.

Having read with 'gender on the agenda' throughout this book, I hope you will have noticed that of the five characters listed, only three are given first names. These are the men. The women are provided only with the names of their husbands. Of course, in many societies women lose their pre-marital names, usually to take their husband's surname on marriage. Glaspell is, at one level, merely following convention when she lists the two female characters without names of their own. But she is also commenting on an aspect of gender and language, which becomes a central theme of the play. As we read the play in detail later, we'll see that the female characters *do* have names of their own and that the revelation of these names becomes important to their understanding of each other, their connection to each other and to women more generally. ∎

Before moving on to the play itself, it is important to remember that the visualization process in which we'll engage will be different for each of us. Some will picture particular actors and others will picture people they know, or perhaps make up faces to match character types. And, I would argue, our own positions with regard to gender (and class and race) will also affect our ways of imagining and interpreting characters.

So, the study of gender and performance can be extended to the 'stage' of our own lives, wherein we all encounter gendered images every day: in television advertisements, billboard campaigns and magazines. Images of women have long been used as visual 'signs' or symbols that rely on stereotypes of female and male gender roles in order to communicate messages. Some communicate traditional messages about women's place in the home, others deliberately subvert such stereotypes. **Is Figure 38, a First World War poster, subversive in this way?**

D i s c u s s i o n

The image of a woman smiling out to the camera (or viewer) wearing male clothing and saying 'Gee!! I wish I were a man ... I'd Join the Navy' is obviously not intended to encourage women to cross-dress or undergo sex changes, nor even to enlist in the navy. One way of reading the image might be to see it as intended within a mainstream heterosexual social context to entice men to join the navy, by implying that it's a sexy thing to do to impress 'the ladies'. (For gay and lesbian viewers of the same image, the implications and range of possible meanings would differ significantly.) Another might be that it reminds male viewers that they are privileged and that their position is enviable (at a time when it might not always have seemed so). Either way, though the image of a female sailor might appear novel for the period, the meanings readable from the image are rather traditional. ∎

So, images of women can be 'read' as 'sign systems', where images represent and suggest many other images and associations. It is these kinds of 'sign systems' upon which drama, or more precisely theatre and

Figure 38 'Gee!! I wish I were a man ...'
United States Navy recruiting poster designed
by Howard Chandler Christy. Imperial War
Museum, London.

performance rely. (Elaine Aston and George Savona offer a much more sophisticated and theoretical framework for analysing theatrical sign systems, or the 'semiotics' of drama, theatre and performance, in *Theatre as Sign System*, 1993.) Costumes signal character-types, single chairs or tables may represent the furniture of an entire household and each hat or chair can also signal the age and class status of its owner. Names are also 'signs' or shorthand identifiers of character-type and status. In the line describing the 'setting' of the play *Trifles* for instance, Glaspell describes 'the abandoned farmhouse of John Wright', not mentioning his wife. We see that Glaspell refers to ownership of the house and the power structures within the house, in her conscious choice language. Glaspell's play *Trifles* operates theatrically by juxtaposing visual sign systems – particular images – with textual or linguistic signs: the language of the play creates images and ideas that require your participation as the play's 'audience'. We'll explore the visual and linguistic 'signs' of the play throughout this chapter.

Susan Glaspell's Trifles: *a case in point*

Susan Glaspell's *Trifles* is arguably one of the most skilfully written one-act plays by any writer (female or male), in any language. The rest of this chapter considers *Trifles*, reprinted in Part Two of this book. Please now read the play. **Write out a brief summary of the setting and action of the play and make a list of all the characters.**

D i s c u s s i o n

The setting of the play is explicit: the kitchen in the now abandoned farmhouse of John Wright. Yet this description is not as clear as it seems to be. Where is this farmhouse and when does the play take place? This kind of information is usually included by playwrights, and the fact that Glaspell chose not to provide it is important, a significant absence.

The briefest summary of the action might read as follows:

> A set of characters converge at an abandoned farmhouse, to investigate
> the murder of the owner, the farmer John Wright. Wright's wife Minnie
> is held in the county jail, accused of the murder. Wright had been
> found strangled in bed, and Minnie is the prime suspect. The men look
> for evidence of Mrs Wright's guilt, while the women discuss her
> emotional state. The men never find the evidence they need in order
> to convict her. The women discover a small but important piece of
> evidence, but they decide not to share it with the men.

Your list of characters probably looks like this:

> George Henderson, County Attorney; Henry Peters, Sheriff; Lewis
> Hale, a neighbouring farmer; Mrs Peters; Mrs Hale.

Indeed, this is the list of characters printed at the opening of the play. But you'll see that the characters mentioned in the plot summary and the list of characters in the play don't match. Two important characters never appear on the stage: Minnie and John Wright. Minnie does not appear in the play because she has been arrested while an investigation into the death of her husband takes place. So, the absence of two characters – one by death and one by incarceration – facilitates the story by bringing the rest of the characters together in the abandoned farmhouse. You may recognize the technique of absenting characters in order to bring others together, as it is now often used in the theatre, television and film. The television detective genre plays on the same rules: in popular mystery series, dead and missing bodies routinely attract the attention, and the presence, of all the other characters in any given episode. What is more – as in the play *Trifles* – the dead or missing characters are often the main topic of the other characters' conversations. ■

Many plays involve characters who do not appear: Shakespeare's *Hamlet* begins with the ghost of Hamlet's dead father. In Ibsen's *A Doll's House*, the main character Nora refers repeatedly to her sense of mistreatment by her absent father. Samuel Beckett's *Waiting for Godot* is the story, or 'non-story' (for it has no 'plot' or 'narrative') of two characters who wait for the arrival of a third character, 'Godot' or 'God', who never arrives. In Glaspell's day, the technique of centring the action of a play around a set of absent characters was not unique but was not yet commonplace; more importantly, it was highly unusual to develop a play as a mystery, or detective story. In this, *Trifles* can be seen as a forerunner to the stage mysteries of Agatha Christie. Indeed, *Trifles* is a detective story in dramatic form. It was also written as prose fiction, in a short story, 'A Jury of her Peers', printed in Part Two of this volume.

Read the short story now and compare it to the play version, *Trifles*. Ask yourself whether there are particular aspects of the use of language in the play which engage with your imagination in ways that compliment the 'detective' form of the story.

Discussion

Both the story and the play make for 'easy' reading – both are enjoyable, entertaining, engaging. Both call for some interaction with the text, in the sense that the element of mystery engages with the reader's imagination more directly than straightforward prose narrative wherein the author tells the reader everything s/he needs to know about the characters and the world of the story. But there are two aspects of the play version which demand more attention of me as I read and which therefore engage with my imagination in a particular way. First there is the way in which the language of the stage directions calls upon me to create the movements of the characters in my mind's eye. At the same time, the play seems to demand a designation of particular voices to the characters, to the extent that I try to hear the voice speaking when I read the play, although in the prose fiction version I'm happy enough to allow the narrator's voice to mediate for all the characters. These two aspects are not particular to the play *Trifles* and the story 'A Jury of her Peers'. In fact, the use of language to evoke action imagined in the mind of the reader is a central part of reading any play text, while the narrative style and voice perform very different functions in prose fiction. We'll look at some specific examples later in this chapter. But here, let's think back to our potted 'plot summary' and ask whether we can develop the outline of the story of *Trifles*, this time saying what's happening between the lines of the text as well as in the lines that the characters actually speak. ■

Let's start with something small: one word. **Skim the text of the play *Trifles* again, looking for the first instance of the word 'trifles'. Consider the meaning of the term for the men who use it and the women who hear it.**

Discussion

The first instance of the word 'trifles' in the play version is on page 362.

HALE Well, women are used to worrying over trifles.

In this line, Hale implies that the preserves that are the subject of this particular remark, are 'trifles': unimportant, frivolous or mundane details of life. Preserves are a metaphorically rich choice of subject for this particular complaint: preserves keep something of value from the summer (in this case, cherries) through the winter. The work that goes into making them is hot and laborious, but the 'fruit' of the labour is valued only after the fact. The men in this scene do not seem to be aware of the work that goes into the making of the preserves, nor the attention required to keep them from freezing and being spoiled. Yet this is not Hale's fault; he simply comments – innocently enough – to the effect that the women's concern over Mrs Wright and Mrs Wright's concern over her preserves, are somehow misplaced, out of proportion to the seriousness of the charge of murder. His is a 'rational' or 'reasonable' view, after all. Yet in considering Humpty Dumpty's view of Alice and Doctor John's view of the nameless narrator in Gilman's *The Yellow Wallpaper* in earlier chapters, we saw that female and male views of the 'reasonable' do not always match up. We may deduce – if we do some detective work of our own – that:

a   while Mr Hale does not seem to mean any harm by what he says and while his words may sound wise to the men, they nevertheless have a negative and condescending ring to the women's ears; whereas readers may also note that

b   Mrs Wright has been removed from her home by 'the law', so is not able to take care of her preserves or defend herself against the criticism of these men who have come uninvited into her house and therefore

c   Mrs Hale wants to defend Mrs Wright, as she does in the exchange that follows Hale's comment about 'trifles'. ■

If you read Hale's comment about 'trifles' in the context of the larger scene (pp.362–3), including the stage directions as well as the characters' actual speeches, what kind of textual or contextual evidence can you find about the relationship between Hale and Mrs Hale? Are the characters sympathetic, or is one or the other in some way unlikeable?

Discussion

A few lines after Hale refers to the preserves the County Attorney criticizes Mrs Wright's soiled kitchen roller-towels. He implies that she was a poor housewife; his tone suggests that this is a reflection on her character and perhaps on women in general. Mrs Hale defends Mrs Wright:

> MRS HALE There's a great deal of work to be done on a farm …

and several lines later:

> Those towels get dirty awful quick. Men's hands aren't always as clean as they might be.

You might argue that Mrs Hale's lines are more a reply to the County Attorney and men in general than to her husband in particular. We might come to the conclusion that the men, as a group, want to find the house in a particular domestic order, that they object when what they view as 'women's work' isn't done – though these are the same men who did not seem to know how much work goes into, for example, making preserves. By contrast, Mrs Hale recognizes the 'trifles' as important parts of a woman's life and is quick to defend Mrs Wright. The relationship between Hale and Mrs Hale does not seem at all strained. She does not seem resentful of him, nor he of her. Both are sympathetic characters in their own way. Glaspell depicts a basic misunderstanding or miscommunication between the sexes: these are good people who do not seem to speak the same language or to value work, emotions and words in quite the same way. It is this misunderstanding or miscommunication that fuels the play and the mystery at its centre. We'll return to this example in Part Three. ■

First, let's consider the unusual career of the writer, as described by J. Ellen Gainor.

Reading Trifles: *the signs of gender*

by J. Ellen Gainor

Playwright, novelist and short story writer Susan Glaspell has recently emerged from comparative literary obscurity, rediscovered by scholars interested in women writers, particularly those whose works evince an understanding of women's roles in society or whose sensibilities we might describe as being in some way 'feminist'. Most probably born on 1 July 1876, in Davenport, Iowa, Glaspell began her writing career as a newspaper columnist. She attended Drake University and after receiving her degree in 1899, worked for the *Des Moines Daily News* as a legislative reporter. She soon decided to devote herself exclusively to creative writing, quickly garnering a reputation as a short-story writer, then publishing her first novel in 1909. In 1913, she married George Cram ('Jig') Cook and the two decided to follow the migration to New York City of many emerging American writers and artists. They settled in the bohemian community of Greenwich Village.

In the summer of 1915, the couple visited the artists' colony of Provincetown, on Cape Cod in Massachusetts. There, they and their friends decided to stage informally some of their plays, and the Provincetown Players were born. Glaspell wrote 11 plays for the company, which began performing in Greenwich Village in 1916, although her work was soon produced by other theatres across the United States and abroad. In 1922, she and Cook, the director of the group, left New York to live in Greece, fulfilling his lifelong dream. Cook died unexpectedly in 1924 and Glaspell returned primarily to fiction writing following his death. In 1931, however, she received the Pulitzer Prize for her play *Alison's House*. She lived on Cape Cod for most of the remainder of her life, producing a series of novels and one last play. She died in 1948.

Glaspell's published account of how *Trifles* came to be has been widely quoted from her biography of Cook:

'Now Susan,' he [Cook] said to me, briskly, 'I have announced a play of yours for the next bill.'
　'But I have no play!'
　'Then you will have to sit down to-morrow and begin one.'
　I protested. I did not know how to write a play. I had never 'studied it.'

'Nonsense,' said Jig. 'You've got a stage, haven't you? ... What playwrights need is a stage ... their own stage.'

(*The Road to the Temple*, 1927, pp.196–7)

This dialogue smacks of condensed theatricalization. It conveys a strange aura of the backstage world of amateur theatre as it was later romanticized in Hollywood, mixed with the ideas of Virginia Woolf's *A Room of One's Own* (as if that text were directed at female playwrights). Glaspell wrote a different account of these events later in her life:

> I began writing plays because my husband ... forced me to. 'I have announced a play of yours for the next bill,' he told me, soon after we started The Provincetown Players. I didn't want my marriage to break up so I wrote *Trifles*.
>
> (Glaspell Papers, Berg Collection)

Taken together, these two narratives demonstrate clearly that Glaspell's play writing career was not originally her idea, regardless of her ultimate success as a dramatist. At the time of the composition of *Trifles*, Glaspell thought of herself primarily as a fiction writer, with three novels and numerous short stories to her credit. When urged to come up with a play, Glaspell used an idea she 'had meant to do ... as a short story' (*The Road to the Temple*, 1927, p.197), the plot derived from a murder trial she had covered as a young reporter in Iowa (see Ben-Zvi, 'Murder, She Wrote', 1992, pp.141–62). Glaspell remarked that 'the stage took it for its own' (*The Road to the Temple*, 1927, p.197), however, indicating the key transition to dramatic writing that occurred at this point in Glaspell's career. Regardless of Glaspell's own sense that her work as a dramatist interrupted her real vocation as a fiction writer, her comments on the creation of *Trifles* reveal the significant alteration in her artistic process that writing for the stage entailed. Although her work to that point had always included vivid detail to spur her readers' imagination, she now had to use her own imagination differently, envisioning real people and environments that she could translate theatrically for actors, directors and designers to recreate. Her description of the composition process details this struggle:

> So I went out on the wharf, sat alone on one of our wooden benches without a back, and looked a long time at that bare little stage. After a time the stage became a kitchen, – a kitchen there all by itself. I saw just where the stove was, the table, and the steps going upstairs. Then the door at the back opened, and people all bundled up came in – two or three men, I wasn't sure which, but sure enough about the two women, who hung back, reluctant to enter that kitchen ... I hurried in from the wharf to write down what I had seen. Whenever I got stuck, I would run across the street to the old wharf, sit in that leaning little theatre under which the sea sounded, until the play was ready to continue. Sometimes things written in my room would not form on the stage, and I must go home and cross them out.
>
> (Ibid., pp.196–7)

Glaspell wrote the play remarkably quickly and it was rehearsed and ready for production in Provincetown by 8 August 1916. Both she and her husband appeared in the first performance, Glaspell in the role of Mrs Hale and Cook as Mr Hale, the neighbouring farm couple. *Trifles* was first produced in New York by another Greenwich Village theatre company, the Washington Square Players, on a bill of one-act plays. Heywood Broun, an influential New York critic, reviewed the performance in the *New York Tribune*:

> 'Trifles' ... is the most noteworthy element of the bill. The play is a striking illustration of the effect which may be produced by a most uncommon method. It shows that indirection need not be denied to the playwright if only he is clever enough to handle this most difficult manner of telling a story for the stage. Playwrights of our day, and of a good many previous days for that matter, have gone ahead in the belief that an off-stage story is a poor story ... No direct statements are made for the benefit of the audience. Like the women, they must piece out the story by inference ... The story is brought to mind vividly enough to induce the audience to share the sympathy of the women for the wife and agree with them that the trifles which tell the story should not be revealed.
>
> It is impossible to give any idea of the effectiveness of the author's slow but steady method of building bit by bit ... 'Trifles' is one of the most absorbing things the Players have ever done.
>
> ('Best bill seen at the comedy', 1916, p.7)

Arthur Hornblow, the critic for *Theatre Magazine*, praised the drama as 'an ingenious study in feminine ability at inductive and deductive analysis by which two women through trifles bring out the motive for a murder ('Mr. Hornblow goes to the play, 1917, p.21).

What do you make of these reviews? What do they say about the way in which the play was received, about its structure and its appeal to different audiences at different levels of understanding? The reviews point to the two levels on which the play works: as an engrossing murder mystery and as a more personal study that allows audiences to discover, along with the characters, the hard realities of their lives. Widely regarded as Glaspell's best overall drama, *Trifles* has been repeatedly anthologized and produced, standing as an exemplar of the one-act play form in numerous studies of the genre. However, some of the broader critical regard for the play ironically derives from the fact that Glaspell subsequently followed her original intent and published the work in short story form within a year. 'A Jury of her Peers' appeared in *Every Week* on 5 March 1917 and was then republished in *The Best Short Stories of 1917*. Thus the fictional account probably had a significantly larger audience than the drama, which was not widely available until Glaspell published her collected drama to date, *Plays*, in 1920.

Comparing genres: short story and play

by J. Ellen Gainor

The critical analysis of this one Glaspell work (in two genres) totally outweighs commentary on all her other writing. Much of this analysis can be attributed to the rediscovery of 'A Jury of her Peers' in the 1970s by feminist critics committed to a re-examination of forgotten women writers. Mary Anne Ferguson's inclusion of the story in her extremely influential collection, *Images of Women in Literature* (1973), was central to this re-emergence of Glaspell, and the appearance of *Trifles* in Sandra Gilbert and Susan Gubar's *Norton Anthology of Literature by Women* (1985) helped redress the balance of Glaspell studies to promote consideration of her drama; Elaine Showalter has since considered Glaspell's *Trifles* alongside literature by Alcott, Dickinson, Plath, Walker and others in her study of *Tradition and Change in American Women's Writing* (1991). Although it is somewhat surprising that comparatively few scholars have considered other Glaspell works, the volume of feminist writing on this short story and one-act play attests to their power and deceptively complex creativity.

Given the early critical response to the drama, it is also surprising that few analysts have considered the work at length within the genre of detective fiction, although Karen F. Stein gestures in that direction. In her essay (contained in a theatrical reference work as influential in its field as Ferguson's), she calls the play 'an anomaly in the murder mystery genre, which is predominantly a masculine *tour de force*' ('The women's world of Glaspell's *Trifles*' in Chinoy and Jenkins, *Women in American Theatre*, 1981, p.251). As the following discussion will demonstrate, I believe Stein errs in both elements of this analysis. We now know that women are and have been popular as well as influential writers in the mystery form and *Trifles* indeed conforms to many elements of the genre, particularly in those written by women.

Furthermore, *Trifles* and 'A Jury of her Peers' have become benchmark texts for an astounding range of critical discussions. Feminist critics have hailed them for their realistic portrait of women's lives in patriarchal society. Literary critics marvel at Glaspell's compact and complex use of metaphor and imagery. And many scholars see them as pivotal works for the examination of the relationship between authorial (gender) identity and theme. Although the issue of 'women's dramaturgy' (whether there is a way of writing and directing theatre specific to women) is complicated and too extensive to discuss in this essay, it is worth noting that Glaspell's focus on women characters and women's perspectives – inverting the traditional pattern of the male point of view – distinguishes her work.

Detective work: Glaspell's form and intent in 'A Jury of her Peers' and Trifles

by J. Ellen Gainor

In an essay on the origins of detective novels in America, B.J. Rahn identifies two women, Anna Katharine Green (*The Leavenworth Case*, 1878) and Seeley Regester (*The Dead Letter*, 1867), as the authors of the first works in the category ('Seeley Regester: America's first detective novelist', 1988, p.49). Critics unanimously trace the development of detective stories to Edgar Allan Poe, whose 'Murders in the Rue Morgue' (1891) and other stories initially defined the mystery genre. Yet the later prominence of women in the field, as writers of both stories and novels, remains unique. The genre of detective fiction is 'read equally and heavily by both men and women and [is] perhaps the only one in which women have excelled as writers of a form *read regularly by men*' (Bargainnier, *Ten Women of Mystery*, 1981, p.2). In the introduction to his book, Bargainnier expands upon this phenomenon:

> For centuries there have been women writers of all sorts whose writings have been almost totally read by other women, but mystery writing is a unique area of popular fiction in the widespread success of women writers, the widespread use of women as important characters and the widespread occurrence of *male* readers.
>
> (Ibid., p.2)

Thus, for Glaspell, one of the keys to the success of *Trifles* and 'A Jury of her Peers' may well have been her choice of genre. Previously (and subsequently) known primarily for stories aimed at women readers, particularly within the subgenre of 'local color' (works detailing a specific, usually suburban or rural and often domestic milieu), Glaspell in these works of 1916–17 probably reached a more varied audience, yet maintained her women's focus and regional orientation by subtle and effective manipulation of the mystery genre's conventions.

Marilyn Stasio, in her analysis of the subgenres of detective fiction, identifies several that are dominated by women writers. The 'village mystery' and the 'historical mystery' are particularly relevant for Glaspell, as her Midwestern farming community setting and slightly distanced time frame establish *Trifles*/'Jury' within both categories. Central to the 'village mystery' is the setting 'in a self-contained society whose way of life is threatened by ... a major disruption of the social order' (Rader and Zettler, *The Sleuth and the Scholar*, p.70). The 'Historical Mystery, often misidentified as a romance,' is important for its female authors' 'extremely perceptive and meaningful social commentary' (Ibid., p.71). Glaspell's orchestration of the events within her play and story exemplifies both the fixed order of life within the farm environment and her view of the issues facing such communities and society overall.

In her study *Sisters in Crime* (1988), Maureen Reddy identifies several tenets of crime narratives by women as distinguished from those of men. She notes that 'in the most interesting mysteries' the solution to the crime often 'lies in character, with its revelation depending upon the investigation of personality and on the conjunction of the personal and the social' (p.5). Reddy, following such feminist theorists as Carol Gilligan and Nancy Chodorow, hypothesizes that

> a woman detective might read clues differently than a male detective would and that her relationship to the problem presented would differ from the male detective's. The detective, whether male or female, is primarily a reader, but a reader more than ordinarily sensitive to nuances of meaning and to implications.
>
> (Ibid., p.10)

Glaspell seems acutely aware of these aspects of her genre and highly sensitive to these gender differences. In fact, she makes the relationship between gender and deduction (or interpretation) a theme of the work and this has larger implications for society's systems of law and justice, all of which have been designed by men. She actively involves her audience in these issues, by constantly juxtaposing the male attempts at detection to the women's and repeatedly demonstrating that, although the audience might initially assume that the men would be superior detectives, this is not necessarily the case. The play neatly demonstrates Reddy's assertion that much fiction 'teaches everyone to read as men', but that there are 'some crime novels [that] teach us how to read as women by focusing on a female detective's thought processes' (Ibid., pp.12–13).

S.E. Sweeney expands this discussion into the area of narrative theory, pointing out that within the mystery genre, the reader and the act of reading are reflected in and by the text ('Locked rooms', in Walker and Frazer, *The Cunning Craft*, pp.12–13). Sweeney explains: 'The detective story ... dramatizes the act of narration ... In other words, the detective story reflects reading itself' (Ibid., p.7). Sweeney's choice of the verb 'dramatizes' unintentionally also explains the success of Glaspell's work in two distinct major genres, drama and fiction. While 'A Jury of her Peers' engages its armchair audience in issues of gender and reading, *Trifles* actively involves them in the detection process as well. It should thus come as no surprise that detection drama has had a long and successful presence in the theatre (see Carlson, *Deathtraps*, 1993).

Structurally and methodologically, there are many parallels – as well as some significant deviations – between Glaspell's work and the mainstays of the detection genre. Many critics of detective fiction point to Britain's Detection Club Oath (1928) as the elemental determinant for the genre:

> Do you promise that your Detectives shall well and truly detect the crimes presented to them, using those wits which it may please you to bestow upon them and not placing reliance on nor making use of Divine Revelation, Feminine Intuition, Mumbo-Jumbo, Jiggery-Pokery, Coincidence or the Act of God?
>
> (Brabazon, *Dorothy L. Sayers,* 1981, p.144)

Other critics, like Rahn, identify a more elaborate formula for the creation of mysteries, a nine-step schema that moves from the occurrence of a murder through the detection process to the denouement (or final unravelling of) a plot or complicated situation.

Does *Trifles* conform to the following schema?

1 A murder occurs within a closed environment – sometimes a locked room.

2 The police are called in to investigate the crime but remain baffled even after examining the circumstantial evidence and interviewing witnesses and suspects. They sometimes arrest an innocent person.

3 A gifted but eccentric amateur detective with encyclopaedic knowledge, intuitive insight and great capacity for deductive reasoning is consulted.

4 He then visits the scene of the crime, examines the physical evidence, conducts research, interviews the witnesses and suspects and forms a hypothesis using logical deduction to explain how the crime was committed – including means, motive and opportunity.

5 He tests his hypothesis by reconstructing the crime and confronting the villain – often the least likely suspect – in a dramatic climax.

6 The ending usually preserves the comic world view, because the culprit is apprehended and the moral and civil order restored.

7 The denouement includes a full explanation of any unanswered questions or obscure points of the mystery.

8 Of course, the balance of the tale is devoted to discovering who-done-it.

9 The sleuth is sometimes assisted by a trusted but less able friend who, in addition to performing minor tasks, may keep a written record of the case and later publish it.

('Seeley Regester' in Rader and Zettler, *Sleuth and the Scholar,* 1988, pp.49–50)

D i s c u s s i o n

On most parts of the schema, *Trifles* does conform. Although there is no firm evidence that Glaspell consciously set out to write in imitation of other works in the mystery genre, *Trifles*/'Jury' demonstrates such strong links to the form that comparison is warranted.

It seems most important, however, in terms of Glaspell's experimentation with form and gender, to analyse the moments of departure from the set formula outlined above. The first differences lie in elements 3 and 4. Rather than have the detection occur in two stages, with incompetent police consulting the detective(s) after their own process stalls, Glaspell has the official and amateur investigations happen simultaneously to highlight for the audience the limitations of the authority figures. Glaspell's men never learn what the women do because that would undermine the reversal of competence at the heart of the story. Both male and female readers must learn to see as the women do and realize that that kind of seeing is different from, and in this case superior to, the men's way. The fact that the secret stays with the women gives them the power and authority denied to the men in the story, although in the author's pedagogical strategy, the capacity to read and see as women do is conveyed to both sexes in the audience. Although the women in the play are amateurs, their knowledge is limited, unlike the usual detective(s). However, this limitation is turned to strength, as the knowledge of their 'women's sphere,' rather than the men's 'public sphere' is exactly what enables them to solve the mystery. Their identification with the absent

Minnie allows them to piece together the mystery, but that process is distinct from the 'feminine intuition' anathema to the Detection Club. Mrs Hale exclaims:

> I might' a' *known* she needed help! I tell you, it's *queer*, Mrs Peters. We live close together, and we live far apart. We all go through the same things – it's all just a different kind of the same thing! If it weren't – why do you and I *understand?* Why do we *know* – what we know this minute?

> (p.383)

The play version of this speech omits the last two sentences, but in performance the connection between the actresses should clearly establish this shared understanding for the audience. The fact that Glaspell makes the women realize their knowledge of Minnie's life and their own lives along with her audience is also key here, for that realization is the process of giving value to women and women's work that the drama celebrates.

Glaspell also revises aspects of elements 5 through 7. The 'world view' of the community – the patriarchal order – is exactly what is being questioned, not only by the women, but by the crime and its motives. Glaspell develops the resolution that that world view must be changed and though order will return to the community, we know that it will never be quite the same as it was before.

Glaspell's decision to make the criminal and victim both offstage characters means that no confrontation or confession can occur. Although the evidence seems to point unquestioningly to Minnie as the murderer, she never admits her guilt nor is the case resolved. The ending of the story suggests that Minnie will be released from jail for lack of motive and conclusive evidence, although what her life in the community or the community itself will be like remains unknown.

Thus Glaspell leaves us with a number of questions, although the play has a strong feel of narrative closure. This is because, for the women who act as amateur detectives, issues have been resolved. They have the answers to the questions they raise and they know much more about themselves and the world they inhabit. In other words, by making the drama more than a murder mystery *per se*, Glaspell has given herself the flexibility to use the detection genre as the springboard for a wider exploration of character and society. ■

Detective work and piece work: the quilt as metaphor

The key symbol connecting the women's concerns with their role as detectives is the unfinished quilt, the clue which also serves as the central metaphor for the play. One critic, Karen Alkalay-Gut, aptly describes the women's detection as quilt-making – piecing together the clues to the mystery ('A Jury of her Peers', 1984, p.2) – while another, Annette Kolodny, sees the character of Minnie herself (as well as the tattered clothes she wears) as 'a pieced quilt' ('Map for rereading', 1985). Elaine Showalter sees the quilt as 'a hieroglyphic or diary for these women who are skilled in its language' ('Piecing and writing' in Miller, *The Poetics of Gender*, 1986, pp.241–2). Thus, through the image of the quilt, the connection of detection and reading – particularly reading as women – has emerged as an important critical nexus for analysis of both story and play.

Two scholars, Judith Fetterley and Annette Kolodny, have figured the act of reading prominently in their analyses of Glaspell's story. For Kolodny, the entire piece functions on both a theoretical and narrative level: it demonstrates the process of 'reading' as women as well as providing the plot that necessitates this activity ('A map for rereading', 1985, p.56). For Fetterley, the story has even broader implications for women's place in society. She believes Glaspell's work demonstrates the dominant tendency for the patriarchy to ignore women's lives. The fact that the men cannot envision any significance to the women renders them incapable of solving the mystery. They are forced to invent a story that they can recognize as important because they are incapable of reading the true story of the women's lives ('Reading about reading' in Flynn and Schweickart, *Gendered Reading*, 1986, pp.147–8).

Fetterley explains Mrs Hale's and Mrs Peter's success simply: 'Women can read women's texts because they live women's lives' (Ibid., p.149) and she also clarifies the men's failure:

> It is not simply the case that men cannot recognize or read women's texts; it is, rather, that they will not ... For the men to find the clue that would convict Minnie ... they would have to confront the figure of John Wright.
>
> (Ibid.)

In other words, the men would have to recognize and acknowledge the male brutality that motivated the woman's response.

The sardonic humour of Minnie's having married 'Mr (W)right' (Gubar and Hedin, 'A jury of our peers', 1981, p.788) cannot mask the harsh reality of his treatment of her. One of the ironies of *Trifles*/'Jury' is that if she had had the companionship of other women, Minnie might not have generated these clues. The other, of course, is that the brutality of her husband compelled her to destroy any semblance of companionship she may have had. Her isolation, in fact, creates the context for the reading of her codes, particularly the quilt.

As Alkalay-Gut has noted, the distinction between 'quilting' and 'knotting' has great significance for the plot. Towards the middle of the play, Mrs Hale mentions that Minnie 'didn't even belong to the Ladies Aid,' as she 'couldn't do her part' (in terms of making financial contributions) and felt 'shabby' and therefore was incapable of enjoying the women's group (p.364). This information is strategic for the women's later discovery of Minnie's method of quilt-making. When they reveal that they 'think she was going to – knot it' (p.367), they are not only referring to their conclusion that Minnie indeed tied the knot that strangled her husband, but also to their understanding of her isolation:

> Patchworking is conceived as a collective activity, for although it is the individual woman who determines the pattern, collects, cuts the scraps,

and pieces them together, quilting work on an entire blanket is too arduous for one person. Minnie's patchwork would have been knotted and not quilted because knotting is easier and can be worked alone.

(Alkalay-Gut, 'A Jury of her Peers', 1984, p.8)

Another ironic element of the quilting image is its connotations for the Wright home. Physical as well as spiritual cold permeates the play; Mrs Hale's memory of John Wright prompts a 'shiver' as she describes him: 'Like a raw wind that gets to the bone' (p.366). Cold and hard, Wright seems unlikely to have been affected by the warmth of Minnie's quilting efforts; it is fitting that she would use the scraps of cloth initially intended for the quilt as coverings for the last bit of warmth in her life, her strangled canary. Given the absence of children in the household, despite Minnie's attempts to create a conducive home environment, one is tempted to cross gendered connotations to attribute the term 'frigid' to her husband.

While a great deal of critical attention has focused on Minnie and her kitchen, less has been said of John Wright and critics do not at all discuss the other key locus of attention in the play, the bedroom. Minnie has been widely identified as the first of Glaspell's 'absent centres' – female characters who never appear on stage but play important roles in the dramas. (See Dymkowski, 'On the edge: the plays of Susan Glaspell,' 1988, pp.91–105.) But John, too, is a significant yet absent male character (readers will note the connections to 'The Yellow Wallpaper').

Furthermore, in *Trifles*, Glaspell establishes a noteworthy 'absent setting,' the room in which the murder occurred and in which the male characters spend much of the time in the play. If the kitchen is coded as the

Figure 39 'A Quilting Bee in the Olden Time', engraving by D.W. Peirce. The Louisa May Alcott Memorial Association, Orchard House, Concord.

Figure 40   Straight furrow variation on the Log Cabin block quilt, 1860s.
Metropolitan Museum of Art, New York. Purchase, Eva Gebhard-Gourgaud
Foundation Gift and funds from various donors, 1974.

'women's sphere' then surely the bedroom must be thought of as the male
arena, a place of importance, as opposed to the locus of 'trifles.' The
bedroom is established, through opposition with the kitchen, as a place of
male interest and dominance, just as Wright must have controlled the
sexuality (or absence thereof) in his marriage. It is the room on top; the
kitchen lies underneath it. Glaspell's choice of keeping this an offstage
space – and the men's activities there hidden – reverses the invisibility of
women and their work in a male-dominated world.

Of course, from the pragmatic standpoint of theatre history, we know
that production limitations also curtailed Glaspell's realization of a setting.
At the Wharf Theater in Provincetown, where the play was first performed,
there would have been no possibility of anything other than a single,
simple set, with only some verbal suggestions to help the audience
envision the other rooms in the house. It is extremely significant, then, that
when Glaspell chose to rework the drama into its short-story form, she
opted to retain the single location, with no expansion of the narrative to
include depictions of the other rooms.

Texts in context: Trifles *in performance*

Glaspell's work evaluated

by J. Ellen Gainor

Glaspell's drama/story stands out as an exemplar for many issues central to women's studies and feminist criticism. *Trifles*/'Jury' has been the focus of numerous feminist analyses concerned with women's role(s) in society, the characterization of women and women's authorship in the late-Victorian and early Modern eras. Yet within the smaller world of Glaspell studies, there is some debate over Glaspell's position in the larger disciplines just described. In her biographical study *Susan Glaspell: Voices From the Heartland* (1983), Marcia Noe asserts that 'First and foremost, Susan Glaspell was not a feminist' (p.10). Rather, Noe accounts for Glaspell's creativity by identifying her as an 'idealist' (Ibid.), a rubric that must support all the various positions Glaspell seems to project through her writing. Thus Noe must be explaining *Trifles* having been 'written from a feminist point of view' (Ibid., p.33) under this name, despite the apparent contradiction these positions suggest.

Several issues emerge here that merit examination, not only for the analysis of *Trifles*, but for a grasp of Glaspell's work in general. Noe makes a strategic error by not seeing Glaspell's writing as a political act. In other words, she distinguishes Glaspell's writing from her other activities, such as her connection with the Federal Theater project (where she served as the Midwest Play Bureau Director from 1936–38), deeming only the latter 'political' (Ibid., pp.9–10). Others would suggest, however, that Glaspell chose her writing, particularly her drama, as her political venue. While it is true that she was not directly involved in the protest activities of her colleagues in Greenwich Village, the public presentation of her concerns in a widely viewed arena such as the theatre must be seen as a political act. Furthermore, it seems illogical to separate the political content of her writing from the act of writing itself, somehow emptying only the latter of its social import.

To call Glaspell a political dramatist is not, however, synonymous with her being a feminist playwright. While we may certainly concur with the critical appraisal of *Trifles*/'Jury' as works of great interest for feminist critics, still a closer examination of the work itself is warranted and consideration of Glaspell herself, as a feminist is in order. We now know that there are multiple 'feminisms' – multiple perspectives on women's lives and women's roles in a culture. Noe, for example, errs in not defining what she means by 'feminist.' By holding to an unspecified and probably narrow notion of the term, she may be misrepresenting the author. It is imperative to grasp such terms contextually, to understand what they mean in a given place and time for a given group of people. Although there are connections between Glaspell's moment and Noe's, it is not at all safe to assume that feminism for an American woman academic in the 1980s is the same as it was in Greenwich Village in the teens.

The issue of Glaspell's point of view in her writing merits similar scrutiny and raises interesting theoretical questions. *Trifles* clearly exemplifies the attempt to make readers and audiences perceive a situation from both the women's and men's perspectives, as opposed to the exclusively male perspective that feminist criticism has identified as the (former) norm. **But does redressing this balance qualify Glaspell as feminist? In other words, do Glaspell's attempts to present both sides of an argument qualify her as feminist? Is introducing the female perspective the strategic point for the definition, especially given her efforts to give both positions?**

D i s c u s s i o n

Although most critics would agree that *Trifles* privileges the women's view of the law and justice and ultimately shows its superiority to the men's (presciently anticipating recent legal debates in spousal murder cases when the wife is a victim of repeated abuse), Glaspell also fairly portrays both sides. ■

Rather than categorize only some of Glaspell's work as feminist – with *Trifles* as the clearest example – it may be more productive to see all Glaspell's dramaturgy as political and to consider that her concern with women is a strong – perhaps the strongest – element of her politics. Within socialist circles in that era, women's issues were one of many concerns, workers' issues theoretically being foremost. Glaspell's embracing of the former, rather than urban working-class or ethnicity issues, is a strategic point for positioning her dramaturgy, as well as her politics. It is important to remember, however, that the women's concerns she dramatizes never arise in a vacuum; they are always part of larger socio-political arenas. Thus *Trifles* stands as an outstanding example of the potential for resistant writing by a woman. Glaspell, understanding extremely well the politics of the American theatre and American fiction, chose to subvert from within. Our continued pleasure in her work derives from our ability to perceive how deftly she achieved her goal.

Re-evaluation through performance: space, speech and silence in Trifles

The division of space in the play is 'gendered'; the movement and conversation of the women in the kitchen is distinct from that of the men upstairs in the bedroom and outside the house. This gendering of space and movement is illustrative of a division of the private and public spheres. The men occupy higher spaces: upstairs and also in symbolic 'official' roles such as Sheriff and County Attorney, while the women occupy lower types of space: the kitchen and the role of 'wife'. Mrs Peters is even described as 'married to the law'. In defining gendered spaces in this way, Glaspell writes in a symbolic shorthand which designates power relations in this relationship and also in the theatre.

Let's return to the roller-towel incident discussed in Part One. This scene provides a very good example of the way in which the language of the play (unlike that of the short story version) indicates movement in space, associated with silent communication between characters. **In the exchange about the roller-towels and the frozen cherries (pp.362–3), is there a non-verbal form of communication – an important clue given by the stage directions – which supports the County Attorney's joking but serious accusation that Mrs Hale is 'loyal to her sex'?**

D i s c u s s i o n

On page 362, just after Hale describes the women's concerns as 'trifles', the stage direction reads:

(The two women move a little closer together.)

and a few lines later, another stage direction indicates that 'The women do not unbend … '. The women's movement and posture ('bent', together and rigid in a defensive body position-language) are both forms of language: a 'sign' in dramatic terms. Their physical movements and gestures demonstrate without spoken words that there is a bond developing between the two women on-stage (Mrs Hale and Mrs Peters) and the third woman who is not present to defend herself, Mrs Wright. The relationship between the women is something you'll want to watch out for throughout the play and will need to consider in Glaspell's language (in her authorial interventions in the stage directions), as well as in the lines and between the lines of the play. ■

Now, taking the idea of the different ways in which the female and male characters in the play define 'trifles' as a clue, can you construct the story of the play in more detail, taking account of what is not said by the characters, what they seem to know but don't tell each other and the way in which language and silence are used playfully by Glaspell?

D i s c u s s i o n

The entire play can be read as a 'playful' investigation into gendered language, speech and silence. A detailed reading of the play's 'plot summary' shows how this is so: three male characters engage in 'reasoned' argument about the lack of evidence to convict Mrs Wright. They move about the house and outside it looking for clues. Meanwhile, the wives of the Sheriff and the neighbouring farmer tidy up the house and collect items to take to Mrs Wright in jail. As they talk about Mrs Wright, they decide that she may have been very lonely, begin to identify with her and discover 'trifles' (small, seemingly unimportant) domestic details which suggest that Mrs Wright may indeed have killed her husband. The women talk in one part of the house while the men talk in another. When the conversations overlap, it seems that the men hear only 'trifles' or insignificance in what the women say. The references to 'quilting or knotting' are ridiculed and the apron is assumed to be 'not very dangerous', for instance. ('Knotting' is a term for a particular loose stitch in quilting; it can be done quickly and is often 'finished' at a later stage with more measured stitches.) But in context, the method of quilting and the uneven stitching offer the women a major piece of evidence and the piece of silk hides the missing clue of the dead canary – the most important piece of evidence. ∎

What is the function of the apron in the play? In particular, what does it mean when Mrs Hale comments that she might take the apron to the jail, as it might make Mrs Wright feel more 'natural' – in what sense could wearing an apron possibly be more 'natural' than not wearing one?

Discussion

The apron, first mentioned on page 361 functions as a 'sign' to the women about Mrs Wright's personality. Since she has asked for it to be brought to her in jail, they infer that Mrs Wright must be domestic, tidy and concerned to have her personal items about her. The women interpret this as a positive sign, something they can understand and sympathize with. In this sense, wearing an apron was 'natural' for all the women – so much a part of their domestic routine that they may have felt 'naked', or at least 'not themselves' without one. ∎

But the apron can also serve another, more sinister, function later in the play. It can have a second 'significance' as well. In the making of the audio version of the play, we decided to give a double meaning to the 'sign' or symbolic function of the apron by allowing it to be a useful item of clothing for a busy woman and also the garment in which the dead bird is hidden (the major clue). Mrs Peters truly transcends her role as 'married to the law' when she allows the two functions of the apron to come together.

Now let's consider the development of one of the play's central ideas: that women and men may value emotions and events differently. **Can you find four major instances in the play when women's experiences and language are depreciated or joked about by the men? Consider the development of these instances and their impact on the mood of the play – does each instance carry the same weight, or do they build in some way, develop a cumulative effect or pattern?**

Discussion

The first instance is contained in the reference to 'trifles' already discussed at length. When we first encounter this idea, it may seem amusing, or at least inoffensive. The second instance occurs on page 365:

> COUNTY ATTORNEY They wonder if she was going to quilt it or just knot it!
> *(The men laugh; the women look abashed.)*

Here, the men imply that women's experience, activities and ways of expressing themselves – indeed their very language, their words – are 'trifling', unimportant, even ridiculous. Mrs Hales's reply is significant: both her words and her actions suggest her growing annoyance with the men's condescending attitude; she replies 'resentfully' and she smoothes out a block of the quilt as she speaks, using her hands in a form of body language which suggests her attempt to hide her annoyance. This small movement also has a much larger significance within the play. Had the men

202

not ridiculed the women at this point, Mrs Hale might not have been motivated to rip out the uneven stitching – a clue that, for the women, had seemed to implicate Minnie Wright – just a few lines later.

The third instance occurs on p.83:

COUNTY ATTORNEY *(As one turning from serious things to little pleasantries)* Well, ladies, have you decided whether she was going to quilt it or knot it?

Here again, the male character's joke undermines the importance of the women's activities and words. But it also adds fuel to the growing fire of irritation which inspires the women's mood of complicity with the accused: Minnie Wright. In my copy of the script – used in the audio production – I have written the word 'laugh' in the margin next to the County Attorney's line above. The first time he delivered the line it did not sound quite sarcastic or dismissive enough to warrant the defensive replies which follow from the two women (both their words and their actions in covering over evidence). The laugh added just the right note to lead into the next lines – yet the laugh is not a laugh of comedy, but rather an inflection in the actor's voice: the audio equivalent of a sarcastic sneer or dismissive shrug.

These three major incidents and many other minor examples weave in and out of the play like a refrain, until the fourth major incident wraps up all the clues into a neat package. This incident is the last line of the play:

MRS HALE *(Her hand against her pocket)* We call it – knot it, Mr. Henderson.

The hand over the pocket hides the missing piece of evidence for which the men search: the dead canary. Had the men listened for its song, appreciated the women's work and ways of speaking, perhaps they would have found that clue themselves, or at least the women would have been more inclined to share their discovery.

By tracing these four examples of the 'trifles' theme throughout the play, we can see that the entire play is riddled with clues to the developing sense of frustration felt by the women at the condescending attitude of the men. Tension builds subtly, forms a pattern of sorts, as the connection between the women grows with the unspoken as well as the spoken 'languages' of the play. ■

Now let's further consider the physical movement of the play in relation to its language. In order to do this we'll need to visualize the performance in our imaginations. If we consider differences between the short story version and the play, we can see that some of what a director might write into the margins of the script is already contained within the omniscient narration of the fiction. That is, the stage directions of the playwright do not go far enough to provide all the contextual clues necessary to an understanding of the story. The rest of that information is encoded in the performance itself. The actions of the characters, their inflections of voice, their movements on stage, all inform the play. All these 'theatrical languages' can be read for meaning, whereas in fiction, it is necessary to use more written words. If you compare the story and the play, you'll see that some scenes are considerably longer in the story.

For instance, look the paragraph beginning with the words, 'The sheriff's wife ...' (p.378). What does this paragraph tell you? How would the performance of this scene differ in a live theatre production and in an audio production?

Discussion

The paragraph in the story contains clues to the growing understanding between the two women and to their developing connection to the absent character Mrs Wright. It describes the location of the characters: the men who can be heard upstairs and the women downstairs, silent. It describes a significant glance passed between the two women. In that glance, the women communicate silently. Without saying so, they begin to see their connection to Minnie Wright: a connection which will later influence their (again unspoken) decision to hide the evidence which might implicate her. This glance, which might seem a 'trifle', is a major clue to the development of the story.

Similarly, on the next page of the story, Glaspell again describes the meeting of the women's eyes: 'Their eyes met – something flashed to life, passed between them; then, as if with an effort they seemed to pull away from each other' (p.379). And then: 'Again their eyes met – startled, questioning, apprehensive. For a moment neither spoke nor stirred. Then Mrs Hale, turning away, said brusquely: 'If they're going to find any evidence, I wish they'd be about it ... ' (p.380).

The same scenes in the play are not described in such detail: they must be performed before they can 'come to life' in any meaningful way. In an audio production, the developing understanding is even harder to convey: without the words on the page or the language of gesture visible in a stage performance, the director of an audio performance must find a way of bringing the words of the text to life so as to convey the significance of the look which passes between the women. In the audio version, the effect of a developing complicity between the women was achieved with sound. The actors playing Mrs Hale and Mrs Peters were instructed to alter their voices in order to suggest complicity: the additional performance direction written in the margin of my script reads simply: 'whisper'. ■

At other points in the play, however, more complex performance directions had to be provided for the actors in our audio version, in order to create a sense of stage space, without the actual visual space. For example, the setting of the scene at the beginning of the play: the director must imagine and delineate the space and indicate the locations of areas and items within the space. Is the closet near to the sink? Where is the stove located? Props that we do not see in an audio production, we may hear when they are used to create sound effects. Such props (jars of cherries, bird cages, quilts, sewing boxes) are important for another reason as well: when characters move across spaces to pick them up and put them down, the movements create pauses and silences in the performance. Such pauses and silences speak volumes – as in the silent glances exchanged between the women.

The sound of rubbing hands suggests the cold of the winter weather and also a sense of isolation (or a lack of 'cheerfulness') in this house. Footsteps can be used to create a sense of space and also to suggest character. The men have loud stomping boots, suggesting confidence of movement; the women enter later, more quietly, suggesting deference. The rising and falling of voices – created by directing actors to stretch away from a microphone, or to lean into one – can suggest moods and relationships between characters.

Finally, it's worth remembering that both the play *Trifles* and the story 'A Jury of her Peers' have been read and interpreted in this chapter as literary texts that have something significant to say about gender. The play has also been analysed as a 'text for performance' which plays with gender roles through spoken language and body language.

You may have noticed that two 'signs' or 'symbols' in *Trifles* have already featured in other literary texts we've studied: the quilt and the bird cage. How are these occurrences connected?

D i s c u s s i o n

Like the Lady of Shalott and the seamstress in Woolf's story, Mrs Wright is a woman who sews. Sewing is for her a form of work (she is poor and needs to mend things rather than buy or make new ones) and it is also, to some extent, a form of creativity or self expression, as Gainor's discussion of the function of quilting bees explains. You will recall that the quilt which Celie makes in *The Color Purple* is a gift of love and friendship, made of the pieces of many women's clothes and household items and you may also recall that Celie's financial independence is finally achieved through the honourable and creative work of sewing: of making 'folkspants'.

The metaphor for the caged bird has cropped up quite frequently: first in reference to Maya Angelou's autobiography (*I Know Why the Caged Bird Sings*) and then in Angus Calder's discussion of some nineteenth- and twentieth-century poets, including Emily Dickinson, as 'caged birds'. The canary first appeared in Woolf's story 'The New Dress': the offending garment is itself a shade of yellow and Mabel seems to compare herself to the canary in the cage at the seamstress's shop. In Gilman's description of *The Yellow Wallpaper*, the colour of the paper (yellow) is probably accidental, but the room's function as a kind of cage is not: though here we must rely on a metaphorical reading. In *Trifles*, the bird is a central part of the story, even though it never appears. The canary was the bird used to test the level of gas in coal mines (if the bird died, it was not safe for ponies or people). In *Trifles*, then, Minnie Wright is like the canary: she used to sing, but was trapped in the lonely house, cut off from her community and eventually suffocated – first by losing hope and her sense of her self and finally by putting herself in the position of possible incarceration by killing her husband. She is saved – or may be saved, as the ending is inconclusive – by the small, seemingly insignificant actions of other women who remove the evidence which might convict her. Nora in Ibsen's *A Doll's House* (another kind of cage) is described as a bird as well, as we shall see in Chapter Seven.

Women writers have indeed been aware of certain images and metaphors for the limits imposed on the freedom of women, in literature and life. I am, of course, reading 'signs' in fiction, engaging in the process of literary interpretation and the authors may not have intended those 'signs' to be read in those ways. Still, each reader interprets as part of the process of reading – and our 'gendered' perspective offers one way of interpreting images and ideas – not the only one, by any means, but an interesting way to approach literature. ■

Let's move on now to consider the emergence of a different set of images and ideas in a play by a man. When female characters are created by men, the representation of gender in performance opens up a whole new area of study. (This area is amply covered by the many available texts about gender relations in Shakespeare's plays and by the comprehensive coverage offered in Cima, *Performing Women*, 1993.) In Ibsen's play *A Doll's House*, a strong female character makes choices of her own.

Before moving on to the next chapter, please read *A Doll's House*. As you read, look for references to Nora in diminutive terms (as a bird, or a doll) and consider the visual implications for playing out these roles: what would Nora look like, how would she move her body, what would her voice sound like? Also consider the larger issue of language and power (recalling our discussion of those issues in Chapter Four), when the central male character uses language in ways which designate his position of authority or power within the play. Pay particular attention to Torvald, the main male character of the play, as well as to Nora and her friend Christine. Gender relations will be explored in relation to both women and men in the next chapter.

Further Reading

Alkalay-Gut, K. '"A Jury of her Peers": the importance of trifles', *Studies in Short Fiction* 21.1, Winter 1984, pp.1–9.

Fetterley, J. 'Reading about reading: 'A Jury of her Peers', 'The Murders in the Rue Morgue' and 'The Yellow Wallpaper', in Flynn and Schweickart (eds) (1986) *Gendered Reading: Essays on Readers, Texts and Contexts*, The Johns Hopkins University Press.

Kolodny, A. 'A map for rereading: gender and the interpretation of literary texts' in Showalter (ed.) (1985) *The New Feminist Criticisms: Essays on Women, Literature and Theory*, Pantheon Books, pp.46–62.

Noe, M. (1983) *Susan Glaspell: Voices from the Heartland*, Western Illinois University Press.

Showalter, E. 'Piecing and writing' in Miller (ed.) (1986) *The Poetics of Gender*, Columbia University Press, pp.222–47.

Stein, K.F. 'The women's world of Glaspell's *Trifles*', in Chinoy and Jenkins (eds) (1981) *Women in American Theatre*, Crown Publishers, pp.251–54.

New women in the theatre

by Richard Allen

A Doll's House was first performed in Copenhagen in 1879. In the next ten years there were a number of performances across Europe before it reached London in 1889. Wherever it was played it caused a sensation. The final offstage slam of the door attacked the certainty that marriage and the bond between mother and child were sacrosanct. In this chapter I want to acknowledge this radicalism but to argue that the play stands on a knife-edge: it slams the door on conventional ideas just as it contains and controls the idea of the 'new woman' in the theatre and in society more generally.

Figure 41   Emil Poulsen as Helmer and Betty Hennings as Nora in the first performance of *A Doll's House*, Royal Theatre, Copenhagen, December 21 1879. Reproduced by courtesy of Teatermuseet, Copenhagen.

Please read *A Doll's House* now if you have not already done so. (For this book we are using an anonymous translation from around 1900 republished by Dover Publications, 1992; page references are to that edition unless specified otherwise.)

Chapter Seven

Performing the opening scenes

For an actor beginning work on the opening scene of the play, that final slam of the door is very much in the future. What is at issue is how each character can be established on the stage. Perhaps the title will be a guide? In the hundred years since the first performance of *A Doll's House*, the title has become a kind of icon summing up women's situation in society and the family and focusing our attention on Nora (the same process seems to happen in the German translation, where the play is often known simply as *Nora*). Should the performance proclaim its feminism from the beginning? Or perhaps someone will go back to the original Norwegian title, *Et Dukkehjem*, which 'does not mean a house for dolls, which in Norwegian is *dukkehus*, or *dukkestue*. Before Ibsen, *et dukkehjem* was a small, cosy, neat home' (Törnqvist, *Ibsen: A Doll's House*, 1995, p.54). Should we see Torvald and Nora Helmers as caught in the same domestic dream?

How might the first exchange between Torvald and Nora pick up these possibilities?

D i s c u s s i o n

'Is it my little lark twittering out there?' (p.1) is a very difficult first line for Torvald; just how much is he addressing a woman and how much a kind of pet? Nora's response and the stage direction which accompanies it seem to suggest she hardly reacts to the words. This impression might be reinforced by the way Nora takes up his words to refer to herself later 'You haven't any idea how many expenses we skylarks and squirrels have' (p.4). The stage direction here is 'smiling quietly and happily'. So the scene might be played as a cosy domestic comedy. Even the little quarrel which breaks out over whether she is a spendthrift or not does not seem serious since it is only 'for a short time longer that there need be any struggle' (p.2). In this comedy the characters are equally close to nineteenth-century stereotypes: Nora is the epitome of the good housewife and mother, putting her energies into ensuring a successful Christmas, while Torvald seems the image of masculine responsibility. From this point of view Torvald's lark and squirrel references bring conventional ideas onto the stage; men should be established before marriage while women should be innocent and young. Even if the couple were the same age, they should play out their relationship in these quasi-father/daughter terms. But the exchange could be worked out differently. The scene might show that Nora is hardly through the door after some rushed Christmas shopping when Torvald asserts his self-satisfied superiority by belittling her with a childish nick-name. Her response could carry an undertone that asks who else Torvald thought it could be; her tone could then become increasingly irritated as she strains against the role of some household pet. ∎

What further scope is there in the opening scene for the actor playing Nora to develop her character? How could this scene be played?

Discussion

The sequence which builds up to Nora asking Torvald for money as a Christmas present could be developed to show Nora as a far from doll-like character. The stage direction requires Nora to toy with the buttons on Torvald's coat – this again might suggest that Nora acts like a child, but it is not necessarily an innocent moment. Using the 'prop' of the buttons, Nora's body language could 'speak' an erotic, seductive moment where she displays a sexual vitality (to be developed later in the tarantella and with Dr Rank). The scene might be played as a kind of suppressed struggle between the two characters where she aims to get her money without giving favours while Torvald expects some return for his money. Juliet Stephenson played up the sexuality of her 'little girl' role in the BBC TV production of 1991 directed by David Thacker (Figure 42). ■

Figure 42 Juliet Stephenson as Nora and Trevor Eve as Torvald in the BBC production of *A Doll's House*, directed by David Thacker, 21 November 1992, as part of the Performance series. Photo: © BBC.

These issues remain important in the next scene between Nora and Christine Linde. Is Nora to continue in some way to be the doll of the title, or are we to see her as awkwardly struggling against the confines of the cosy little house? In the first part of the scene (pp.6–10) there seems to be quite a strong parallel with her opening scene with Torvald. Mrs Linde becomes a kind of parent figure, describing herself as 'much, much older' (p.6), stroking Nora's hair in a way which is potentially companionate and parental, then shadowing Torvald in describing Nora as a spendthrift. She casts herself as the one who has had to work hard and portrays Nora as cosseted and useless. **When does this balance change and how might it be registered in performance?**

Discussion

Nora begins to turn the tables on Christine when she reveals to her friend and to the audience what she has done to save Torvald's life. The key stage direction here is 'Pulls her down on the sofa beside her' (p.10). The two women characters then begin to talk together in a different way and Nora's behaviour differs from the role she played with Torvald. The dialogue is at first more or less even, carrying forward our knowledge in a series of questions and answers, but eventually the balance shifts again. In working out the performance, the two actors have contrasting problems: the person playing Nora has to work out how to animate long speeches when the stage directions suggest she remains static on the sofa, while the person playing Christine has to manage the fact that her character is suddenly reduced to the simplest kind of interventions. Christine cannot, however, disappear from the stage – she must stay on the sofa in full view of the audience. The workshop production recorded by the BBC in association with this book shows how the sofa and Christine can form a structure which confines Nora. At the end of the scene, Nora is apparently given words that are positive and outgoing, 'it's a wonderful thing to be alive and be happy' (p.13), but she must struggle to make them sound genuinely so. ■

Figure 43   Janet Maw as Nora and Julie Covington as Christine in the BBC Open University workshop production of *A Doll's House*, directed by Tony Coe, 1995.

The 'new woman'

In the 1880s and 1890s a wave of feminist thinking and agitation – always fiercely contested – swept across Europe. A new, more independent, kind of woman seemed to many to be emerging; in Britain she was referred to as the 'new woman'. This phrase occurred increasingly regularly in discussions of the situation of women in Britain, though never in a neutral way. It might have come into the minds of members of the first audience of *A Doll's House* by the end of the scene between Nora and Mrs Linde in Act 1. **What is there in the scene that might have called up the phrase in either a positive or a negative sense?**

D i s c u s s i o n

Nora and Christine Linde have both earned and managed money and kept a family together without a man – this in particular makes them 'new women'. To some in the audience these signs of independence would have been very positive, but for others they may have seemed to be merely unconventional qualities that threatened the stability of patriarchal society. As a widow, Christine Linde's behaviour could be seen as excusable, but Nora's actions of borrowing money and managing the repayment simply pushes her husband to one side. This is just what makes her – for good and bad – a 'new woman'. In a period when 'votes for women' had not yet been won, Nora's story made contemporary audiences pause to reflect that women could act independently – could, for example, cast a vote secretly – beyond the knowledge and control of their husbands. The sensation caused by *A Doll's House* indicates the strength of feeling on both sides. For anyone supportive of rights for women, 'new' signified something good, an opening out of a new world order; to anyone with conservative views the word 'new' and indeed the whole phrase had a sarcastic tone. ■

Although Ibsen does not explicitly refer to the 'new woman' in *A Doll's House*, the term occurs as the subject and title of a roughly contemporary British play. This play, which is discussed in *The New Woman and Her Sisters: Feminism and Theatre 1850–1914* (1992) by Viv Gardner and Susan Rutherford, provides further evidence of the conflicting ideas about gender embodied in the term:

> Sydney Grundy's play, *The New Woman*, opened at the Comedy Theatre on 1 September 1894. The poster for the performance shows a rather severe young woman in black, pince-nez perched on her nose. On the wall behind her in a cabinet is a large latchkey, in the margins of the poster a smouldering cigarette. This image of the New Woman was instantly recognizable to the public at large in 1894 – the latchkey and the cigarette already infamous tokens of her 'advanced' nature ... The New Woman of the play's title is Mrs Sylvester, a married female of progressive views and conduct ... [she spends] her time with the play's hero, Gerald Cazenove, collaborating on another work of radical, sexual philosophy ... Three other members of the New Woman sisterhood are regular [visitors with] consequences for his masculinity ... These three women are variously referred to as 'Frankensteins', 'of a new gender' and 'badly in need of a husband' ... All four characters

are drawn with something more than general satirical intent. The play demonstrates an underlying hostility to the whole notion of the New Woman.

But, the authors note, there was a 'profound irony' in the participation of working actresses in Grundy's hostile portrayal:

> The women who played these roles were themselves, in many ways, New Women. Simply by working they were transgressing the social boundaries that required middle-class women to be dependent on either father, husband or brother. To be working on the stage doubled the offence and alienated these women from 'normal' female society.
>
> (pp.2–3)

In Rutherford and Gardner's account, the problem lay in the institution of the theatre itself. For actors of both sexes, the best way to exercise control over their work was through management; for those who were female this meant putting themselves under the control of male managers. But in the 1880s and 1890s, forms of alternative theatre emerged and 'at least two of the female cast of *The New Woman*', namely Alma Murray and Gertrude Warden, 'were associated with radical theatre experiments of the day':

> Alma Murray ... had played Portia with Irving at the Lyceum. More interestingly, in 1886 she had been involved with the Shelley Society's production of Shelley's banned play, *The Cenci* ... Murray became an associate of Shaw and played Raina in the première of *Arms and the Man* in Florence Farr's experimental theatre season at the Avenue in 1894 ... Gertrude Warden, who played Victoria Vivash [one of the 'new women' in the play] as 'a *garçon manqué*, who smokes and wears her hair short', was Mrs Linden [*sic*] in the first British production of *A Doll's House*. The part of Gerald's wife, the 'real woman', was taken by Winifred Emery, who was later to become a member of the Actresses' Franchise League. These actresses were conspicuously independent, creative women involved in politically and artistically progressive ventures, playing roles diametrically opposed to the reality of their own lives, roles that denigrated women who crossed conventional boundaries.
>
> (Ibid.)

Sometimes these women actors did become involved in producing and directing plays, but usually in connection with a new kind of privately sub-sidized experimental theatre rather than with major West End productions. The Free Theatre movement 'began in England with performances of Ibsen's plays':

> The most notable were Janet Achurch and Charles Carrington's *A Doll's House* (1889) and *Hedda Gabler* (1891), Florence Farr's production of *Rosmerholm* (1891) [etc.] ... Florence Farr ran an experimental season of plays at the Avenue Theatre in 1894, including plays by Todhunter, Shaw and Yeats. The venture was secretly funded by one of the most important theatre managers of the period, Annie Horniman, who went on to fund the Abbey Theatre in Dublin.
>
> (Ibid., pp.10–11)

1 **How does this historical information help us to understand the impact of the first performances of** *A Doll's House*?

2 **What does it tell us about the women who made a living, as it were, acting the 'new woman' on the stage? How does this information relate to the situation of Nora in** *A Doll's House*?

D i s c u s s i o n

1 This account reveals how different *A Doll's House* was from other plays being performed in London around 1890 and suggests the diversity of opinions available on how women should behave. Seeing Ibsen's plays as part of a feminist and experimental theatre project – as works to be performed outside the commercial theatre – helps us understand the reception given to them. The subject-matter challenged social convention and, as importantly, the actual performances themselves challenged the traditional male-controlled London theatre system.

2 The account suggests that when a woman like Gertrude Warden took part in a play like *The New Woman* she had to act a hostile stereotype of her real self. If, like Gertrude Warden, she was also able to act in plays like *A Doll's House*, her life in the theatre fell into two parts: playing a caricature of a woman in one kind of play and the new truth of women's lives in the other. Off stage her life might be said to have been marked by a similar duality; at times she had to behave in a way that would fit in with the demands of a generally male theatre management, while at other times she might be involved in 'free' women's theatre. There is a parallel here with Nora's situation: as a wife she sometimes has to act as if she is a squirrel or a skylark, at other times she has to take charge. Nora's situation can in turn cast a shadow on how we see the possibilities open to women actors like Gertrude Warden. For some it might have been possible to hold the two parts of their lives in balance, but for many the more independent part of their lives would be likely to be more suppressed – like Nora they might have had to play the doll parts for years. ■

For all the differences in subject-matter and style *The New Woman* and *A Doll's House* have a parallel: both are men's depictions of women's roles. The performance given by a woman in either play can be said to have been 'scripted' and 'produced' by a man (or men) at three different levels. First, the part of a wife is determined by her husband or her father on stage as in life (as part of Nora's character is determined by her father and then Torvald). Second, the possibilities and choices she faces as an actor arise within the institution of the theatre in which men dominate as producers. Third, the words that she speaks to express her woman's character are produced by a male imagination. In the case of *A Doll's House* these facts have a particularly importance. The problem of the new woman comes in the end to be the problem of Nora. In other words *A Doll's House* seems to set up the issue of the new woman – and gender generally – as an issue for and about woman. There is little sense on the surface that the problem of the new woman has anything to do with men. We will go on to question this idea and to see whether the play can be seen as a text in which we see enacted the problem of masculine identity.

This section has considered what the phrase 'new woman' meant in the period of the first performances of *A Doll's House*, particularly in England. An understanding of women's involvement in the theatre at this time throws light on Ibsen's play. It has also been suggested that there are continuities between the way women were involved (or not involved) in the management of the theatre and the actual parts they played. In both cases there are elements pulling in opposite directions – on the one hand working to control women and on the other to give them freedom.

Playing A Doll's House: *masculinity and misogyny*

Earlier chapters of this book have shown how the questions of gender and identity that women writers like Alcott and Gilman faced in their lives spill over into the questions of gender and femininity they write about. Perhaps Ibsen's writing about gender will involve questions of masculinity that somehow relate to his own life? Evidence that this might be the case comes in details of Ibsen's relationship with a woman called Laura Petersin and a series of incidents which seem to show the text shadowing the life as it does in 'The Yellow Wallpaper'. Ibsen first met Laura in 1871: 'they saw a good deal of each other ... he called her his "skylark" and encouraged her to write more' (the story is told in Meyer, *Henrik Ibsen,* 1992, pp.461–4). Their ways separated, however, and they did not meet again until 1876 when Ibsen learnt that Laura had married a man called Victor Kieler. Her husband had contracted tuberculosis, but it had been cured by a move to a warmer climate. Later, in 1878, Ibsen discovered that Laura had secretly obtained a loan to pay for the trip, 'the matter weighed on her mind and Ibsen noted sadly that his little skylark "could no longer sing her happy songs"' (Ibid., p.462). When they met in 1878 Laura asked Ibsen to help her to get a book published to avoid a crisis in her secret financial affairs; she could not repay the loan which was now due and the friend who had guaranteed it would be ruined if he became liable. At this point Ibsen himself took on the role he was to assign to Mrs Linde in the play, refusing the help with the book and insisting she tell her husband: 'he must take on his shoulders the sorrows and problems which now torment you' (Ibid., p.462). With no faith in the book or in Victor Kieler, Laura instead tried to solve things by forging a cheque, but this was discovered. Now she had to tell her husband the whole story. Her lack of faith in him turned out to be entirely correct; he ignored the fact that the whole business had been done for his sake, 'treated her like a criminal, told her she was unworthy to have charge of their children, and when she in consequence had a nervous breakdown, had her committed to a public asylum ... and demanded a separation' (Ibid., p.464). Only after her friends intervened, and very grudgingly, did he agree to her release and allow her to return to look after the children.

From this point of view the play seems like a rewriting of experience, but there is no evidence that Ibsen himself saw it in these terms. His written down thoughts have a much more abstract tone. In 1878, for example, he wrote some 'Notes for a Modern Tragedy' in his notebook: 'a woman cannot be herself in modern society. It is an exclusively male society, with laws made by men ... and judges who assess feminine conduct from a masculine standpoint' (Ibid., p.466). **How does Ibsen show this male society and this masculine viewpoint in** *A Doll's House*?

Discussion

Male society is represented through Torvald, Krogstad and Dr Rank. Together Torvald and Krogstad represent marriage, family and money – the principle means by which men control women. ■ **Dr Rank at first seems outside this masculine standpoint; how is his character built up?**

Discussion

The first references to Dr Rank show him to be almost part of the family – a close enough friend to be 'as a matter of course' (p.5) invited to Christmas dinner. What soon becomes clear is that Rank is dying of syphilis and that this is not the result of his own behaviour but has been inherited from his father. Syphilis was a common theme in the literature of the 1880s and 1890s, usually viewed as something hereditary; it features centrally in Ibsen's later play *Ghosts*. Literature tended to explain the infection according to the double standard of sexual behaviour then current: before marrying, men had sex with prostitutes who carried the disease and then passed syphilis on to their still-virgin wives. Every age seems to have a connection with a particular disease and syphilis often seems to be a metaphor for a pessimistic view prevalent in the period – destruction would not come through some sudden catastrophe but was a process being worked out gradually as generation succeeded generation. (Such ideas might make it seem that Dr Rank is a character very much tied to the original period of the play, but it might be possible to achieve similar effects in a production set in the twentieth century by translating syphilis into Aids, for example.) ■

How does Dr Rank fit into the play as a whole?

Discussion

Dr Rank has a particular importance as a confidant for both Torvald and Nora. The first scene between Nora and Torvald leads directly into the scene between Nora and Christine and a parallel one between Torvald and Rank which happens off stage. Relations between the two women on stage seem as intimate and as confidential as those between man and wife; perhaps we can infer something similar happening off stage. On both counts this would be entirely in accord with the situation in almost all Western European culture at the end of the nineteenth century, in which same sex relationships (often formed in adolescence) remained powerful throughout women's and men's lives. Such ties were often lived at a deeper level than the relationship between husband and wife (for examples of this amongst the British upper middle class see Hyam, *Empire and Sexuality*, 1990, p.38ff.). Publicly at least, the idea of a sexual element to these relationships was taboo. In contrast, there is an open sexual charge between Nora and Dr Rank in the scene in Act 2 (pp.37–42). When they speak of Rank's illness, Nora appears all innocence, suggesting that his illness comes from too many truffles and oysters, but only a few moments later the tone is quite different as she teases him with her flesh-coloured silk stockings and the prospect of a sight of her legs. His response – 'and what other nice things am I to be allowed to see?' – surely lacks any ambiguity. Dr Rank, Torvald and Nora are an emotional/erotic triangle, with the two men as rivals for the woman. The remainder of the play carries this rivalry along; in the tarantella scene in Act 2 Torvald appears to be the director of Nora's performance, but it is Rank who is playing when she dances most wildly. In Act 3, after the off-stage tarantella, we see Torvald's sexuality at its most aroused: 'when I watched the seductive figures of the tarantella my blood was on fire' (p.58), he cries as he pursues Nora. She tries to escape him; only the coincidence of his 'rival' Dr Rank knocking on the door breaks up the scene. ■

The triangle of Nora, Dr Rank and Torvald is important throughout the play, but at various times the relationships within the triangle shift. In Act 2, for example, Rank and Nora are established as parallel, with Torvald as a kind of centre. As Rank suffers because of his father's acts, so Nora seems to have been committed to the disastrous marriage to Torvald by her own father's treatment of her (p.66). In the scene between Nora and Dr Rank early in Act 2, he forecasts his own immediate death, while at the very end of the act Nora imagines her own death. In Act 3, during Rank's last appearance on the stage, the triangle reforms around him. Rank's last request is that Torvald give him a fine cigar, but there is then a kind of quiet tussle when Nora insists on being the one to light it and then demands that she receive her farewell in the same affectionate terms that Rank had used with Torvald.

The play uses the matter of the debt and Nora's saving Torvald's life to set up an exploration of how 'a woman cannot be herself in modern society'. **But does it also offer a way of exploring whether men – these 'judges who assess feminine conduct' – can be themselves?**

Discussion

The play provides scope for a performance which suggests that a gap exists – for men, as for women – between the real self and that which society expects. This idea can be developed through what we see of the sexuality of Dr Rank and Torvald in Acts 2 and 3. In the scene between Rank and Nora, his sexual desire focuses on Nora's silk stockings (p.39); she rouses Rank initially with the stockings and then 'hits him lightly on the ear' with them. In the language of psychoanalysis his desire depends on a fetish – 'a part of the body … or an inanimate object [i.e. underclothes] contiguous to the female genitalia' (Wright, *Feminism and Psychoanalysis*, 1992, p.114). And in psychoanalytic terms a relationship which operates through a fetish inevitably conceals its true nature. For Freud, the presence of a fetish signals that the man has within him an unresolved relationship with his mother; any boy has a 'fantasy of a hidden maternal omnipotence' (Ibid.), a sense that his mother is powerful enough to provide everything for him.

This belief is shattered when the boy realizes that his mother is not male and cannot be such a source of power in a patriarchal world. The loss of belief makes the child reject his mother. For some men this rejection, according to Freud, is transformed into 'the most primal form of misogyny, the "aversion, which is never absent in any fetishist, to the real female genitalia"' (Ibid., p.115; the author cites Freud's 1927 essay, 'Fetishism'). To see Rank as excited by the silk stockings is to see his desire for Nora as containing a strong misogynist streak under the playful surface. If this were the case, Rank's peculiarly mild reference to his father's part in catching the disease – what he calls his father's 'youthful amusements' (p.38) – would confirm his concurrence with (misogynistic) contemporary ways of thinking about syphilis. In cases of syphilis, as I have said, blame was apportioned to the women who infected men, rather than the men themselves or the men who infected those women. ■

My discussion here may have reminded you of the discussions earlier in the book of how red shoes can suggest gender and sexuality. **Can you think of another point in *A Doll's House* when an erotic relationship seems to turn on something like a fetish?**

D i s c u s s i o n

In being closely involved in male sexual desire, the dress Nora wears for the tarantella seems to have something of the same quality as the silk stockings. In retrospect we might notice how in Act 1 Torvald readily agrees to design the dress for Nora. More importantly, in the tarantella rehearsal – which leaves Torvald quite unsatisfied – we notice that she is wearing only an outer part of the dress, a shawl, rather than the whole thing. Torvald is only fully aroused when she wears the whole costume for the tarantella, and when he can show her off as a kind of dramatic 'turn'. Making the dance specifically a tarantella is significant in this context: the tarantella is a solo dance – a wild display – not something that can allow two people to express their love together. More importantly, the dance derives from the supposed behaviour of someone bitten by the deadly tarantula spider – an appropriate association since Nora is feeling suicidal when she dances. The effect, however, is ultimately misogynistic – to link erotic excitement with a woman's death. We see a softened form of this in Torvald's insistence on his rights as a husband in Act 3 – things come close to what we might today call rape (p.58). ■

Psychoanalytic thought (which, we should remember, was produced in just the kind of bourgeois culture that Ibsen depicts in his realistic plays) can again provide a pattern to what lies suppressed in the relationhips between Torvald, Rank and Nora. Freud and his co-workers saw growing up as involving the channelling and repressing of sexual desire and the erotic into forms and practices approved by society – especially heterosexuality leading to marriage. One of them in particular, Sandor Ferenczi, suggested that homoerotic desire often remained active for men even though society demanded it be suppressed. This desire is displaced into feelings and ways of behaving which are approved and accepted in society – into 'obsessively heterosexual' behaviour by men, for example. Ferenczi wrote 'I quite seriously believe that the men of today are one and all obsessively heterosexual as the result of this affective displacement; in order to free themselves from men, they become the slaves of women' (see Stanton, *Sandor Ferenczi*, 1990, p.121). **Ferenczi's view might seem sweeping, but can you see how it might describe how the characters of Torvald and Rank could be performed as embodying suppressed homo-erotic desires inadmissible in society?**

The text certainly enables both characters to be slaves to Nora and there are also signs of a strong bond of some sort between Torvald and Rank, so it is not difficult to see a degree of displacement here. Torvald's behaviour in Act 3 could be interpreted as obsessively heterosexual, both in his desire for Nora and his desire to hold on to his position in the heterosexual family. Nora's leaving is the principle threat to this, but remember that in much of the play her destiny is presented in parallel to that of Dr Rank. When Torvald hears of Rank's death we see first the deep feeling he has for his dead friend, but this is rapidly displaced into his feelings for Nora. Torvald says he 'can't think of him [Rank] as having gone out of their lives', but then shifts to a fantasy in which Nora is 'threatened by some great danger, so that I might risk my life's blood and everything for your sake' (p.60). Torvald's gendered identity and feelings are surely as much at issue as Nora's. ■

This section has argued that having gender in mind need not be equated solely with thinking about women's issues. Though patriarchy works by making masculinity appear the 'normal' state (as mankind slips into being a synonym for humankind) and femininity the 'problem', this is not something achieved easily and the stresses, tensions and prohibitions of the process show. I have suggested that the focus on the woman question in *A Doll's House* – which makes female gender identity problematic – also opens up questions about male gender. The play provides possibilities for performing male and female gender roles and exploring both in active comparison.

Playing A Doll's House: *femininity, power and the male gaze*

The tarantella scenes

In this section we shall look more closely at the character of Nora and the possibilities for performance there. First, continuing the idea that there are suppressed erotic and misogynistic elements in the play: **How much do we know about Nora? Does it seem that some possibilities for her have been suppressed by authorial choice?**

The play gives us a good deal of information about Nora; by the end we know her past in some detail, see her present dilemma and can understand her motives for her behaviour. The play sets things up so that whatever we think of her motives, beneath everything lie strongly admirable elements. She became embroiled in the debt to save her husband's life; when she thinks of the future she dwells on education. Generally her character has a serious cast even when she turns her life upside down in the last scene. What is largely absent from the themes of the plot is any sense of sexual threat to Nora. In stories and plays written around the same time as *A Doll's House,* the failure of a marriage would often be associated with some real or supposed infidelity by the woman. Nora's guilty secret is not an affair; there is no sexual element to her relation with Krogstad and no suggestion that the future involves her meeting anyone new. Her sexuality is expressed primarily with Dr Rank and in the tarantella scenes. ∎

We considered the tarantella scenes in the previous section from the point of view mostly of the men involved; **how significant are they for Nora's character and thus for the presentation of female identity in the play? Think particularly of the dance scene which happens on stage**.

D i s c u s s i o n

In a play that works mostly realistically and through conversation, the on-stage tarantella stands out as something different; this can make it extremely difficult to perform especially for the person playing Nora. While the actor playing Nora is dancing she cannot speak, but this does not mean the scene is silent about her situation or that she is entirely under the control of the men. On the contrary, in the tarantella dance Nora could be performing her own situation and that of women in general – her dance could speak as powerfully as spoken dialogue. The dance is to be performed as part of a fancy dress party, so it requires Nora to dress up and adopt a role, as well to perform certain movements. I suggested above that this could represent how she becomes a kind of object, here a mechanical doll, for Torvald and Rank. We could add that the playing of this role represents the way that in patriarchal society 'feminity' involves playing a series of roles – particularly those of daughter, wife, housewife and mother. These roles require the disguising of the self and the wearing of a costume; the traditional roles and costumes may be designed by men, but women also collude in their making. In the tarantella, Nora's role and costume are designed by Torvald, but as things get more out of control, it seems to be her driving things on. Nora's dancing becomes wilder and wilder; Torvald insists that she stop. She seems overwhelmed by the 'hysteria' that was seen by male medical knowledge in the nineteenth century as particularly the property of the female. ∎

In all these ways the scenes could project a critique of the way in which femininity is defined in society; even as she dances Nora is under the control of men. But the idea that Nora's performance ends up hysterical might have brought back to your mind the discussion about women and madness in Chapter 4. Juliet Mitchell there says, for example, that 'hysteria is the woman's simultaneous acceptance *and refusal* of the organization of sexuality under patriarchal capitalism' (p.116, my emphasis). In the same section Helen Small concludes that 'the madwoman' can be 'antithetical to Victorian ideals of femininity in a way that can be interpreted as feminist' (p.120). **Can these ideas help us understand how Nora's tarantella can be performed?**

Discussion

If the dance acts out women's role play in society, it can also be seen to represent her ability to refuse its constraints – the tarantella becomes as full of resistance to stereotypical images of women's behaviour as the scene between Nora and Mrs Linde. Looking back on that earlier scene, we may now see it as marked – like the tarantella – by an ambiguity; on the one hand Nora literally breaks the (man-made) law to borrow money and then appears to break a stereotype by managing finances and repaying the debt. On the other hand, saving money from her housekeeping to repay the debit fits in with a stereotype of the way a woman was expected to behave in a marriage, silently putting herself last. In the tarantella scene the emphasis is more on the physical and sexual. Nora is the object of Torvald and Dr Rank's male fantasies but the dance also enables her to act out an energetic and sexual self. Here, perhaps, Nora is manipulated to the point that she becomes hysterical and can bear it no longer – she has to get out. But perhaps the energy that she displays as she dances demonstrates a strength that will be fully expressed in the final scene when she again dominates the stage, reducing Torvald almost to the position of a bystander. We need to remember that there are two audiences for Nora's dancing: the two men on the stage and the public audience in the theatre. Any production of the scene is likely to put Nora at the centre of the stage, so we in the larger audience can either join in with the erotic excitement of the men on the stage or feel detached, responding more to the fact that she now dominates the stage. Finally, the style of the on-stage performance feeds into the playing of the scenes after the off-stage dance. Nora seems to put herself into Torvald's power, insisting that he 'coach' her 'up to the last minute' in the movements set for the dance (p.49). On the other hand she asserts her power, holding him in a kind of spell; he will only be 'free' after she has danced. A similar ambiguity surrounds the dance itself as it is reported. Torvald appears in control, 'An exit ought to be effective', he says, as any director might. Yet the player seems almost to have escaped the stage: Nora has been more 'realistic … than was strictly compatible with the limitations of art' (p.56). He in turn seems to avoid the limits of the aesthetic, asserting his own power over her by trying to force her to have sex. ■

Mother and children

The focus in the final scene is not on sexuality but on other aspects of Nora's self and her feminine identity. The play comes close to ending as it began, namely with the focus on Nora as a mother. To help understand the impact of this look again at Act 1; **how does Ibsen build our initial sense of Nora as a mother in Act 1?**

Discussion

The opening scene seems designed to show Nora as a good mother. Later, at the end of the scene with Mrs Linde, part of the delight in having enough money would be having the time to 'romp with the children' (p.13). The idea that Nora is a good mother – and that motherhood itself is a good thing – seems to be further developed in the scene where the children appear on the stage to play with their mother. Then, as the act draws towards its end, a darker moral tone is introduced into the issue when Torvald explains that a man who behaves like Krogstad has to live with a sense of guilt not only for his own fault but because he has contaminated his family – 'Each breath the children take is full of the germs of evil' (p.27). Torvald accidentally catches a raw nerve and Nora has a moment of panic. Almost immediately Torvald leaves the stage and the act comes to an end. The curtain falls on Nora, horrified, trying to defuse the possibility that the judgement can apply to her – 'it's *not* true ...' she cries (p.28). This completes the image we have of her as completely devoted to her children. Depending on the way that the words are spoken, Nora's final words may also engender a sense of foreboding for the audience. They might be performed assertively, to deny the possibility that she might corrupt her children, whatever Torvald says, or they might be performed with a tone of despair and horror, suggesting a futile attempt to deny what must come to pass. ■

A number of days seem to have passed between the end of Act 1 and the beginning of Act 2. In terms of theme, the action seems continuous since Act 2 opens with Nora talking to her maid. She speaks about her own children but also about the nursemaid's child who has been passed on to foster parents, as was the custom with those who came to nurse and often breastfeed the children of wealthier parents. **What effect does Ibsen's clear assertion of Nora's motherhood have on the final scene between Torvald and Nora?**

Discussion

The ending of the play seems constructed as a debate about Nora. On the one hand her duty to herself requires that she do whatever will enable her to be a 'reasonable human being' as opposed to the kind of woman she has been made, first by her father and then by Torvald; on the other hand she has a duty to be a 'wife and mother'. In some respects Ibsen seems to want the debate to be open, but the earlier images of Nora as a mother have a powerful influence. In retrospect the actual representation of the children on the stage is a charge of dynamite in the play, ready to explode beneath Nora's bid for freedom. We can hear the ticking of this bomb from Nora's first entry with the Christmas presents. ■

In fact, Ibsen was later forced to increase the amount of powder in the charge and even to detonate it, exploding any possibility of escape for Nora. A famous actress in Germany in 1880 announced she would play the part of Nora, but insisted that Nora should not slam the door on Torvald and her children. Social expectations regarding representations of gender demanded a new ending here, just as Louisa May Alcott was coerced into providing a happier ending for her adult novel *Moods* (see Chapter Three). Rather than have someone else savage his work, Ibsen wrote a new ending himself. In this 'happy' ending the children play a key part; sentiment is used to blackmail Nora and seal her fate. Torvald prevents her leaving with the melodramatic cry 'first you shall see your children for the last time'; he forces her to the door of the children's bedroom. Opening it, he follows through with 'Look, there they are asleep … Tomorrow, when they wake up and call for their mother, they will be – motherless'. Nora is made to repeat this word not once but twice, as she 'half sinks down by the door' and the curtain falls (for further details see Ibsen, *Four Major Plays*, 1981, pp.87–8). Ibsen's description of what he had done as a 'barbaric outrage' seems apt. But it is worth remembering that the new ending would not have worked if he had not sown the seeds for it by drawing the children on to the stage in the earlier scene.

Nora's fate

Please read the following extracts; the first comes from an interview given by Janet Achurch who played Nora in the first proper production of the play in 1889; the second, written by Ibsen himself in 1878, is a continuation of the *Notes for a Modern Tragedy* to which I referred earlier. **Do the extracts give us any clue as to how Nora's ambiguous fate can be understood?**

> [What will happen after the end of the play?] I think she will come back after a time and try again the experiment of living with Helmer. But it will fail. That man is impossible … She did right to leave him … [But what about the children?] I don't think that was right, but you should remember that it was partly for the sake of the children she went away. She felt herself so utterly unworthy of undertaking their education, and she left them with a very good nurse.
>
> (Egan, *Ibsen*, 1972, p.125)

> Moral conflict. Weighed down and confused by her trust in authority, [Nora] loses faith in her own morality, and in her fitness to bring up her children. Bitterness. A mother in modern society, like certain insects, retires and dies once she has done her duty by propagating the race. Love of life, of home, of husband and children and family. Now and then, as women do, she shrugs off her thoughts. Sudden anguish and fear return. Everything must be borne alone. The catastrophe approaches, mercilessly, inevitably. Despair, conflict, and defeat.
>
> (quoted in Meyer, *Ibsen*, 1992, p.466)

D i s c u s s i o n

Janet Achurch's comments seem to restate the ambiguity in different terms from the play. On the one hand she seems to agree with the ending – Torvald is 'impossible' – but on the other hand she seems to agree with Torvald's moral pronouncements at the end of Act 1 – Nora feels 'unworthy' of being a mother to the children. They show perhaps just how far the bond of mother and child was viewed in moral rather than simply emotional terms at the time that the play was first produced. Ibsen's comments share something of the same sentiments when he speaks of Nora losing 'faith in her own morality'. It suggests that the dominant note of the final scene should be that of a 'catastrophe'. This perhaps does allow a resolution of the dilemma I described. Nora is to be a tragic heroine, the equivalent of the tragic hero to be found in Shakespeare, a great character, like King Lear or Hamlet, at odds with the society in which he lives. Conventionally tragedy shows a character who, because of a single flaw, becomes involved in a plot which leads to his or her death. But at the end of the play the audience still feels such a character has greater stature than those – like Krogstad and, in particular, Mrs Linde – who compromise and survive. Seen in these terms Nora's departure from the stage is a kind of tragic death. ■

To see the events as tragic is to see them as noble – and making Nora an excellent mother early in the play contributes to this. But seeing Nora in these rather grand terms also has the effect of distancing her from the everyday. Beside this possibility, we can put another, which is closer to the realism of the play and which might link the attitudes represented in the play to Gilman's 'Yellow Wallpaper'. **Looking back to the discussion of Gilman's story in Chapter Four (pp.120–25), what seems particularly relevant to Ibsen's play?**

Discussion

Gilman's heroine is 'depicted as an intelligent and articulate woman who has been … asked to conform to a norm of "feminine" behaviour and domesticity that stifles her' (p.123). Nora – like a number of other Ibsen heroines – follows Gilman's heroine by implicitly rejecting the self-sacrificial archetype of the wife and mother. The unmistakable signs of individuality she shows could only strike other characters – and a considerable part of the audience – as mad, because the kind of future she demands for herself would have been seen – at the least – as 'odd or peculiar in so far as female individuality was literally unthinkable' (Velissariou, 'Mental illness and the problem of female identity in Ibsen' in Redmond, *Madness in Drama*, 1993, p.71).

We can sense this possibility in Ibsen's mind because he brings it onto the stage when he makes Torvald say in the final scene, 'You are ill, Nora; you are delirious; I almost think you are out of your mind' (p.69). Perhaps you will think Torvald is hardly a reliable judge at this point and that the audience would not take his comment seriously. But, equally, Torvald's plight might create sympathy in other parts of the audience. For these people, the hysteria Nora showed at the end of the tarantella has become delirium. One of the many derogatory comments on the first London performance may be unintentionally illuminating in this respect: the *Licensed Victuallers' Mirror* observed that 'seldom, outside a doctor's consulting room, have such candid and plain-spoken revelations been heard' (Egan, *Ibsen: The Critical Heritage,* 1972, p.105). ■

Ibsen's male gaze

I hope you will agree that the ending of *A Doll's House* can be seen in a number of different ways. It may be seen as demonstrating the problems of the new woman; as Nora's tragedy – her independent spirit broken by the constrictions of the world; or as the end of a case-history – Nora is afflicted by some medical disorder, subject to intermittent hysteria and delirium. All these seem to me to embody a 'male gaze' – that is, they are interpretations derived from a male point of view. If she is a new woman, she is some kind of freak; if she is a tragic heroine, she stands on an aesthetic or ethical pedestal; if she is a 'case history', she is as much on display as one of Charcot's patients. Along with this distancing of Nora from everyday reality goes a strong sense of contradiction. One critic has described Nora's situation like this:

> Ibsen's conviction [is] that women find themselves excluded from the
> social spheres of action, decision-making and power which are
> unquestionably men's territory. The tragic irony is that [his heroines]
> are equally subjected to the middle-class rhetoric of individuality
> proclaiming the individual's right to freedom, to which, however, they
> are denied access
>
> (Velissariou, 'Mental illness and the problem of female identity in
> Ibsen' in Redmond, *Madness in Drama*, 1993, p.80)

How does this help us create Nora's character and a mood for the ending of the play?

Discussion

The opening sentence seems quite straightforward, echoing as it does Ibsen's own words quoted earlier. The next sentence is a little more complex. It refers to the idea that middle-class values in the later nineteenth century included a strong sense that each person was an individual with particular rights. Ibsen certainly allows Nora to share in this set of ideas, building a strong sense of her individual identity right through to the final scene. We see this in her sense of her separateness from Torvald – 'You are not to feel yourself bound in the slightest way, any more than I shall. There must be freedom on both sides' (p.71) – and her confident sense that she can sort things out for herself. She says about religion 'when I am away from all this and am alone I will look into that too' (p.68). The audience sees nothing of the freedom behind the door, as I have said; Velissariou goes further to say that Nora herself is denied access to understanding that world. This means that while the play is tragic, it is also ironic. The play offers a possibility of individual freedom and takes that possibility away. ∎

Conclusion

How might the irony of this ending be brought out in performance? This may seem a complex question, but it is not too different from that we asked about the beginning of the first scene: how do the actors find a way of speaking and acting the text? Perhaps Nora needs to speak the lines that suggest she is on the verge of finding a new self in a much less certain and much more anxious way. Perhaps, too, more weight can be given to an exchange like:

> NORA ... I can't bear to think of it! I could tear myself into little bits!
>
> TORVALD I see, I see. An abyss has opened up between us ...

(p.70)

If this kind of exchange determines the style of the performance, how might the play develop?

D i s c u s s i o n

The actors might develop their movements to match the idea of a great violence behind the everyday language. Why not break the realistic convention to allow Nora a larger stage presence, with more dramatic gestures which allow her to hold the centre of the stage at other times? Why not also allow the actors an agitated kind of delivery in which speeches within the dialogue overlap to show the fragility of the relationship. Why not allow Nora's public tarantella to be shown using a back projection – giving it something of the same force, perhaps, as the Dance of the Seven Veils in Oscar Wilde's *Salome* of 1893. ∎

How might the setting of the play (the physical appearance of the stage and the period chosen for the sets and costumes) be used to make a similar point?

D i s c u s s i o n

Perhaps faithfully following the realistic sets described in Ibsen's stage directions prevents us from thinking about the freedoms lying beyond the door for Nora. Certainly one can easily imagine a production which distorted those realistic settings. Why not allow some sight of the inside of Torvald's study but represent it in some way as a place of stress – a room filled with anxiety, repression and potential violence rather than domestic normality? The set might be out of proportion to the actors. Making the furniture like doll's house furniture would emphasize the way that Nora and Torvald's feelings crash around in their bourgeois household. Making the domestic objects bigger – over-large and threatening – would emphasize that Nora and Torvald are trapped in this world. Edward Munch (1863–1944), the famous Norwegian painter of *The Scream*, did not produce designs for *A Doll's House*, but he did produce some for other plays which would express exactly this kind of disturbed and disturbing feeling. As witness of her escape from this world, Nora might then be given access to freedom at the end by leaving through a conventionally-sized door, while Torvald remains alone trying to continue the fantasy he has built and to which he clings, to escape the sense that

> [he has been] the doll all along. Torvald has regarded himself as the breadwinner ... When he discovers that it was Nora who sustained the family during the crucial months of his illness ... His whole concept of

Figure 44 Edvard Munch, stage design for Ibsen's *Ghosts* : Oswald, Mrs Alving, Pastor Manders and Engstrand, 1906, tempera on canvas, 60 x 102 cm. Sketch for production (never realised) by Max Reinhardt and his Kammerspieltheater in Berlin. Munch-Museet, Oslo Kommunes Kunstsamlinger M.1038 © 1995 BONO, Oslo, DACS, London.

himself has been shattered – a concept imposed upon him by society. He has unknowingly been the wife in the family.

> (Sprinchorn, 'Ibsen and the actors' in Durbach, *Ibsen and the Theatre*, 1980, p.122)

In these ways the doll's house becomes not simply a title for the play but a persisting symbol provoking the audience to thought. ∎

For myself I would turn my attention to the way Nora's children appear in the play. In the past, the scene in which they are on stage has been cut for purely practical reasons – having child actors available each night is not always easy. If the scene remains, I would want to suggest it was played in an exaggerated way – perhaps in an over-sentimental way – so that the audience is pushed back from the scene and understands its manipulative potential. Or again the children might appear in over-large projections to emphasize how they dominate Nora's (and other women's) gendered actions and feelings. A final possibility, perhaps to be used along with this last, requires simply the removal from the play of some twelve words (far fewer than are usually removed in most reverential modern productions of Shakespeare). Cutting the final words of the play would throw weight onto Nora's leaving. This may sound like violence to the text, but most productions inevitably make free with the text here because it presents such a problem to the actor playing Torvald. The stage direction instructs the actor that 'A hope flashes across his mind'. How is he to do this? How is he to know what his last words ('The most wonderful thing of all −') mean, when the text itself tails off before the end of the sentence? Why not simply allow Nora's flat 'Good-bye', the slam of the door and the fall of the curtain to comment on the possibility that the domestic world can be restored?

This chapter has taken a key text regularly described as one of the earliest feminist plays and attempted to unpick some of the complex ways in which issues of gender were involved in the original production and in the text itself. It has also explored the special possibilities the play text offers now for performing gender − for example, in its focus on role playing. We move in the next chapter to *Top Girls*, a twentieth-century play by one of Britain's leading playwrights, Caryl Churchill. *Top Girls* explores the world of women without reference to any male characters. Even so, it is also a play dealing with masculinity at some level, in the sense that the female characters live in a 'male' world and, like Nora, struggle to gain status and approval within it.

Further Reading

Egan, M. (ed.) (1972) *Ibsen: The Critical Heritage*, Routledge.

Gardner, V. and Rutherford, S. (1992) *The New Woman and Her Sisters: Feminism and Theatre 1850–1914*, Harvester Wheatsheaf.

Ibsen, H. (1981) *Four Major Plays*, translated by JW McFarlane and J Arup, Oxford University Press.

Meyer, M. (1992) *Ibsen*, Cardinal Books.

Sprinchorn, E. 'Ibsen and the actors' in Durbach (ed.) (1980) *Ibsen and the Theatre*, Macmillan.

Stanton, M. (1990) *Sandor Ferenczi: Reconsidering Active Intervention*, Free Association Books.

Törnqvist, Egil (1995) *Ibsen: A Doll's House*, Cambridge University Press.

Velissariou, A., 'Mental illness and the problem of female identity in Ibsen' in Redmond (ed.) (1993) *Themes in Drama*, vol. 15: *Madness in Drama*, Cambridge University Press.

Wright, E. (ed.) (1992) *Feminism and Psychoanalysis*, Blackwell.

Contemporary women's theatre: Top Girls

by Lizbeth Goodman, with Juli Thompson Burk

The texts studied in this book so far have offered insights into gender issues; most have also been relevant to discussion of the impact of feminist thought on literary study. But few of them could be called 'feminist texts'. The distinction between literature that can be read and interpreted as feminist, and literature that is intended by its author to be feminist, is a thorny issue. In this chapter we will explore it through close study of one contemporary playwright, Caryl Churchill, and her relationship to feminism and the theatre.

There are three main reasons why it can be difficult to label texts, or authors, as 'feminist':

1   the term has been defined differently from generation to generation, culture to culture;

2   modern usage tends to refer to inherently political texts, usually written by women, with the concerns of contemporary women on the agenda;

3   even texts which fit the definition above may not be intended by their authors to be 'feminist' or even 'political' – what we take from a text is partly a function of social context and partly a matter of individual interpretation.

For all these reasons, it is awkward to label much early writing (by women or men) as 'feminist', though we can say that texts, the ideas they convey and the characters they depict, offer insights into the situation of women and are illuminated by study with a contemporary feminist approach. To return to a term defined and discussed in the Introduction to this book, we can also say that some modern writers have written literature in the context of the 'feminist critical revolution'. The 'revolution' has influenced what we read and study today and has highlighted a number of themes and issues which recur with compelling frequency in the literature of women writers, past and present.

Uneasy alliances: Caryl Churchill and the feminist critical revolution

Where does the work of playwright Caryl Churchill sit in relation to the 'revolution'? This is a complex question, which we will address by reference to Churchill's career and statements about her work and then through analysis of one of her best known plays, *Top Girls*.

Caryl Churchill, born in London in 1938, is one of England's best-known and most respected contemporary playwrights. She began by writing short plays which were given small-scale productions when she was a student at Oxford University; this was followed by a period of writing radio plays when her three sons were small, and later by a number of stage

Figure 45   Caryl Churchill, from *Top Girls*, Open University/BBC video, 1995.
Photo: BBC.

productions for the London theatre. Her first big break was acceptance into
the small group of writers working at the Royal Court Theatre, which was
known in the 1960s and 1970s as the most radical venue for new work by
'angry young men' and a handful of women, including Churchill. This
period was influential for theatre generally, as well as for Churchill: 'From
1970 to 1985, new writing formed 12 per cent of all plays performed on the
main stage of London's and regional repertory theatres: between 1985 and
1990 this fell to 7 per cent' (Waugh, *Harvest of the Sixties*, 1995, p.200).
These statistics suggest that playwrights faced an uphill battle to get their
work produced towards the end of the twentieth century, when arts
funding was being cut by a Conservative government so that many
repertory theatres closed and many London theatres reverted to producing
plays with tried and tested success rates, including transfers from Broadway
and the revival of 'classics'. This trend, coupled with the increasing
popularity of cinema and home video in the period, added an element of
commercial pressure on playwrights to write plays likely to capture the
public imagination: a pressure which tended to mitigate against the success
of what were (and are) considered 'minority' areas of theatre, including
women's theatre. (The status of women in contemporary theatre has been
analysed in detail, in relation to the work of Churchill, Sarah Daniels,
Timberlake Wertenbaker and many other women mentioned in this book in
Goodman, *Contemporary Feminist Theatres*, 1993.)

Of course, the work of women represents only a small percentage of
new work produced, even at the 'radical' Royal Court. According to the

long-term Artistic Director at the Royal Court in the 1980s, Max Stafford-Clark, the percentage of plays by women rose from 8% in the 1970s to 30% in the 1980s: 'still not 50%, but a sizeable increase which reflects what was happening to women in the period' (Stafford-Clark interviewed by Lizbeth Goodman, 1995). The 1980s, as Stafford-Clark suggests, were years of rapid advancement for women in many areas of the business world, but one which saw little corresponding advancement in organized child-care systems or benefits for working mothers. In this climate the idea of the 'superwoman' emerged: one who excelled in all areas of life, public and private, professional and domestic – she was, perhaps, another version of the 'New Woman' discussed in Chapter Seven. But of course, real women suffered under the strain of the 'superwoman' image.

It was in the 1980s that Caryl Churchill, by then a successful playwright and mother of three, began a long-term collaboration with Max Stafford-Clark. They worked together on several of Churchill's plays, including the one which became known as her ultimate statement about women's status in the 1980s, *Top Girls*. (The quality of roles for women and women's status in contemporary theatre are discussed by a range of women in the theatre and by Max Stafford-Clark on a BBC audio-cassette produced in conjunction with this book. Many of these women speak for themselves in Goodman, *Feminist Stages*, 1996.)

Labels, intentions and theatrical impact

While the theme of *Top Girls* is a feminist one, Caryl Churchill herself does not embrace the word 'feminism'. Churchill, like many contemporary writers, has pointed out that the label is not necessarily liberating – it sometimes evokes a negative critical response, or can be a limiting categorization of work and ideas. Yet Churchill's work can be seen as strongly feminist. In fact, she has been widely recognized as a leading 'socialist feminist' playwright. While she would prefer her work to be read and produced for itself rather than for its politics, she does not deny its feminist impact.

Churchill's early experiences of working at the Royal Court can be seen to have influenced the style of her writing generally and also the theme of women's status in society (recurrent in many of her plays) in two ways. The Royal Court writers in the 1960s and 1970s were almost exclusively men, dedicated on the whole to social realist theatre. From the post-war period onwards, social realist theatre aimed to represent issues of concern in society, to offer characters at odds with that society and to challenge the increasing move towards capitalist economic and political systems. Churchill was greatly influenced by this school of thought. Her 'socialism' (her politics) is related but not identical to the 'social realist' techniques of many of her contemporaries, such as Arnold Wesker and John Osborne. Her work is not 'social realist'; it does not offer characters who you might expect to meet in real life, nor does it aim to produce a 'slice of life' on the stage. Rather, her socialism intersects with her views on the status of women in society and her theatre offers a unique mixture of 'realist' scenes with surreal exchanges between mythical, even fantastic, characters. *Top Girls* illustrates this point, as we shall see.

The theme of women's status in society is obviously influenced to some extent by Churchill's experience of writing as one of the only female members of the writers' group at the Royal Court during her formative years as a mainstream playwright. But she also perceived the isolation and survival strategies of women working in other professions. In her own words:

> I remember before I wrote *Top Girls* thinking about women barristers – and how they were in a minority and had to imitate men to succeed – and I was thinking of them as different from me. And then I thought, 'wait a minute, my whole concept of what plays might be is from plays written by men ...' And I remember long before that thinking of the 'maleness' of the traditional structure of plays, with conflict and building in a certain way to a climax. But it's not something I think about very often
>
> (Churchill quoted in Naismith, *Commentary and Notes to Caryl Churchill's* Top Girls, 1991, p.xxii)

1   What does it mean that women might have to 'imitate men to succeed'?

2   How might this perception have affected the development of Churchill's writing?

3   Why is it significant that Churchill points out that she does not often think about these issues?

Discussion

1   If women have to 'imitate men' to succeed, in the legal profession as in writing and all areas of professional or creative work, it may mean that a particularly 'female' way of working or of writing is stifled. It is a controversial question whether women and men are 'essentially' different in their ways of dealing with people, or whether we all learn to act gendered roles in society. But in this context, what Churchill identifies is a social positioning of women's experience as second rate, assuming that the 'right' way to succeed is to 'act like a man'. *Top Girls* is set in a very specific decade and political context: Britain in the 1980s. The tabloid press of the time frequently represented the Prime Minister, Margaret Thatcher, as a self-made career woman, the daughter of a grocer and mother of two, transformed into the ultimate symbol of the capitalist 'superwoman' politician. As we shall see, *Top Girls* features a character called Marlene, a symbol of the 1980s career woman, or 'superwoman' in Thatcher's Britain. The parallel between Margaret Thatcher and the character in the play is clear.

2   Churchill notes that she recognized that she was not different from the isolated female barristers she describes, but actually had a lot in common with them. In recognizing the similarities as well as the differences between her situation and those of other women, Churchill's statement positions her quite comfortably within a contemporary framework of feminist consciousness. Her comments about the structuring of plays also bear on our concern with gender. Many critics have argued that there is a 'female'

Figure 46   (left) Margaret Thatcher at the Conservative Party conference, 1980. Photo: BBC. (right) Lesley Manville as Marlene, from *Top Girls* in the 1991 production directed by Max Stafford-Clark, recorded for BBC television and included on an Open University/BBC video, 1995. Photo: BBC.

way of speaking, writing and reading, which is influenced by innate gender characteristics and/or by culturalization and learned gender roles. The work of French theorists Hélène Cixous, Luce Irigiray and Julia Kristeva was mentioned briefly in Chapter Three, with reference to the idea that women may have a distinct way of using language and of writing prose fiction. The theoretical ideas of these and other critics are too complex for the limited scope of this book, but it is important to pursue a few ideas briefly, as they will inform our subsequent reading of *Top Girls*. Churchill refers to her sudden realization that she writes plays in a tradition that has been defined and structured by male writers. When she makes this realization, she takes the first step towards seeing her own writing as having a different flow, a different pattern, a structure that is less linear, less concerned with building to a climax and more concerned with representing the rhythms of women's lives. Hélène Cixous's theories are apt here: she argues that women's writing is different from men's because women write with their bodies, so their writing has a rhythm closer to that of female sexual pleasure (Cixous, *The Newly Born Woman,* 1975). While Churchill's statement is not theorized, it does imply that she thinks about her writing as influenced by gender, even if she does not think of herself as a 'feminist writer'. *Top Girls*, as we shall see, is an example of a play without a traditional structure, which ebbs and flows from one time frame to another. In it women's voices rise and fall like waves, or like the strains of a musical composition. This kind of writing differs markedly from that offered in Ibsen's *A Doll's House*, for instance, where characters speak one at a time and where the plot builds to a climax followed by a dramatic resolution. Cixous would argue that this structure mimics the rhythm of male sexual pleasure. Another common way of viewing the difference is to see the non-linear pattern of Churchill's play and of much writing by women as closer to the typical structure of women's lives: often interrupted by child-rearing and housekeeping, so that both the overall life trajectory and the individual days which make it up will tend to be less linear, composed of repeated gestures and actions, more like a series of musical refrains than one grand opera.

3   Churchill does not see her role as the 'authority' on her own work. Indeed she prefers not to be interviewed, in part because spoken words take on an authority of their own when set in print. Still, we can see that the statement quoted says a great deal about Churchill's view of writing plays, as well as about her views on women's status and women's creativity. But it does so indirectly, in the context of a casual remark, so it is necessary to include Churchill's disclaimer in the last sentence, to remind readers of the informal status of her remarks. ■

If you have not already done so, stop now and read the opening scene of _Top Girls_.

Churchill on the origins of Top Girls

What follows is an extract from an interview in which Churchill agreed to put down on record the origins of the dinner party scene in _Top Girls_. **Can you see any way in which her comments support the idea that she writes in a non-linear, perhaps distinctively 'female' way?**

> _Top Girls_ was a play whose ideas came together over a period of time and in quite separate parts. I think some years before I wrote it, I had an idea for a play where a whole lot of people from the past, a whole lot of dead women, came and had cups of coffee with someone who was alive now. That ideas was just floating around as something quite separate, by itself. Then I started thinking about a play possibly to do with women at work and went and talked to quite a lot of people doing different jobs and one of the places I visited was an employment agency, which later became the focus of the play.
>
> (Churchill, interviewed by Lizbeth Goodman, 1995)

D i s c u s s i o n

Churchill's description offers an image of one scene, sketched lightly and filled in over a long period of time as the characters developed and their voices began to be audible. That scene 'floated' around, separate, while she outlined her ideas for a play about women at work. The two elements came together in _Top Girls_, a play about contemporary women at work which explores the effects of modern 'superwoman' status on individual women, their families and society more generally. Within that, the opening scene of the play stands out and remains quite separate; it is the dinner party scene, where a host of characters from myth and history converge over plates of food, rather than cups of coffee.

Except for Marlene, these characters do not reappear later in the play. The scene moves to the present day and a different set of characters appears to frame Marlene in a contemporary context. We next encounter Marlene at work in the Top Girls employment agency. ■

If you have not read the rest of the play, please do so now.

The basic story of the play can be summarized as follows: a 1980s career woman, Marlene, throws a dinner party to celebrate her promotion to the post of Managing Director at the Top Girls employment agency. She shares dinner and life stories with a host of women from myth and history. Meanwhile, the 'real' story of her life develops in the agency, where she competes for success against a management board and business world which is primarily male. We see her interact with her colleagues at work, with young women seeking employment and later, with her sister and Angie, the child whom we eventually discover to be Marlene's daughter. When we realize that Marlene gave her daughter up to be raised by her sister in order to succeed in her career, the complicated and compromising situation of the modern 'superwoman' is made explicit.

If we were to add some value judgements to this bland description, we might note that it is significant that Marlene has no real friends to invite to her party; her success within the agency has cost her a family and a social life. Later, we see how her absence has affected her sister's life and that of her daughter. But rather than depict Marlene as a 'bad mother' or a 'flawed character', Churchill seems to suggest that Marlene is a character at odds with a world which expects too much of women and offers too little support. In this reading, I have defined the play as in part 'social realist' – but it also contains surreal elements and non-traditional uses of language and structure. For instance, the storyline of the play is difficult to follow at first reading, since we only learn all the facts in the final scene of the play, which is the first of the realistic scenes in terms of the play's chronology.

Marlene is clearly the main character – the only character who appears in both the surreal dinner party scene and the realistic modern scenes. She is the centre of the play's focus, but her position is also somehow symbolic of the position of women in the 1980s – she is an individual character and also a stock figure or representative of an age.

Which of the characters seem 'realistic' (defining 'realism' at a basic level as 'truthful to life')?

Discussion

The most obvious way of assessing the 'realism' of characters is to say that those who appear in the main text of the play (in the modern world) are 'realistic' while the guests at the dinner party are not realistic. But this is too simple. Marlene appears in both the surreal and 'realistic' scenes while the waitress who serves at the dinner party is quite realistic.

Nothing Isabella says is too fantastic; it is only her appearance as a character who returns from the dead for dinner which renders her 'unrealistic'. The other characters are less and less realistic. Next there is Lady Nijo, the Buddhist Nun and Emperor's concubine (born in 1258). She is a historical character, known to have travelled by foot across Japan, but her story is embroidered by Churchill. She is followed by characters whose existence in history is less and less certain, and whose stories become more and more fantastic: from Pope Joan (thought to have been Pope between 854–856) and her story of birth and death by stoning, to Dull Gret, a figure taken from a painting by Brueghel, pictured wearing an apron and armour (symbolizing her dual roles as woman and warrior), leading a crowd of women through Hell and fighting Devils.

Figure 47   Deborah Findlay as Isabella Bird and Lesley Sharp as Dull Gret, from *Top Girls* in the 1991 production directed by Max Stafford-Clark, recorded for BBC television and included on an Open University/BBC video, 1995. Photo: BBC.

Figure 48   Pieter Brueghel the Elder, *Dulle Griet*, c.1562, oil on canvas, 115 x 161 cm. Museum Mayer van den bergh, Antwerp.

Dull Gret's one big speech, late in the scene, is a mad rave, with a prophetic quality. Dull Gret is present for a considerable amount of time before she speaks; she is the least articulate of the characters (which may be appropriate, as in many productions the part is doubled with that of Angie, another inarticulate but somehow 'visionary' character). Gret plays the role of the wise fool for much of the scene, the silent witness who only speaks when she really has something to say. In the 1991 televised production of the play discussed below, this aspect of Gret's character is emphasized by her actions; she eats voraciously with her hands and stuffs food into her satchel while the camera frames her as a comic figure who only later has something serious to say.

What all these characters have in common is their activity: they are travellers, mothers who have lost children, adventurers, even leaders. The last guest to enter Churchill's scene also comes from what critic Carolyn Heilbrun refers to as 'the houses and the fictions of men': she is Patient Griselda, known as a character in the literary texts of Boccaccio, Petrarch and Chaucer. Even Griselda is granted some 'realistic' elements in the play, as Churchill depicts her as the model of the self-sacrificing women transplanted into the 1980s, denying herself both food and the right to express her own emotions.

The characters who appear later in the play, at the *Top Girls* agency and at Joyce's house, are more 'realistic' or similar to people we might know. Yet they are also less realistic in the sense that they are purely characters invented by Churchill; they never really existed at all. ■

With these points in mind, it is interesting to consider the author's views on the relationship between the characters:

> A long time before I wrote the play I had the idea of having people from the past who might just turn up and have a cup of coffee with someone in the present. I noticed in this particular play that this was a way of putting Marlene in context, as someone who was celebrating extraordinary achievements – and I thought we could look at her as a sort of feminist heroine who had done things against extraordinary odds so that we could then have a different attitude to her as the play went on and we began to question what her values actually were.
>
> The choice of women was fairly arbitrary. It was a collection of people who happened to have caught my fancy at the time. I started to look at what they might talk about, what they had in common and I began to realise that they had all made big changes in their lives, quite often they had travelled and quite often they had difficulties about combining children with the other things they'd done.
>
> (Churchill, interviewed by Lizbeth Goodman, 1995)

Here, Churchill demonstrates again that the creation of the characters was not structured in any linear way and that the selection of characters was not premeditated – each one serves a purpose, but the purpose was defined as the play developed and is redefined as we read and analyse the play today. It is also significant that Churchill describes Marlene as a 'sort of feminist heroine' in the context of a play which explodes the myth that such heroines have easy, satisfactory lives in a 'real world' that does not offer support for the domestic, familial roles they also play.

How does the language of the play work to create a sense of 'realistic conversation'?

D i s c u s s i o n

Churchill uses the technique of 'overlapping dialogue'. The insertion of a 'backslash' (/) in the text indicates the place where one character begins speaking over the top of another, just as 'real' conversation tends to include a cross-fertilization of voices and a modicum of interruption. In fact, Churchill was the 'inventor' of the technique of overlapping dialogue, which has since been adapted for use by other playwrights, including Harold Pinter. Stage directions printed in parentheses in the text show that Churchill intended some speeches to be delivered primarily to particular characters, but of course the group setting means that all the characters present hear each line and may respond to it in their own speeches, however indirectly. In this way, speeches are spoken to identifiable characters, but the impact of each speech is wider and becomes part of the subtext of the general scene. Churchill's explanation for the choice of setting the scene around a dinner table helps to show why the technique of overlapping dialogue seemed most suitable:

> I suppose I set them around a dinner table because it's a place where you can celebrate and I wanted it to be a festive scene where they were celebrating what they'd done as well as talking about the hard times. It was to be at a level of amusing anecdotes, sharing something, entertaining each other.

> (Churchill, interviewed by Lizbeth Goodman, 1995)

Here, we find that there is a precise, structured aspect to the technique of overlapping dialogue: it functions at one level as a form of 'realistic' speech, but it is artistically orchestrated so that the strains and main ideas of each line can be heard above the others. The points of interruption and overlap are carefully planned, so that the overall effect is one of noisy celebration and shared story-telling by women seated around a table. The consumption of alcohol as the dinner proceeds brings the experiences of the women together in a physical sense – wherever they have come from, they all become present in the same space, drinking and getting more free with their speech as the scene develops. As each woman speaks, the others listen to only part of each speech; they also think about their stories and interrupt when a line from one story becomes a cue to tell another. The dinner party scene becomes a kind of patchwork of characters, a quilt of sorts which stitches together the stories of women from myth, history and fiction, past and present, making one creative image of community and of diversity within that community. The image is contained in a production photograph (Figure 49). ■

Let's now look more closely at the structure of the play:

What is the effect of the all-female cast of characters?
What difference would it make if one or more male characters were represented in this play?

Figure 49   A unified image of the Top Girls (left to right: Pope Joan, Patient Griselda, Marlene, Lady Nijo, Waitress, Isabella Bird and Dull Gret), from *Top Girls* in the 1991 production directed by Max Stafford-Clark, recorded for BBC television and included on an Open University/BBC video, 1995. Photo: BBC.

D i s c u s s i o n

The effect of the all-female cast of characters is the creation of a world in which women's experiences and stories are given full attention, where men's ways of thinking and speaking are not relevant. There is a practical element to this exclusion of male voices as well as a thematic one: men's voices tend to be deeper, lower and louder. The introduction of even one male voice to this artfully orchestrated symphony of women's voices would have altered the rhythm entirely and probably interrupted the entire scene mid-flow. (Many linguistic and sociological studies of conversational interaction have found that, on the whole, men interrupt more frequently and with more persistence than do women. For a summary and analysis of these studies, see Swann, 'Ways of speaking', in Bonner, *Imagining Women*, 1972, pp.56–66.) In addition, the women's stories are very personal, sometimes quite graphic. It is unlikely that the characters would speak so freely in the presence of men. Once the all-female world is established in the dinner party scene, the idea of women competing in a 'man's world' is emphasized by the lack of men on stage. The introduction of one male character would set Marlene up in competition with him, whereas the scene stresses her internalized sense of competition, which manifests itself in her relationship with other women. ■

Are any of the characters 'feminist'? (Do any of the main characters seem politically motivated to argue for the equal representation of women, or to advocate a sense of women's solidarity and community more generally)?

In what is widely known as a 'feminist play', it is interesting to note that none of the characters can be defined as particularly 'feminist' in her actions towards others. Churchill calls Marlene a 'sort of feminist heroine', but the 'sort of' is important – Marlene is active, strong and motivated to succeed, but her treatment of other women, including her sister and daughter, is hardly 'sisterly' or supportive. Joyce comes closest to being a 'feminist character' in her dedication to the 'feminist cause' of working together with other women. Yet Joyce also shows signs of strain – there is a crumbling of her faith in 'sisterhood' as she remains trapped in a working-class culture and in her role as adoptive mother, so is unable to connect with many other women, or to make much of a career for herself. Most of the female characters in the opening scene are active, interesting and worth considering from a feminist perspective, but none is very useful as a 'feminist role model' – they all lost out on something along their various roads to the collective table. If Marlene and Joyce were combined as one character, she might be seen as 'feminist', but as the separation of the characters points out, such 'superwomen' are rare in real life. It may be Angie and Kit, the girls soon to be women, who stand some chance of combining success in their personal and professional lives, though neither is particularly intelligent and neither has a strong 'feminist role model' to help them. ■

In our discussion thus far we have raised the issue of social class. How is the theme of class difference expressed in the play?

D i s c u s s i o n

It is expressed in the positioning of the waitress as the character who serves but does not speak and in the division of roles and experience of Marlene (who has worked her way to a successful career) and her sister Joyce (who has remained within the working-class culture of their childhood in order to offer a home to Marlene's daughter). A third expression of class difference is illustrated in the scene in which Marlene instructs the job applicant, Jeanine, on how to dress for success and 'convince her' of her potential and worth. Here, Marlene is the middle-class woman looking down on the working-class woman, implying that her appearance and values are unacceptable, even embarrassing. So the theme of class and the theme of appearance are closely linked. We see this again in the final scene, when Angie reveals that she admires Marlene partly because of her fancy clothes and polished appearance: Joyce is not impressed. It is Joyce who knows what style of dress Angie prefers, while Marlene gives the gift of clothes, forgetting that Angie is not a doll but a real live girl who has grown significantly since Marlene's last visit and developed an older girl's preferences. ■

What themes do you think emerge as important in the play?

D i s c u s s i o n

Many themes emerge as important, including women's work, competition in a man's world, connections between women across cultures and generations, motherhood and the conflict between domestic responsibility and work outside the home (whether creative or careerist). In addition, the theme of appearance crops up: Griselda and some of the other characters are overly concerned about their size (a parallel to the modern woman's form of self-denial: eating disorders), while Jeanine is instructed on how to dress for success and Marlene is concerned about appearing to be successful and popular (hence her carefully planned positioning of herself at the centre of a dinner party). ■

What visual images are created in the language of the play?

Discussion

This question asks you to consider the 'semiotics' of the play – the appearance of symbolic visual images. 'Semiotic' symbols are readable between the lines of *Top Girls*, and some signs are more evident by their absence. For instance, Marlene's home is never shown – she has been so successful in escaping her 'doll's house', the confining space of domestic life, that her house cannot be found. She is represented in a restaurant, at work and at her sister's house only. The other image which recurs in language is that of the mother with child, it is never actually represented in the play, but many of the characters speak of their experiences of having and losing children. The visual presence of a mother with child is what is missing from the play and that absence speaks volumes. ■

But in studying *Top Girls*, we must invent our own visual images in our own imagined productions. If you were directing the play, what symbols or images would you use to represent key themes in the play?

Discussion

You may have thought of all manner of things, but two images flashed immediately into my mind: the briefcase, which would symbolize Marlene's obsessive working life and the related absence of her home life, and the mirror, which would frame all the women as they talk in turn about their appearance, their lost youth, their lost children, their search for themselves. Perhaps, at one level, we as the audience become the mirror for the characters in *Top Girls* – as we watch the play, we see what the characters cannot see and can reflect on the play in our own cultural and generational contexts. ■

Finally, why do you think this particular play has been selected for study in this book?

Discussion

In fact, the play was chosen for several reasons. Churchill's work – and this play in particular – offers numerous strong women's parts, a fact which is itself some sort of statement. The politics of the play are contained in the subtext: in what the characters don't say, as much as in what they do say. The style of the play is original; indeed Churchill's innovation in the use of overlapping dialogue and the structure of the scenes opened the way for a whole new form of expression in the theatre. Also, *Top Girls* illustrates many of the themes and ideas developed throughout this book, in this case with reference to the work of a contemporary writer who is very much aware of the impact of feminist thought and whose work can be usefully evaluated within that context. ■

Playing Top Girls: *from the page to the stage*

In this section, we'll consider a range of factors affecting the interpretation of the text in performance, but it will help to outline three main ideas before we move on.

Firstly, you will need to consider how the playing space and set, props and costumes will appear, since they will inevitably affect the way a play is performed and received. *Top Girls* is very clearly set in the 1980s, a relatively short time before the writing of this book. But as we think about the play in the following decades, we may want to consider the costumes, ways of dressing and speaking and even the postures of the different characters as 'historically specific', even though this is comparatively recent history.

At another level, imagining plays in performance always involves consideration of the text (the spoken language of the characters, delivered by the actors) and its context (including silences and pauses in the dialogue). Space is important here as well, since the text is always 'played' in three dimensions, in a physical space. While we usually know which characters are present or absent, the positions of characters become significant if we want to consider who hears whom, who listens to whom and why.

Thirdly, we will want to keep in mind the idea that a text can create visual images, which take on semiotic significance in performance.

If you have access to a video production of the play, or even better, to a live production, then do make use of that resource to analyse directorial decisions. We have commissioned Juli Thompson Burk, an American theatre director and teacher, to describe her personal experience of directing *Top Girls*. As you read her account, keep three questions in mind:

1 **Can you find an example of the set affecting the action?**
2 **Can you find an example of a semiotic sign or meaningful visual symbol which Burk adds to the play in her interpretation?**
3 **How does the context of performance in a multiracial community affect the choices Burk makes in casting?**

Staging Top Girls *in the late 1980s*

by Juli Thompson Burk

In the fall of 1987, I directed Caryl Churchill's *Top Girls* at the University of Hawaii as part of the main stage season of the Department of Theatre and Dance. My production of the play, based on a feminist reading, investigated the price women pay for their success and the ways in which they often participate in their own oppression. In it, the figure of the child, in this case Angie, was designated as the theatrical locus or centre of attention, in the sense that she occupies the crucial intersection where the personal inevitably becomes political. The characterizations, staging and production design that I chose were intended to prevent the audience from relaxing into a traditional patriarchal (or male-centred) reading of the play, which would render Marlene little more than a 'bad mommy' who abandoned her child for life in the fast lane. As I was convinced that the text problematizes Marlene's success, the challenge was to create a performance that did not rely completely on the last scene to establish that Marlene is as much a victim as she is victimizer – that she is as alienated as alienating and that her spectrum of opportunity has been severely limited by the options available to her as a woman.

In presenting *Top Girls*, I wanted to interrogate the nature of Marlene's success and its consequences for herself and others. Instead of creating a drama that glorified or crucified this career woman, I attempted to demonstrate how Marlene can only be considered successful within a patriarchal model. Within this system Marlene's appointment to Managing Director, over a male colleague of greater seniority, appears to be a banner of achievement for women, what some might call a feminist victory. Her new position prompts her to comment in the first scene, 'Well, it's not Pope ... [but] it's worth a party' (*Top Girls*, p.13). Close examination of Marlene's victory celebration in the first scene reveals an unusual situation – all of her guests are from the distant past, none of them co-workers, real-life friends or family. While this lack of personal relationships is irrelevant to success in a patriarchal setting, Marlene's lack of friends, family and co-workers at the celebration resonates sharply. It becomes clear that the path to Marlene's success has been paved with the hard reality of Joyce's labour.

Visual elements: set design and staging

I sought to bring resonances of my production concept into the visual elements on the stage, to create an atmosphere of little comfort and few options. Each of the locations of the play, the restaurant, the employment agency (an office and an interviewing room), Joyce's back yard and Joyce's flat were scaled down to the least number of objects necessary for the action. I felt this would underscore the barrenness of the sisters' lives, punctuate the idea that they lived to survive rather than enjoy, having no other options. While Joyce had no money for decorations or small comforts, Marlene had no interest in such objects, making the office at the employment agency extremely institutional and impersonal. The only location in which there were objects not directly related to the action of the scene was in the restaurant. There we used a few objects related to the historical characters, placing them carefully so as to suggest as little ambience as possible. Joyce's back yard was completely devoid of vegetation and the fort built by the two young girls consisted of a shopping trolley on its side, a tattered sheet and a few bricks. The emptiness of each location was intended to add to the sense of emptiness in life when there are few options and great responsibilities. The furniture was all painted grey and the floor was also a shade of grey. The lack of color was intended to reinforce the lack of choice, just as the poor choice of places to sit suggested the lack of real options for the women in the play.

We built all the furniture for the production, using nothing commercially available as commercial pieces are generally designed for comfort and ease. The chairs, desks and tables onstage were without round edges or cushions. Not only did this create a visual image to support the production concept, but what these lines did to the bodies of the actors who used the furniture was also evident – the actors were uncomfortable and they looked it. We also used exactly the same furniture design for the employment offices and Joyce's flat as a means to equalize the two environments. While Joyce's 'home' was not more comfortable than the employment agency, neither was the office more sophisticated and high-tech than Joyce's flat. It was important that neither location become identified as a haven, that both appeared as alienated and alienating spaces.

Characterization: interpreting the text in performance

The text of *Top Girls* provides the audience with few moments in which Marlene is other than her impersonal, business-like self. There is only a brief section of her exchange with Joyce in the final scene where Marlene lets down her powerful demeanour to reveal a desire to be wanted by her sister, needed in some undistinguished way. Structurally, this moment occurs very late in the text and therefore it was important for me to provide a double edge to Marlene's hardened exterior throughout the production. Instead of relying on this moment to erode her tough image entirely through her tears, I worked to question her take-charge attitude. My first step in this effort was to 'cast against' Marlene's hard exterior – that is, to look for an actress who might work against the grain of the 'hard' side of the character. I was fortunate enough to find a talented actress who was able to play against her own distaste for the kind of woman Marlene had become. In addition, Marlene was comfortable only when she was in an exchange in a business rather than personal situation. This included the play's opening scene, which I interpreted to be a sort of professional 'survivors hall of fame', created by Marlene and comprised of women who had experienced emotional or physical oppression, now 'reborn' to tell about it.

While the terms of Marlene's success would appear completely justified within a patriarchal society valuing commercialism, I made those commercial values the object of examination in my production. As the play progressed, I wanted to show that her success rests on her acceptance of those patriarchal patterns of behaviour needed to succeed within the male-dominated world of offices and careers. Marlene completely rejects any possibility of value in the domestic realm to which the patriarchy relegates women. Believing that their mother had a 'wasted' life, she tells Joyce, 'I had to get out, I knew when I was thirteen, out of their house, out of them, never let that happen to me, never let him, make my own way, out' (*Top Girls*, p.85). In this scene, the tenuous connection Marlene maintains with the domestic world she has rejected is illustrated in the hugely inappropriate belated Christmas presents she brings. While the dress for Angie is the correct size, it is more appropriate for the nine-year-old Marlene last visited than for the sixteen-year-old she finds. The difference is illustrative: Angie at sixteen must soon, like Marlene, face the possibility of unwanted pregnancy. Time moves quickly and these women and the girls who are soon-to-be women aren't close enough to keep tabs on each other's lives, each other's development.

In this chronologically displaced final scene, we see Marlene in a personal environment for the first time. The final moment of the play, when Angie comes back downstairs after Joyce has gone to bed, calling 'Mum?' reinforced Marlene's earlier discomfort with Angie's surprise visit. Unable to acknowledge her position as birth mother, she responds, 'No, she's gone to bed. It's Aunty Marlene'. At this point Marlene was seated on the upstage edge of the sofa, wrapped in a blanket having a last drink before sleep. Angie came into the room, crossed to the sofa, sat beside her for the last exchange of conversation and after her final word, 'Frightening', laid herself across Marlene's lap. This positioning allowed a final confirmation of Marlene's inability to tolerate physical closeness and evoked a powerful Christian image of maternity: Michelangelo's Pietà (Figure 50). This choice

Figure 50   Michelangelo, *Pietà*, 1397–1400, marble, height 174 cm. Photo: Mansell-Alinari.

was particularly successful in Hawaii, a heavily Catholic state, as an image intended to call to mind the sacrifices women make as well as to illustrate the extent of Marlene's alienation from herself as a mother and from her child. Marlene remained quite stiff, a demeanour contrasting with the image of the ultimate Christian mother, Mary, who cradles her son lovingly in her lap.

While refusing to vilify Marlene, I also felt it necessary to resist the temptation to idealize Joyce or portray her simply as a victim. While neither sister is ultimately sympathetic, Joyce has fed, clothed and looked after Marlene's illegitimate child. Motivated by family loyalty, she has remained all her life in a closed domestic environment. But to portray Joyce simply as the victim ignores her emotional battering of Angie, her acceptance of her father's physical battering of her mother and Marlene's challenge, 'You could have left' (p.76). Instead of portraying Joyce as a martyr to the needs of her family, in production I worked to emphasize the bitterness that results from her self-martyring. Accepting the traditional role of wife and mother has brought Joyce nothing but hardship, no rewards save her own convictions of righteousness. In withholding a positive protagonist for the audience to identify with, I hoped to problematize the choices both sisters made. At the same time, I wanted to emphasize the fact that once each woman chose between career and family, there were few options open to them, regardless of the twentieth-century societal myth that anything is possible.

Women's roles in theatre and society: creative casting

The women with whom Marlene celebrates her promotion serve to highlight the similarities in women's lives throughout history. What I tried to do was to position them as successful (for the most part) in Marlene's opinion, while from the perspective of the audience providing the opportunity to see how each woman's apparent success rested upon her ultimate oppression. We portrayed the historical characters as contradictions, not successes. They rarely even appeared to listen to one another, being happier to relate their own stories than to try to understand one another's experiences. And their party, as a prediction for the ultimate quotient of satisfaction in Marlene's life, degenerates into complete chaos. Producing the play in Hawaii enabled me to make one point clear in the casting of the historical women. Because these women were for me Marlene's fiction, created from her sense of what is successful, I cast a Caucasian woman as Lady Nijo, the woman from tenth-century Japan. The ethnic mix in this university made it highly probable that had I wanted an Asian woman to play Nijo, I could have found one without any problem, a fact obvious to my audience. So my decision to cast a 'white' Nijo and an Indian woman as Mrs Kidd allowed me to make political statements about race as well as gender in a particular production and cultural context. My point was to emphasize the *historical* characters as figments of Marlene's (white middle-class English) imagination, as opposed to the 'real' characters Marlene encounters (such as Mrs Kidd) who may be of any ethnic origin in twentieth-century London.

Reading *Top Girls* as a feminist text helped me to find ways to dramatize the price women pay for success in a patriarchal society. For me, and, I hope, for the spectators who attended this production, Marlene and the other women of the play embodied the dangerous and complex situation faced by many women in today's world, a world in which the consequences of success are almost as frightening as those of failure.

Analysing the text in performance

At the beginning of this section, I asked you to consider three questions in relation to Burk's account of her production:

1 Can you find an example of the set affecting the action?

2 Can you find an example of a semiotic sign or meaningful visual symbol which Burk adds to the play in her interpretation?

3 How does the context of performance in a multiracial community affect the choices Burk makes in casting?

D i s c u s s i o n

1 An example of the set affecting the action is provided in Burk's description of the straight-backed chairs and sparse furnishing of the set to 'create an atmosphere of little comfort and few options', both in a literal sense (the actors cannot make themselves comfortable on this set) and in a symbolic sense (the audience cannot see the play in this production without considering the limitations imposed by Marlene's struggle for success, which alienates her from any sense of domestic comfort).

2 An example of a semiotic sign of meaningful visual symbol which Burk adds to the play in her interpretation is that of the *Pietà* (see Figure 50): the image of mother with child, which Burk creates in the mind's eye of her audience, by positioning Angie across the lap of the physically awkward, reluctant Marlene.

3 The context of performance in a multiracial community affected the choices Burk made in casting in very real ways. It influenced her consideration the theme of racial difference as represented in the character of Lady Nijo: a theme largely ignored in many productions. The deliberate casting against the grain of racial difference emphasizes Lady Nijo's status as a fictional character who exists only in Marlene's (conservative, English) imagination. By contrast, Burk cast an Indian actor in the part of Mrs Kidd, one of the 'realistic' characters who appears only briefly, in a scene in the Top Girls agency. This choice of casting deliberately emphasizes that in relation to 1980s London, there is no reason to assume that a character should be Caucasian. ■

Juli Thompson Burk describes the process of interpreting the play for performance by a particular group of people to a particular audience in a particular setting. Each production adds a new interpretation of the play. In fact, *Top Girls* may be seen to exist not only as the text written by the playwright, Caryl Churchill, but also as the collected body of theatre productions and individual interpretations of its readers and audiences. The play is much more than a literary text.

Recording Top Girls: *from page to stage to camera to life*

While there is very little space left in this chapter, it is important to offer some account, however brief, of the adaptation of Churchill's play for television and video. What follows is an abbreviated version of the 'inside story' of the recording of the play for both media. (The process is described in detail in Boireau, *Drama On Drama*, 1996.) Recorded drama on video and television, like film, takes visual images in three dimensions but somehow flattens out the three-dimensional quality on the screen. One effect is that actions which seem small or subtle on stage suddenly seem noticeable, perhaps even exaggerated, on screen. When stage plays are recorded, then, many actors struggle with the transition of media, taking time to minimalize their gestures and facial expressions, lowering their voices and limiting their range of movements, following the maxim that 'less is more'.

In *Top Girls*, the transition poses another problem. The first production was staged in 1982, directed by Max Stafford-Clark at the Royal Court Theatre. The revival of the play for BBC television and the stage in 1991 was also directed by Stafford-Clark, with some of the same actors. By 1991, times had changed and what had been in 1982 a provocative play about women's current status was suddenly re-viewed as a prophetic play about the conflicts faced by women in the modern age more generally. The Thatcherite aspect of Marlene's character and all its negative associations were highlighted in 1991, not due to a difference in direction of the play, but rather due to the altered political and social climate in which the play was performed and received.

With that in mind, it is interesting to trace the development of the productions from 1982 and 1991 in terms of the 'actioning' provided by the director for the actors. For each line of the text, Stafford-Clark encourages actors to think of separate motivations, of some action which the character wants to make, or some change which the character wants to impose. Lesley Manville, who played Patient Griselda, Nell and Jeanine in the 1982 production and Marlene in the 1991 production, describes her experience of Stafford-Clark's 'actioning' process as a way of enabling actors to find the meaning of each line in its potential for performance by 'attaching a transitive verb' to each idea, speech or action in order to 'determine how your character would present each line' (Manville, in interview with Lizbeth Goodman, 1995).

Here, it is also important to recall that the 1991 stage version was recorded for television before it was performed on stage – normally, the reverse order might have been more satisfactory, as the performance on stage would have functioned as a 'rehearsal' for the recorded version. But economies of scale dictated that the budget to cover rehearsal of the stage revival would have to be met by recording the play first. In this case, then, the actions and gestures began small and had to be enlarged and expanded for the stage version (Stafford-Clark, Sharp and Findlay, in interview with Lizbeth Goodman, 1995).

The transitions from one medium to another (page, stage and recorded performance) and the change in reception from the audience of 1982 to that of 1991 can be read between the lines (or in the margins, in this case) in extracts from the working scripts of an actor who performed in both productions. Deborah Findlay played the same three parts in both productions: Isabella Bird, Joyce and Mrs Kidd. Her annotated scripts reveal different sets of marginal directions. Please look at Figure 51.

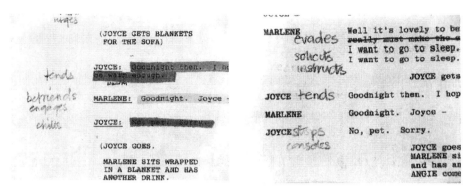

Figure 51   *Top Girls* annotated script extracts, courtesy Deborah Findlay.

These extracts illustrate the very different interpretations that an actor can bring to her part by the use of facial expression, gesture, body language, tone of voice or other means of conveying the attitude behind the lines of the text. The hand-written words in the left-hand margins of these extracts are 'director's notes', containing the 'actioning' cues recorded by the actors as aids to finding meaning in the play. That meaning is determined not only by the lines themselves, or even by the relationship between the characters who interact in this exchange, but also by the cultural context of production.

The two extracts have not been identified with dates in Figure 51. **Can you tell which extract comes from which production? Which set of directions seem most relevant to the play as produced for an audience in the 1980s and which seem more relevant to the 1990s?**

D i s c u s s i o n

You might be surprised to learn that the extract on the left comes from the 1982 production and the one on the right from the 1991 production. You might have thought it appropriate for Joyce in the 1991 production to chill Marlene with the finality of her last line: 'No, pet. Sorry.' – Marlene ought to know better. In fact it is the 1982 script which has the cues 'tends, befriends, engages, chills'. By 1991 the cues are 'tends, stops, consoles'. This 1991 Joyce feels able to offer Marlene consolation in the final line, as both women have been trapped by the choices they were forced to make in the political climate of the 1980s. The actor Deborah Findlay offered this explanation for the changed action: 'in the second version I was much more expansive with both characters [Isabella Bird and Joyce]. On reflection I wanted to make both of them much warmer than I had in the original production.' ∎

Both versions are faithful to the text Churchill wrote. It is the social context of performance that determines the most appropriate way of interpreting those lines, for each generation of readers and viewers. (For further information about the transfer of the play to video, including interviews with the playwright, director, cast and crew, see Goodman, 'Overlapping dialogue in overlapping media', in Rabillard, *Caryl Churchill*, 1996.)

Conclusion: speaking for a gender and a generation

Earlier, we considered the inarticulacy of the character Angie, noting the significance of that role being played in many productions by the same actor who plays Dull Gret. It should be said that Churchill and the actors are unanimously uncertain about whether the doubling of characters matters (Churchill, Stafford-Clark, Manville, Findlay, Sharp, in interview with Lizbeth Goodman, 1995). Churchill argues that the doubling was never intentional – sixteen actors could have been hired to play the sixteen different parts – so doubling is at least not conscious – more a matter of production values, as it is less expensive to hire a small cast and more satisfying to actors to have the opportunity to play several parts. Deliberate or not, there is a strong parallel between the visionary inarticulacy of Dull Gret and her raving battle cry for women to take arms and the abrasive, provocative, sometimes apocalyptic ideas which Angie utters to her friend Kit (she even speaks of killing her 'mother', in fact her Aunt, Joyce). The visionary warrior Gret and the imaginative girl Angie both look to the future. Angie has the very last word of the play and that word, appropriately enough, is 'frightening'.

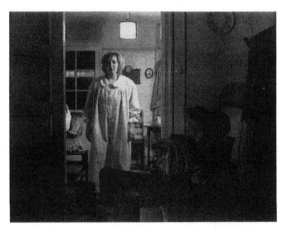 

Figure 52   Lesley Sharp as Angie: 'frightening', from *Top Girls* in the 1991 production directed by Max Stafford-Clark, recorded for BBC television and included on an Open University/BBC video, 1995. Photo: BBC.

If Angie overheard the adults' conversation, that would provide one explanation for her 'fear'. Stafford-Clark contends that Angie has not overheard, but has rather woken from a nightmare. Churchill, provocatively, claims that while she did not intend for Angie to overhear, it is equally

If Angie overheard the adults' conversation, that would provide one explanation for her 'fear'. Stafford-Clark contends that Angie has not overheard, but has rather woken from a nightmare. Churchill, provocatively, claims that while she did not intend for Angie to overhear, it is equally possible that she does. It is left to the reader of the play to interpret that line, just as the director of any performance must do so. Churchill leaves the final act of interpretation to us. Perhaps the 'actioning' of Angie's final line will resonate differently for each generation who hears it.

Further Reading

Burk, J.T. '*Top Girls* in performance', in Donkin and Clements (eds) (1993) *Directing Theatre as if Gender and Race Matter*, University of Michigan Press.

Cixous, H. and Catherine Clément (1986) *The Newly Born Woman*, translated by Betsy Wing with an introduction by Sandra Gilbert, Manchester University Press, first published (1975) as *La Jeune Née*.

Cousin, G. (1989) *Churchill: The Playwright*, Methuen.

Fitzsimmons, L. (1989) *File on Churchill*, Methuen.

Goodman, L. (ed.) (1997) *Mythic Women/Real Women: Plays and Performance Pieces by Women*, Faber and Faber (includes comparative analysis of other plays by contemporary women writers from around the world).

Irigiray, L. (1985) *This Sex Which Is Not One*, translated by Catherine Porter with Carolyn Burke, Cornell University Press; first published in 1977.

Kritzer, A.H. (1991) *The Plays of Caryl Churchill: Theatre of Empowerment*, Macmillan.

Marks, E. and Isobel de Courtivron (eds) (1981) *New French Feminisms*, Harvester.

Moi, T. (ed.) (1986) *The Kristeva Reader*, Blackwell.

Conclusion: Piecing and quilting

Piecework: finding the pattern(s)

The texts studied in this book were written by a wide range of authors, in different times and places and for different reasons. What is, perhaps, most compelling is the way in which all of them share concerns, themes, and ideas.

An insight into the process of writing about these texts and authors may help to illustrate my point. When I initially chose them, I made deliberate choices about covering the three main literary genres, offering a range of voices from women of different periods and cultures, and so on. But when I compared the lives and work of six of these women (Alcott, Dickinson, Gilman, Woolf, Plath and Walker), the connections between them leapt off the page: all experienced isolation of one kind or another; all recognized the need for mental and physical space for writing or dealt with ideas of confinement, hidden writing or suppressed creativity; some lost children; some suffered mental and emotional breakdowns after bearing children or because they found that raising children and writing competed for their time and energy. Perhaps most striking was the way in which it became impossible to 'mask' the fact that three of these talented women had committed suicide (albeit for very different reasons and at different points in their lives). Though I did not want 'madness' or suicide to take greater significance than the writing of the women, it seemed to write itself into their stories, as one form of 'escape' from the cages or enclosed spaces (mental and emotional) in which some of them wrote. Each of the six women, and indeed most of the others studied in this book, can be seen as part of a larger pattern of women's literature. But at the same time, as we have argued throughout the book, each writer must also be studied for her individual contribution and literary achievement.

Domestic fiction, and its representation of a conflict between domesticity and creativity, has emerged as a key theme in the book. Many of the female characters discussed have been seen as trapped in the 'houses and fictions of men' or as trapped in a social code of feminine behaviour defined by patriarchy, even in stories written by women. Early domestic fiction, for instance, included novels by Jane Austen, the Brontë sisters and Alcott, all of whom are known primarily for stories which focus on women's culturally specified roles in the home. In a genre like this, with particular conventions defined by period and culture, it is interesting to notice the way that changing values and expectations for women have shifted over time: Jane Eyre searched for a home; Gilman's stricken wife was imprisoned in the home; Ibsen's Nora slammed the door on her home; Churchill's Marlene had 'lost' hers altogether. Today, authors of both sexes are free to represent the domestic in all manner of once unthinkable ways. It is intriguing that Alcott's work, which includes the ultra-conventional scenes of *Little Women*, also provides an early example of non-conformism, the anti-domestic thriller 'Behind a Mask'.

Domestic themes, including that of motherhood, are still at issue in modern texts by women. If we look only at our three play texts, we can trace a progression from the entrapment of Minnie Wright in *Trifles*, to Nora's escape, to Marlene's troubled success in *Top Girls*. But all of these plays offer images of women in conflict with cultural expectation.

The theme of having and losing children also emerges strongly. Motherhood and creativity are the intertwined subjects of some of the poetry discussed in Chapter Two. Clearly, motherhood is a role that has often come into conflict with women's work outside the home, but this conflict has nevertheless found expression as a theme in women's literature. Lost babies are also, of course, at the centre of *The Color Purple*. In her account of the process of writing her book, Walker referred to her idea of selling apples to support herself and her daughter – so long as she could earn enough to write. Curiously, Alcott, writing over a century earlier, also considered selling apples – in fact, the apples which she and her sisters grew were transferred to the fictional world of *Little Women* to be munched by Jo March as she sat in her attic room 'scribbling' stories. Alcott referred to her own stories as her 'children', as she never had time or energy to bear children of her own. Here, the writing represents the birth process and the fiction represents the missing or lost child – a metaphor which may be familiar from Mary Shelley's 'monstrous birth' with her novel, *Frankenstein* (see Walder, *The Realist Novel*, 1996). In the experiences of the female characters we find the roots of the experiences of their female authors. While the texts are still fascinating in and of themselves, it is difficult to resist peeking beneath the surface. And when we do, we see that the roots are tangled up with a whole range of conflicting energies, experiences and desires, all at odds with social expectations for women.

Is this why women's writing is so little represented in the traditional literary canon? Early in the book we looked at the poem 'The Lady of Shalott', a firmly canonized text selected by earlier generations of scholars and authors as a work of considerable literary and aesthetic merit. Newly canonized works are selected by a different set of people, including teachers and contemporary readers, and the grounds of selection may include aesthetic considerations, but may also focus on thematic issues of relevance at the time. As the wider canon continues to grow, new forms and styles of writing are included, and critical issues about literary value are often raised. Having studied the relationship between literature and gender, do you think there are valid reasons for expanding the traditional canon? If so, is it the case that the criteria for inclusion need to be reconsidered? And do ideas about what constitutes aesthetic worth also need to be reconsidered? I hope that this book will have helped you to answer these questions in your own way.

Everyone reads in a different way, and learns through different processes. I tend to remember ideas associated with visual images, so I have included as many images as possible in the hope that these might enrich the material, and perhaps also the learning process, for others as well. But the poems and stories are themselves illustrated, not with pictures or photographs, but with visual images conjured through the use of words. Like the shoes represented on this book's cover, a wide range of props, accessories and seemingly unimportant objects have taken on a cumulative significance through their repeated occurrence in the writings of women in this book. Among them are dresses, costumes, masks, veils, mirrors, windows, houses, birds, cages and quilts: all items to do with the artifice of living as women, when the notion of womanhood, or of 'femininity', is defined by men. But once characters have come to life in our imaginations anything can happen. Minnie Wright may be freed or imprisoned, depending on us. Nora may succeed or be locked out in the cold after she slams the door; it's up to us. Marlene's future, and Angie's, are frightening

Figure 53 *Re-member Us*, etching by Judith Anderson, Fall Equinox 1990, 18 x 24 in. Photo: Jim Colando.

but also potentially exciting; it depends what we make of them in our own imaginations. We decide what happens to all these characters after the proverbial curtain falls. The next generation of readers and writers may invent new endings to these plays to reflect the times. But the final 'act' of interpretation will be 'performed' by the reader, whatever his or her gender.

The image of the quilt: fragment and whole

Some critics have argued that the metaphor of the quilt as a symbol for women's creativity is overly simplistic. I would argue, however, that the metaphor works to show the differences between women writers as well as their similarities. To borrow a phrase from Elaine Showalter, we can see the 'family resemblance' between writers even as we see individual features in each author and work of fiction. In the process of reading and interpreting, each of us will find our pieces to add to the fabric, or perhaps the stitching, of the quilt which is the study of literature and gender.

Contemporary visual artist Judith Anderson created the image of a quilt (Figure 53), symbolizing women's history, women's literature and culture, all stitched loosely together as a new piece of artwork. This quilt has a very specific function: it brings together the images of a wide range of women, famous and unknown, asking us all to 're-member' how women's history has been ignored, but can now be pieced together and made permanent. Anderson's quilt takes the face of Virginia Woolf as its centre piece. It also includes bits and pieces of different cultures and generations. You might recognize the face of Soujourner Truth, the illiterate African-American woman whose cry 'Ain't I a Woman?' still echoes in current writing by women such as Alice Walker and Maya Angelou.

This book is itself a bit like a patchwork quilt: stitched together of the bits and pieces of stories and ideas, in a small contribution to the evolving body of writing by and about literature and gender. The many women and men whose literary writing has been discussed all contributed to the quilt; their images and ideas enrich its fabric, and the inspiration they offer is like a way of stitching, taught by doing, passed on like an heirloom. All readers will, of course, have discovered different patterns: perhaps the little yellow stars, perhaps the bright purple patches, perhaps the plain white muslin which acts as the backdrop, perhaps the threads which hold it all together. Those threads are composed of words, which form poems and stories and plays, and the stories of the lives of the women and men who imagine them and write them into being.

Part Two

Poetry Anthology

This poetry anthology includes all the poems discussed in Chapter Two of this book, and a few which extend and amplify the themes and issues discussed in other chapters. Some of them are read and discussed on the BBC television programme and audio-cassette produced in association with this book. Poems printed elsewhere in the book are: Charlotte Perkins Gilman, 'An Obstacle' (p.vii); Sylvia Plath, 'The Bull of Bendylaw' (p.7); James Joyce, extract from 'Chamber Music' (pp.7–8); A.S. Byatt, extract from *Possession* (p.24). The anthology is organized in five sections: I Men and women; II From antiquity to the Victorians; III Nineteenth-century Welsh, Scottish and Irish Poetry; IV Emily Dickinson; V Contemporary poets.

I   Men and women

The Lady of Shalott

Part I

On either side the river lie
Long fields of barley and of rye,
That clothe the wold and meet the sky;
And through the field the road runs by
　　To many-towered Camelot,
And up and down the people go,
Gazing where the lilies blow
Round an island there below,
　　The island of Shalott.

Willows whiten, aspens quiver,
Little breezes dusk and shiver
Through the wave that runs forever
By the island in the river
　　Flowing down to Camelot.
Four gray walls, and four gray towers,
Overlook a space of flowers,
And the silent isle imbowers
　　The Lady of Shalott.

By the margin, willow-veiled,
Slide the heavy barges trailed
By slow horses; and unhailed
The shallop flitteth silken-sailed
　　Skimming down to Camelot:
But who hath seen her wave her hand?
Or at the casement seen her stand?
Or is she known in all the land,
　　The Lady of Shalott?

Only reapers, reaping early
In among the bearded barley,
Hear a song that echoes cheerly
From the river winding clearly,

Down to towered Camelot;
And by the moon the reaper weary,
Piling sheaves in uplands airy,
Listening, whispers ''Tis the fairy
        Lady of Shalott.'

Part II

There she weaves by night and day
A magic web with colours gay.
She has heard a whisper say,
A curse is on her if she stay
        To look down to Camelot.
She knows not what the curse may be,
And so she weaveth steadily,
And little other care hath she,
        The Lady of Shalott.

And moving through a mirror clear
That hangs before her all the year,
Shadows of the world appear.
There she sees the highway near
        Winding down to Camelot;
There the river eddy whirls,
And there the surly village churls,
And the red cloaks of market girls,
        Pass onward from Shalott.

Sometimes a troop of damsels glad,
An abbot on an ambling pad.
Sometimes a curly shepherd lad,
Or long-haired page in crimson clad,
        Goes by to towered Camelot;
And sometimes through the mirror blue
The knights come riding two and two:
She hath no loyal knight and true,
        The Lady of Shalott.

But in her web she still delights
To weave the mirror's magic sights,
For often through the silent nights
A funeral, with plumes and lights
        And music, went to Camelot;
Or when the moon was overhead,
Came two young lovers lately wed:
'I am half sick of shadows,' said
        The Lady of Shalott.

Part III

A bowshot from her bower eaves,
He rode between the barley sheaves.
The sun came dazzling through the leaves,
And flamed upon the brazen greaves
        Of bold Sir Lancelot.

A red-cross knight forever kneeled
To a lady in his shield,
That sparkled on the yellow field,
    Beside remote Shalott.

The gemmy bridle glittered free,
Like to some branch of stars we see
Hung in the golden Galaxy.
The bridle bells rang merrily
    As he rode down to Camelot;
And from his blazoned baldric slung
A mighty silver bugle hung,
And as he rode his armour rung,
    Beside remote Shalott.

All in the blue unclouded weather
Thick-jeweled shone the saddle leather,
The helmet and the helmet-feather
Burned like one burning flame together,
    As he rode down to Camelot;
As often through the purple night,
Below the starry clusters bright,
Some bearded meteor, trailing light,
    Moves over still Shalott.

His broad clear brow in sunlight glowed;
On burnished hooves his war horse trode;
From underneath his helmet flowed
His coal-black curls as on he rode,
    As he rode down to Camelot.
From the bank and from the river
He flashed into the crystal mirror,
'Tirra lirra,' by the river
    Sang Sir Lancelot.

She left the web, she left the loom,
She made three paces through the room,
She saw the water lily bloom,
She saw the helmet and the plume,
    She looked down to Camelot.
Out flew the web and floated wide;
The mirror cracked from side to side;
'The curse is come upon me,' cried
    The Lady of Shalott.

Part IV

In the stormy east wind straining,
The pale yellow woods were waning,
The broad stream in his banks complaining,
Heavily the low sky raining
    Over towered Camelot;
Down she came and found a boat
Beneath a willow left afloat,
And round about the prow she wrote
    The Lady of Shalott.

And down the river's dim expanse
Like some bold seër in a trance,
Seeing all his own mischance —
With a glassy countenance
    Did she look to Camelot.
And at the closing of the day
She loosed the chain, and down she lay;
The broad stream bore her far away,
    The Lady of Shalott.

Lying, robed in snowy white
That loosely flew to left and right —
The leaves upon her falling light —
Through the noises of the night
    She floated down to Camelot;
And as the boat-head wound along
The willowy hills and fields among,
They heard her singing her last song,
    The Lady of Shalott.

Heard a carol, mournful, holy,
Chanted loudly, chanted lowly,
Till her blood was frozen slowly,
And her eyes were darkened wholly,
    Turned to towered Camelot.
For ere she reached upon the tide
The first house by the waterside,
Singing in her song she died,
    The Lady of Shalott.

Under tower and balcony,
By garden wall and gallery,
A gleaming shape she floated by,
Dead-pale between the houses high,
    Silent into Camelot.
Out upon the wharfs they came,
Knight and burgher, lord and dame,
And round the prow they read her name,
    The Lady of Shalott.

Who is this? and what is here?
And in the lighted palace near
Died the sound of royal cheer;
And they crossed themselves for fear,
    All the knights at Camelot:
But Lancelot mused a little space;
He said, 'She has a lovely face;
God in his mercy lend her grace,
    The Lady of Shalott'.

Alfred, Lord Tennyson (1809–1892)
From: Ricks, C. (ed.) (1987) *The Poems of Tennyson,* 3 vols, Longman.

The Gentleman of Shalott

Which eye's his eye?
Which limb lies
next the mirror?
For neither is clearer
nor a different color
than the other,
nor meets a stranger
in this arrangement
of leg and leg and
arm and so on.
To his mind
it's the indication
of a mirrored reflection
somewhere along the line
of what we call the spine.

He felt in modesty
his person was
half looking-glass,
for why should he
be doubled?
The glass must stretch
down his middle,
or rather down the edge.
But he's in doubt
as to which side's in or out
of the mirror.
There's little margin for error,
but there's no proof, either.
And if half his head's reflected,
thought, he thinks, might be affected.

But he's resigned
to such economical design.
If the glass slips
he's in a fix—
only one leg, etc. But
while it stays put
he can walk and run
and his hands can clasp one
another. The uncertainty
he says he
finds exhilarating. He loves
that sense of constant re-adjustment.
He wishes to be quoted as saying at present:
'Half is enough.'

Elizabeth Bishop (1911–1979)
From: Bishop, E. (1970) *Complete Poems,* Chatto and Windus.

My Last Duchess
FERRARA

That's my last Duchess painted on the wall,
Looking as if she were alive. I call
That piece a wonder, now: Frà Pandolfs hands
Worked busily a day, and there she stands.
Will't please you sit and look at her? I said
'Frà Pandolf' by design, for never read
Strangers like you that pictured countenance,
The depth and passion of its earnest glance,
But to myself they turned (since none puts by
The curtain I have drawn for you, but I)
And seemed as they would ask me, if they durst,
How such a glance came there; so, not the first
Are you to turn and ask thus Sir, 'twas not
Her husband's presence only, called that spot
Of joy into the Duchess' cheek: perhaps
Frà Pandolf chanced to say 'Her mantle laps
Over my lady's wrist too much,' or 'Paint
Must never hope to reproduce the faint
Half-flush that dies along her throat': such stuff
Was courtesy, she thought, and cause enough
For calling up that spot of joy. She had
A heart—how shall I say?—too soon made glad,
Too easily impressed; she liked whate'er
She looked on, and her looks went everywhere.
Sir, 'twas all one! My favour at her breast,
The dropping of the daylight in the West,
The bough of cherries some officious fool
Broke in the orchard for her, the white mule
She rode with round the terrace—all and each
Would draw from her alike the approving speech,
Or blush, at least. She thanked men—good! but thanked
Somehow—I know not how—as if she ranked
My gift of a nine-hundred-years-old name
With anybody's gift. Who'd stoop to blame
This sort of trifling? Even had you skill
In speech—(which I have not)—to make your will
Quite clear to such an one, and say, 'Just this
Or that in you disgusts me; here you miss,
Or there exceed the mark'—and if she let
Herself be lessoned so, nor plainly set
Her wits to yours, forsooth, and made excuse
—E'en then would be some stooping; and I choose
Never to stoop. Oh sir, she smiled, no doubt,
Whene'er I passed her; but who passed without
Much the same smile? This grew; I gave commands;
Then all smiles stopped together. There she stands
As if alive. Will't please you rise? We'll meet
The company below, then. I repeat,
The Count your master's known munificence
Is ample warrant that no just pretence
Of mine for dowry will be disallowed;
Though his fair daughter's self, as I avowed

At starting, is my object. Nay, we'll go
Together down, sir. Notice Neptune, though,
Taming a sea horse, thought a rarity,
Which Claus of Innsbruck cast in bronze for me!

Robert Browning (1812–1889)
From: Abrams, M.H. (ed.) (1974) *The Norton Anthology of English Literature,*
vol. 2, Norton.

The Reincarnation of Captain Cook

Earlier than I could learn
the maps had been coloured in.
When I pleaded, the kings told me
nothing was left to explore.

I set out anyway, but
everywhere I went
there were historians, wearing
wreaths and fake teeth
belts; or in the deserts, cairns

and tourists. Even the caves had
candle stubs, inscriptions quickly
scribbled in darkness. I could

never arrive. Always
the names got there before.

Now I am old I know my
mistake was my acknowledging
of maps. The eyes raise
tired monuments.

Burn down
the atlases, I shout
to the park benches; and go

past the cenotaph
waving a blank banner
across the street, beyond
the corner

into a land cleaned of geographies,
its beach gleaming with arrows.

Margaret Atwood (1939–)
From: Rumens, C. (ed.) (1985) *Making for the Open: The Chatto Book of
Post-Feminist Poetry 1964–1984*, Chatto and Windus.

Sonnet LXXIII

That time of year thou mayst in me behold
When yellow leaves, or none, or few, do hang
Upon those boughs which shake against the cold,
Bare ruin'd choirs, where late the sweet birds sang.
In me thou see'st the twilight of such day
As after sunset fadeth in the west;
Which by and by black night doth take away,
Death's second self, that seals up all in rest.

In me thou see'st the glowing of such fire,
That on the ashes of his youth doth lie,
As the death-bed whereon it must expire
Consum'd with that which it was nourish'd by.
This thou perceiv'st, which makes thy love more strong,
To love that well which thou must leave ere long.

William Shakespeare (1564–1616)
From: Kerrigan, J. (ed.) (1986) *The Sonnets and A Lover's Complaint*, New
Penguin Shakespeare.

Sonnets from the Portuguese
XIV

If thou must love me, let it be for nought
Except for love's sake only. Do not say
'I love her for her smile ... her look ... her way
Of speaking gently, ... for a trick of Thought
That falls in well with mine, and certes brought
A sense of pleasant ease on such a day' –
For these things in themselves, Beloved, may
Be changed, or change for thee, – and love so wrought,
May be unwrought so. Neither love me for
Thine own dear pity's wiping my cheeks dry,
Since one might well forget to weep who bore
Thy comfort long, and lose thy love thereby.
But love me for love's sake, that evermore
Thou mayst love all through love's eternity.

Elizabeth Barrett Browning (1806–1861)
From: *The Poetical Works of Elizabeth Barrett Browning*, Oxford University
Press, 1904.

II   From antiquity to the Victorians

Sappho: An Extract

My mother always said
that in her youth she was
exceedingly in fashion

wearing a purple ribbon
looped in her hair. But
the girl whose hair is yellower

than torchlight need wear no colorful ribbons from Sardis –
but a garland of fresh flowers.

Sappho (b. *c.*650 BC)
From: Barnstone, A. and Barnstone, W. (eds) (1980) *Women Poets*,
translation by Willis Barnstone, Schoken Books.

A Suttee

Gather her raven hair in one rich cluster,
Let the white champac light it, as a star   *champac – a species of magnolia flower*
Gives to the dusky night a sudden lustre,
Shining afar.

Shed fragrant oils upon her fragrant bosom,
Until the breathing air around grows sweet;
Scatter the languid jasmine's yellow blossom
Beneath her feet.

Those small white feet are bare – too soft are they
To tread on aught but flowers; and there is roll'd
Round the slight ankle, meet for such display,
The band of gold.

Chains and bright stones are on her arms and neck;
What pleasant vanities are linked with them,
Of happy hours, which youth delights to deck
With gold and gem.

She comes! So comes the Moon, when she has found
A silvery path wherein thro' heaven to glide.
Fling the white veil – a summer cloud – around;
She is a bride!

And yet the crowd that gather at her side
Are pale, and every gazer holds his breath.
Eyes fill with tears unbidden for the bride –
The bride of Death!

She gives away the garland from her hair,
She gives the gems that she will wear no more;
All the affections whose love-signs they were
Are gone before.

The red pile blazes – let the bride ascend,
And lay her head upon her husband's heart,
Now in a perfect unison to blend –
No more to part.

Letitia Elizabeth Landon (1802–1838)
From: Bell Scott, W. (ed.) (1874) *Poetical Works*

To George Sand
A RECOGNITION

True genius, but true woman! dost deny
Thy woman's nature with a manly scorn,
And break away the gauds and armlets worn
By weaker women in captivity?
Ah, vain denial! that revolted cry
Is sobbed in by a woman's voice forlorn: –
Thy woman's hair, my sister, all unshorn,
Floats back dishevelled strength in agony,
Disproving thy man's name. And while before
The world thou burnest in a poet-fire,
We see thy woman-heart beat evermore
Through the large flame. Beat purer, heart,
and higher,
Till God unsex thee on the spirit-shore;
To which alone unsexing, purely aspire.

Elizabeth Barrett Browning (1806–1861)
From: Browning, E.B. (1904 edn) *Poetical Works*, Oxford University Press.

Aurora Leigh

Aurora Leigh is a novel in verse. Aurora is an aspiring writer, daughter of an English father and Italian mother. She is brought up in Italy but returns to England to live in the countryside with her aunt. She receives a proposal of marriage from her cousin Romney, who asks her to give up poetry and join him in his crusade for political reform. At the heart of the poem is Aurora's eloquent defence of a woman's right to choose her own career.

[Extract 1   Aurora meets her English aunt and guardian, First Book]

I think I see my father's sister stand
Upon the hall-step of her country-house
To give me welcome. She stood straight and calm,
Her somewhat narrow forehead braided tight
As if for taming accidental thoughts
From possible pulses; brown hair pricked with grey
By frigid use of life (she was not old,
Although my father' elder by a year),
A nose drawn sharply, yet in delicate lines;
A close mild mouth, a little soured about
The ends, through speaking unrequited loves,
Or peradventure niggardly half-truths;
Eyes of no colour,—once they might have smiled,
but never, never have forgot themselves
In smiling; cheeks, in which was yet a rose

Of perished summers, like a rose in a book,
Kept more for ruth than pleasure,—if past bloom,
Past fading also.
She had lived, we'll say,
A harmless life, she called a virtuous life,
A quiet life, which was not life at all
(But that, she had not lived enough to know),
Between the vicar and the county squires,
The lord-lieutenant looking down sometimes
From the empyreal, to assure their souls
Against chance-vulgarisms, and, in the abyss,
The apothecary, looked on once a year,
To prove their soundness of humility.
The poor-club exercised her Christian gifts
Of knitting stockings, stitching petticoats,
Because we are of one flesh, after all
And need one flannel (with a proper sense
Of difference in the quality) —and still
The book-club, guarded from your modern trick
Of shaking dangerous questions from the crease,
Preserved her intellectual. She had lived
A sort of cage-bird life, born in a cage,
Accounting that to leap from perch to perch
Was act and joy enough for any bird.
Dear heaven, how silly are the things that live
In thickets, and eat berries!
I, alas,
A wild bird scarcely fledged, was brought to her cage,

And she was there to meet me. Very kind.
Bring the clean water; give out the fresh seed.

[Extract 2   The poet, on her art and its penalties, Fifth Book]

The artist's part is both to be and do,
Transfixing with a special, central power
The flat experiences of the common man,
And turning outward, with sudden wrench,

Half agony, half ecstasy, the thing
He feels the inmost: never felt the less
Because he sings it. Does a torch less burn
For burning next reflectors of blue steel,
That *he* should be the colder for his place
'Twixt two incessant fires, –his personal life's,
And that intense refraction which burns back
Perpetually against him from the round
Of crystal conscience he was born into
If artist-born? O sorrowful great gift
Conferred on poets, of a twofold life,
When one life has been found enough for pain!
We, staggering 'neath our burden as mere men,
Being called to stand up straight as demi-gods,
Support the intolerable strain and stress
Of the universal, and send clearly up,
With voices broken by the human sob,
Our poems to find rhymes among the stars!
But soft! – a 'poet' is a word soon said;
A book's a thing soon written. Nay, indeed,
The more the poet shall be questionable,
The more unquestionably comes his book!
And this of mine –well, granting to myself
Some passion in it, furrowing up the flats,
Mere passsion will not prove a volume worth
Its gall and rags even. Bubbles round a keel
Mean nought, excepting that the vessel moves.
There's more than passion goes to make a man,
Or book, which is a man too [...]
[...]   To have our books
Appraised by love, associated with love,
While *we* sit loveless! is it hard, you think?
At least 'tis mournful. Fame, indeed, 'twas said,
Means simply love. It was a man said that.
And then, there's love and love: the love of all
(To risk, in turn, a woman's paradox,)
Is but a small thing to the love of one.
You bid a hungry child be satisfied
With a heritage of many corn-fields: nay,
He says he's hungry,—he would rather have
That little barley-cake you keep from him
While reckoning up his harvests.

Elizabeth Barrett Browning (1806–1861)
From: Reynolds, M. (ed.) (1992) *Aurora Leigh,* Ohio University Press; the
poem was first published in 1856.

'No coward soul is mine'

No coward soul is mine
No trembler in the world's storm-troubled sphere.
I see Heaven's glories shine
And Faith shines equal arming me from Fear

O God within my breast
Almighty ever-present Deity
Life, that in me hast rest
As I Undying Life, have power in thee

Vain are the thousand creeds
That move men's hearts, unutterably vain.
Worthless as withered weeds
Or idlest froth amid the boundless main

To waken doubt in one
Holding so fast by thy infinity
So surely anchored on
The steadfast rock of Immortality

With wide-embracing love
Thy spirit animates eternal years
Pervades and broods above.
Changes, sustains, dissolves, creates and rears

Though Earth and moon were gone
and suns and universe ceased to be
And thou wert left alone
Every Existence would exist in thee

There is not room for Death
Nor atom that his might could render void
Since Thou art Being and Breath
And what thou art may never be destroyed

Emily Brontë (1818–1848)
From: Lloyd-Evans, B. (ed.) (1992) *The Poems of Emily Brontë*, Batsford; the
poem is dated January 2 1846.

The Winged Soul

My Soul is like some cage-born bird, that hath
A restless prescience – howsoever won –
Of a broad pathway leading to the sun,
With promptings of an oft-reproved faith
In sun-ward yearnings. Stricken through her breast,
And faint her wing, with beating at the bars
Of sense, she looks beyond outlying stars,
And only in the Infinite sees rest.
Sad soul! If ever thy desire be bent
Or broken to thy doom, and made to share
The ruminant's beatitude, – content, –
Chewing the cud of knowledge, with no care
For germs of life within; *then* will I say,
Thou art not caged, but fitly *stall'd* in clay.

Emily Pfeiffer (1827–1890)
From: Pfeiffer, E. (1886) *Sonnets*, Field and Tuer.

The Last Light

I never touched thy royal hand, dead queen,
But from afar have looked upon thy face,
Which, calm with conquest, carried still the trace
Of many a hard-fought battle that had been.
Since thou hast done with life, its toil and teen,
Its pains and gains, and that no further grace
Can come to us of thee, a poorer place
Shows the lorn world, – a dimlier lighted scene.

Lost queen and captain, Pallas of our band,
Who late upon the height of glory stood,
Guarding from scorn – the aegis in thy hand –
The banner of insurgent womanhood;
Who of our cause may take the high command?
Who make with shining front our victory good?

Emily Pfeiffer (1827–1890)
Pfeiffer, E. (1886) *Sonnets*, Field and Tuer; the poem is dated 29 December 1880, in memory of George Eliot.

In An Artist's Studio

ONE face looks out from all his canvases,
One selfsame figure sits or walks or leans:
We found her hidden just behind those screens,
That mirror gave back all her loveliness.
A queen in opal or in ruby dress,
A nameless girl in freshest summer-greens,
A saint, an angel—every canvas means
The same one meaning, neither more nor less.
He feeds upon her face by day and night,
And she with true kind eyes looks back on him,
Fair as the moon and joyful as the light:
Not wan with waiting, not with sorrow dim;
Not as she is, but was when hope shone bright;
Not as she is, but as she fills his dream.

Christina Rossetti (1830–1894)
From: Crump, W.R. (ed.) (1979–1990) *The Complete Poems of Christina Rossetti*, 3 vols, Louisiana University Press; the poem is dated 24 December 1856.

L. E. L.

'Whose heart was breaking for a little love.'

Downstairs I laugh, I sport and jest with all;
But in my solitary room above
I turn my face in silence to the wall;
My heart is breaking for a little love.
Though winter frosts are done,
And birds pair every one,
And leaves peep out, for springtide is begun.

I feel no spring, while spring is well-nigh blown,
I find no nest, while nests are in the grove:
Woe's me for mine own heart that dwells alone,

My heart that breaketh for a little love.
While golden in the sun
Rivulets rise and run,
While lilies bud, for springtide is begun.

All love, are loved, save only I; their hearts
Beat warm with love and joy, beat full thereof:
They cannot guess, who play the pleasant parts,
My heart is breaking for a little love.
While bee-hives wake and whirr,
And rabbit thins his fur,
In living spring that sets the world astir.

I deck myself with silks and jewelry,
I plume myself like any mated dove:
They praise my rustling show, and never see
My heart is breaking for a little love.
While sprouts green lavender
With rosemary and myrrh,
For in quick spring the sap is all astir.

Perhaps some saints in glory guess the truth,
Perhaps some angels read it as the move,
And cry one to another full of ruth,
'Her heart is breaking for a little love.'
Though other things have birth,
And leap and sing for mirth,
When springtime wakes and clothes and feeds the earth.

Yet saith a saint, 'Take patience for thy scathe';
Yet saith an angel: 'Wait, and thou shalt prove
True best is last, true life is born of death,
O thou, heart-broken for a little love.
Then love shall fill thy girth,
And love make fat thy dearth,
When new spring builds new heaven and clean new earth.'

Christina Rossetti (1830–1894)
From: Crump, W.R. (ed.) (1979–1990) *The Complete Poems of Christina Rossetti*, 3 vols, Louisiana University Press; the poem is dated 15 February 1859.

Goblin Market

Goblin Market is the story of two sisters, Laura and Lizzie, who are tempted by goblin men to buy their orchard fruits. Lizzie warns Laura not to look at the goblins, but Laura cannot resist the temptation and exchanges a 'golden curl' for a taste of the luscious fruit. Laura falls ill with a desperate craving for the fruit, and is close to death when Lizzie seeks out the goblins and attempts to buy fruit for her sister. The goblins try to force Lizzie to eat the fruit herself, but she escapes and helps to save Laura with the juices that have run down her face. At one level a fairy tale for children, *Goblin Market* is also a subtle allegory of temptation.

[Extract 1]

Laura reared her glossy head,
and whispered like the restless brook:
'Look, Lizzie, look, Lizzie,
Down the glen tramp little men.
One hauls a basket,
One bears a plate,
One lugs a golden dish
of many pounds' weight.
How fair the vine must grow
Whose grapes are so luscious
How warm the wind must blow
Through those fruit bushes.'
'No' said Lizzie: 'No, no, no;
Their offers should not charm us,
Their evil gifts would harm us.'
She thrust a dimpled finger
In each ear, shut eyes and ran:
Curious Laura chose to linger
Wondering at each merchant man.
One had a cat's face,
One whisked a tail,
One tramped at a rat's pace,
One crawled like a snail,
One like a wombat prowled obtuse and furry,
One like a ratel tumbled hurryskurry.   *ratel – honey badger*
She heard a voice like voice of doves
Cooing all together:
They sounded kind and full of loves
In the pleasant weather.

Laura stretched her gleaming neck
Like a rush-imbedded swan,
Like a lily from the beck,
Like a moonlit poplar branch,
Like a vessel at the launch
When its last restraint is gone.

Backwards up the mossy glen
Turned and trooped the goblin men,
With their shrill repeated cry,
Come buy, come buy.
When they reached where Laura was
They stood stock still upon the moss,
Leering at each other,
Brother with queer brother;
Signalling each other,
Brother with sly brother.
One set his basket down,
One reared his plate;
One began to weave a crown
Of tendrils, leaves, and rough nuts brown
[Men sell not such in any town];
One heaved the golden weight of dish and fruit to offer her:
'Come buy, come buy,' was still their cry.

Laura stared but did not stir,
Longed but had no money.
The whisk-tailed merchant bade her taste
In tones as smooth as honey,
The ,cat-faced purr'd
The rat-paced spoke a word
Of welcome, and the snail-paced even was heard;
One parrot-voiced and jolly
Cried 'Pretty Goblin' still for 'Pretty Polly';
One whistled like a bird.

But sweet-tooth Laura spoke in haste:
'Good Folk, I have no coin;
To take were to purloin:
I have no copper in my purse,
I have no silver either,
And all my gold is on the furze
That shakes in windy weather
Above the rusty heather.'
'You have much gold upon your head,'
They answered all together:
'Buy from us with a golden curl.'
She clipped a precious golden lock,
She dropped a tear more rare than pearl,
Then sucked their fruit globes fair or red.
Sweeter than honey from the rock,
Stronger than man-rejoicing wine,
Clearer than water flowed that juice;
She never tasted such before,
How should it cloy with length of use?
She sucked and sucked and sucked the more
Fruits which that unknown orchard bore;
She sucked until her lips were sore;
Then flung the emptied rinds away
But gathered up one kernel stone,
And knew not was it night or day
As she turned home alone.

Extract 2

Though the goblins cuffed and caught her,
Coaxed and fought her,
Bullied and besought her,
Scratched her, pinched her black as ink,
Kicked and knocked her,
Mauled and mocked her,
Lizzie uttered not a word;
Would not open lip from lip
Lest they should cram a mouthful in:
But laughed in heart to feel the drip
Of juice thay syruped all her face,
And lodged in dimples of her chin,
And streaked her neck which quaked like curd,
At last the evil people,
Worn out by her resistance,
Fling back her penny, kicked their fruit

Along whichever road they took,
Not leaving root or stone or shoot;
Some writhed into the ground,
Some dived into the brook
With ring and ripple,
Some scudded on the gale without a sound,
Some vanished in the distance.

In a smart, ache, tingle,
Lizzie went her way;
Knew not was it night or day;
Sprang up the bank, tore thro' the furze,
Threaded copse and dingle,
And heard her penny jingle
Bouncing in her purse, –
Its bounce was music to her ear.
She ran and ran
As if she feared some goblin man
Dogged her with gibe or curse
Or something worse:
But not one goblin skurried after,
Nor was she pricked by fear;
The kind heart made her windy-paced
That urged her home quite out of breath with haste
And inward laughter.

She cried, 'Laura,' up the garden,
'Did you miss me ?
Come and kiss me.
Never mind my bruises,
Hug me, kiss me, suck my juices
Squeezed from goblin fruits for you,
Goblin pulp and goblin dew.
Eat me, drink me, love me;
Laura, make much of me;
For your sake I have braved the glen
And had to do with goblin merchant men.'

Laura started from her chair,
Flung her arms up in the air,
Clutched her hair:
'Lizzie, Lizzie, have you tasted
For my sake the fruit forbidden ?
Must your light like mine be hidden,
Your young life like mine be wasted,
Undone in mine undoing,
and ruined in my ruin,
Thirsty, cankered, goblin-ridden?' –
She clung about her sister,
Kissed and kissed and kissed her:
Tears once again
Refreshed her shrunken eyes,
Dropping like rain
After long sultry drouth;
Shaking with anguish fear, and pain,
She kissed and kissed her her with a hungry mouth.

Her lips began to scorch,
That juice was wormwood to her tongue,
She loathed the feast:
Writhing as one possessed she leaped and sung,
Rent all her robe, and wrung
Her hands in lamentable haste,
And beat her breast.
Her locks streamed like the torch
Borne by a racer at full speed,
Or like the mane of horses in their flight,
Or like an eagle when she stems the light
Straight toward the sun,
Or like a caged thing freed,
Or like a flying flag when armies run.

Christina Rossetti (1830–1894)
From: Crump, W.R. (ed.) (1979–1990) *The Complete Poems of Christina Rossetti*, 3 vols, Louisiana University Press.

III   Nineteenth-century Scottish and Irish poetry

The Weary Spinnin O't

Sittin spinnin, sittin spinnin
A' the lea-lang day,
Hearin the bit burnie rinnin,   *bit burnie – little stream*
And the bairns at play.
I'm sweir to get my leg let loose,   *sweir – reluctant*
To do a turn about the hoose;
Oh, amna I a waefu wife
To spin awa my threid of life?
Spinnin, spinnin, ever spinnin,
Never endin, aye beginnin;
Hard at wark wi hand and fuit,
Oh, the weary spinnin o't!

Sittin spinnin, sittin spinnin,
Vow but I am thrang,   *Vow – an exclamation   thrang – busy*
My wee pickle siller winnin,   *pickle siller – bit of money*
Croonin some auld sang.
Leese me o my spinnin-wheel,   *leese – release*
Gie's us a' oor milk and meal;
Weet or dry, or het or cauld,
I maun spin till I grow auld.
Spinnin, spinnin, ever spinnin,
Never endin, aye beginnin,
Hard at wark wi hand and fuit
At the weary spinnin o't.

Sittin spinnin, sittin spinnin,
Sic a wear and tear,
Taps of tow for wabs o linen,   *taps of tow – tufts of flax wabs – webs*
Till my heid is sair.

Mony a wiselike wab I've spun,   *wiselike – nice-looking*
Spreid and sortit i the sun;
Puirtith cauld is ill to bear;   *puirtith – poverty*
Mony bairns bring mickle care.   *mickle – much*
Spinnin, spinnin, ever spinnin,
Never endin, aye beginnin,
Hard at wark wi hand and fuit,
Oh! the weary spinnin o't!

Dorothea Maria Ogilvy of Clova (1823–1895)
From: Kerrigan, C. (ed.) (1991) *An Anthology of Scottish Women Poets*,
Edinburgh University Press.

A Legend of Tyrone

Among those green hills where O'Neill in his pride,
Rules in high state, with his fair English bride.
A quaint cottage stood, till swept down by some gale,
And of that vanished home the old wives tell this tale.

***

Crouched round a bare hearth in hard, frosty weather,
Three lone, helpless weans cling close together;
Tangled those gold locks, once bonnie and bright,
There's no one to fondle the baby to-night.

'My mammie I want! Oh! my mammie I want!'
The big tears stream down with low wailing chaunt;
Sweet Ely's slight arms enfold the gold head;
'Poor weeny Willie, sure mammie is dead —

And daddie is crazy from drinking all day,
Come down, holy angels, and take us away!'
Eily and Eddie keep kissing and crying —
Outside the weird winds are sobbing and sighing.

All in a moment the children are still,
Only a quick coo of gladness from Will.
The sheiling no longer seems empty and bare,   *sheiling – homestead*
For, clothed in white raiment, the mother stands there.

They gather around her, they cling to her dress;
She rains down soft kisses for each shy caress,
Her light, loving touches smooth out tangled locks,
And pressed to her bosom the baby she rocks.

He lies in his cot, there's a fire on the hearth;
To Eily and Eddy 'tis heaven on earth,
For mother's deft fingers have been everywhere,
She lulls them to rest in the low sugaun chair.   *sugaun – rush-seated*

They gaze open-eyed, then the eyes gently close,
As petals fold into the heart of a rose;
But ope soon again in awe, love, but not fear,
And fondly they murmur, 'Our mammie is here!'

She lays them down softly, she wraps them around,
They lie in sweet slumbers, she starts at a sound!
The cock loudly crows, and the spirits away —
The drunkard steals in at the dawning of day.

Again and again 'tween the dark and the dawn
Glides in the dead mother to nurse Willie bawn,   *bawn – fair*
Or is it an angel who sits by the hearth?
An angel in heaven, a mother on earth.

Ellen O'Leary (1831–1889)
From: Miles, A.H. (ed.) (1892) *The Poets and Poetry of the Century*,
Hutchinson.

The Shade of the Past

Could he appear—the grand majestic Spirit,
Telling the tale, so little prized before,
He, from the babbling present, did inherit—
All that our fathers heard, *yet* did not hear, of yore!

They who lived, acted, in the world's turmoil—
Who threw their passions' colouring o'er each scene—
Shone with may-flies, or with true sons of toil
Built up a life which tells that they have been.

Fragments they leave us of the world's old story
Fragments we muse and gaze upon and sigh—
Had we been there—in those bright days of glory!
Had we a faithful record 'neath our eye!

We sit and dim our eyes in vainly guessing—
In spelling olden letters half effaced—
All that thine eyes have watched in the progressing,
Seen every letter in succession traced!

Silent, still silent – never prayer hath moved thee
Calm look'st thou down on our laborious hours
Have ne'er thy votaries worn-out lives reproved thee,
Thou cruel miser, for thy hoarded powers?

One word of thine were worth ten thousand pages,
Brilliant, but doubtful, of historic guess
One living relic of those far-off ages
We vainly strive in fancy's robes to dress.

Ah! niggard, sullen Ghost, where o'er thy treasures
Dost thou sit gloating, callous to all prayer?
While cruel Time, yielding to thee, outmeasures
Days, months and years all passing to thy care.

I know thou art even as I know God living
I know thou livest on, though seeming still to die
And all the treasure Time to thee is giving
Will it be ours then, in Eternity?

Like a spread map, may we unfold before us
The story of our earth from morn to night?
And shall a mightier power compel thee to restore us
The darkened page—all gleaming into light?

Christina Leslie Burnett (1818–1866)
Source: C.L.B., (1867?) *Songs of a Caged Bird*, privately printed in Inverurie;
the poem is dated 1857.

The Last Sark

Gude guide me, are ye hame again, and hae ye got nae wark?
We've naething noo tae pit awa, unless your auld blue sark.   *sark – shirt*
My heid is rinnin roond aboot, far lichter nor a flee   *lichter nor a flee – lighter than a fly*
What care some gentry if they're weel though a' the puir wad dee?

Our merchants and mill-masters they wad never want a meal
Though a' the banks in Scotland wad for a twalmonth fail;
For some o them hae far mair gowd than ony ane can see.   *gowd – gold*
What care some gentry if they're weel though a' the puir wad dee?

Oor hoose aince bien and cosy, John, oor beds aince snug and warm,   *bien – thriving*
Feels unco cauld and dismal noo, and empty as a barn;   *unco – uncommonly*
The weans sit greetin in our face, and we hae nocht tae gie.   *greetin – crying*
What care some gentry if they're weel though a' the puir wad dee?

It is the puir man's hard-won cash that fills the rich man's purse;
I'm sure his gowden coffers they are het wi mony a curse   *het – assailed*
Were it no for the workin man what wad the rich man be?
What care some gentry if they' weel though a' the puir wad dee?

My head is licht, my heart is weak, my een are growing blin';
The bairn is faen' aff my knee – oh! John, catch haud o' him,
You ken I hinna tasted meat for days far mair than three;
Were it no for my helpless bairns I wadna care to dee.

Ellen Johnston (*c*.1835–1873)
From: Johnston, E. (1867) *Autobiography, Poems and Songs,* publisher
unknown.

Any Woman

I am the pillars of the house;
The keystone of the arch am I.
Take me away, and roof and wall
Would fall to ruin utterly.

I am the fire upon the hearth,
I am the light of the good sun,
I am the heat that warms the earth,
Which else were colder than a stone.

At me the children warm their hands;
I am their light of love alive.
Without me cold the hearthstone stands,
Nor could the precious children thrive.

I am the twist that holds together
The children in its sacred ring,
Their knot of love, from whose close tether
No lost child goes a-wandering.

I am the house from floor to roof,
I deck the walls, the board I spread;
I spin the curtains, warp and woof,
And shake the down to be their bed.

I am their wall against all danger,
Their door against the wind and snow,
Thou Whom a woman laid in manger,
Take me not till the children grow!

Katharine Tynan (1861–1931)
From: Gibbon, M. (ed.) (1963) *The Poems of Katharine Tynan*, Allen Figgis.

IV   Emily Dickinson (1830–1886)

All poems in this section are taken from Johnson, T.H. (ed.) (1970) *The Complete Poems of Emily Dickinson*, Faber and Faber.

280

I felt a Funeral, in my Brain,
And Mourners to and fro
Kept treading – treading – till it seemed
That Sense was breaking through –

And when they all were seated,
A Service, like a Drum –
Kept beating – beating – till I thought
My Mind was going numb –

And then I heard them lift a Box
And creak across my Soul
With those same Boots of Lead, again,
Then Space – began to toll,

As all the Heavens were a Bell,
And Being, but an Ear,
And I, and Silence, some strange Race
Wrecked, solitary, here –

And then a Plank in Reason, broke,
And I dropped down, and down –
And hit a World, at every plunge,
And Finished knowing – then –

c. 1861

486

I was the slightest in the House –
I took the smallest Room –
At night, my little Lamp, and Book –
And one Geranium –

So stationed I could catch the Mint
That never ceased to fall –
And just my Basket –
Let me think – I'm sure
That this was all –

I never spoke – unless addressed –
And then, 'twas brief and low –
I could not bear to live – aloud –
The Racket shamed me so –

And if it had not been so far –
And any one I knew
Were going – I had often thought
How noteless – I could die –

303

The Soul selects her own Society –
Then – shuts the Door –
To her divine Majority –
Present no more –

Unmoved – she notes the Chariots – pausing –
At her low Gate –
Unmoved – an Emperor be kneeling
Upon her Mat –

I've known her – from an ample nation –
Choose One –
Then – close the Valves of her attention –
Like Stone –

c. 1862

712

Because I could not stop for Death –
He kindly stopped for me –
The Carriage held but just Ourselves –
And Immortality.

We slowly drove – He knew no haste
And I had put away
My labor and my leisure too,
For His Civility –

We passed the School, where Children strove
At Recess – in the Ring –
We passed the Fields of Gazing Grain –
We passed the Setting Sun –

Or rather – He Passed Us –
The Dews drew quivering and chill –
For only Gossamer, my Gown –
My Tippet – only Tulle –

We paused before a House that seemed
A swelling of the Ground –
The Roof was scarcely visible –
The Cornice – in the Ground –

Since then – 'tis Centuries – and yet
Feels shorter than the Day
I first surmised the Horses' Heads
Were toward Eternity –

c. 1863

108

Surgeons must be very careful
When they take the knife!
Underneath their fine incisions
Stirs the culprit – *LIFE!*

1737

Rearrange a 'Wife's' affection!
When they dislocate my Brain!
Amputate my freckled Bosom!
Make me bearded like a man!

Blush, my spirit, in thy Fastness –
Blush, my unacknowledged clay –
Seven years of troth have taught thee
More than Wifehood ever may!

Love that never leaped its socket –
Trust entrenched in narrow pain –
Constancy thro' fire – awarded –
Anguish – bare of anodyne!

Burden – borne so far triumphant –
None suspect me of the crown,
For I wear the 'Thorns' till *Sunset* –
Then – my Diadem put on.

Big my Secret but it's *bandaged* –
It will never get away
Till the Day its Weary Keeper
Leads it through the Grave to thee.

1261

A Word dropped careless on a Page
May stimulate an eye
When folded in perpetual seam
The Wrinkled Maker lie

Infection in the sentence breeds
We may inhale Despair
At distances of Centuries
From the Malaria –

77

I never hear the word 'escape'
Without a quicker blood,
A sudden expectation,
A flying attitude.

I never hear of prisons broad
By soldiers battered down,
But I tug childish at my bars, –
Only to fail again!

441

This is my letter to the World
That never wrote to Me –
The simple News that Nature told –
With tender Majesty

Her Message is committed
To Hands I cannot see –
For love of her – Sweet – countrymen –
Judge tenderly – of Me

593

I think I was enchanted
When first a sombre Girl –
I read that Foreign lady –
The Dark – felt beautiful –

And whether it was noon at night –
Or only Heaven – at Noon –
For very Lunacy of Light
I had not power to tell –

The Bees – became as Butterflies –
The Butterflies – as Swans –
Approached – and spurned the narrow Grass –
And just the meanest Tunes

The Nature murmured to herself
To keep herself in Cheer –
I took for Giants – practising
Titanic Opera –

The Days – to Mighty Metres stept –
The Homeliest – adorned
As if unto a Jubilee
'Twere suddenly confirmed –

I could not have defined the change –
Conversion of the Mind
Like Sanctifying in the Soul –
Is witnessed – not explained –

'Twas a Divine Insanity –
The Danger to be Sane
Should I again experience –
'Tis Antidote to turn –

To Tomes of solid Witchcraft –
Magicians be asleep –
But Magic – hath an Element
Like Deity – to keep –

435

Much Madness is divinest Sense –
To a discerning Eye –
Much Sense – the starkest Madness –
'Tis the Majority
In this, as All, prevail –
Assent – and you are sane –
Demur – you're straightway dangerous –
And handled with a Chain –

67

Success is counted sweetest
By those who ne'er succeed.
To comprehend a nectar
Requires sorest need.

Not one of all the purple Host
Who took the Flag today
Can tell the definition
So clear of Victory

As he defeated – dying –
On whose forbidden ear
The distant strains of triumph
Burst agonized and clear!

288

I'm Nobody! Who are you?
Are you – Nobody – Too?
Then there's a pair of us?
Don't tell! they'd advertise – you know!

How dreary – to be – Somebody!
How public – like a Frog –
To tell one's name – the livelong June –
To an admiring Bog!

512

The Soul has Bandaged moments –
When too appalled to stir –
She feels some ghastly Fright come up
And stop to look at her –

Salute her – with long fingers –
Caress her freezing hair –
Sip, Goblin, from the very lips
The Lover – hovered – o'er –
Unworthy, that a thought so mean
Accost a Theme – so – fair –

The soul has moments of Escape –
When bursting all the doors –
She dances like a Bomb, abroad,
And swings upon the Hours,

As do the Bee – delirious borne –
Long Dungeoned from his Rose –
Touch Liberty – then know no more,
But Noon, and Paradise –

The Soul's retaken moments –
When, Felon led along,
With shackles on the plumed feet,
And staples, in the Song,

The Horror welcomes her, again,
These, are not brayed of Tongue –

V Contemporary poets

The Colossus

I shall never get you put together entirely,
Pieced, glued, and properly jointed.
Mule-bray, pig-grunt and bawdy cackles
Proceed from your great lips.
It's worse than a barnyard.

Perhaps you consider yourself an oracle,
Mouthpiece of the dead, or of some god or other.
Thirty years now I have laboured
To dredge the silt from your throat.
I am none the wiser.

Scaling little ladders with gluepots and pails of lysol
I crawl like an ant in mourning
Over the weedy acres of your brow
To mend the immense skull-plates and clear
The bald, white tumuli of your eyes.

A blue sky out of the Oresteia
Arches above us. O father, all by yourself
You are pithy and historical as the Roman Forum.
I open my lunch on a hill of black cypress.
Your fluted bones and acanthine hair are littered

In their old anarchy to the horizon-line.
It would take more than a lightning-stroke
To create such a ruin.
Nights, I squat in the cornucopia
Of your left ear, out of the wind,

Counting the red stars and those of plum-colour.
The sun rises under the pillar of your tongue.
My hours are married to shadow.
No longer do I listen for the scrape of a keel
On the blank stones of the landing.

Sylvia Plath (1932–1963)
From: Plath, S. (1960) *The Colossus,* Faber and Faber.

Lady Lazarus

I have done it again.
One year in every ten
I manage it —

A sort of walking miracle, my skin
Bright as a Nazi lampshade,
My right foot

A paperweight,
My face a featureless, fine
Jew linen.

Peel off the napkin
O my enemy.
Do I terrify? —

The nose, the eye pits, the full set of teeth?
The sour breath
Will vanish in a day.

Soon, soon the flesh
The grave cave ate will be
At home on me

And I a smiling woman.
I am only thirty.
And like the cat I have nine times to die.

This is Number Three.
What a trash
To annihilate each decade.

What a million filaments.
The peanut-crunching crowd
Shoves in to see

Them unwrap me hand and foot —
The big strip tease.
Gentlemen, ladies

These are my hands
My knees.
I may be skin and bone,

Nevertheless, I am the same, identical woman.
The first time it happened I was ten.
It was an accident.

The second time I meant
To last it out and not come back at all.
I rocked shut

As a seashell.
They had to call and call
And pick the worms off me like sticky pearls.

Dying
Is an art, like everything else.
I do it exceptionally well.

I do it so it feels like hell.
I do it so it feels real.
I guess you could say I've a call.

It's easy enough to do it in a cell.
It's easy enough to do it and stay put.
It's the theatrical

Comeback in broad day
To the same place, the same face, the same brute
Amused shout:

'A miracle!'
That knocks me out.
There is a charge

For the eyeing of my scars, there is a charge
For the hearing of my heart –
It really goes.

And there is a charge, a very large charge
For a word or a touch
Or a bit of blood

Or a piece of my hair or my clothes.
So, so, Herr Doktor.
So, Herr Enemy.

I am your opus,
I am your valuable,
The pure gold baby

That melts to a shriek.
I turn and burn.
Do not think I underestimate your great concern.

Ash, ash –
You poke and stir.
Flesh, bone, there is nothing there –

A cake of soap,
A wedding ring,
A gold filling.

Herr God, Herr Lucifer
Beware
Beware.

Out of the ash
I rise with my red hair
And I eat men like air.

Sylvia Plath (1932–1963)
From: Plath, S. (1965) *Ariel*, Faber and Faber.

Autobiographical

Right now, here it comes.
I killed my father when I was three.
I have muddled through several affairs
and always come out badly.
I've learned almost nothing from experience.
I head for the abyss with
monotonous regularity.

My enemies say I'm a critic because
really I'm writhing with envy
and anyway need to get married.

My friends say I'm not
entirely without talent.

Yes, I've tried suicide,
I tidied my clothes but
left no notes. I was surprised
to wake up in the morning.

One day my soul
stood outside me
watching me twitch
and grin and gibber
the skin tight
over my bones

I thought the whole world
was trying to rip me up
cut me down go through me
with a razor blade

then I discovered
a cliché: that's what I wanted
to do to the world.

Eunice de Souza (1940–)
From: Rumens, C. (ed.) (1985) *Making for the Open: The Chatto Book of
Post-Feminist Poetry 1964–1984*, Chatto and Windus.

Against Coupling

I write in praise of the solitary act:
of not feeling a trespassing tongue
forced into one's mouth, one's breath
smothered, nipples crushed against the
ribcage, and that metallic tingling
in the chin set off by a certain odd nerve:

unpleasure. Just to avoid those eyes would help –
such eyes as a young girl draws life from,
listening to the vegetal
rustle within her, as his gaze
stirs polypal fronds in the obscure   *polypal – like the arms of an octopus*
sea-bed of her body, and her own eyes blur.

There is much to be said for abandoning
this no longer novel exercise –
for not 'participating in
a total experience' – when
one feels like the lady in Leeds who
had seen *The Sound of Music* eighty-six times;

or more, perhaps, like the school drama mistress
producing *A Midsummer Night's Dream*
for the seventh year running, with
yet another cast from 5B.
Pyramus and Thisbe are dead, but
the hole in the wall can still be troublesome.

I advise you, then, to embrace it without
encumbrance. No need to set the scene,
dress up (or undress), make speeches.
Five minutes of solitude are
enough – in the bath, or to fill
that gap between the Sunday papers and lunch.

Fleur Adcock (1934–)
From: Morrison, B. and Motion, A. (eds) (1982) *The Penguin Book of Contemporary Poetry*, Penguin Books.

Hanging Curtains with an Abstract Pattern in a Child's Room

I chose these for you –
not the precinct of the unicorn, nor

the half-torn
singlet of a nursery rhyme prince, but

the signals of enigma:
Ellipse. Triangle. A music of ratio.

Draw these lines
against a winter dusk. Let them stand in for

frost on the spider's web and on
bicycle sheds.

Observe
how the season enters pure line

like a soul: all the signs we know
are only ways

of coming to our senses.
I can see

the distances off-loading colour now
into angles as

I hang their weather in
your room, all the time wondering

just how I look from the road –
my blouse off-white and

my skirt the colour of
all the disappointments of a day when

the curtains are pulled back on
a dull morning.

Eavan Boland, Ireland (1944–)
From: Boland, E. (1990) *Outside History*, Carcanet.

Sleeping

Under the dark warm waters of sleep
your hands part me.
I am dreaming you anyway.

Your mouth is hot fruit, wet, strange,
night-fruit I taste with my opening mouth;
my eyes closed.

You, you. Your breath flares into fervent words
which explode in my head. Then you ask, push,
for an answer.

And this is how we sleep. You're in now, hard,
demanding; so I dream more fiercely, dream
till it hurts

that this is for real, yes, I feel it.
When you hear me, you hold on tight, frantic,
as if we were drowning.

Carol Ann Duffy (1955–)
From: Duffy, C.A. (1993) *Mean Time,* Anvil Press.

Reflection
'I Love My Children More Than Anyone'

How I wish I could discern
why
children once arriving
overturn our world,
disqualifying ourselves
to them, – reproachless
and how we turn our
necks inward
on their depth,
like swans relishing
to capture lives underneath.

But I understand
though the need
of lover and friend
that they do not possess
the gleam
which gilds the lake
with innocence;
when we protect
the small ones from the snatching world
of coarse grass:

for in them
are our tomorrows,
unnerving dives,
floaters of calm.

And in their gaze
absence of arrogance,
which is more than
a bait for our being.

Menna Elfyn (1951–)
From: Elfyn, M. (1990) *In the Gold of the Flesh,* translated from the Welsh by
the author, Womens Press

The Telling Part

Ma mammy bot me oot a shop
Ma mammy says I was a luvly baby

Ma mammy picked me (I wiz the best)
your mammy had to take you (she'd no choice)
Ma mammy says she's no really ma mammy

(just kid on)

It's a bit like a part you've rehearsed so well
you can't play it on the opening night
She says my real mammy is away far away
Mammy why aren't you and me the same colour
    But I love my mammy whether she's real or no
My heart started rat tat tat like a tin drum
all the words took off to another planet
Why

But I love ma mammy whether she's real or no

I could hear the upset in her voice
I says *I'm not your real mother*
though Christ knows why I said that
If I'm not who is, but all my planned speech
went out the window

    She took me when I'd nowhere to go
    my mammy is the best mammy in the world OK

After mammy telt me she wisnae my real mammy
I was scared to death she was gonnie melt
or something or mibbe disappear in the dead
of night and somebody would say she wis a fairy
godmother. So the next morning I felt her skin
to check it was flesh, but mibbe it was just
a good imitation. How could I tell if my mammy
was a dummy with a voice spoken by someone else
So I searches the whole house for clues
but I never found nothing. Anyhow a day after
I got my guinea pig and forgot all about it.

I always believed in the telling anyhow.
You can't keep something like that secret
I wanted her to think of her other mother
out here thinking that child I had will be
seven today eight today all the way up to
god knows when. I told my daughter –
I bet your mother's never missed your birthday
How could she?

Jackie Kay (1961–)
From: Rumens, C. (ed.) (1990) *New Women Poets*, Bloodaxe.

Wherever I Hang

I leave me people, me land, me home
For reasons, I not too sure
I forsake de sun
And de humming-bird splendour
Had big rats in de floorboard
So I pick up me new-world-self
And come, to this place call England
At first I feeling like I in dream –
De misty greyness
I touching de walls to see if they real
They solid to de seam
And de people pouring from de underground system
Like beans
And when I look up to de sky
I see Lord Nelson high – too high to lie

And is so I sending home photos of myself
Among de pigeons and de snow
And is so I warding off de cold
And is so, little by little
I begin to change my calypso ways
Never visiting nobody
Before giving them clear warning
And waiting me turn in queue
Now, after all this time
I get accustom to de English life
But I still miss back-home side
To tell you de truth
I don't know really where I belaang
    Yes, divided to de ocean
    Divided to de bone
Wherever I hang me knickers – that's my home.

Grace Nichols (1950–)
From: Nichols, G. (1989) *Lazy Thoughts of a Lazy Woman and Other Poems*,
Virago Press.

The Bridge Poem

I've had enough
I'm sick of seeing and touching
Both sides of things
Sick of being the damn bridge for everybody

Nobody can talk to anybody without me Right

I explain my mother to my father my father to my little sister my
little sister to my brother my brother to the White Feminists the
White Feminists to the Black Church Folks the Black Church Folks
to the ex-Hippies the ex-Hippies to the Black Separatists the Black
Separatists to the Artists and the Artists to the parents of my
friends ...

Then
I've got to explain myself
To everybody

I do more translating than the UN

Forget it
I'm sick of filling in your gaps
Sick of being your insurance against
The isolation of your self-imposed limitations
Sick of being the crazy at your Holiday Dinners
The odd one at your Sunday Brunches
I am sick of being the sole Black friend to
Thirty-four Individual White Folks

Find another connection to the rest of the world
Something else to make you legitimate
Some other way to be political and hip
I will not be the bridge to your womanhood
Your manhood
Your human-ness

I'm sick of reminding you not to
Close off too tight for too long

Sick of mediating with your worst self
On behalf of your better selves

Sick
Of having
To remind you
To breathe
Before you
Suffocate
Your own
Fool self

Forget it
Stretch or drown
Evolve or die

You see it's like this
The bridge I must be
Is the bridge to my own power
I must translate
My own fears
Mediate
My own weaknesses

I must be the bridge to nowhere
But my own true self
It's only then
I can be
Useful

Kate Rushin (1951–)
From: Rushin, K. (1993) *The Black Back-Ups*, Firebrand Books.

Dialogue

She sits with one hand poised against her head, the
other turning an old ring to the light
for hours our talk has beaten
like rain against the screens
a sense of August and heat-lightning
I get up, go to make tea, come back
we look at each other
then she says (and this is what I live through
over and over) – she says: *I do not know*
if sex is an illusion
I do not know
who I was when I did those things
or who I said I was
or whether I willed to feel
what I had read about
or who in fact was there with me
or whether I knew, even then
that there was doubt about these things

Adrienne Rich (1929–)
From: Rumens, C. (ed.) (1985) *Making for the Open: The Chatto Book of
Post-Feminist Poetry 1964–1984*, Chatto; the poem is dated 1972.

Ain't I a Woman?

That man over there say
    a woman needs to be helped into carriages
and lifted over ditches
    and to have the best place everywhere.
Nobody ever helped me into carriages
    or over mud puddles
        or gives me a best place …

And ain't I a woman?
    Look at me
Look at my arm!
    I have plowed and planted
and gathered into barns
    and no man could head me …
And ain't I a woman?
    I could work as much
and eat as much as a man –
    when I could get to it –
and bear the lash as well
    and ain't I a woman?
I have born 13 children
    and seen most all sold into slavery
and when I cried out a mother's grief
    none but Jesus heard me …
and ain't I a woman?
    that little man in black there say
a woman can't have as much rights as a man
    cause Christ wasn't a woman
Where did your Christ come from?
    From God and a woman!

Man had nothing to do with him!
    If the first woman God ever made
was strong enough to turn the world
    upside down, all alone

From: Linthwaite, I. (ed.) *Ain't I a Woman: A Book of Women's Poetry from Around the World.*

Anniversary

Suppose I took out a slender ketch from
under the spokes of Palace pier tonight to
catch a sea going fish for you

or dressed in antique goggles and wings and
flew down through sycamore leaves into the park

or luminescent through some planetary strike
put one delicate flamingo leg over the sill of your lab

Could I surprise you? or would you insist on
keeping a pattern to link every transfiguration?

Listen, I shall have to whisper it
into your heart directly: we are all
supernatural / every day
we rise new creatures / cannot be predicted

Elaine Feinstein (1930–)
Feinstein, E. (1977) *Unease and Angels*, Carcanet.

Ce'st na Teangan

Cuirim mo dhóchas ar snámh
i mbáidín teangan
faoi mar a leagfá naíonán
i gcliabhán
a bheadh fite fuaite
de dhuilleoga feileastraim
is bitiúman agus pic
bheith cuimilte lena thóin

ansan é leagadh síos
i measc na ngiolcach
is coigeal na mban si
le taobh na habhann,
féachaint n'fheadaraís
cá dtabharfaidh an sruth é,
féachaint, dála Mhaoise,
an bhfóirfidh iníon Fharoinn?

The Language Issue

I place my hope on the water
in this little boat
of the language, the way a body might put
an infant

in a basket of intertwined
iris leaves,
its underside proofed
with bitumen and pitch,

then set the whole thing down amidst
the sedge
and bulrushes by the edge
of a river

only to have it borne hither and thither,
not knowing where it might end up;
in the lap, perhaps,
of some Pharaoh's daughter.

Nuala ni Dhomnaill (1952–)
From: Hulse, M., et al. (eds) (1993) *The New Poetry,* translated from the Irish by Paul Muldoon, Bloodaxe Books.

The New Dress

by Virginia Woolf

From: Cahill, S. (ed.) (1975) *Women and Fiction*, Mentor Books, pp.51–8.

Mabel had her first serious suspicion that something was wrong as she took her cloak off and Mrs Barnet, while handing her the mirror and touching the brushes and thus drawing her attention, perhaps rather markedly, to all the appliances for tidying and improving hair, complexion, clothes, which existed on the dressing table, confirmed the suspicion – that it was not right, not quite right, which growing stronger as she went upstairs and springing at her, with conviction as she greeted Clarissa Dalloway, she went straight to the far end of the room, to a shaded corner where a looking-glass hung and looked. No! It was not *right*. And at once the misery which she always tried to hide, the profound dissatisfaction – the sense she had had, ever since she was a child, of being inferior to other people – set upon her, relentlessly, remorselessly, with an intensity which she could not beat off, as she would when she woke at night at home, by reading Borrow or Scott; for oh these men, oh these women, all were thinking – 'What's Mabel wearing? What a fright she looks! What a hideous new dress!' – their eyelids flickering as they came up and then their lids shutting rather tight. It was her own appalling inadequacy; her cowardice; her mean, water-sprinkled blood that depressed her. And at once the whole of the room where, for ever so many hours, she had planned with the little dressmaker how it was to go, seemed sordid, repulsive; and her own drawing-room so shabby, and herself, going out, puffed up with vanity as she touched the letters on the hall table and said: 'How dull!' to show off – all this now seemed unutterably silly, paltry, and provincial. All this had been absolutely destroyed, shown up, exploded, the moment she came into Mrs Dalloway's drawing-room.

What she had thought that evening when, sitting over the teacups, Mrs Dalloway's invitation came, was that, of course, she could not be fashionable. It was absurd to pretend it even – fashion meant cut, meant style, meant thirty guineas at least – but why not be original? Why not be herself, anyhow? And, getting up, she had taken that old fashion book of her mother's, a Paris fashion book of the time of the Empire, and had thought how much prettier, more dignified, and more womanly they were then, and so set herself – oh, it was foolish – trying to be like them, pluming herself in fact, upon being modest and old-fashioned, and very charming, giving herself up, no doubt about it, to an orgy of self-love, which deserved to be chastised, and so rigged herself out like this.

But she dared not look in the glass. She could not face the whole horror – the pale yellow, idiotically old-fashioned silk dress with its long skirt and its high sleeves and its waist and all the things that looked so charming in the fashion book, but not on her, not among all these ordinary people. She felt like a dressmaker's dummy standing there, for young people to stick pins into.

'But, my dear, it's perfectly charming!' Rose Shaw said, looking her up and down with that little satirical pucker of the lips which she expected –

Rose herself being dressed in the height of fashion, precisely like everybody else, always.

We are all like flies trying to crawl over the edge of the saucer, Mabel thought, and repeated the phrase as if she were crossing herself, as if she were trying to find some spell to annul this pain, to make this agony endurable. Tags of Shakespeare, lines from books she had read ages ago, suddenly came to her when she was in agony, and she repeated them over and over again. 'Flies trying to crawl,' she repeated. If she could say that over often enough and make herself see the flies, she would become numb, chill, frozen, dumb. Now she could see flies crawling slowly out of a saucer of milk with their wings stuck together; and she strained and strained (standing in front of the looking-glass, listening to Rose Shaw) to make herself see Rose Shaw and all the other people as flies, trying to hoist themselves out of something, or into something, meagre, insignificant, toiling flies. But she could not see them like that, not other people. She saw herself like that – she was a fly, but the others were dragonflies, butterflies, beautiful insects, dancing, fluttering, skimming, while she alone dragged herself up out of the saucer. (Envy and spite, the most detestable of the vices, were her chief faults.)

'I feel like some dowdy, decrepit, horribly dingy old fly,' she said, making Robert Haydon stop just to hear her say that, just to reassure herself by furbishing up a poor weak-kneed phrase and so showing how detached she was, how witty, that she did not feel in the least out of anything. And, of course, Robert Haydon answered something, quite polite, quite insincere, which she saw through instantly, and said to herself, directly he went (again from some book), 'Lies, lies, lies!' For a party makes things either much more real, or much less real, she thought; she saw in a flash to the bottom of Robert Haydon's heart; she saw through everything. She saw the truth. *This* was true, this drawing-room, this self, and the other false. Miss Milan's little workroom was really terribly hot, stuffy, sordid. It smelt of clothes and cabbage cooking; and yet, when Miss Milan put the glass in her hand, and she looked at herself with the dress on, finished, an extraordinary bliss shot through her heart. Suffused with light, she sprang into existence. Rid of cares and wrinkles, what she had dreamed of herself was there – a beautiful woman. Just for a second (she had not dared look longer, Miss Milan wanted to know about the length of the skirt), there looked at her, framed in the scrolloping mahogany, a grey-white, mysteriously smiling, charming girl, the core of herself, the soul of herself; and it was not vanity only, not only self-love that made her think it good, tender, and true. Miss Milan said that the skirt could not well be longer; if anything the skirt, said Miss Milan, puckering her forehead, considering with all her wits about her, must be shorter; and she felt, suddenly, honestly, full of love for Miss Milan, much, much fonder of Miss Milan than of any one in the whole world, and could have cried for pity that she should be crawling on the floor with her mouth full of pins, and her face red and her eyes bulging – that one human being should be doing this for another, and she saw them all as human beings merely, and herself going off to her party, and Miss Milan pulling the cover over the canary's cage, or letting him pick a hempseed from between her lips, and the thought of it, of this side of human nature and its patience and its endurance and its being content with such miserable, scanty, sordid, little pleasures filled her eyes with tears.

And now the whole thing had vanished. The dress, the room, the lover, the pity, the scrolloping looking-glass, and the canary's cage – all had vanished, and here she was in a corner of Mrs Dalloway's drawing-room, suffering tortures, woken wide awake to reality.

But it was all so paltry, weak-blooded, and petty-minded to care so much at her age with two children, to be still so utterly dependent on people's opinions and not have principles or convictions, not to be able to say as other people did, 'There's Shakespeare! There's death! We're all weevils in a captain's biscuit' – or whatever it was that people did say.

She faced herself straight in the glass; she pecked at her left shoulder; she issued out into the room, as if spears were thrown at her yellow dress from all sides. But instead of looking fierce or tragic, as Rose Shaw would have done – Rose would have looked like Boadicea – she looked foolish and self-conscious, and simpered like a schoolgirl and slouched across the room, positively slinking, as if she were a beaten mongrel, and looked at a picture, an engraving. As if one went to a party to look at a picture! Everybody knew why she did it – it was from shame, from humiliation.

'Now the fly's in the saucer,' she said to herself, 'right in the middle, and can't get out, and the milk,' she thought, rigidly staring at the picture, 'is sticking its wings together.'

'It's so old-fashioned,' she said to Charles Burt, making him stop (which by itself he hated) on his way to talk to some one else.

She meant, or she tried to make herself think that she meant, that it was the picture and not her dress, that was old-fashioned. And one word of praise, one word of affection from Charles would have made all the difference to her at the moment. If he had only said, 'Mabel, you're looking charming tonight!' it would have changed her life. But then she ought to have been truthful and direct. Charles said nothing of the kind, of course. He was malice itself. He always saw through one, especially if one were feeling particularly mean, paltry, or feeble-minded.

'Mabel's got a new dress!' he said, and the poor fly was absolutely shoved into the middle of the saucer. Really, he would like her to drown, she believed. He had no heart, no fundamental kindness, only a veneer of friendliness. Miss Milan was much more real, much kinder. If only one could feel that and stick to it, always. 'Why,' she asked herself – replying to Charles much too pertly, letting him see that she was out of temper, or 'ruffled' as he called it. ('Rather ruffled?' he said and went on to laugh at her with some woman over there) – 'Why,' she asked herself, 'can't I feel one thing always, feel quite sure that Miss Milan is right, and Charles wrong and stick to it, feel sure about the canary and pity and love and not be whipped all round in a second by coming into a room full of people?' It was her odious, weak, vacillating character again, always giving at the critical moment and not being seriously interested in conchology, etymology, botany, archaeology, cutting up potatoes and watching them fructify like Mary Dennis, like Violet Searle.

Then Mrs Holman, seeing her standing there, bore down upon her. Of course a thing like a dress was beneath Mrs Holman's notice, with her family always tumbling downstairs or having the scarlet fever. Could Mabel tell her if Elmthorpe was ever let for August and September? Oh, it was a conversation that bored her unutterably! – it made her furious to be treated like a house agent or a messenger boy, to be made use of. Not to have value, that was it, she thought, trying to grasp something hard, something real, while she tried to answer sensibly about the bathroom and the south aspect and the hot water to the top of the house; and all the time she could see little bits of her yellow dress in the round looking-glass which made them all the size of boot-buttons or tadpoles; and it was amazing to think how much humiliation and agony and self-loathing and effort and passionate ups and downs of feeling were contained in a thing the size of a threepenny bit. And what was still odder, this thing, this Mabel Waring, was separate, quite disconnected: and though Mrs Holman (the black button) was leaning forward and telling her how her eldest boy had strained his heart running, she could see her, too, quite detached in the looking-glass, and it was impossible that the black dot, leaning forward, gesticulating, should make the yellow dot, sitting solitary, self-centred, feel what the black dot was feeling, yet they pretended.

'So impossible to keep boys quiet' – that was the kind of thing one said.

And Mrs Holman, who could never get enough sympathy and snatched what little there was greedily, as if it were her right (but she deserved much more for, there was her little girl who had come down this morning with a swollen knee-joint), took this miserable offering and looked at it suspiciously, grudgingly, as if it were a half-penny when it ought to have been a pound and put it away in her purse, must put up with it, mean and miserly though it was, times being hard, so very hard; and on she went, creaking, injured Mrs Holman, about the girl with the swollen joints. Ah, it was tragic, this greed, this clamour of human beings, like a row of cormorants, barking and flapping their wings for sympathy – it was tragic, could one have felt it and not merely pretended to feel it!

But in her yellow dress to-night she could not wring out one drop more; she wanted it all, all for herself. She knew (she kept on looking into the glass, dipping into that dreadfully showing-up blue pool) that she was condemned, despised, left like this in a backwater, because of her being like this a feeble, vacillating creature: and it seemed to her that the yellow dress was a penance which she had deserved, and if she had been dressed like Rose Shaw, in lovely, clinging green with a ruffle of swansdown, she would have deserved that; and she thought that there was no escape for her – none whatever. But it was not her fault altogether, after all. It was being one of a family of ten; never having money enough, always skimping and paring; and her mother carrying great cans, and the linoleum worn on the stair edges, and one sordid little domestic tragedy after another – nothing catastrophic, the sheep farm failing, but not utterly; her eldest brother marrying beneath him but not very much – there was no romance, nothing extreme about them all. They petered out respectably in seaside resorts; every watering-place had one of her aunts even now asleep in some lodging with the front windows not quite facing the sea. That was so like them – they had to squint at things always. And she had done the same – she was just like her aunts. For all her dreams of living in India, married to some hero like Sir Henry Lawrence, some empire builder (still the sight of a native in a turban filled her with romance), she had failed utterly. She had married Hubert, with his safe, permanent underling's job in the Law Courts, and they managed tolerably in a smallish house, without proper maids, and hash when she was alone or just bread and butter, but now and then – Mrs Holman was off, thinking her the most dried-up unsympathetic twig she had ever met, absurdly dressed, too, and would tell every one about Mabel's fantastic appearance – now and then, thought Mabel Waring, left alone on the blue sofa, punching the cushion in order to look occupied, for she would not join Charles Burt and Rose Shaw, chattering like magpies and perhaps laughing at her by the fireplace – now and then, there did come to her delicious moments, reading the other night in bed, for instance, or down by the sea on the sand in the sun, at Easter – let her recall it – a great tuft of pale sand-grass standing all twisted like a shock of spears against the sky, which was blue like a smooth china egg, so firm, so hard, and then the melody of the waves – 'Hush, hush,' they said, and the children's shouts paddling – yes, it was a divine moment, and there she lay, she felt, in the hand of the Goddess who was the world; rather a hard-hearted, but very beautiful Goddess, a little lamb laid on the altar (one did think these silly things, and it didn't matter so long as one never said them). And also with Hubert sometimes she had quite unexpectedly – carving the mutton for Sunday lunch, for no reason, opening a letter, coming into a room – divine moments, when she said to herself (for she would never say this to anybody else), 'This is it. This has happened. This is it!' And the other way about it was equally surprising – that is, when everything was arranged – music, weather, holidays, every reason for happiness was there – then nothing happened at all. One wasn't happy. It was flat, just flat, that was all.

Her wretched self again, no doubt! She had always been a fretful, weak, unsatisfactory mother, a wobbly wife, lolling about in a kind of twilight existence with nothing very clear or very bold, or more one thing than another, like all her brothers and sisters, except perhaps Herbert – they were all the same poor water-veined creatures who did nothing. Then in the midst of this creeping, crawling life, suddenly she was on the crest of a wave. That wretched fly – where had she read the story that kept coming into her mind about the fly and the saucer? – struggled out. Yes, she had those moments. But now that she was forty, they might come more and more seldom. By degrees she would cease to struggle any more. But that was deplorable! That was not to be endured! That made her feel ashamed of herself!

She would go to the London Library tomorrow. She would find some wonderful, helpful, astonishing book, quite by chance, a book by a clergyman, by an American no one had every heard of; or she would walk down the Strand and drop, accidentally, into a hall where a miner was telling about the life in the pit, and suddenly she would become a new person. She would be absolutely transformed. She would wear a uniform; she would be called Sister Somebody; she would never give a thought to clothes again. And for ever after she would be perfectly clear about Charles Burt and Miss Milan and this room and that room; and it would be always, day after day, as if she were lying in the sun or carving the mutton. It would be it!

So she got up from the blue sofa, and the yellow button in the looking-glass got up too, and she waved her hand to Charles and Rose to show them she did not depend on them one scrap, and the yellow button moved out of the looking-glass, and all the spears were gathered into her breast as she walked towards Mrs Dalloway and said, 'Good night'.

'But it's too early to go,' said Mrs Dalloway, who was always so charming.

'I'm afraid I must,' said Mabel Waring. 'But,' she added in her weak, wobbly voice which only sounded ridiculous when she tried to strengthen it, 'I have enjoyed myself enormously.'

'I have enjoyed myself,' she said to Mr Dalloway, whom she met on the stairs.

'Lies, lies, lies!' she said to herself, going downstairs, and 'Right in the saucer!' she said to herself as she thanked Mrs Barnet for helping her and wrapped herself, round and round and round, in the Chinese cloak she had worn these twenty years.

Girl

by Jamaica Kincaid

From: Carter, A. (ed) (1986) *Wayward Girls and Wicked Women*, Virago, pp.326–7.

Wash the white clothes on Monday and put them on the stone heap; wash the colour clothes on Tuesday and put them on the clothes-line to dry; don't walk barehead in the hot sun; cook pumpkin fritters in very hot sweet oil; soak your little cloths right after you take them off; when buying cotton to make yourself a nice blouse, be sure that it doesn't have gum on it, because that way it won't hold up well after a wash; soak salt fish overnight before you cook it; is it true that you sing benna in Sunday school?; always eat your food in such a way that it won't turn someone else's stomach; on Sundays try to walk like a lady and not like the slut you are so bent on becoming; don't sing benna in Sunday school; you mustn't speak to wharf-rat boys, not even to give directions; don't eat fruits on the street – flies will follow you; *but I don't sing benna on Sundays at all and never in Sunday school*; this is how to sew on a button; this is how to make a buttonhole for the button you have just sewed on; this is how to hem a dress when you see the hem coming down and so to prevent yourself from looking like the slut I know you are so bent on becoming; this is how you iron your father's khaki shirt so that it doesn't have a crease; this is how you iron your father's khaki pants so that they don't have a crease; this is how you grow okra – far from the house, because okra tree harbours red ants; when you are growing dasheen, make sure it gets plenty of water or else it makes your throat itch when you are eating it; this is how you sweep a corner; this is how you sweep a whole house; this is how you sweep a yard; this is how you smile to someone you don't like too much; this is how you smile to someone you don't like at all; this is how you smile to someone you like completely; this is how you set a table for tea; this is how you set a table for dinner; this is how you set a table for dinner with an important guest; this is how you set a table for lunch; this is how you set a table for breakfast; this is how to behave in the presence of men who don't know you very well, and this way they won't recognize immediately the slut I have warned you against becoming; be sure to wash every day, even if it is with your own spit; don't squat down to play marbles – you are not a boy, you know; don't pick people's flowers – you might catch something; don't throw stones at blackbirds, because it might not be a blackbird at all; this is how to make a bread pudding; this is how to make doukona; this is how to make pepper pot; this is how to make a good medicine for a cold; this is how to make a good medicine to throw away a child before it even becomes a child; this is how to catch a fish; this is how to throw back a fish you don't like, and that way something bad won't fall on you; this is how to bully a man; this is how a man bullies you; this is how to love a man, and if this doesn't work there are other ways, and if they don't work don't feel too bad about giving up; this is how to spit up in the air if you feel like it, and this is how to move quick so that it doesn't fall on you; this is how to make ends meet; always squeeze bread to make sure it's fresh; *but what if the baker won't let me feel the bread?*; you mean to say that after all you are really going to be the kind of woman who the baker won't let near the bread?

Behind a Mask or A Woman's Power

by A.M. Barnard

Abridged from: Stern, M.B. (ed.) (1984) *Behind A Mask: The Unknown Thrillers of Louisa May Alcott*, Quill.

I   Jean Muir

'Has she come?'

'No, Mamma, not yet.'

'I wish it were well over. The thought of it worries and excites me. A cushion for my back, Bella.'

And poor, peevish Mrs. Coventry sank into an easy chair with a nervous sigh and the air of a martyr, while her pretty daughter hovered about her with affectionate solicitude.

'Who are they talking of, Lucia?' asked the languid young man lounging on a couch near his cousin, who bent over her tapestry work with a happy smile on her usually haughty face.

'The new governess, Miss Muir. Shall I tell you about her?'

'No, thank you. I have an inveterate aversion to the whole tribe. I've often thanked heaven that I had but one sister, and she a spoiled child, so that I have escaped the infliction of a governess so long.'

'How will you bear it now?' asked Lucia.

'Leave the house while she is in it.'

'No, you won't. You're too lazy, Gerald,' called out a younger and more energetic man, from the recess where he stood teasing his dogs.

'I'll give her a three days' trial; if she proves endurable I shall not disturb myself; if, as I am sure, she is a bore, I'm off anywhere, anywhere out of her way.'

'I beg you won't talk in that depressing manner, boys. I dread the coming of a stranger more than you possibly can, but Bella *must* not be neglected; so I have nerved myself to endure this woman, and Lucia is good enough to say she will attend to her after tonight.'

'Don't be troubled, Mamma. She is a nice person, I dare say, and when once we are used to her, I've no doubt we shall be glad to have her, it's so dull here just now. Lady Sydney said she was a quiet, accomplished, amiable girl, who needed a home, and would be a help to poor stupid me, so try to like her for my sake.'

'I will, dear, but isn't it getting late? I do hope nothing has happened. Did you tell them to send a carriage to the station for her, Gerald?'

'I forgot it. But it's not far, it won't hurt her to walk' was the languid reply.

'It was indolence, not forgetfulness, I know. I'm very sorry; she will think it so rude to leave her to find her way so late. Do go and see to it, Ned.'

'Too late, Bella, the train was in some time ago. Give your orders to me next time, Mother, and I'll see that they are obeyed,' said Edward.

'Ned is just at an age to make a fool of himself for any girl who comes in his way. Have a care of the governess, Lucia, or she will bewitch him.'

Gerald spoke in a satirical whisper, but his brother heard him and answered with a good-humored laugh.

'I wish there was any hope of your making a fool of yourself in that way, old fellow. Set me a good example, and I promise to follow it. As for the governess, she is a woman, and should be treated with common civility. I should say a little extra kindness wouldn't be amiss, either, because she is poor, and a stranger.'

'That is my dear, good-hearted Ned! We'll stand by poor little Muir, won't we?' And running to her brother, Bella stood on tiptoe to offer him a kiss which he could not refuse, for the rosy lips were pursed up invitingly, and the bright eyes full of sisterly affection.

'I do hope she has come, for, when I make an effort to see anyone, I hate to make it in vain. Punctuality is *such* a virtue, and I know this woman hasn't got it, for she promised to be here at seven, and now it is long after,' began Mrs. Coventry, in an injured tone.

Before she could get breath for another complaint, the clock struck seven and the doorbell rang.

'There she is!' cried Bella, and turned toward the door as if to go and meet the newcomer.

But Lucia arrested her, saying authoritatively, 'Stay here, child. It is her place to come to you, not yours to go to her.'

'Miss Muir,' announced a servant, and a little black-robed figure stood in the doorway. For an instant no one stirred, and the governess had time to see and be seen before a word was uttered. All looked at her, and she cast on the household group a keen glance that impressed them curiously; then her eyes fell, and bowing slightly she walked in. Edward came forward and received her with the frank cordiality which nothing could daunt or chill.

'Mother, this is the lady whom you expected. Miss Muir, allow me to apologize for our apparent neglect in not sending for you. There was a mistake about the carriage, or, rather, the lazy fellow to whom the order was given forgot it. Bella, come here.'

'Thank you, no apology is needed. I did not expect to be sent for.' And the governess meekly sat down without lifting her eyes.

'I am glad to see you. Let me take your things,' said Bella, rather shyly, for Gerald, still lounging, watched the fireside group with languid interest, and Lucia never stirred. Mrs. Coventry took a second survey and began:

'You were punctual, Miss Muir, which pleases me. I'm a sad invalid, as Lady Sydney told you, I hope; so that Miss Coventry's lessons will be directed by my niece, and you will go to her for directions, as she knows what I wish. You will excuse me if I ask you a few questions, for Lady Sydney's note was very brief, and I left everything to her judgment.'

'Ask anything you like, madam,' answered the soft, sad voice.

'You are Scotch, I believe.'

'Yes, madam.'

'Are your parents living?'

'I have not a relation in the world.'

'Dear me, how sad! Do you mind telling me your age?'

'Nineteen.' And a smile passed over Miss Muir's lips, as she folded her hands with an air of resignation, for the catechism was evidently to be a long one.

'So young! Lady Sydney mentioned five-and-twenty, I think, didn't she, Bella?'

'No, Mamma, she only said she thought so. Don't ask such questions. It's not pleasant before us all,' whispered Bella.

A quick, grateful glance shone on her from the suddenly lifted eyes of Miss Muir, as she said quietly, 'I wish I was thirty, but, as I am not, I do my best to look and seem old.'

Of course, every one looked at her then, and all felt a touch of pity at the sight of the pale-faced girl in her plain black dress, with no ornament but a little silver cross at her throat. Small, thin, and colorless she was, with yellow hair, gray eyes, and sharply cut, irregular, but very expressive features. Poverty seemed to have set its bond stamp upon her, and life to have had for her more frost than sunshine. But something in the lines of the mouth betrayed strength, and the clear, low voice had a curious mixture of command and entreaty in its varying tones. Not an attractive woman, yet not an ordinary one; and, as she sat there with her delicate hands lying in her lap, her head bent, and a bitter look on her thin face, she was more interesting than many a blithe and blooming girl. Bella's heart warmed to her at once, and she drew her seat nearer, while Edward went back to his dogs that his presence might not embarrass her.

'You have been ill, I think,' continued Mrs. Coventry, who considered this fact the most interesting of all she had heard concerning the governess.

'Yes, madam, I left the hospital only a week ago.'

'Are you quite sure it is safe to begin teaching so soon?'

'I have no time to lose, and shall soon gain strength here in the country, if you care to keep me.'

'And you are fitted to teach music, French, and drawing?'

'I shall endeavor to prove that I am.'

'Be kind enough to go and play an air or two. I can judge by your touch; I used to play finely when a girl.'

Miss Muir rose, looked about her for the instrument, and seeing it at the other end of the room went toward it, passing Gerald and Lucia as if she did not see them. Bella followed, and in a moment forgot everything in admiration. Miss Muir played like one who loved music and was perfect mistress of her art. She charmed them all by the magic of this spell; even indolent Gerald sat up to listen, and Lucia put down her needle, while Ned watched the slender white fingers as they flew, and wondered at the strength and skill which they possessed.

'Please sing,' pleaded Bella, as a brilliant overture ended.

With the same meek obedience Miss Muir complied, and began a little Scotch melody, so sweet, so sad, that the girl's eyes filled, and Mrs. Coventry looked for one of her many pocket-handkerchiefs. But suddenly the music ceased, for, with a vain attempt to support herself, the singer slid from her seat and lay before the startled listeners, as white and rigid as if struck with death. Edward caught her up, and, ordering his brother off the couch, laid her there, while Bella chafed her hands, and her mother rang for her maid. Lucia bathed the poor girl's temples, and Gerald, with unwonted energy, brought a glass of wine. Soon Miss Muir's lips trembled, she sighed, then murmured, tenderly, with a pretty Scotch accent, as if wandering in the past, 'Bide wi' me, Mither, I'm sae sick an, sad here all alone.'

'Take a sip of this, and it will do you good, my dear,' said Mrs. Coventry, quite touched by the plaintive words.

The strange voice seemed to recall her. She sat up, looked about her, a little wildly, for a moment, then collected herself and said, with a pathetic look and tone, 'Pardon me. I have been on my feet all day, and, in my eagerness to keep my appointment, I forgot to eat since morning. I'm better now; shall I finish the song?'

'By no means. Come and have some tea,' said Bella, full of pity and remorse.

'Scene first, very well done,' whispered Gerald to his cousin.

Miss Muir was just before them, apparently listening to Mrs. Coventry's remarks upon fainting fits; but she heard, and looked over her shoulders with a gesture like Rachel. Her eyes were gray, but at that instant they seemed black with some strong emotion of anger, pride, or defiance. A curious smile passed over her face as she bowed, and said in her penetrating voice, 'Thanks. The last scene shall be still better.'

Young Coventry was a cool, indolent man, seldom conscious of any emotion, any passion, pleasurable or otherwise; but at the look, the tone of the governess, he experienced a new sensation, indefinable, yet strong. He colored and, for the first time in his life, looked abashed. Lucia saw it, and hated Miss Muir with a sudden hatred; for, in all the years she had passed with her cousin, no look or word of hers had possessed such power. Coventry was himself again in an instant, with no trace of that passing change, but a look of interest in his usually dreamy eyes, and a touch of anger in his sarcastic voice.

'What a melodramatic young lady! I shall go tomorrow.'

Lucia laughed, and was well pleased when he sauntered away to bring her a cup of tea from the table where a little scene was just taking place. Mrs. Coventry had sunk into her chair again, exhausted by the flurry of the fainting fit. Bella was busied about her; and Edward, eager to feed the pale governess, was awkwardly trying to make the tea, after a beseeching glance at his cousin which she did not choose to answer. As he upset the caddy and uttered a despairing exclamation, Miss Muir quietly took her place behind the urn, saying with a smile, and a shy glance at the young man, 'Allow me to assume my duty at once, and serve you all. I understand the art of making people comfortable in this way. The scoop, please. I can gather this up quite well alone, if you will tell me how your mother likes her tea.'

Edward pulled a chair to the table and made merry over his mishaps, while Miss Muir performed her little task with a skill and grace that made it pleasant to watch her. Coventry lingered a moment after she had given him a steaming cup, to observe her more nearly, while he asked a question or two of his brother. She took no more notice of him than if he had been a statue, and in the middle of the one remark he addressed to her, she rose to take the sugar basin to Mrs. Coventry, who was quite won by the modest, domestic graces of the new governess.

'Really, my dear, you are a treasure; I haven't tasted such tea since my poor maid Ellis died. Bella never makes it good, and Miss Lucia always forgets the cream. Whatever you do you seem to do well, and that is *such* a comfort.'

'Let me always do this for you, then. It will be a pleasure, madam.' And Miss Muir came back to her seat with a faint color in her cheek which improved her much.

'My brother asked if young Sydney was at home when you left,' said Edward, for Gerald would not take the trouble to repeat the question.

Miss Muir fixed her eyes on Coventry, and answered with a slight tremor of the lips, 'No, he left home some weeks ago.'

The young man went back to his cousin, saying, as he threw himself down beside her, 'I shall not go tomorrow, but wait till the three days are out.'

'Why?' demanded Lucia.

Lowering his voice he said, with a significant nod toward the governess, 'Because I have a fancy that she is at the bottom of Sydney's mystery. He's not been himself lately, and now he is gone without a word. I rather like romances in real life, if they are not too long, or difficult to read.'

'Do you think her pretty?'

'Far from it, a most uncanny little specimen.'

'Then why fancy Sydney loves her?'

'He is an oddity, and likes sensations and things of that sort.'

'What do you mean, Gerald?'

'Get the Muir to look at you, as she did at me, and you will understand. Will you have another cup, Juno?'

'Yes, please.' She liked to have him wait upon her, for he did it to no other woman except his mother.

Before he could slowly rise, Miss Muir glided to them with another cup on the salver; and, as Lucia took it with a cold nod, the girl said under her breath, 'I think it honest to tell you that I possess a quick ear, and cannot help hearing what is said anywhere in the room. What you say of me is of no consequence, but you may speak of things which you prefer I should not hear; therefore, allow me to warn you.' And she was gone again as noiselessly as she came.

'How do you like that?' whispered Coventry, as his cousin sat looking after the girl, with a disturbed expression.

'What an uncomfortable creature to have in the house! I am very sorry I urged her coming, for your mother has taken a fancy to her, and it will be hard to get rid of her,' said Lucia, half angry, half amused.

'Hush, she hears every word you say. I know it by the expression of her face, for Ned is talking about horses, and she looks as haughty as ever you did, and that is saying much. Faith, this is getting interesting.'

'Hark, she is speaking; I want to hear,' and Lucia laid her hand on her cousin's lips. He kissed it, and then idly amused himself with turning the rings to and fro on the slender fingers.

'I have been in France several years, madam, but my friend died and I came back to be with Lady Sydney, till –' Muir paused an instant, then added, slowly, 'till I fell ill. It was a contagious fever, so I went of my own accord to the hospital, not wishing to endanger her.'

'Very right, but are you sure there is no danger of infection now?' asked Mrs. Coventry anxiously.

'None, I assure you. I have been well for some time, but did not leave because I preferred to stay there, than to return to Lady Sydney.'

'No quarrel, I hope? No trouble of any kind?'

'No quarrel, but – well, why not? You have a right to know, and I will not make a foolish mystery out of a very simple thing. As your family, only, is present, I may tell the truth. I did not go back on the young gentleman's account. Please ask no more.'

'Ah, I see. Quite prudent and proper, Miss Muir. I shall never allude to it again. Thank you for your frankness. Bella, you will be careful not to mention this to your young friends; girls gossip sadly, and it would annoy Lady Sydney beyond everything to have this talked of.'

'Very neighborly of Lady S. to send the dangerous young lady here, where there are *two* young gentlemen to be captivated. I wonder why she didn't keep Sydney after she had caught him,' murmured Coventry to his cousin.

'Because she had the utmost contempt for a titled fool.' Miss Muir dropped the words almost into his ear, as she bent to take her shawl from the sofa corner.

'How the deuce did she get there?' ejaculated Coventry, looking as if he had received another sensation. 'She has spirit, though, and upon my word I pity Sydney, if he did try to dazzle her, for he must have got a splendid dismissal.'

'Come and play billiards. You promised, and I hold you to your word,' said Lucia, rising with decision, for Gerald was showing too much interest in another to suit Miss Beaufort.

'I am, as ever, your most devoted. My mother is a charming woman, but I find our evening parties slightly dull, when only my own family are present. Good night, Mamma.' He shook hands with his mother, whose pride and idol he was, and, with a comprehensive nod to the others, strolled after his cousin.

'Now they are gone we can be quite cozy, and talk over things, for I don't mind Ned any more than I do his dogs,' said Bella, settling herself on her mother's footstool.

'I merely wish to say, Miss Muir, that my daughter has never had a governess and is sadly backward for a girl of sixteen. I want you to pass the mornings with her, and get her on as rapidly as possible. In the afternoon you will walk or drive with her, and in the evening sit with us here, if you like, or amuse yourself as you please. While in the country we are very quiet, for I cannot bear much company, and when my sons want gaiety, they go away for it. Miss Beaufort oversees the servants, and takes my place as far as possible. I am very delicate and keep my room till evening, except for an airing at noon. We will try each other for a month, and I hope we shall get on quite comfortably together.'

'I shall do my best, madam.'

One would not have believed that the meek, spiritless voice which uttered these words was the same that had startled Coventry a few minutes before, nor that the pale, patient face could ever have kindled with such sudden fire as that which looked over Miss Muir's shoulder when she answered her young host's speech.

Edward thought within himself, Poor little woman! She has had a hard life. We will try and make it easier while she is here; and began his charitable work by suggesting that she might be tired. She acknowledged she was, and Bella led her away to a bright, cozy room, where with a pretty little speech and a good-night kiss she left her.

When alone Miss Muir's conduct was decidedly peculiar. Her first act was to clench her hands and mutter between her teeth, with passionate force, 'I'll not fail again if there is power in a woman's wit and will!' She stood a moment motionless, with an expression of almost fierce disdain on her face, then shook her clenched hand as if menacing some unseen enemy. Next she laughed, and shrugged her shoulders with a true French shrug, saying low to herself, 'Yes, the last scene *shall* be better than the first. *Mon dieu,* how tired and hungry I am!'

Kneeling before the one small trunk which held her worldly possessions, she opened it, drew out a flask, and mixed a glass of some ardent cordial, which she seemed to enjoy extremely as she sat on the carpet, musing, while her quick eyes examined every corner of the room.

'Not bad! It will be a good field for me to work in, and the harder the task the better I shall like it. *Merci,* old friend. You put heart and courage into me when nothing else will. Come, the curtain is down, so I may be myself for a few hours, if actresses ever are themselves.'

Still sitting on the floor she unbound and removed the long abundant braids from her head, wiped the pink from her face, took out several pearly teeth, and slipping off her dress appeared herself indeed, a haggard, worn, and moody woman of thirty at least. The metamorphosis was wonderful, but the disguise was more in the expression she assumed than in any art of costume or false adornment. Now she was alone, and her mobile features settled into their natural expression, weary, hard, bitter. She had been lovely once, happy, innocent, and tender; but nothing of all this remained to the gloomy woman who leaned there brooding over some wrong, or loss, or disappointment which had darkened all her life. For an hour she sat so, sometimes playing absently with the scanty locks that hung about her face, sometimes lifting the glass to her lips as if the fiery draught warmed her cold blood; and once she half uncovered her breast to eye with a terrible glance the scar of a newly healed wound. At last she rose and crept to bed, like one worn out with weariness and mental pain.

II   A Good Beginning

Only the housemaids were astir when Miss Muir left her room next morning and quietly found her way into the garden. As she walked, apparently intent upon the flowers, her quick eye scrutinized the fine old house and its picturesque surroundings.

'Not bad,' she said to herself, adding, as she passed into the adjoining park, 'but the other may be better, and I will have the best.'

Walking rapidly, she came out at length upon the wide green lawn which lay before the ancient hall where Sir John Coventry lived in solitary splendor. A stately old place, rich in oaks, well-kept shrubberies, gay gardens, sunny terraces, carved gables, spacious rooms, liveried servants, and every luxury befitting the ancestral home of a rich and honorable race. Miss Muir's eyes brightened as she looked, her step grew firmer, her carriage prouder, and a smile broke over her face; the smile of one well pleased at the prospect of the success of some cherished hope. Suddenly her whole air changed, she pushed back her hat, clasped her hands loosely before her, and seemed absorbed in girlish admiration of the fair scene that could not fail to charm any beauty-loving eye. The cause of this rapid change soon appeared. A hale, handsome man, between fifty and sixty, came through the little gate leading to the park, and, seeing the young stranger, paused to examine her. He had only time for a glance, however; she seemed conscious of his presence in a moment, turned with a startled look, uttered an exclamation of surprise, and looked as if hesitating whether to speak or run away. Gallant Sir John took off his hat and said, with the old-fashioned courtesy which became him well, 'I beg your pardon for disturbing you, young lady. Allow me to atone for it by inviting you to walk where you will, and gather what flowers you like. I see you love them, so pray make free with those about you.'

With a charming air of maidenly timidity and artlessness, Miss Muir replied, 'Oh, thank you, sir! But it is I who should ask pardon for trespassing. I never should have dared if I had not known that Sir John was absent. I always wanted to see this fine old place, and ran over the first thing, to satisfy myself.'

'And *are* you satisfied?' he asked, with a smile.

'More than satisfied – I'm charmed; for it is the most beautiful spot I ever saw, and I've seen many famous seats, both at home and abroad,' she answered enthusiastically.

'The Hall is much flattered, and so would its master be if he heard you,' began the gentleman, with an odd expression.

'I should not praise it to him – at least, not as freely as I have to you, sir,' said the girl, with eyes still turned away.

'Why not?' asked her companion, looking much amused.

'I should be afraid. Not that I dread Sir John; but I've heard so many beautiful and noble things about him, and respect him so highly, that I should not dare to say much, lest he should see how I admire and –'

'And what, young lady? Finish, if you please.'

'I was going to say, love him. I will say it, for he is an old man, and one cannot help loving virtue and bravery.'

Miss Muir looked very earnest and pretty as she spoke, standing there with the sunshine glinting on her yellow hair, delicate face, and downcast eyes. Sir John was not a vain man, but he found it pleasant to hear himself commended by this unknown girl, and felt redoubled curiosity to learn who she was. Too well-bred to ask, or to abash her by avowing what she seemed unconscious of, he left both discoveries to chance; and when she turned, as if to retrace her steps, he offered her the handful of hothouse flowers which he held, saying, with a gallant bow, 'In Sir John's name let me give you my little nosegay, with thanks for your good opinion, which, I assure you, is not entirely deserved, for I know him well.'

Miss Muir looked up quickly, eyed him an instant, then dropped her eyes, and, coloring deeply, stammered out, 'I did not know – I beg your pardon – you are too kind, Sir John.'

He laughed like a boy, asking, mischievously, 'Why call me Sir John? How do you know that I am not the gardener or the butler?'

'I did not see your face before, and no one but yourself would say that any praise was undeserved,' murmured Miss Muir, still overcome with girlish confusion.

'Well, well, we will let that pass, and the next time you come we will be properly introduced. Bella always brings her friends to the Hall, for I am fond of young people.'

'I am not a friend. I am only Miss Coventry's governess.' And Miss Muir dropped a meek curtsy. A slight change passed over Sir John's manner. Few would have perceived it, but Miss Muir felt it at once, and bit her lips with an angry feeling at her heart. With a curious air of pride, mingled with respect, she accepted the still offered bouquet, returned Sir John's parting bow, and tripped away, leaving the old gentleman to wonder where Mrs. Coventry found such a piquant little governess.

'That is done, and very well for a beginning,' she said to herself as she approached the house.

In a green paddock close by fed a fine horse, who lifted up his head and eyed her inquiringly, like one who expected a greeting. Following a sudden impulse, she entered the paddock and, pulling a handful of clover, invited the creature to come and eat. This was evidently a new proceeding on the part of a lady, and the horse careered about as if bent on frightening the newcomer away.

'I see,' she said aloud, laughing to herself. 'I am not your master, and you rebel. Nevertheless, I'll conquer you, my fine brute.'

Seating herself in the grass, she began to pull daises, singing idly the while, as if unconscious of the spirited prancings of the horse. Presently he drew nearer, sniffing curiously and eyeing her with surprise. She took no notice, but plaited the daisies and sang on as if he was not there. This seemed to pique the petted creature, for, slowly approaching, he came at length so close that he could smell her little foot and nibble at her dress. Then she offered the clover, uttering caressing words and making smoothing sounds, till by degrees and with much coquetting, the horse permitted her to stroke his glossy neck and smooth his mane.

It was a pretty sight – the slender figure in the grass, the high-spirited horse bending his proud head to her hand. Edward Coventry, who had watched the scene, found it impossible to restrain himself any longer and, leaping the wall, came to join the group, saying, with mingled admiration and wonder in countenance and voice, 'Good morning, Miss Muir. If I had not seen your skill and courage proved before my eyes, I should be alarmed for your safety. Hector is a wild, wayward beast, and has damaged more than one groom who tried to conquer him.'

'Good morning, Mr. Coventry. Don't tell tales of this noble creature, who has not deceived my faith in him. Your grooms did not know how to win his heart, and so subdue his spirit without breaking it.'

Miss Muir rose as she spoke, and stood with her hand on Hector's neck while he ate the grass which she had gathered in the skirt of her dress.

'You have the secret, and Hector is your subject now, though heretofore he has rejected all friends but his master. Will you give him his morning feast? I always bring him bread and play with him before breakfast.'

'Then you are not jealous?' And she looked up at him with eyes so bright and beautiful in expression that the young man wondered he had not observed them before.

'Not I. Pet him as much as you will; it will do him good. He is a solitary fellow, for he scorns his own kind and lives alone, like his master,' he added, half to himself.

'Alone, with such a happy home, Mr. Coventry?' And a softly compassionate glance stole from the bright eyes.

'That was an ungrateful speech, and I retract it for Bella's sake. Younger sons have no position but such as they can make for themselves, you know, and I've had no chance yet.'

'Younger sons! I thought – I beg pardon.' And Miss Muir paused, as if remembering that she had no right to question.

Edward smiled and answered frankly, 'Nay, don't mind me. You thought I was the heir, perhaps. Whom did you take my brother for last night?'

'For some guest who admired Miss Beaufort. I did not hear his name, nor observe him enough to discover who he was. I saw only your kind mother, your charming little sister, and –'

She stopped there, with a half-shy, half-grateful look at the young man which finished the sentence better than any words. He was still a boy, in spite of his one-and-twenty years, and a little color came into his brown cheek as the eloquent eyes met his and fell before them.

'Yes, Bella is a capital girl, and one can't help loving her. I know you'll get her on, for, really, she is the most delightful little dunce. My mother's ill health and Bella's devotion to her have prevented our attending to her education before. Next winter, when we go to town, she is to come out, and must be prepared for that great event, you know,' he said, choosing a safe subject.

'I shall do my best. And that reminds me that I should report myself to her, instead of enjoying myself here. When one has been ill and shut up a long time, the country is so lovely one is apt to forget duty for pleasure. Please remind me if I am negligent, Mr. Coventry.'

'That name belongs to Gerald. I'm only Mr. Ned here,' he said as they walked toward the house, while Hector followed to the wall and sent a sonorous farewell after them.

Bella came running to meet them, and greeted Miss Muir as if she had made up her mind to like her heartily. 'What a lovely bouquet you have got! I never can arrange flowers prettily, which vexes me, for Mamma is so fond of them and cannot go out herself. You have charming taste,' she said, examining the graceful posy which Miss Muir had much improved by adding feathery grasses, delicate ferns, and fragrant wild flowers to Sir John's exotics.

Putting them into Bella's hand, she said, in a winning way, 'Take them to your mother, then, and ask her if I may have the pleasure of making her a daily nosegay; for I should find real delight in doing it, if it would please her.'

'How kind you are! Of course it would please her. I'll take them to her while the dew is still on them.' And away flew Bella, eager to give both the flowers and the pretty message to the poor invalid.

Edward stopped to speak to the gardener, and Miss Muir went up the steps alone. The long hall was lined with portraits, and pacing slowly down it she examined them with interest. One caught her eye, and, pausing before it, she scrutinized it carefully. A young, beautiful, but very haughty female face. Miss Muir suspected at once who it was, and gave a decided nod, as if she saw and caught at some unexpected chance. A soft rustle behind her made her look around, and, seeing Lucia, she bowed, half turned, as if for another glance at the picture, and said, as if involuntarily, 'How beautiful it is! May I ask if it is an ancestor, Miss Beaufort?'

'It is the likeness of my mother' was the reply, given with a softened voice and eyes that looked up tenderly.

'Ah, I might have known, from the resemblance, but I scarcely saw you last night. Excuse my freedom, but Lady Sydney treated me as a friend, and I forget my position. Allow me.'

As she spoke, Miss Muir stooped to return the handkerchief which had fallen from Lucia's hand, and did so with a humble mien which touched the other's heart; for, though a proud, it was also a very generous one.

'Thank you. Are you better, this morning?' she said, graciously. And having received an affirmative reply, she added, as she walked on, 'I will show you to the breakfast room, as Bella is not here. It is a very informal meal with us, for my aunt is never down and my cousins are very irregular in their hours. You can always have yours when you like, without waiting for us if you are an early riser.'

Bella and Edward appeared before the others were seated, and Miss Muir quietly ate her breakfast, feeling well satisfied with her hour's work. Ned recounted her exploit with Hector, Bella delivered her mother's thanks for the flowers, and Lucia more than once recalled, with pardonable vanity, that the governess had compared her to her lovely mother, expressing by a look as much admiration for the living likeness as for the painted one. All kindly did their best to make the pale girl feel at home, and their cordial manner seemed to warm and draw her out; for soon she put off her sad, meek air and entertained them with gay anecdotes of her life in Paris, her travels in Russia when governess in Prince Jermadoff's family, and all manner of witty stories that kept them interested and merry long after the meal was over. In the middle of an absorbing adventure, Coventry came in, nodded lazily, lifted his brows, as if surprised at seeing the governess there, and began his breakfast as if the ennui of another day had already taken possession of him. Miss Muir stopped short, and no entreaties could induce her to go on.

'Another time I will finish it, if you like. Now Miss Bella and I should be at our books.' And she left the room, followed by her pupil, taking no notice of the young master of the house, beyond a graceful bow in answer to his careless nod.

'Merciful creature! she goes when I come, and does not make life unendurable by moping about before my eyes. Does she belong to the moral, the melancholy, the romantic, or the dashing class, Ned?' said Gerald, lounging over his coffee as he did over everything he attempted.

'To none of them; she is a capital little woman. I wish you had seen her tame Hector this morning.' And Edward repeated his story.

'Not a bad move on her part,' said Coventry in reply. 'She must be an observing as well as an energetic young person, to discover your chief weakness and attack it so soon. First tame the horse, and then the master. It will be amusing to watch the game, only I shall be under the painful necessity of checkmating you both, if it gets serious.'

'You needn't exert yourself, old fellow, on my account. If I was not above thinking ill of an inoffensive girl, I should say you were the prize best worth winning, and advise you to take care of your own heart, if you've got one, which I rather doubt.'

'I often doubt it, myself; but I fancy the little Scotchwoman will not be able to satisfy either of us upon that point. How does your highness like her?' asked Coventry of his cousin, who sat near him.

'Better than I thought I should. She is well-bred, unassuming, and very entertaining when she likes. She has told us some of the wittiest stories I've heard for a long time. Didn't our laughter wake you?' replied Lucia.

'Yes. Now atone for it by amusing me with a repetition of these witty tales.'

'That is impossible; her accent and manner are half the charm,' said Ned. 'I wish you had kept away ten minutes longer, for your appearance spoilt the best story of all.'

'Why didn't she go on?' asked Coventry, with a ray of curiosity.

'You forget that she overheard us last night, and must feel that you consider her a bore. She has pride, and no woman forgets speeches like those you made,' answered Lucia.

'Or forgives them, either, I believe. Well, I must be resigned to languish under her displeasure then. On Sydney's account I take a slight interest in her; not that I expect to learn anything from her, for a woman with a mouth like that never confides or confesses anything. But I have a fancy to see what captivated him; for captivated he was, beyond a doubt, and by no lady whom he met in society. Did you ever hear anything of it, Ned?' asked Gerald.

'I'm not fond of scandal or gossip, and never listen to either.' With which remark Edward left the room.

Lucia was called out by the housekeeper a moment after, and Coventry left to the society most wearisome to him, namely his own. As he entered, he had caught a part of the story which Miss Muir had been telling, and it had excited his curiosity so much that he found himself wondering what the end could be and wishing that he might hear it.

What the deuce did she run away for, when I came in? he thought. If she *is* amusing, she must make herself useful; for it's intensely dull, I own, here, in spite of Lucia. Hey, what's that?

It was a rich, sweet voice, singing a brilliant Italian air, and singing it with an expression that made the music doubly delicious. Stepping out of the French window, Coventry strolled along the sunny terrace, enjoying the song with the relish of a connoisseur. Others followed, and still he walked and listened, forgetful of weariness or time. As one exquisite air ended, he involuntarily applauded. Miss Muir's face appeared for an instant, then vanished, and no more music followed, though Coventry lingered, hoping to hear the voice again. For music was the one thing of which he never wearied, and neither Lucia nor Bella possessed skill enough to charm him. For an hour he loitered on the terrace or the lawn, basking in the sunshine, too indolent to seek occupation or society. At length Bella came out, hat in hand, and nearly stumbled over her brother, who lay on the grass.

'You lazy man, have you been dawdling here all this time?' she said, looking down at him.

'No, I've been very busy. Come and tell me how you've got on with the little dragon.'

'Can't stop. She bade me take a run after my French, so that I might be ready for my drawing, and so I must.'

'It's too warm to run. Sit down and amuse your deserted brother, who has had no society but bees and lizards for an hour.'

He drew her down as he spoke, and Bella obeyed; for, in spite of his indolence, he was one to whom all submitted without dreaming of refusal.

'What have you been doing? Muddling your poor little brains with all manner of elegant rubbish?'

'No, I've been enjoying myself immensely. Jean is *so* interesting, so kind and clever. She didn't bore me with stupid grammar, but just talked to me in such pretty French that I got on capitally, and like it as I never expected to, after Lucia's dull way of teaching it.'

'What did you talk about?'

'Oh, all manner of things. She asked questions, and I answered, and she corrected me.'

'Questions about our affairs, I suppose?'

'Not one. She don't care two sous for us or our affairs. I thought she might like to know what sort of people we were, so I told her about Papa's sudden death, Uncle John, and you, and Ned; but in the midst of it she said, in her quiet way, "You are getting too confidential, my dear. It is not best to talk too freely of one's affairs to strangers. Let us speak of something else."'

'What were you talking of when she said that, Bell?'

'You.'

'Ah, then no wonder she was bored.'

'She was tired of my chatter, and didn't hear half I said; for she was busy sketching something for me to copy, and thinking of something more interesting than the Coventrys.'

'How do you know?'

'By the expression of her face. Did you like her music, Gerald?'

'Yes. Was she angry when I clapped?'

'She looked surprised, then rather proud, and shut the piano at once, though I begged her to go on. Isn't Jean a pretty name?'

'Not bad; but why don't you call her Miss Muir?'

'She begged me not. She hates it, and loves to be called Jean, alone. I've imagined such a nice little romance about her, and someday I shall tell her, for I'm sure she has had a love trouble.'

'Don't get such nonsense into your head, but follow Miss Muir's well-bred example and don't be curious about other people's affairs. Ask her to sing tonight; it amuses me.'

'She won't come down, I think. We've planned to read and work in my boudoir, which is to be our study now. Mamma will stay in her room, so you and Lucia can have the drawing room all to yourselves.'

'Thank you. What will Ned do?'

'He will amuse Mamma, he says. Dear old Ned! I wish you'd stir about and get him his commission. He is so impatient to be doing something and yet so proud he won't ask again, after you have neglected it so many times and refused Uncle's help.'

'I'll attend to it very soon; don't worry me, child. He will do very well for a time, quietly here with us.'

'You always say that, yet you know he chafes and is unhappy at being dependent on you. Mamma and I don't mind; but he is a man, and it frets him. He said he'd take matters into his own hands soon, and then you may be sorry you were so slow in helping him.'

'Miss Muir is looking out of the window. You'd better go and take your run, else she will scold.'

'Not she. I'm not a bit afraid of her, she's so gentle and sweet. I'm fond of her already. You'll get as brown as Ned, lying here in the sun. By the way, Miss Muir agrees with me in thinking him handsomer than you.'

'I admire her taste and quite agree with her.'

'She said he was manly, and that was more attractive than beauty in a man. She does express things so nicely. Now I'm off.' And away danced Bella, humming the burden of Miss Muir's sweetest song.

'"Energy is more attractive than beauty in a man." She is right, but how the deuce *can* a man be energetic, with nothing to expend his energies upon?' mused Coventry, with his hat over his eyes.

A few moments later, the sweep of a dress caught his ear. Without stirring, a sidelong glance showed him Miss Muir coming across the terrace, as if to join Bella. Two stone steps led down to the lawn. He lay near them, and Miss Muir did not see him till close upon him. She started and slipped on the last step, recovered herself, and glided on, with a glance of unmistakable contempt as she passed the recumbent figure of the apparent sleeper. Several things in Bella's report had nettled him, but this look made him angry, though he would not own it, even to himself.

'Gerald, come here, quick!' presently called Bella, from the rustic seat where she stood beside her governess, who sat with her hand over her face as if in pain.

Gathering himself up, Coventry slowly obeyed, but involuntarily quickened his pace as he heard Miss Muir say, 'Don't call him; *he* can do nothing'; for the emphasis on the word 'he' was very significant.

'What is it, Bella?' he asked, looking rather wider awake than usual.

'You startled Miss Muir and made her turn her ankle. Now help her to the house, for she is in great pain; and don't lie there anymore to frighten people like a snake in the grass,' said his sister petulantly.

'I beg your pardon. Will you allow me?' And Coventry offered his arm.

Miss Muir looked up with the expression which annoyed him and answered coldly, 'Thank you, Miss Bella will do as well.'

'Permit me to doubt that.' And with a gesture too decided to be resisted, Coventry drew her arm through his and led her into the house. She submitted quietly, said the pain would soon be over, and when settled on the couch in Bella's room dismissed him with the briefest thanks. Considering the unwonted exertion he had made, he thought she might have been a little more grateful, and went away to Lucia, who always brightened when he came.

No more was seen of Miss Muir till teatime; for now, while the family were in retirement, they dined early and saw no company. The governess had excused herself at dinner, but came down in the evening a little paler than usual and with a slight limp in her gait. Sir John was there, talking with his nephew, and they merely acknowledged her presence by the sort of bow which gentlemen bestow on governesses. As she slowly made her way to her place behind the urn, Coventry said to his brother, 'Take her a footstool, and ask her how she is, Ned.' Then, as if necessary to account for his politeness to his uncle, he explained how he was the cause of the accident.

'Yes, yes. I understand. Rather a nice little person, I fancy. Not exactly a beauty, but accomplished and well-bred, which is better for one of her class.'

'Some tea, Sir John?' said a soft voice at his elbow, and there was Miss Muir, offering cups to the gentlemen.

'Thank you, thank you,' said Sir John, sincerely hoping she had overheard him.

As Coventry took his, he said graciously, 'You are very forgiving, Miss Muir, to wait upon me, after I have caused you so much pain.'

'It is my duty, sir' was her reply, in a tone which plainly said, 'but not my pleasure.' And she returned to her place, to smile, and chat, and be charming, with Bella and her brother.

Lucia, hovering near her uncle and Gerald, kept them to herself, but was disturbed to find that their eyes often wandered to the cheerful group about the table, and that their attention seemed distracted by the frequent bursts of laughter and fragments of animated conversation which reached them. In the midst of an account of a tragic affair which she endeavored to make as interesting and pathetic as possible, Sir John burst into a hearty laugh, which betrayed that he had been listening to a livelier story than her own. Much annoyed, she said hastily, 'I knew it would be so! Bella has no idea of the proper manner in which to treat a governess. She and Ned will forget the difference of rank and spoil that person for her work. She is inclined to be presumptuous already, and if my aunt won't trouble herself to give Miss Muir a hint in time, I shall.'

'Wait till she has finished that story, I beg of you,' said Coventry, for Sir John was already off.

'If you find that nonsense so entertaining, why don't you follow Uncle's example? I don't need you.'

'Thank you. I will.' And Lucia was deserted.

But Miss Muir had ended and, beckoning to Bella, left the room, as if quite unconscious of the honor conferred upon her or the dullness she left behind her. Ned went up to his mother, Gerald returned to make his peace with Lucia, and, bidding them good night, Sir John turned homeward. Strolling along the terrace, he came to the lighted window of Bella's study, and, wishing to say a word to her, he half pushed aside the curtain and looked in. A pleasant little scene. Bella working busily, and near her in a low chair, with the light falling on her fair hair and delicate profile, sat Miss Muir, reading aloud. 'Novels!' thought Sir John, and smiled at them for a pair of romantic girls. But pausing to listen a moment before he spoke, he found it was no novel, but history, read with a fluency which made every fact interesting, every sketch of character memorable, by the dramatic effect given to it. Sir John was fond of history, and failing eyesight often curtailed his favorite amusement. He had tried readers, but none suited him, and he had given up the plan. Now as he listened, he thought how pleasantly the smoothly flowing voice would while away his evenings, and he envied Bella her new acquisition.

A bell rang, and Bella sprang up, saying, 'Wait for me a minute. I must run to Mamma, and then we will go on with this charming prince.'

Away she went, and Sir John was about to retire as quietly as he came, when Miss Muir's peculiar behavior arrested him for an instant. Dropping the book, she threw her arms across the table, laid her head down upon them, and broke into a passion of tears, like one who could bear restraint no longer. Shocked and amazed, Sir John stole away; but all that night the kindhearted gentleman puzzled his brains with conjectures about his niece's interesting young governess, quite unconscious that she intended he should do so.

[In Chapter III, Passion and Pique, Jean makes her presence known at Coventry House, alternately charming and alarming all she encounters. Not long after her arrival, she drops hints that a young man at her previous post (Sydney) had had a passion for her. These hints, and Jean's manners, intrigue Ned Coventry, who falls in love with her. Jean shows a love letter from Ned to his elder brother, Gerald. The brothers come to blows; Gerald is wounded and Ned is sent away. This leaves Jean free to play on Gerald's heart, which she begins to do by pretending to be what he wants her to be: pretty, witty and above all, mysterious. She wins over the child, Bella, as well – and uses her to 'set her scene', or trap, in the next chapter.

In Chapter IV, A Discovery, Bella innocently helps Jean to win Gerald's admiration by criticizing Lucia as 'cold and uninteresting'. Gerald, quite unconsciously, falls into the trap. He wants to be intriguing – to win the respect of Jean Muir. She alternately flirts with and scorns him, teasing him with the carefully dropped hint that she may have descended from a titled family. As Jean rises in Gerald's estimation, he drops in hers – but she uses her advantage over Gerald to set her sights more accurately on her next target: 'old' Sir John Coventry. The chapter ends with Gerald musing: 'How the deuce does the girl do it?']

V How the Girl Did It

At home he found a party of young friends, who hailed with delight the prospect of a revel at the Hall. An hour later, the blithe company trooped into the great saloon, where preparations had already been made for a dramatic evening.

Good Sir John was in his element, for he was never so happy as when his house was full of young people. Several persons were chosen, and in a few moments the curtains were withdrawn from the first of these impromptu tableaux. A swarthy, darkly bearded man lay asleep on a tiger skin, in the shadow of a tent. Oriental arms and drapery surrounded him; an antique silver lamp burned dimly on a table where fruit lay heaped in costly dishes, and wine shone redly in half-emptied goblets. Bending over the sleeper was a woman robed with barbaric splendor. One hand turned back the embroidered sleeve from the arm which held a scimitar; one slender foot in a scarlet sandal was visible under the white tunic; her purple mantle swept down from snowy shoulders; fillets of gold bound her hair, and jewels shone on neck and arms. She was looking over her shoulder toward the entrance of the tent, with a steady yet stealthy look, so effective that for a moment the spectators held their breath, as if they also heard a passing footstep.

'Who is it?' whispered Lucia, for the face was new to her.

'Jean Muir,' answered Coventry, with an absorbed look.

'Impossible! She is small and fair,' began Lucia, but a hasty 'Hush, let me look!' from her cousin silenced her.

Impossible as it seemed, he was right nevertheless; for Jean Muir it was. She had darkened her skin, painted her eyebrows, disposed some wild black locks over her fair hair, and thrown such an intensity of expression into her eyes that they darkened and dilated till they were as fierce as any southern eyes that ever flashed. Hatred, the deepest and bitterest, was written on her sternly beautiful face, courage glowed in her glance, power spoke in the nervous grip of the slender hand that held the weapon, and the indomitable will of the woman was expressed – even the firm pressure of the little foot half hidden in the tiger skin.

'Oh, isn't she splendid?' cried Bella under her breath.

'She looks as if she'd use her sword well when the time comes,' said someone admiringly.

'Good night to Holofernes; his fate is certain,' added another.

'He is the image of Sydney, with that beard on.'

'Doesn't she look as if she really hated him?'

'Perhaps she does.'

Coventry uttered the last exclamation, for the two which preceded it suggested an explanation of the marvelous change in Jean. It was not all art: the intense detestation mingled with a savage joy that the object of her hatred was in her power was too perfect to be feigned; and having the key to a part of her story, Coventry felt as if he caught a glimpse of the truth. It was but a glimpse, however, for the curtain dropped before he had half analyzed the significance of that strange face.

'Horrible! I'm glad it's over,' said Lucia coldly.

'Magnificent! Encore! Encore!' cried Gerald enthusiastically.

But the scene was over, and no applause could recall the actress. Two or three graceful or gay pictures followed, but Jean was in none, and each lacked the charm which real talent lends to the simplest part.

'Coventry, you are wanted,' called a voice. And to everyone's surprise, Coventry went, though heretofore he had always refused to exert himself when handsome actors were in demand.

'What part am I to spoil?' he asked, as he entered the green room, where several excited young gentlemen were costuming and attitudinizing.

'A fugitive cavalier. Put yourself into this suit, and lose no time asking questions. Miss Muir will tell you what to do. She is in the tableau, so no one will mind you,' said the manager pro tem, throwing a rich old suit toward Coventry and resuming the painting of a moustache on his own boyish face.

A gallant cavalier was the result of Gerald's hasty toilet, and when he appeared before the ladies a general glance of admiration was bestowed upon him.

'Come along and be placed; Jean is ready on the stage.' And Bella ran before him, exclaiming to her governess, 'Here he is, quite splendid. Wasn't he good to do it?'

Miss Muir, in the charmingly prim and puritanical dress of a Roundhead damsel, was arranging some shrubs, but turned suddenly and dropped the green branch she held, as her eye met the glittering figure advancing toward her.

'You!' she said with a troubled look, adding low to Bella, 'Why did you ask *him*? I begged you not.'

'He is the only handsome man here, and the best actor if he likes. He won't play usually, so make the most of him.' And Bella was off to finish powdering her hair for 'The Marriage à la Mode.'

'I was sent for and I came. Do you prefer some other person?' asked Coventry, at a loss to understand the half-anxious, half-eager expression of the face under the little cap.

It changed to one of mingled annoyance and resignation as she said. 'It is too late. Please kneel here, half behind the shrubs; put down your hat, and –allow me – you are too elegant for a fugitive.'

As he knelt before her, she disheveled his hair, pulled his lace collar awry, threw away his gloves and sword, and half untied the cloak that hung about his shoulders.

'That is better; your paleness is excellent – nay, don't spoil it. We are to represent the picture which hangs in the Hall. I need tell you no more. Now, Roundheads, place yourselves, and then ring up the curtain.'

With a smile, Coventry obeyed her; for the picture was of two lovers, the young cavalier kneeling, with his arm around the waist of the girl, who tries to hide him with her little mantle, and presses his head to her bosom in an ecstasy of fear, as she glances back at the approaching pursuers. Jean hesitated an instant and shrank a little as his hand touched her; she blushed deeply, and her eyes fell before his. Then, as the bell rang, she threw herself into her part with sudden spirit. One arm half covered him with her cloak, the other pillowed his head on the muslin kerchief folded over her bosom, and she looked backward with such terror in her eyes that more than one chivalrous young spectator longed to hurry to the rescue. It lasted but a moment; yet in that moment Coventry experienced another new sensation. Many women had smiled on him, but he had remained heart-whole, cool, and careless, quite unconscious of the power which a woman possesses and knows how to use, for the weal or woe of man. Now, as he knelt there with a soft arm about him, a slender waist yielding to his touch, and a maiden heart throbbing against his cheek, for the first time in his life he felt the indescribable spell of womanhood, and looked the ardent lover to perfection. Just as his face assumed this new and most becoming aspect, the curtain dropped, and clamorous encores recalled him to the fact that Miss Muir was trying to escape from his hold, which had grown painful in its unconscious pressure. He sprang up, half bewildered, and looking as he had never looked before.

'Again! Again!' called Sir John. And the young men who played the Roundheads, eager to share in the applause begged for a repetition in new attitudes.

'A rustle has betrayed you, we have fired and shot the brave girl, and she lies dying, you know. That will be effective; try it, Miss Muir,' said one. And with a long breath, Jean complied.

The curtain went up, showing the lover still on his knees, unmindful of the captors who clutched him by the shoulder, for at his feet the girl lay dying. Her head was on his breast, now, her eyes looked full into his; no longer wild with fear, but eloquent with the love which even death could not conquer. The power of those tender eyes thrilled Coventry with a strange delight, and set his heart beating as rapidly as hers had done. She felt his hands tremble, saw the color flash into his cheek, knew that she had touched him at last, and when she rose it was with a sense of triumph which she found it hard to conceal. Others thought it fine acting; Coventry tried to believe so; but Lucia set her teeth, and, as the curtain fell on that second picture, she left her place to hurry behind the scenes, bent on putting an end to such dangerous play. Several actors were complimenting the mimic lovers. Jean took it merrily, but Coventry, in spite of himself, betrayed that he was excited by something deeper than mere gratified vanity.

As Lucia appeared, his manner changed to its usual indifference; but he could not quench the unwonted fire of his eyes, or keep all trace of emotion out of his face, and she saw this with a sharp pang.

'I have come to offer my help. You must be tired, Miss Muir. Can I relieve you?' said Lucia hastily.

'Yes, thank you. I shall be very glad to leave the rest to you, and enjoy them from the front.'

So with a sweet smile Jean tripped away, and to Lucia's dismay Coventry followed.

'I want you, Gerald; please stay,' she cried.

'I've done my part – no more tragedy for me tonight.' And he was gone before she could entreat or command.

There was no help for it; she must stay and do her duty, or expose her jealousy to the quick eyes about her. For a time she bore it; but the sight of her cousin leaning over the chair she had left and chatting with the governess, who now filled it, grew unbearable, and she dispatched a little girl with a message to Miss Muir.

'Please, Miss Beaufort wants you for Queen Bess, as you are the only lady with red hair. Will you come?' whispered the child, quite unconscious of any hidden sting in her words.

'Yes, dear, willingly though I'm not stately enough for Her Majesty, nor handsome enough,' said Jean, rising with an untroubled face, though she resented the feminine insult.

'Do you want an Essex? I'm all dressed for it,' said Coventry, following to the door with a wistful look.

'No, Miss Beaufort said *you* were not to come. She doesn't want you both together,' said the child decidedly.

Jean gave him a significant look, shrugged her shoulders, and went away smiling her odd smile, while Coventry paced up and down the hall in a curious state of unrest, which made him forgetful of everything till the young people came gaily out to supper.

'Come, bonny Prince Charlie, take me down, and play the lover as charmingly as you did an hour ago. I never thought you had so much warmth in you,' said Bella, taking his arm and drawing him on against his will.

'Don't be foolish, child. Where is – Lucia?'

Why he checked Jean's name on his lips and substituted another's, he could not tell; but a sudden shyness in speaking of her possessed him, and though he saw her nowhere, he would not ask for her. His cousin came down looking lovely in a classical costume; but Gerald scarcely saw her, and, when the merriment was at its height, he slipped away to discover what had become of Miss Muir.

Alone in the deserted drawing room he found her, and paused to watch her a moment before he spoke; for something in her attitude and face struck him. She was leaning wearily back in the great chair which had served for a throne. Her royal robes were still unchanged, though the crown was off and all her fair hair hung about her shoulders. Excitement and exertion made her brilliant, the rich dress became her wonderfully, and an air of luxurious indolence changed the meek governess into a charming woman. She leaned on the velvet cushions as if she were used to such support; she played with the jewels which had crowned her as carelessly as if she were born to wear them; her attitude was full of negligent grace, and the expression of her face half proud, half pensive, as if her thoughts were bitter-sweet.

One would know she was wellborn to see her now. Poor girl, what a burden a life of dependence must be to a spirit like hers! I wonder what she is thinking of so intently. And Coventry indulged in another look before he spoke.

'Shall I bring you some supper, Miss Muir?'

'Supper!' she ejaculated, with a start. 'Who thinks of one's body when one's soul is –' She stopped there, knit her brows, and laughed faintly as she added, 'No, thank you. I want nothing but advice, and that I dare not ask of anyone.'

'Why not?'

'Because I have no right.'

'Everyone has a right to ask help, especially the weak of the strong. Can I help you? Believe me, I most heartily offer my poor services.'

'Ah, you forget! This dress, the borrowed splendor of these jewels, the freedom of this gay evening, the romance of the part you played, all blind you to the reality. For a moment I cease to be a servant, and for a moment you treat me as an equal.'

It was true; he *had* forgotten. That soft, reproachful glance touched him, his distrust melted under the new charm, and he answered with real feeling in voice and face, 'I treat you as an equal because you *are* one; and when I offer help, it is not to my sister's governess alone, but to Lady Howard's daughter.'

'Who told you that?' she demanded, sitting erect.

'My uncle. Do not reproach him. It shall go no further, if you forbid it. Are you sorry that I know it?'

'Yes.'

'Why?'

'Because I will not be pitied!' And her eyes flashed as she made a half-defiant gesture.

'Then, if I may not pity the hard fate which has befallen an innocent life, may I admire the courage which meets adverse fortune so bravely, and conquers the world by winning the respect and regard of all who see and honor it?'

Miss Muir averted her face, put up her hand, and answered hastily, 'No, no, not that! Do not be kind; it destroys the only barrier now left between us. Be cold to me as before, forget what I am, and let me go on my way, unknown, unpitied, and unloved!'

Her voice faltered and failed as the last word was uttered, and she bent her face upon her hand. Something jarred upon Coventry in this speech, and moved him to say, almost rudely, 'You need have no fears for me. Lucia will tell you what an iceberg I am.'

'Then Lucia would tell me wrong. I have the fatal power of reading character; I know you better than she does, and I see –' There she stopped abruptly.

'What? Tell me and prove your skill,' he said eagerly.

Turning, she fixed her eyes on him with a penetrating power that made him shrink as she said slowly, 'Under the ice I see fire, and warn you to beware lest it prove a volcano.'

For a moment he sat dumb, wondering at the insight of the girl; for she was the first to discover the hidden warmth of a nature too proud to confess its tender impulses, or the ambitions that slept till some potent voice awoke them. The blunt, almost stern manner in which she warned him away from her only made her more attractive; for there was no conceit or arrogance in it, only a foreboding fear emboldened by past suffering to be frank. Suddenly he spoke impetuously:

'You are right! I am not what I seem, and my indolent indifference is but the mask under which I conceal my real self. I could be as passionate, as energetic and aspiring as Ned, if I had any aim in life. I have none, and so I am what you once called me, a thing to pity and despise.'

'I never said that!' cried Jean indignantly.

'Not in those words, perhaps; but you looked it and thought it, though you phrased it more mildly. I deserved it, but I shall deserve it no longer. I am beginning to wake from my disgraceful idleness, and long for some work that shall make a man of me. Why do you go? I annoy you with my confessions. Pardon me. They are the first I ever made; they shall be the last.'

'No, oh no! I am too much honored by your confidence; but is it wise, is it loyal to tell *me* your hopes and aims? Has not Miss Beaufort the first right to be your confidante?'

Coventry drew back, looking intensely annoyed, for the name recalled much that he would gladly have forgotten in the novel excitement of the hour. Lucia's love, Edward's parting words, his own reserve so strangely thrown aside, so difficult to resume. What he would have said was checked by the sight of a half-open letter which fell from Jean's dress as she moved away. Mechanically he took it up to return it, and, as he did so, he recognized Sydney's handwriting. Jean snatched it from him, turning pale to the lips as she cried, 'Did you read it? What did you see? Tell me, tell me, on your honor!'

'On my honor, I saw nothing but this single sentence, "By the love I bear you, believe what I say," No more, as I am a gentleman. I know the hand, I guess the purport of the letter, and as a friend of Sydney, I earnestly desire to help you, if I can. Is this the matter upon which you want advice?'

'Yes.'

'Then let me give it?'

'You cannot, without knowing all, and it is so hard to tell!'

'Let me guess it, and spare you the pain of telling. May I?' And Coventry waited eagerly for her reply, for the spell was still upon him.

Holding the letter fast, she beckoned him to follow, and glided before him to a secluded little nook, half boudoir, half conservatory. There she paused, stood an instant as if in doubt, then looked up at him with confiding eyes and said decidedly, 'I will do it; for, strange as it may seem, you are the only person to whom I *can* speak. You know Sydney, you have discovered that I am an equal, you have offered your help. I accept it; but oh, do not think me unwomanly! Remember how alone I am, how young, and how much I rely upon your sincerity, your sympathy!'

'Speak freely. I am indeed your friend.' And Coventry sat down beside her, forgetful of everything but the soft-eyed girl who confided in him so entirely.

Speaking rapidly, Jean went on, 'You know that Sydney loved me, that I refused him and went away. But you do not know that his importunities nearly drove me wild, that he threatened to rob me of my only treasure, my good name, and that, in desperation, I tried to kill myself. Yes, mad, wicked as it was, I did long to end the life which was, at best, a burden, and under his persecution had become a torment. You are shocked, yet what I say is the living truth. Lady Sydney will confirm it, the nurses at the hospital will confess that it was not a fever which brought me there; and here, though the external wound is healed, my heart still aches and burns with the shame and indignation which only a proud woman can feel.'

She paused and sat with kindling eyes, glowing cheeks, and both hands pressed to her heaving bosom, as if the old insult roused her spirit anew. Coventry said not a word, for surprise, anger, incredulity, and admiration mingled so confusedly in his mind that he forgot to speak, and Jean went on, 'That wild act of mine convinced him of my indomitable dislike. He went away, and I believed that this stormy love of his would be cured by absence. It is not, and I live in daily fear of fresh entreaties, renewed persecution. His mother promised not to betray where I had gone, but he found me out and wrote to me. The letter I asked you to take to Lady Sydney was a reply to his, imploring him to leave me in peace. You failed to deliver it, and I was glad, for I thought silence might quench hope. All in vain; this is a more passionate appeal than ever, and he vows he will never desist from his endeavors till I give another man the right to protect me. I *can* do this – I am sorely tempted to do it, but I rebel against the cruelty. I love my freedom, I have no wish to marry at this man's bidding. What can I do? How can I free myself? Be my friend, and help me!'

Tears streamed down her cheeks, sobs choked her words, and she clasped her hands imploringly as she turned toward the young man in all the abandonment of sorrow, fear, and supplication. Coventry found it hard to meet those eloquent eyes and answer calmly, for he had no experience in such scenes and knew not how to play his part. It is this absurd dress and that romantic nonsense which makes me feel so unlike myself, he thought, quite unconscious of the dangerous power which the dusky room, the midsummer warmth and fragrance, the memory of the 'romantic nonsense,' and, most of all, the presence of a beautiful, afflicted woman had over him. His usual self-possession deserted him, and he could only echo the words which had made the strongest impression upon him:

'You *can* do this, you are tempted to do it. Is Ned the man who can protect you?'

'No' was the soft reply.

'Who then?'

'Do not ask me. A good and honorable man; one who loves me well, and would devote his life to me; one whom once it would have been happiness to marry, but now –'

There her voice ended in a sigh, and all her fair hair fell down about her face, hiding it in a shining veil.

'Why not now? This is a sure and speedy way of ending your distress. Is it impossible?'

In spite of himself, Gerald leaned nearer, took one of the little hands in his, and pressed it as he spoke, urgently, compassionately, nay, almost tenderly. From behind the veil came a heavy sigh, and the brief answer, 'It is impossible.'

'Why, Jean?'

She flung her hair back with a sudden gesture, drew away her hand, and answered, almost fiercely, 'Because I do not love him! Why do you torment me with such questions? I tell you I am in a sore strait and cannot see my way. Shall I deceive the good man, and secure peace at the price of liberty and truth? Or shall I defy Sydney and lead a life of dread? If he menaced my life, I should not fear; but he menaces that which is dearer than life – my good name. A look, a word can tarnish it; a scornful smile, a significant shrug can do me more harm than any blow; for I am a woman – friendless, poor, and at the mercy of his tongue. Ah, better to have died, and so have been saved the bitter pain that has come now!'

She sprang up, clasped her hands over her head, and paced despairingly through the little room, not weeping, but wearing an expression more tragical than tears. Still feeling as if he had suddenly stepped into a romance, yet finding a keen pleasure in the part assigned him, Coventry threw himself into it with spirit, and heartily did his best to console the poor girl who needed help so much. Going to her, he said as impetuously as Ned ever did, 'Miss Muir – nay, I will say Jean, if that will comfort you – listen, and rest assured that no harm shall touch you if I can ward if off. You are needlessly alarmed. Indignant you may well be, but, upon my life, I think you wrong Sydney. He is violent, I know, but he is too honorable a man to injure you by a light word, an unjust act. He did but threaten, hoping to soften you. Let me see him, or write to him. He is my friend; he will listen to me. Of that I am sure.'

'Be sure of nothing. When a man like Sydney loves and is thwarted in his love, nothing can control his headstrong will. Promise me you will not see or write to him. Much as I fear and despise him, I will submit, rather than any harm should befall you – or your brother. You promise me, Mr. Coventry?'

He hesitated. She clung to his arm with unfeigned solicitude in her eager, pleading face, and he could not resist it.

'I promise; but in return you must promise to let me give what help I can; and, Jean, never say again that you are friendless.'

'You are so kind! God bless you for it. But I dare not accept your friendship, *she* will not permit it, and I have no right to mar her peace.'

'Who will not permit it?' he demanded hotly.

'Miss Beaufort.'

'Hang Miss Beaufort!' exclaimed Coventry, with such energy that Jean broke into a musical laugh, despite her trouble. He joined in it, and, for an instant they stood looking at one another as if the last barrier were down, and they were friends indeed. Jean paused suddenly, with the smile on her lips, the tears still on her cheek, and made a warning gesture. He listened: the sound of feet mingled with calls and laughter proved that they were missed and sought.

'That laugh betrayed us. Stay and meet them. I cannot.' And Jean darted out upon the lawn. Coventry followed; for the thought of confronting so many eyes, so many questions, daunted him, and he fled like a coward. The sound of Jean's flying footsteps guided him, and he overtook her just as she paused behind a rose thicket to take breath.

'Fainthearted knight! You should have stayed and covered my retreat. Hark! they are coming! Hide! Hide!' she panted, half in fear, half in merriment, as the gay pursuers rapidly drew nearer.

'Kneel down; the moon is coming out and the glitter of your embroidery will betray you,' whispered Jean, as they cowered behind the roses.

'Your arms and hair will betray you. "Come under my plaiddie," as the song says.' And Coventry tried to make his velvet cloak cover the white shoulders and fair locks.

'We are acting our parts in reality now. How Bella will enjoy the thing when I tell her!' said Jean as the noises died away.

'Do not tell her,' whispered Coventry.

'And why not?' she asked, looking up into the face so near her own, with an artless glance.

'Can you not guess why?'

'Ah, you are so proud you cannot bear to be laughed at.'

'It is not that. It is because I do not want you to be annoyed by silly tongues; you have enough to pain you without that. I am your friend, now, and I do my best to prove it.'

'So kind, so kind! How can I thank you?' murmured Jean. And she involuntarily nestled closer under the cloak that sheltered both.

Neither spoke for a moment, and in the silence the rapid beating of two hearts was heard. To drown the sound, Coventry said softly, 'Are you frightened?'

'No, I like it,' she answered, as softly, then added abruptly, 'But why do we hide? There is nothing to fear. It is late. I must go. You are kneeling on my train. Please rise.'

'Why in such haste? This flight and search only adds to the charm of the evening. I'll not get up yet. Will you have a rose, Jean?'

'No, I will not. Let me go, Mr. Coventry, I insist. There has been enough of this folly. You forget yourself.'

She spoke imperiously, flung off the cloak, and put him from her. He rose at once, saying, like one waking suddenly from a pleasant dream, 'I do indeed forget myself.'

Here the sound of voices broke on them, nearer than before. Pointing to a covered walk that led to the house, he said, in his usually cool, calm tone, 'Go in that way; I will cover your retreat.' And turning, he went to meet the merry hunters.

Half an hour later, when the party broke up, Miss Muir joined them in her usual quiet dress, looking paler, meeker, and sadder than usual. Coventry saw this, though he neither looked at her nor addressed her. Lucia saw it also, and was glad that the dangerous girl had fallen back into her proper place again, for she had suffered much that night. She appropriated her cousin's arm as they went through the park, but he was in one of his taciturn moods, and all her attempts at conversation were in vain. Miss Muir walked alone, singing softly to herself as she followed in the dusk. Was Gerald so silent because he listened to that fitful song? Lucia thought so, and felt her dislike rapidly deepening to hatred.

When the young friends were gone, and the family were exchanging good-nights among themselves, Jean was surprised by Coventry's offering his hand, for he had never done it before, and whispering, as he held it, though Lucia watched him all the while, 'I have not given my advice, yet.'

'Thanks, I no longer need it. I have decided for myself.'

'May I ask how?'

'To brave my enemy'.

'Good! But what decided you so suddenly?'

'The finding of a friend.' And with a grateful glance she was gone.

[In Chapter VI, On the Watch, Jean continues to manipulate: she orchestrates mysterious letters and stages 'accidental' encounters. The men continue to fall for her, but both Lucia and her maid, Dean, are suspicious. Dean openly refers to Jean's 'play-acting'. Meanwhile, Gerald becomes so entranced with Jean that he sets out to impress her by becoming more responsible about the care of the estate, while he pays less and less attention to Lucia. Eventually, he declares his love for Jean, and Jean leads him on. Dean spies on Jean and Gerald together, and threatens to tell Sir John. Jean determines to use this threat to her own advantage.]

VII The Last Chance

'She will tell Sir John, will she? Then I must be before her, and hasten events. It will be as well to have all sure before there can be any danger. My poor Dean, you are no match for me, but you may prove annoying, nevertheless.'

These thoughts passed through Miss Muir's mind as she went down the hall, pausing an instant at the library door, for the murmur of voices was heard. She caught no word, and had only time for an instant's pause as Dean's heavy step followed her. Turning, Jean drew a chair before the door, and, beckoning to the woman, she said, smiling still, 'Sit here and play watchdog. I am going to Miss Bella, so you can nod if you will.'

'Thank you, miss. I will wait for my young lady. She may need me when this hard time is over.' And Dean seated herself with a resolute face.

Jean laughed and went on; but her eyes gleamed with sudden malice, and she glanced over her shoulder with an expression which boded ill for the faithful old servant.

'I've got a letter from Ned, and here is a tiny note for you,' cried Bella as Jean entered the boudoir. 'Mine is a very odd, hasty letter, with no news in it, but his meeting with Sydney. I hope yours is better, or it won't be very satisfactory.'

As Sydney's name passed Bella's lips, all the color died out of Miss Muir's face, and the note shook with the tremor of her hand. Her very lips were white, but she said calmly, 'Thank you. As you are busy, I'll go and read my letter on the lawn.' And before Bella could speak, she was gone.

Hurrying to a quiet nook, Jean tore open the note and read the few blotted lines it contained.

> I have seen Sydney; he has told me all; and, hard as I found it to believe, it was impossible to doubt, for he has discovered proofs which cannot be denied. I make no reproaches, shall demand no confession or atonement, for I cannot forget that I once loved you. I give you three days to find another home, before I return to tell the family who you are. Go at once, I beseech you, and spare me the pain of seeing your disgrace.

Slowly, steadily she read it twice over, then sat motionless, knitting her brows in deep thought. Presently she drew a long breath, tore up the note, and rising, went slowly toward the Hall, saying to herself, 'Three days, only three days! Can it be accomplished in so short a time? It shall be, if wit and will can do it, for it is my last chance. If this fails, I'll not go back to my old life, but end all at once.'

Setting her teeth and clenching her hands, as if some memory stung her, she went on through the twilight, to find Sir John waiting to give her a hearty welcome.

'You look tired, my dear. Never mind the reading tonight; rest yourself, and let the book go,' he said kindly, observing her worn look.

'Thank you, sir. I am tired, but I'd rather read, else the book will not be finished before I go.'

'Go, child! Where are you going?' demanded Sir John, looking anxiously at her as she sat down.

'I will tell you by-and-by, sir.' And opening the book, Jean read for a little while.

But the usual charm was gone; there was no spirit in the voice of the reader, no interest in the face of the listener, and soon he said, abruptly, 'My dear, pray stop! I cannot listen with a divided mind. What troubles you? Tell your friend, and let him comfort you.'

As if the kind words overcame her, Jean dropped the book, covered up her face, and wept so bitterly that Sir John was much alarmed; for such a demonstration was doubly touching in one who usually was all gaiety and smiles. As he tried to soothe her, his words grew tender, his solicitude full of a more than paternal anxiety, and his kind heart overflowed with pity and affection for the weeping girl. As she grew calmer, he urged her to be frank, promising to help and counsel her, whatever the affliction or fault might be.

'Ah, you are too kind, too generous! How can I go away and leave my one friend?' sighed Jean, wiping the tears away and looking up at him with grateful eyes.

'Then you do care a little for the old man?' said Sir John with an eager look, an involuntary pressure of the hand he held.

Jean turned her face away, and answered, very low, 'No one ever was so kind to me as you have been. Can I help caring for you more than I can express?'

Sir John was a little deaf at times, but he heard that, and looked well pleased. He had been rather thoughtful of late, had dressed with unusual care, been particularly gallant and gay when the young ladies visited him, and more than once, when Jean paused in the reading to ask a question, he had been forced to confess that he had not been listening; though, as she well knew, his eyes had been fixed upon her. Since the discovery of her birth, his manner had been peculiarly benignant, and many little acts had proved his interest and goodwill. Now, when Jean spoke of going, a panic seized him, and desolation seemed about to fall upon the old Hall. Something in her unusual agitation struck him as peculiar and excited his curiosity. Never had she seemed so interesting as now, when she sat beside him with tearful eyes, and some soft trouble in her heart which she dared not confess.

'Tell me everything, child, and let your friend help you if he can.' Formerly he said 'father' or 'the old man,' but lately he always spoke of himself as her 'friend.'

'I will tell you, for I have no one else to turn to. I must go away because Mr. Coventry has been weak enough to love me.'

'What, Gerald?' cried Sir John, amazed.

'Yes; today he told me this, and left me to break with Lucia; so I ran to you to help me prevent him from disappointing his mother's hopes and plans.'

Sir John had started up and paced down the room, but as Jean paused he turned toward her, saying, with an altered face, 'Then you do not love him? Is it possible?'

'No, I do not love him,' she answered promptly.

'Yet he is all that women usually find attractive. How is it that you have escaped, Jean?'

'I love someone else' was the scarcely audible reply.

Sir John resumed his seat with the air of a man bent on getting at a mystery, if possible.

'It will be unjust to let you suffer for the folly of these boys, my little girl. Ned is gone, and I was sure that Gerald was safe; but now that his turn has come, I am perplexed, for he cannot be sent away.'

'No, it is I who must go; but it seems so hard to leave this safe and happy home, and wander away into the wide, cold world again. You have all been too kind to me, and now separation breaks my heart.'

A sob ended the speech, and Jean's head went down upon her hands again. Sir John looked at her a moment, and his fine old face was full of genuine emotion, as he said slowly, 'Jean, will you stay and be a daughter to the solitary old man?'

'No, sir' was the unexpected answer.

'And why not?' asked Sir John, looking surprised, but rather pleased than angry.

'Because I could not be a daughter to you; and even if I could, it would not be wise, for the gossips would say you were not old enough to be the adopted father of a girl like me. Sir John, young as I am, I know much of the world, and am sure that this kind plan is impractical; but I thank you from the bottom of my heart.'

'Where will you go, Jean?' asked Sir John, after a pause.

'To London, and try to find another situation where I can do no harm.'

'Will it be difficult to find another home?'

'Yes. I cannot ask Mrs. Coventry to recommend me, when I have innocently brought so much trouble into her family; and Lady Sydney is gone, so I have no friend.'

'Except John Coventry. I will arrange all that. When will you go, Jean?'

'Tomorrow.'

'So soon!' And the old man's voice betrayed the trouble he was trying to conceal.

Jean had grown very calm, but it was the calmness of desperation. She had hoped that the first tears would produce the avowal for which she waited. It had not, and she began to fear that her last chance was slipping from her. Did the old man love her? If so, why did he not speak? Eager to profit by each moment, she was on the alert for any hopeful hint, any propitious word, look, or act, and every nerve was strung to the utmost.

'Jean, may I ask one question?' said Sir John.

'Anything of me, sir.'

'This man whom you love – can he not help you?'

'He could if he knew, but he must not.'

'If he knew what? Your present trouble?'

'No. My love.'

'He does know this, then?'

'No, thank heaven! And he never will.'

'Why not?'

'Because I am too proud to own it.'

'He loves you, my child?'

'I do not know – I dare not hope it,' murmured Jean.

'Can I not help you here? Believe me, I desire to see you safe and happy. Is there nothing I can do?'

'Nothing, nothing.'

'May I know the name?'

'No! No! Let me go; I cannot bear this questioning!' And Jean's distressful face warned him to ask no more.

'Forgive me, and let me do what I may. Rest here quietly. I'll write a letter to a good friend of mine, who will find you a home, if you leave us.'

As Sir John passed into his inner study, Jean watched him with despairing eyes and wrung her hands, saying to herself, Has all my skill deserted me when I need it most? How can I make him understand, yet not overstep the bounds of maiden modesty? He is so blind, so timid, or so dull he will not see, and time is going fast. What shall I do to open his eyes?

Her own eyes roved about the room, seeking for some aid from inanimate things, and soon she found it. Close behind the couch where she sat hung a fine miniature of Sir John. At first her eye rested on it as she contrasted its placid comeliness with the unusual pallor and disquiet of the living face seen through the open door, as the old man sat at his desk trying to write and casting covert glances at the girlish figure he had left behind him. Affecting unconsciousness of this, Jean gazed on as if forgetful of everything but the picture, and suddenly, as if obeying an irresistible impulse, she took it down, looked long and fondly at it, then, shaking her curls about her face, as if to hide the act, pressed it to her lips and seemed to weep over it in an uncontrollable paroxysm of tender grief. A sound startled her, and like a guilty thing, she turned to replace the picture; but it dropped from her hand as she uttered a faint cry and hid her face, for Sir John stood before her, with an expression which she could not mistake.

'Jean, why did you do that?' he asked, in an eager, agitated voice.

No answer, as the girl sank lower, like one overwhelmed with shame. Laying his hand on the bent head, and bending his own, he whispered, 'Tell me, is the name John Coventry?'

Still no answer, but a stifled sound betrayed that his words had gone home.

'Jean, shall I go back and write the letter, or may I stay and tell you that the old man loves you better than a daughter?'

She did not speak, but a little hand stole out from under the falling hair, as if to keep him. With a broken exclamation he seized it, drew her up into his arms, and laid his gray head on her fair one, too happy for words. For a moment Jean Muir enjoyed her success; then, fearing lest some sudden mishap should destroy it, she hastened to make all secure. Looking up with well-feigned timidity and half-confessed affection, she said softly, 'Forgive me that I could not hide this better. I meant to go away and never tell it, but you were so kind it made the parting doubly hard. Why did you ask such dangerous questions? Why did you look, when you should have been writing my dismissal?'

'How could I dream that you loved me, Jean, when you refused the only offer I dared make? Could I be presumptuous enough to fancy you would reject young lovers for an old man like me?' asked Sir John, caressing her.

'You are not old, to me, but everything I love and honor!' interrupted Jean, with a touch of genuine remorse, as this generous, honorable gentleman gave her both heart and home, unconscious of deceit. 'It is I who am presumptuous, to dare to love one so far above me. But I did not know how dear you were to me till I felt that I must go. I ought not to accept this happiness. I am not worthy of it; and you will regret your kindness when the world blames you for giving a home to one so poor, and plain, and humble as I.'

'Hush, my darling. I care nothing for the idle gossip of the world. If you are happy here, let tongues wag as they will. I shall be too busy enjoying the sunshine of your presence to heed anything that goes on about me. But, Jean, you are sure you love me? It seems incredible that I should win the heart that has been so cold to younger, better men than I.'

'Dear Sir John, be sure of this, I love you truly. I will do my best to be a good wife to you, and prove that, in spite of my many faults, I possess the virtue of gratitude.'

If he had known the strait she was in, he would have understood the cause of the sudden fervor of her words, the intense thankfulness that shone in her face, the real humility that made her stoop and kiss the generous hand that gave so much. For a few moments she enjoyed and let him enjoy the happy present, undisturbed. But the anxiety which devoured her, the danger which menaced her, soon recalled her, and forced her to wring yet more from the unsuspicious heart she had conquered.

'No need of letters now,' said Sir John, as they sat side by side, with the summer moonlight glorifying all the room. 'You have found a home for life; may it prove a happy one.'

'It is not mine yet, and I have a strange foreboding that it never will be,' she answered sadly.

'Why, my child?'

'Because I have an enemy who will try to destroy my peace, to poison your mind against me, and to drive me out from my paradise, to suffer again all I have suffered this last year.'

'You mean that mad Sydney of whom you told me?'

'Yes. As soon as he hears of this good fortune to poor little Jean, he will hasten to mar it. He is my fate; I cannot escape him, and wherever he goes my friends desert me; for he has the power and uses it for my destruction. Let me go away and hide before he comes, for, having shared your confidence, it will break my heart to see you distrust and turn from me, instead of loving and protecting.'

'My poor child, you are superstitious. Be easy. No one can harm you now, no one would dare attempt it. And as for my deserting you, that will soon be out of my power, if I have my way.'

'How, dear Sir John?' asked Jean, with a flutter of intense relief at her heart, for the way seemed smoothing before her.

'I will make you my wife at once, if I may. This will free you from Gerald's love, protect you from Sydney's persecution, give you a safe home, and me the right to cherish and defend with heart and hand. Shall it be so, my child?'

'Yes; but oh, remember that I have no friend but you! Promise me to be faithful to the last – to believe in me, to trust me, protect and love me, in spite of all misfortunes, faults, and follies. I will be true as steel to you, and make your life as happy as it deserves to be. Let us promise these things now, and keep the promises unbroken to the end.'

Her solemn air touched Sir John. Too honorable and upright himself to suspect falsehood in others, he saw only the natural impulse of a lovely girl in Jean's words, and, taking the hand she gave him in both of his, he promised all she asked, and kept that promise to the end. She paused an instant, with a pale, absent expression, as if she searched herself, then looked up clearly in the confiding face above her, and promised what she faithfully performed in afteryears.

'When shall it be, little sweetheart? I leave all to you, only let it be soon, else some gay young lover will appear, and take you from me,' said Sir John, playfully, anxious to chase away the dark expression which had stolen over Jean's face.

'Can you keep a secret?' asked the girl, smiling up at him, all her charming self again.

'Try me.'

'I will. Edward is coming home in three days. I must be gone before he comes. Tell no one of this; he wishes to surprise them. And if you love me, tell nobody of your approaching marriage. Do not betray that you care for me until I am really yours. There will be such a stir, such remonstrances, explanations, and reproaches that I shall be worn out, and run away from you all to escape the trial. If I could have my wish, I would go to some quiet place tomorrow and wait till you come for me. I know so little of such things, I cannot tell how soon we may be married; not for some weeks, I think.'

'Tomorrow, if we like. A special license permits people to marry when and where they please. My plan is better than yours. Listen, and tell me if it can be carried out. I will go to town tomorrow, get the license, invite my friend, the Reverend Paul Fairfax, to return with me, and tomorrow evening you come at your usual time, and, in the presence of my discreet old servants, make me the happiest man in England. How does this suit you, my little Lady Coventry?'

The plan which seemed made to meet her ends, the name which was the height of her ambition, and the blessed sense of safety which came to her filled Jean Muir with such intense satisfaction that tears of real feeling stood in her eyes, and the glad assent she gave was the truest word that had passed her lips for months.

'We will go abroad or to Scotland for our honeymoon, till the storm blows over,' said Sir John, well knowing that this hasty marriage would surprise or offend all his relations, and feeling as glad as Jean to escape the first excitement.

'To Scotland, please. I long to see my father's home,' said Jean, who dreaded to meet Sydney on the continent.

They talked a little longer, arranging all things, Sir John so intent on hurrying the event that Jean had nothing to do but give a ready assent to all his suggestions. One fear alone disturbed her. If Sir John went to town, he might meet Edward, might hear and believe his statements. Then all would be lost. Yet this risk must be incurred, if the marriage was to be speedily and safely accomplished; and to guard against the meeting was Jean's sole care. As they went through the park – for Sir John insisted upon taking her home – she said, clinging to his arm:

'Dear friend, bear one thing in mind, else we shall be much annoyed, and all our plans disarranged. Avoid your nephews; you are so frank your face will betray you. They both love me, are both hot-tempered, and in the first excitement of the discovery might be violent. You must incur no

danger, no disrespect for my sake; so shun them both till we are safe –
particularly Edward. He will feel that his brother has wronged him, and that
you have succeeded where he failed. This will irritate him, and I fear a
stormy scene. Promise to avoid both for a day or two; do not listen to them,
do not see them, do not write to or receive letters from them. It is foolish, I
know; but you are all I have, and I am haunted by a strange foreboding
that I am to lose you.'

Touched and flattered by her tender solicitude, Sir John promised
everything, even while he laughed at her fears. Love blinded the good
gentleman to the peculiarity of the request; the novelty, romance, and
secrecy of the affair rather bewildered though it charmed him; and the
knowledge that he had outrivaled three young and ardent lovers gratified
his vanity more than he would confess. Parting from the girl at the garden
gate, he turned homeward, feeling like a boy again, and loitered back,
humming a love lay, quite forgetful of evening damps, gout, and the
five-and-fifty years which lay so lightly on his shoulders since Jean's arms
had rested there. She hurried toward the house, anxious to escape
Coventry; but he was waiting for her, and she was forced to meet him.

'How could you linger so long, and keep me in suspense?' he said
reproachfully, as he took her hand and tried to catch a glimpse of her face
in the shadow of her hat brim. 'Come and rest in the grotto. I have so much
to say, to hear and enjoy.'

'Not now; I am too tired. Let me go in and sleep. Tomorrow we will
talk. It is damp and chilly, and my head aches with all this worry.' Jean
spoke wearily, yet with a touch of petulance, and Coventry, fancying that
she was piqued at his not coming for her, hastened to explain with eager
tenderness.

'My poor little Jean, you do need rest. We wear you out, among us,
and you never complain. I should have come to bring you home, but
Lucia detained me, and when I got away I saw my uncle had forestalled
me. I shall be jealous of the old gentleman, if he is so devoted. Jean, tell
me one thing before we part; I am free as air, now, and have a right to
speak. Do you love me? Am I the happy man who has won your heart? I
dare to think so, to believe that this telltale face of yours has betrayed
you, and to hope that I have gained what poor Ned and wild Sydney have
lost.'

'Before I answer, tell me of your interview with Lucia. I have a right to
know,' said Jean.

Coventry hesitated, for pity and remorse were busy at his heart when
he recalled poor Lucia's grief. Jean was bent on hearing the humiliation of
her rival. As the young man paused, she frowned, then lifted up her face
wreathed in softest smiles, and laying her hand on his arm, she said, with
most effective emphasis, half shy, half fond, upon his name, 'Please tell me,
Gerald!'

He could not resist the look, the touch, the tone, and taking the little
hand in his, he said rapidly, as if the task was distasteful to him, 'I told her
that I did not, could not love her; that I had submitted to my mother's wish,
and, for a time, had felt tacitly bound to her, though no words had passed
between us. But now I demanded my liberty, regretting that the separation
was not mutually desired.'

'And she – what did she say? How did she bear it?' asked Jean, feeling in her own woman's heart how deeply Lucia's must have been wounded by that avowal.

'Poor girl! It was hard to bear, but her pride sustained her to the end. She owned that no pledge tied me, fully relinquished any claim my past behavior had seemed to have given her, and prayed that I might find another woman to love me as truly, tenderly as she had done. Jean, I felt like a villain; and yet I never plighted my word to her, never really loved her, and had a perfect right to leave her, if I would.'

'Did she speak of me?'

'Yes.'

'What did she say?'

'Must I tell you?'

'Yes, tell me everything. I know she hates me and I forgive her, knowing that I should hate any woman whom *you* loved.'

'Are you jealous, dear?'

'Of you, Gerald?' And the fine eyes glanced up at him, full of a brilliancy that looked like the light of love.

'You make a slave of me already. How do you do it? I never obeyed a woman before. Jean, I think you are a witch. Scotland is the home of weird, uncanny creatures, who take lovely shapes for the bedevilment of poor weak souls. Are you one of those fair deceivers?'

'You are complimentary,' laughed the girl. 'I *am* a witch, and one day my disguise will drop away and you will see me as I am, old, ugly, bad and lost. Beware of me in time. I've warned you. Now love me at your peril.'

Coventry had paused as he spoke, and eyed her with an unquiet look, conscious of some fascination which conquered yet brought no happiness. A feverish yet pleasurable excitement possessed him; a reckless mood, making him eager to obliterate the past by any rash act, any new experience which his passion brought. Jean regarded him with a wistful, almost woeful face, for one short moment; then a strange smile broke over it, as she spoke in a tone of malicious mockery, under which lurked the bitterness of a sad truth. Coventry looked half bewildered, and his eye went from the girl's mysterious face to a dimly lighted window, behind whose curtains poor Lucia hid her aching heart, praying for him the tender prayers that loving women give to those whose sins are all forgiven for love's sake. His heart smote him, and a momentary feeling of repulsion came over him, as he looked at Jean. She saw it, felt angry, yet conscious of a sense of relief; for now that her own safety was so nearly secured, she felt no wish to do mischief, but rather a desire to undo what was already done, and be at peace with all the world. To recall him to his allegiance, she sighed and walked on, saying gently yet coldly, 'Will you tell me what I ask before I answer your question, Mr. Coventry?'

'What Lucia said of you? Well, it was this. "Beware of Miss Muir. We instinctively distrusted her when we had no cause. I believe in instincts, and mine have never changed, for she has not tried to delude me. Her art is wonderful; I feel yet cannot explain or detect it, except in the working of events which her hand seems to guide. She has brought sorrow and dissension into this hitherto happy family. We are all changed, and this girl has done it. Me she can harm no further; you she will ruin, if she can.

Beware of her in time, or you will bitterly repent your blind infatuation!"

'And what answer did you make?' asked Jean, as the last words came reluctantly from Coventry's lips.

'I told her that I loved you in spite of myself, and would make you my wife in the face of all opposition. Now, Jean, your answer.'

'Give me three days to think of it. Good night.' And gliding from him, she vanished into the house, leaving him to roam about half the night, tormented with remorse, suspense, and the old distrust which would return when Jean was not there to banish it by her art.

VIII   Suspense

All the next day, Jean was in a state of the most intense anxiety, as every hour brought the crisis nearer, and every hour might bring defeat, for the subtlest human skill is often thwarted by some unforeseen accident. She longed to assure herself that Sir John was gone, but no servants came or went that day, and she could devise no pretext for sending to glean intelligence. She dared not go herself, lest the unusual act should excite suspicion, for she never went till evening. Even had she determined to venture, there was no time, for Mrs. Coventry was in one of her nervous states, and no one but Miss Muir could amuse her; Lucia was ill, and Miss Muir must give orders; Bella had a studious fit, and Jean must help her. Coventry lingered about the house for several hours, but Jean dared not send him, lest some hint of the truth might reach him. He had ridden away to his new duties when Jean did not appear, and the day dragged on wearisomely. Night came at last, and as Jean dressed for the late dinner, she hardly knew herself when she stood before her mirror, excitement lent such color and brilliancy to her countenance. Remembering the wedding which was to take place that evening, she put on a simple white dress and added a cluster of white roses in bosom and hair. She often wore flowers, but in spite of her desire to look and seem as usual, Bella's first words as she entered the drawing room were 'Why, Jean, how like a bride you look; a veil and gloves would make you quite complete!'

'You forget one other trifle, Bell,' said Gerald, with eyes that brightened as they rested on Miss Muir.

'What is that?' asked his sister.

'A bridegroom.'

Bella looked to see how Jean received this, but she seemed quite composed as she smiled one of her sudden smiles, and merely said, 'That trifle will doubtless be found when the time comes. Is Miss Beaufort too ill for dinner?'

'She begs to be excused, and said you would be willing to take her place, she thought.'

As innocent Bella delivered this message, Jean glanced at Coventry, who evaded her eye and looked ill at ease.

A little remorse will do him good, and prepare him for repentance after the grand *coup,* she said to herself, and was particularly gay at dinnertime, though Coventry looked often at Lucia's empty seat, as if he missed her. As soon as they left the table, Miss Muir sent Bella to her mother; and, knowing that Coventry would not linger long at his wine, she hurried away to the Hall. A servant was lounging at the door, and of him she asked, in a tone which was eager in spite of all efforts to be calm, 'Is Sir John at home?'

'No, miss, he's just gone to town.'

'Just gone! When do you mean?' cried Jean, forgetting the relief she felt in hearing of his absence in surprise at his late departure.

'He went half an hour ago, in the last train, miss.'

'I thought he was going early this morning; he told me he should be back this evening.'

'I believe he did mean to go, but was delayed by company. The steward came up on business, and a load of gentlemen called, so Sir John could not get off till night, when he wasn't fit to go, being worn out, and far from well.'

'Do you think he will be ill? Did he look so?' And as Jean spoke, a thrill of fear passed over her, lest death should rob her of her prize.

'Well, you know, miss, hurry of any kind is bad for elderly gentlemen inclined to apoplexy. Sir John was in a worry all day, and not like himself. I wanted him to take his man, but he wouldn't; and drove off looking flushed and excited like. I'm anxious about him, for I know something is amiss to hurry him off in this way.'

'When will he be back, Ralph?'

'Tomorrow noon, if possible; at night, certainly, he bid me tell anyone that called.'

'Did he leave no note or message for Miss Coventry, or someone of the family?'

'No, miss, nothing.'

'Thank you.' And Jean walked back to spend a restless night and rise to meet renewed suspense.

The morning seemed endless, but noon came at last, and under the pretense of seeking coolness in the grotto, Jean stole away to a slope whence the gate to the Hall park was visible. For two long hours she watched, and no one came. She was just turning away when a horseman dashed through the gate and came galloping toward the Hall. Heedless of everything but the uncontrollable longing to gain some tidings, she ran to meet him, feeling assured that he brought ill news. It was a young man from the station, and as he caught sight of her, he drew bridle, looking agitated and undecided.

'Has anything happened?' she cried breathlessly.

'A dreadful accident on the railroad, just the other side of Croydon. News telegraphed half an hour ago,' answered the man, wiping his hot face.

'The noon train? Was Sir John in it? Quick, tell me all!'

'It was that train, miss, but whether Sir John was in it or not, we don't know; for the guard is killed, and everything is in such confusion that nothing can be certain. They are at work getting out the dead and wounded. We heard that Sir John was expected, and I came up to tell Mr. Coventry, thinking he would wish to go down. A train leaves in fifteen minutes; where shall I find him? I was told he was at the Hall.'

'Ride on, ride on! And find him if he is there. I'll run home and look for him. Lose no time. Ride! Ride!' And turning, Jean sped back like a deer, while the man tore up the avenue to rouse the Hall.

Coventry was there, and went off at once, leaving both Hall and house in dismay. Fearing to betray the horrible anxiety that possessed her, Jean shut herself up in her room and suffered untold agonies as the day wore on and no news came. At dark a sudden cry rang through the house, and Jean rushed down to learn the cause. Bella was standing in the hall, holding a letter, while a group of excited servants hovered near her.

'What is it?' demanded Miss Muir, pale and steady, though her heart died within her as she recognized Gerald's handwriting. Bella gave her the note, and hushed her sobbing to hear again the heavy tidings that had come.

> Dear Bella:
>   Uncle is safe; he did not go in the noon train. But several persons are sure that Ned was there. No trace of him as yet, but many bodies are in the river, under the ruins of the bridge, and I am doing my best to find the poor lad, if he is there. I have sent to all his haunts in town, and as he has not been seen, I hope it is a false report and he is safe with his regiment. Keep this from my mother till we are sure. I write you, because Lucia is ill. Miss Muir will comfort and sustain you. Hope for the best, dear.
>   Yours, G. C.

Those who watched Miss Muir as she read these words wondered at the strange expressions which passed over her face, for the joy which appeared there as Sir John's safety was made known did not change to grief or horror at poor Edward's possible fate. The smile died on her lips, but her voice did not falter, and in her downcast eyes shone an inexplicable look of something like triumph. No wonder, for if this was true, the danger which menaced her was averted for a time, and the marriage might be consummated without such desperate haste. This sad and sudden event seemed to her the mysterious fulfilment of a secret wish; and though startled she was not daunted but inspirited, for fate seemed to favor her designs. She did comfort Bella, control the excited household, and keep the rumors from Mrs. Coventry all that dreadful night.

At dawn Gerald came home exhausted, and bringing no tiding of the missing man. He had telegraphed to the headquarters of the regiment and received a reply, stating that Edward had left for London the previous day, meaning to go home before returning. The fact of his having been at the London station was also established, but whether he left by the train or not was still uncertain. The ruins were still being searched, and the body might yet appear.

'Is Sir John coming at noon?' asked Jean, as the three sat together in the rosy hush of dawn, trying to hope against hope.

'No, he had been ill, I learned from young Gower, who is just from town, and so had not completed his business. I sent him word to wait till night, for the bridge won't be passable till then. Now I must try and rest an hour; I've worked all night and have no strength left. Call me the instant any messenger arrives.'

With that Coventry went to his room, Bella followed to wait on him, and Jean roamed through house and grounds, unable to rest. The morning was far spent when the messenger arrived. Jean went to receive his tidings, with the wicked hope still lurking at her heart.

'Is he found?' she asked calmly, as the man hesitated to speak.

'Yes, ma'am.'

'You are sure?'

'I am certain, ma'am, though some won't say till Mr. Coventry comes to look.'

'Is he alive?' And Jean's white lips trembled as she put the question.

'Oh no, ma'am, that warn't possible, under all them stones and water. The poor young gentleman is so wet, and crushed, and torn, no one would know him, except for the uniform, and the white hand with the ring on it.'

Jean sat down, very pale, and the man described the finding of the poor shattered body. As he finished, Coventry appeared, and with one look of mingled remorse, shame, and sorrow, the elder brother went away, to find and bring the younger home. Jean crept into the garden like a guilty thing, trying to hide the satisfaction which struggled with a woman's natural pity, for so sad an end for this brave young life.

'Why waste tears or feign sorrow when I must be glad?' she muttered, as she paced to and fro along the terrace. 'The poor boy is out of pain, and I am out of danger.'

She got no further, for, turning as she spoke, she stood face to face with Edward! Bearing no mark of peril on dress or person, but stalwart and strong as ever, he stood there looking at her, with contempt and compassion struggling in his face. As if turned to stone, she remained motionless, with dilated eyes, arrested breath, and paling cheek. He did not speak but watched her silently till she put out a trembling hand, as if to assure herself by touch that it was really he. Then he drew back, and as if the act convinced as fully as words, she said slowly, 'They told me you were dead.'

'And you were glad to believe it. No, it was my comrade, young Courtney, who unconsciously deceived you all, and lost his life, as I should have done, if I had not gone to Ascot after seeing him off yesterday.'

'To Ascot?' echoed Jean, shrinking back, for Edward's eye was on her, and his voice was stern and cold.

'Yes; you know the place. I went there to make inquiries concerning you and was well satisfied. Why are you still here?'

'The three days are not over yet. I hold you to your promise. Before night I shall be gone; till then you will be silent, if you have honor enough to keep your word.'

'I have.' Edward took out his watch and, as he put it back, said with cool precision, 'It is now two, the train leaves for London at half-past six; a carriage will wait for you at the side door. Allow me to advise you to go then, for the instant dinner is over I shall speak.' And with a bow he went into the house, leaving Jean nearly suffocated with a throng of contending emotions.

For a few minutes she seemed paralyzed; but the native energy of the woman forbade utter despair, till the last hope was gone. Frail as that now was, she still clung to it tenaciously, resolving to win the game in defiance of everything. Springing up, she went to her room, packed her few valuables, dressed herself with care, and then sat down to wait. She heard a joyful stir below, saw Coventry come hurrying back, and from a garrulous maid learned that the body was that of young Courtney. The uniform being the same as Edward's and the ring, a gift from him, had caused the men to believe the disfigured corpse to be that of the younger Coventry. No one but the maid came near her; once Bella's voice called her, but some one checked the girl, and the call was not repeated. At five an envelope was brought her, directed in Edward's hand, and containing a check which more than paid a year's salary. No word accompanied the gift, yet the generosity of it touched her, for Jean Muir had the relics of a once honest nature and despite her falsehood could still admire nobleness and respect virtue. A tear of genuine shame dropped on the paper, and real gratitude filled her heart, as she thought that even if all else failed, she was not thrust out penniless into the world, which had no pity for poverty.

As the clock struck six, she heard a carriage drive around and went down to meet it. A servant put on her trunk, gave the order, 'To the station, James,' and she drove away without meeting anyone, speaking to anyone, or apparently being seen by anyone. A sense of utter weariness came over her, and she longed to lie down and forget. But the last chance still remained, and till that failed, she would not give up. Dismissing the carriage, she seated herself to watch for the quarter-past-six train from London, for in that Sir John would come if he came at all that night. She was haunted by the fear that Edward had met and told him. The first glimpse of Sir John's frank face would betray the truth. If he knew all, there was no hope, and she would go her way alone. If he knew nothing, there was yet time for the marriage; and once his wife, she knew she was safe, because for the honor of his name he would screen and protect her.

Up rushed the train, out stepped Sir John, and Jean's heart died within her. Grave, and pale, and worn he looked, and leaned heavily on the arm of a portly gentleman in black. The Reverend Mr. Fairfax, why has he come, if the secret is out? thought Jean, slowly advancing to meet them and fearing to read her fate in Sir John's face. He saw her, dropped his friend's arm, and hurried forward with the ardor of a young man, exclaiming, as he seized her hand with a beaming face, a glad voice, 'My little girl! Did you think I would never come?'

She could not answer, the reaction was too strong, but she clung to him, regardless of time or place, and felt that her last hope had not failed. Mr. Fairfax proved himself equal to the occasion. Asking no questions, he hurried Sir John and Jean into a carriage and stepped in after them with a bland apology. Jean was soon herself again, and, having told her fears at his delay, listened eagerly while he related the various mishaps which had detained him.

'Have you seen Edward?' was her first question.

'Not yet, but I know he has come, and have heard of his narrow escape. I should have been in that train, if I had not been delayed by the indisposition which I then cursed, and now bless. Are you ready, Jean? Do you repent your choice, my child?'

'No, no! I am ready, I am only too happy to become your wife, dear, generous Sir John,' cried Jean, with a glad alacrity, which touched the old man to the heart, and charmed the Reverend Mr. Fairfax, who concealed the romance of a boy under his clerical suit.

They reached the Hall. Sir John gave orders to admit no one and after a hasty dinner sent for his old housekeeper and his steward, told them of his purpose, and desired them to witness his marriage. Obedience had been the law of their lives, and Master could do nothing wrong in their eyes, so they played their parts willingly, for Jean was a favorite at the Hall. Pale as her gown, but calm and steady, she stood beside Sir John, uttering her vows in a clear tone and taking upon herself the vows of a wife with more than a bride's usual docility. When the ring was fairly on, a smile broke over her face. When Sir John kissed and called her his 'little wife,' she shed a tear or two of sincere happiness; and when Mr. Fairfax addressed her as 'my lady,' she laughed her musical laugh, and glanced up at a picture of Gerald with eyes full of exultation. As the servants left the room, a message was brought from Mrs. Coventry, begging Sir John to come to her at once.

'You will not go and leave me so soon?' pleaded Jean, well knowing why he was sent for.

'My darling, I must.' And in spite of its tenderness, Sir John's manner was too decided to be withstood.

'Then I shall go with you,' cried Jean, resolving that no earthly power should part them.

IX   *Lady Coventry*

When the first excitement of Edward's return had subsided, and before they could question him as to the cause of this unexpected visit, he told them that after dinner their curiosity should be gratified, and meantime he begged them to leave Miss Muir alone, for she had received bad news and must not be disturbed. The family with difficulty restrained their tongues and waited impatiently. Gerald confessed his love for Jean and asked his brother's pardon for betraying his trust. He had expected an outbreak, but Edward only looked at him with pitying eyes, and said sadly, 'You too! I have no reproaches to make, for I know what you will suffer when the truth is known.'

'What do you mean?' demanded Coventry.

'You will soon know, my poor Gerald, and we will comfort one another.'

Nothing more could be drawn from Edward till dinner was over, the servants gone, and all the family alone together. Then pale and grave, but very self-possessed, for trouble had made a man of him, he produced a packet of letters, and said, addressing himself to his brother, 'Jean Muir has deceived us all. I know her story; let me tell it before I read her letters.'

'Stop! I'll not listen to any false tales against her. The poor girl has enemies who belie her!' cried Gerald, starting up.

'For the honor of the family, you must listen, and learn what fools she has made of us. I can prove what I say, and convince you that she has the art of a devil. Sit still ten minutes, then go, if you will.'

Edward spoke with authority, and his brother obeyed him with a foreboding heart.

'I met Sydney, and he begged me to beware of her. Nay, listen, Gerald! I know she has told her story, and that you believe it; but her own letters convict her. She tried to charm Sydney as she did us, and nearly succeeded in inducing him to marry her. Rash and wild as he is, he is still a gentleman, and when an incautious word of hers roused his suspicions, he refused to make her his wife. A stormy scene ensued, and, hoping to intimidate him, she feigned to stab herself as if in despair. She did wound herself, but failed to gain her point and insisted upon going to a hospital to die. Lady Sydney, good, simple soul, believed the girl's version of the story, thought her son was in the wrong, and when he was gone, tried to atone for his fault by finding Jean Muir another home. She thought Gerald was soon to marry Lucia, and that I was away, so sent her here as a safe and comfortable retreat.'

'But, Ned, are you sure of all this? Is Sydney to be believed?' began Coventry, still incredulous.

'To convince you, I'll read Jean's letters before I say more. They were written to an accomplice and were purchased by Sydney. There was a compact between the two women, that each should keep the other informed of all adventures, plots and plans, and share whatever good fortune fell to the lot of either. Thus Jean wrote freely, as you shall judge. The letters concern us alone. The first was written a few days after she came.

> 'Dear Hortense:
>
> 'Another failure. Sydney was more wily than I thought. All was going well, when one day my old fault beset me, I took too much wine, and I carelessly owned that I had been an actress. He was shocked, and retreated. I got up a scene, and gave myself a safe little wound, to frighten him. The brute was not frightened, but coolly left me to my fate. I'd have died to spite him, if I dared, but as I didn't, I lived to torment him. As yet, I have had no chance, but I will not forget him. His mother is a poor, weak creature, whom I could use as I would, and through her I found an excellent place. A sick mother, silly daughter, and two eligible sons. One is engaged to a handsome iceberg, but that only renders him more interesting in my eyes, rivalry adds so much to the charm of one's conquests. Well, my dear, I went, got up in the meek style, intending to do the pathetic; but before I saw the family, I was so angry I could hardly control myself. Through the indolence of Monsieur the young master, no carriage was sent for me, and I intend he shall atone for that rudeness by-and-by. The younger son, the mother, and the girl received me patronizingly, and I understood the simple souls at once. Monsieur (as I shall call him, as names are unsafe) was unapproachable, and took no pains to conceal his dislike of governesses. The cousin was lovely, but detestable with her pride, her coldness, and her very visible adoration of Monsieur, who let her worship him, like an inanimate idol as he is. I hated them both, of course, and in return for their insolence shall torment her with jealousy, and teach him how to woo a woman by making his heart ache. They are an intensely proud family, but I can humble them all, I think, by captivating the sons, and when they have committed themselves, cast them off, and marry the old uncle, whose title takes my fancy.'

'She never wrote that! It is impossible. A woman could not do it,' cried Lucia indignantly, while Bella sat bewildered and Mrs. Coventry supported herself with salts and fan. Coventry went to his brother, examined the writing, and returned to his seat, saying, in a tone of suppressed wrath, 'She did write it. I posted some of those letters myself. Go on, Ned.'

'I made myself useful and agreeable to the amiable ones, and overheard the chat of the lovers. It did not suit me, so I fainted away to stop it, and excite interest in the provoking pair. I thought I had succeeded, but Monsieur suspected me and showed me that he did. I forgot my meek role and gave him a stage look. It had a good effect, and I shall try it again. The man is well worth winning, but I prefer the title, and as the uncle is a hale, handsome gentleman, I can't wait for him to die, though Monsieur is very charming, with his elegant languor, and his heart so fast asleep no woman has had power to wake it yet. I told my story, and they believed it, though I had the audacity to say I was but nineteen, to talk Scotch, and bashfully confess that Sydney wished to marry me. Monsieur knows S. and evidently suspects something. I must watch him and keep the truth from him, if possible.

'I was very miserable that night when I got alone. Something in the atmosphere of this happy home made me wish I was anything but what I am. As I sat there trying to pluck up my spirits, I thought of the days when I was lovely and young, good and gay. My glass showed me an old woman of thirty, for my false locks were off, my paint gone, and my face was without its mask. Bah! how I hate sentiment! I drank your health from your own little flask, and went to bed to dream that I was playing Lady Tartuffe – as I am. Adieu, more soon.'

No one spoke as Edward paused, and taking up another letter, he read on:

'My Dear Creature:
'All goes well. Next day I began my task, and having caught a hint of the character of each, tried my power over them. Early in the morning I ran over to see the Hall. Approved of it highly, and took the first step toward becoming its mistress, by piquing the curiosity and flattering the pride of its master. His estate is his idol; I praised it with a few artless compliments to himself, and he was charmed. The cadet of the family adores horses. I risked my neck to pet his beast, and *he* was charmed. The little girl is romantic about flowers; I made a posy and was sentimental, and *she* was charmed. The fair icicle loves her departed mamma, I had raptures over an old picture, and she thawed. Monsieur is used to being worshipped. I took no notice of him, and by the natural perversity of human nature, he began to take notice of me. He likes music; I sang, and stopped when he'd listened long enough to want more. He is lazily fond of being amused; I showed him my skill, but refused to exert it in his behalf. In short, I gave him no peace till he began to wake up. In order to get rid of the boy, I fascinated him, and he was sent away. Poor lad, I rather liked him, and if the title had been nearer would have married him.

'Many thanks for the honor.' And Edward's lip curled with intense scorn. But Gerald sat like a statue, his teeth set, his eyes fiery, his brows bent, waiting for the end.

'The passionate boy nearly killed his brother, but I turned the affair to good account, and bewitched Monsieur by playing nurse, till Vashti (the icicle) interfered. Then I enacted injured virtue, and kept out of his way, knowing that he would miss me. I mystified him about S. by sending a letter where S. would not get it, and got up all manner of soft scenes to win this proud creature. I get on well and meanwhile privately fascinate Sir J. by being daughterly and devoted. He is a worthy old man, simple as a child, honest as the day, and generous as a prince. I shall be a happy woman if I win him, and you shall share my good fortune; so wish me success.

'This is the third, and contains something which will surprise you,' Edward said, as he lifted another paper.

'Hortense:

'I've done what I once planned to do on another occasion. You know my handsome, dissipated father married a lady of rank for his second wife. I never saw Lady H_____d but once, for I was kept out of the way. Finding that this good Sir J. knew something of her when a girl, and being sure that he did not know of the death of her little daughter, I boldly said I was the child, and told a pitiful tale of my early life. It worked like a charm; he told Monsieur, and both felt the most chivalrous compassion for Lady Howard's daughter, though before they had secretly looked down on me, and my real poverty and my lowliness. That boy pitied me with an honest warmth and never waited to learn my birth. I don't forget that and shall repay it if I can. Wishing to bring Monsieur's affair to a successful crisis, I got up a theatrical evening and was in my element. One little event I must tell you, because I committed an actionable offense and was nearly discovered. I did not go down to supper, knowing that the moth would return to flutter about the candle, and preferring that the fluttering should be done in private, as Vashti's jealousy is getting uncontrollable. Passing through the gentlemen's dressing room, my quick eye caught sight of a letter lying among the costumes. It was no stage affair, and an odd sensation of fear ran through me as I recognized the hand of S. I had feared this, but I believe in chance; and having found the letter, I examined it. You know I can imitate almost any hand. When I read in this paper the whole story of my affair with S., truly told, and also that he had made inquiries into my past life and discovered the truth, I was in a fury. To be so near success and fail was terrible, and I resolved to risk everything. I opened the letter by means of a heated knife blade under the seal, therefore the envelope was perfect; imitating S.'s hand, I penned a few lines in his hasty style, saying he was at Baden, so that if Monsieur answered, the reply would not reach him, for he is in London, it seems. This letter I put into the pocket whence the other must have fallen and was just congratulating myself on this narrow escape, when Dean, the maid of Vashti, appeared as if watching me. She had evidently seen the letter in my hand, and suspected something. I took no notice of her, but must be careful, for she is on the watch. After this the evening closed with strictly private theatricals, in which Monsieur and myself were the only actors. To make sure that he received my version of the story first, I told him a romantic story of S.'s persecution, and he believed it. This I followed up by a moonlight episode behind a rose hedge, and sent the young gentleman home in a half-dazed condition. What fools men are!'

'She is right!' muttered Coventry, who had flushed scarlet with shame and anger, as his folly became known and Lucia listened in astonished silence.

'Only one more, and my distasteful task will be nearly over,' said Edward, unfolding the last of the papers. 'This is not a letter, but a copy of one written three nights ago. Dean boldly ransacked Jean Muir's desk while she was at the Hall, and, fearing to betray the deed by keeping the letter, she made a hasty copy which she gave me today, begging me to save the family from disgrace. This makes the chain complete. Go now, if you will, Gerald. I would gladly spare you the pain of hearing this.'

'I will not spare myself; I deserve it. Read on,' replied Coventry, guessing what was to follow and nerving himself to hear it. Reluctantly his brother read these lines:

> The enemy has surrendered! Give me joy, Hortense; I can be the wife
> of this proud monsieur, if I will. Think what an honor for the divorced
> wife of a disreputable actor. I laugh at the farce and enjoy it, for I only
> wait till the prize I desire is fairly mine, to turn and reject this lover
> who has proved himself false to brother, mistress, and his own
> conscience. I resolved to be revenged on both, and I have kept my
> word. For my sake he cast off the beautiful woman who truly loved
> him; he forgot his promise to his brother, and put by his pride to beg
> of me the worn-out heart that is not worth a good man's love. Ah well,
> I am satisfied, for Vashti has suffered the sharpest pain a proud woman
> can endure, and will feel another pang when I tell her that I scorn her
> recreant lover, and give him back to her, to deal with as she will.

Coventry started from his seat with a fierce exclamation, but Lucia bowed her face upon her hands, weeping, as if the pang had been sharper than even Jean foresaw.

'Send for Sir John! I am mortally afraid of this creature. Take her away; do something to her. My poor Bella, what a companion for you! Send for Sir John at once!' cried Mrs. Coventry incoherently, and clasped her daughter in her arms, as if Jean Muir would burst in to annihilate the whole family. Edward alone was calm.

'I have already sent, and while we wait, let me finish this story. It is true that Jean is the daughter of Lady Howard's husband, the pretended clergyman, but really a worthless man who married her for her money. Her own child died, but this girl, having beauty, wit and a bold spirit, took her fate into her own hands, and became an actress. She married an actor, led a reckless life for some years; quarreled with her husband, was divorced, and went to Paris; left the stage, and tried to support herself as governess and companion. You know how she fared with the Sydneys, how she has duped us, and but for this discovery would have duped Sir John. I was in time to prevent this, thank heaven. She is gone; no one knows the truth but Sydney and ourselves; he will be silent, for his own sake; we will be for ours, and leave this dangerous woman to the fate which will surely overtake her.'

'Thank you, it has overtaken her, and a very happy one she finds it.'

A soft voice uttered the words, and an apparition appeared at the door, which made all start and recoil with amazement – Jean Muir leaning on the arm of Sir John.

'How dare you return?' began Edward, losing the self-control so long preserved. 'How dare you insult us by coming back to enjoy the mischief you have done? Uncle, you do not know that woman!'

'Hush, boy, I will not listen to a word, unless you remember where you are,' said Sir John, with a commanding gesture.

'Remember your promise: love me, forgive me, protect me, and do not listen to their accusations,' whispered Jean, whose quick eye had discovered the letters.

'I will; have no fears, my child,' he answered, drawing her nearer as he took his accustomed place before the fire, always lighted when Mrs. Coventry was down.

Gerald, who had been pacing the room excitedly, paused behind Lucia's chair as if to shield her from insult; Bella clung to her mother; and Edward, calming himself by a strong effort, handed his uncle the letters, saying briefly, 'Look at those, sir, and let them speak.'

'I will look at nothing, hear nothing, believe nothing which can in any way lessen my respect and affection for this young lady. She has prepared me for this. I know the enemy who is unmanly enough to belie and threaten her. I know that you both are unsuccessful lovers, and this explains your unjust, uncourteous treatment now. We all have committed faults and follies. I freely forgive Jean hers, and desire to know nothing of them from your lips. If she has innocently offended, pardon it for my sake, and forget the past.'

'But, Uncle, we have proofs that this woman is not what she seems. Her own letters convict her. Read them, and do not blindly deceive yourself,' cried Edward, indignant at his uncle's words.

A low laugh startled them all, and in an instant they saw the cause of it. While Sir John spoke, Jean had taken the letters from the hand which he had put behind him, a favorite gesture of his, and, unobserved, had dropped them on the fire. The mocking laugh, the sudden blaze, showed what had been done. Both young men sprang forward, but it was too late; the proofs were ashes, and Jean Muir's bold, bright eyes defied them, as she said, with a disdainful little gesture, 'Hands off, gentlemen! You may degrade yourselves to the work of detectives, but I am not a prisoner yet. Poor Jean Muir you might harm, but Lady Coventry is beyond your reach.'

'Lady Coventry!' echoed the dismayed family, in varying tones of incredulity, indignation, and amazement.

'Aye, my dear and honored wife,' said Sir John, with a protecting arm about the slender figure at his side; and in the act, the words, there was a tender dignity that touched the listeners with pity and respect for the deceived man. 'Receive her as such, and for my sake, forbear all further accusation,' he continued steadily. 'I know what I have done. I have no fear that I shall repent it. If I am blind, let me remain so till time opens my eyes. We are going away for a little while, and when we return, let the old life return again, unchanged, except that Jean makes sunshine for me as well as for you.'

No one spoke, for no one knew what to say. Jean broke the silence, saying coolly, 'May I ask how those letters came into your possession?'

'In tracing out your past life, Sydney found your friend Hortense. She was poor, money bribed her, and your letters were given up to him as soon as received. Traitors are always betrayed in the end,' replied Edward sternly.

Jean shrugged her shoulders, and shot a glance at Gerald, saying with her significant smile, 'Remember that, monsieur, and allow me to hope that in wedding you will be happier than in wooing. Receive my congratulations, Miss Beaufort, and let me beg of you to follow my example, if you would keep your lovers.'

Here all the sarcasm passed from her voice, the defiance from her eye, and the one unspoiled attribute which still lingered in this woman's artful nature shone in her face, as she turned toward Edward and Bella at their mother's side.

'You have been kind to me,' she said, with grateful warmth. 'I thank you for it, and will repay it if I can. To you I will acknowledge that I am not worthy to be this good man's wife, and to you I will solemnly promise to devote my life to his happiness. For his sake forgive me, and let there be peace between us.'

There was no reply, but Edward's indignant eyes fell before hers. Bella half put out her hand, and Mrs. Coventry sobbed as if some regret mingled with her resentment. Jean seemed to expect no friendly demonstration, to understand that they forbore for Sir John's sake, not for hers, and to accept their contempt as her just punishment.

'Come home, love, and forget all this,' said her husband, ringing the bell, and eager to be gone. 'Lady Coventry's carriage.'

And as he gave the order, a smile broke over her face, for the sound assured her that the game was won. Pausing an instant on the threshold before she vanished from their sight, she looked backward, and fixing on Gerald the strange glance he remembered well, she said in her penetrating voice, 'Is not the last scene better than the first?'

The Yellow Wallpaper

by Charlotte Perkins Gilman

From: Gilman, C.P. (1973 edn) *The Yellow Wallpaper*, The Feminist Press.

It is very seldom that mere ordinary people like John and myself secure ancestral halls for the summer.

A colonial mansion, a hereditary estate, I would say a haunted house, and reach the height of romantic felicity – but that would be asking too much of fate!

Still I will proudly declare that there is something queer about it.

Else, why should it be let so cheaply? And why have stood so long untenanted?

John laughs at me, of course, but one expects that in marriage.

John is practical in the extreme. He has no patience with faith, an intense horror of superstition, and he scoffs openly at any talk of things not to be felt and seen and put down in figures.

John is a physician, and *perhaps* – (I would not say it to a living soul, of course, but this is dead paper and a great relief to my mind) – *perhaps* that is one reason I do not get well faster.

You see he does not believe I am sick!

And what can one do?

If a physician of high standing, and one's own husband, assures friends and relatives that there is really nothing the matter with one but temporary nervous depression – a slight hysterical tendency – what is one to do?

My brother is also a physician, and also of high standing, and he says the same thing.

So I take phosphates or phospites – whichever it is, and tonics, and journeys, and air, and exercise, and am absolutely forbidden to 'work' until I am well again.

Personally, I disagree with their ideas.

Personally, I believe that congenial work, with excitement and change, would do me good.

But what is one to do?

I did write for a while in spite of them; but it *does* exhaust me a good deal – having to be so sly about it, or else meet with heavy opposition.

I sometimes fancy that in my condition if I had less opposition and more society and stimulus – but John says the very worst thing I can do is to think about my condition, and I confess it always makes me feel bad.

So I will let it alone and talk about the house.

The most beautiful place! It is quite alone, standing well back from the road, quite three miles from the village. It makes me think of English places that you read about, for there are hedges and walls and gates that lock, and lots of separate little houses for the gardeners and people.

There is a *delicious* garden! I never saw such a garden – large and shady, full of box-bordered paths, and lined with long grape-covered arbors with seats under them.

There were greenhouses, too, but they are all broken now.

There was some legal trouble, I believe, something about the heirs and coheirs; anyhow, the place has been empty for years.

That spoils my ghostliness, I am afraid, but I don't care – there is something strange about the house – I can feel it.

I even said so to John one moonlight evening, but he said what I felt was a *draught,* and shut the window.

I get unreasonably angry with John sometimes. I'm sure I never used to be so sensitive. I think it is due to this nervous condition.

But John says if I feel so, I shall neglect proper self-control; so I take pains to control myself – before him, at least, and that makes me very tired.

I don't like our room a bit. I wanted one downstairs that opened on the piazza and had roses all over the window, and such pretty old-fashioned chintz hangings! but John would not hear of it.

He said there was only one window and not room for two beds, and no near room for him if he took another.

He is very careful and loving, and hardly lets me stir without special direction.

I have a schedule prescription for each hour in the day; he takes all care from me, and so I feel basely ungrateful not to value it more.

He said we came here solely on my account, that I was to have perfect rest and all the air I could get. 'Your exercise depends on your strength, my dear,' said he, 'and your food somewhat on your appetite; but air you can absorb all the time.' So we took the nursery at the top of the house.

It is a big, airy room, the whole floor nearly, with windows that look all ways, and air and sunshine galore. It was nursery first and then playroom and gymnasium, I should judge; for the windows are barred for little children, and there are rings and things in the walls.

The paint and paper look as if a boys' school had used it. It is stripped off – the paper – in great patches all around the head of my bed, about as far as I can reach, and in a great place on the other side of the room low down. I never saw a worse paper in my life.

One of those sprawling flamboyant patterns committing every artistic sin.

It is dull enough to confuse the eye in following, pronounced enough to constantly irritate and provoke study, and when you follow the lame uncertain curves for a little distance they suddenly commit suicide – plunge off at outrageous angles, destroy themselves in unheard of contradictions.

The color is repellent, almost revolting; a smouldering unclean yellow, strangely faded by the slow-turning sunlight.

It is a dull yet lurid orange in some places, a sickly sulphur tint in others.

No wonder the children hated it! I should hate it myself if I had to live in this room long.

There comes John, and I must put this away, – he hates to have me write a word.

We have been here two weeks, and I haven't felt like writing before, since that first day.

I am sitting by the window now, up in this atrocious nursery, and there is nothing to hinder my writing as much as I please, save lack of strength.

John is away all day, and even some nights when his cases are serious. I am glad my case is not serious!

But these nervous troubles are dreadfully depressing.

John does not know how much I really suffer. He knows there is no *reason* to suffer, and that satisfies him.

Of course it is only nervousness. It does weigh on me so not to do my duty in any way!

I meant to be such a help to John, such a real rest and comfort, and here I am a comparative burden already!

Nobody would believe what an effort it is to do what little I am able, – to dress and entertain, and order things.

It is fortunate Mary is so good with the baby. Such a dear baby!

And yet I *cannot* be with him, it makes me so nervous.

I suppose John never was nervous in his life. He laughs at me so about this wall-paper!

At first he meant to repaper the room, but afterwards he said that I was letting it get the better of me, and that nothing was worse for a nervous patient than to give way to such fancies.

He said that after the wall-paper was changed it would be the heavy bedstead, and then the barred windows, and then that gate at the end of the stairs, and so on.

'You know the place is doing you good,' he said, 'and really, dear, I don't care to renovate the house just for a three months' rental.'

'Then do let us go downstairs,' I said, 'there are such pretty rooms there.'

Then he took me in his arms and called me a blessed little goose, and said he would go down to the cellar, if I wished, and have it whitewashed into the bargain.

But he is right enough about the beds and windows and things.

It is an airy and comfortable room as any one need wish, and, of course, I would not be so silly as to make him uncomfortable just for a whim.

I'm really getting quite fond of the big room, all but that horrid paper.

Out of one window I can see the garden, those mysterious deep-shaded arbors, the riotous old-fashioned flowers, and bushes and gnarly trees.

Out of another I get a lovely view of the bay and a little private wharf belonging to the estate. There is a beautiful shaded lane that runs down there from the house. I always fancy I see people walking in these numerous paths and arbors, but John has cautioned me not to give way to fancy in the least. He says that with my imaginative power and habit of story-making, a nervous weakness like mine is sure to lead to all manner of excited fancies, and that I ought to use my will and good sense to check the tendency. So I try.

I think sometimes that if I were only well enough to write a little it would relieve the press of ideas and rest me.

But I find I get pretty tired when I try.

It is so discouraging not to have any advice and companionship about my work. When I get really well, John says we will ask Cousin Henry and

Julia down for a long visit; but he says he would as soon put fireworks in my pillow-case as to let me have those stimulating people about now.

I wish I could get well faster.

But I must not think about that. This paper looks to me as if it *knew* what a vicious influence it had!

There is a recurrent spot where the pattern lolls like a broken neck and two bulbous eyes stare at you upside down.

I get positively angry with the impertinence of it and the everlastingness. Up and down and sideways they crawl, and those absurd, unblinking eyes are everywhere. There is one place where two breadths didn't match, and the eyes go all up and down the line, one a little higher than the other.

I never saw so much expression in an inanimate thing before, and we all know how much expression they have! I used to lie awake as a child and get more entertainment and terror out of blank walls and plain furniture than most children could find in a toy-store.

I remember what a kindly wink the knobs of our big, old bureau used to have, and there was one chair that always seemed like a strong friend.

I used to fell that if any of the other things looked too fierce I could always hop into that chair and be safe.

The furniture in this room is no worse than inharmonious, however, for we had to bring it all from downstairs. I suppose when this was used as a playroom they had to take the nursery things out, and no wonder! I never saw such ravages as the children have made here.

The wall-paper, as I said before, is torn off, in spots, and it sticketh closer than a brother – they must have had perseverance as well as hatred.

Then the floor is scratched and gouged and splintered, the plaster itself is dug out here and there, and this great heavy bed which is all we found in the room, looks as if it had been through the wars.

But I don't mind it a bit – only the paper.

There comes John's sister. Such a dear girl as she is, and so careful of me! I must not let her find me writing.

She is a perfect and enthusiastic housekeeper, and hopes for no better profession. I verily believe she thinks it is the writing which made me sick!

But I can write when she is out, and see her a long way off from these windows.

There is one that commands the road, a lovely shaded winding road, and one that just looks off over the country. A lovely country, too, full of great elms and velvet meadows.

This wall-paper has a kind of sub-pattern in a different shade, a particularly irritating one, for you can only see it in certain lights, and not clearly then.

But in the places where it isn't faded and where the sun is just so – I can see a strange, provoking, formless sort of figure, that seems to skulk about behind that silly and conspicuous front design.

There's sister on the stairs!

Well, the Fourth of July is over! The people are all gone and I am tired out. John thought it might do me good to see a little company, so we just had mother and Nellie and the children down for a week.

Of course I didn't do a thing. Jennie sees to everything now.

But it tired me all the same.

John says if I don't pick up faster he shall send me to Weir Mitchell in the fall.

But I don't want to go there at all. I had a friend who was in his hands once, and she says he is just like John and my brother, only more so!

Besides, it is such an undertaking to go so far.

I don't feel as if it was worth while to turn my hand over for anything, and I'm getting dreadfully fretful and querulous.

I cry at nothing, and cry most of the time.

Of course I don't when John is here, or anybody else, but when I am alone.

And I am alone a good deal just now. John is kept in town very often by serious cases, and Jennie is good and lets me alone when I want her to.

So I walk a little in the garden or down that lovely lane, sit on the porch under the roses, and lie down up here a good deal.

I'm getting really fond of the room in spite of the wall-paper. Perhaps *because* of the wall-paper.

It dwells in my mind so!

I lie here on this great immovable bed – it is nailed down, I believe – and follow that pattern about by the hour. It is as good as gymnastics, I assure you. I start, we'll say, at the bottom, down in the corner over there where it has not been touched, and I determine for the thousandth time that I *will* follow that pointless pattern to some sort of a conclusion.

I know a little of the principle of design, and I know this thing was not arranged on any laws of radiation, or alternation, or repetition, or symmetry, or anything else that I ever head of.

It is repeated, of course, by the breadths, but not otherwise.

Looked at in one way each breadth stands alone, the bloated curves and flourishes – a kind of 'debased Romanesque' with *delirium tremens* – go waddling up and down in isolation columns of fatuity.

But, on the other hand, they connect diagonally, and the sprawling outlines run off in great slanting waves of optic horror, like a lot of wallowing seaweeds in full chase.

The whole thing goes horizontally, too, at least it seems so, and I exhaust myself in trying to distinguish the order of its going in that direction.

They have used a horizontal breadth for a frieze, and that adds wonderfully to the confusion.

There is one end of the room where it is almost intact, and there, when the crosslights fade and the low sun shines directly upon it, I can almost fancy radiation after all, – the interminable grotesques seem to form around a common centre and rush off in headlong plunges of equal distraction.

It makes me tired to follow it. I will take a nap I guess.

I don't know why I should write this.

I don't want to.

I don't feel able.

And I know John would think it absurd. But I *must* say what I feel and think in some way – it is such a relief!

But the effort is getting to be greater than the relief.

Half the time now I am awfully lazy, and lie down ever so much.

John says I mustn't lose my strength, and has me take cod liver oil and lots of tonics and things, to say nothing of ale and wine and rare meat.

Dear John! He loves me very dearly, and hates to have me sick. I tried to have a real earnest reasonable talk with him the other day, and tell him how I wish he would let me go and make a visit to Cousin Henry and Julia.

But he said I wasn't able to go, nor able to stand it after I got there; and I did not make out a very good case for myself, for I was crying before I had finished.

It is getting to be a great effort for me to think straight. Just this nervous weakness I suppose.

And dear John gathered me up in his arms, and just carried me upstairs and laid me on the bed, and sat by me and read to me till it tired my head.

He said I was his darling and his comfort and all he had, and that I must take care of myself for his sake, and keep well.

He says no one but myself can help me out of it, that I must use my will and self-control and not let any silly fancies run away with me.

There's one comfort, the baby is well and happy, and does not have to occupy this nursery with the horrid wall-paper.

If we had not used it, that blessed child would have! What a fortunate escape! Why, I wouldn't have a child of mine, an impressionable little thing, live in such a room for worlds.

I never thought of it before, but it is lucky that John kept me here after all, I can stand it so much easier than a baby, you see.

Of course I never mention it to them any more – I am too wise, – but I keep watch of it all the same.

There are things in that paper that nobody knows but me, or ever will.

Behind that outside pattern the dim shapes get clearer every day.

It is always the same shape, only very numerous.

And it is like a woman stopping down and creeping about behind that pattern. I don't like it a bit. I wonder – I begin to think – I wish John would take me away from here!

It is so hard to talk with John about my case, because he is so wise, and because he loves me so.

But I tried it last night.

It was moonlight. The moon shines in all around just as the sun does.

I hate to see it sometimes, it creeps so slowly, and always comes in by one window or another.

John was asleep and I hated to waken him, so I kept still and watched the moonlight on that undulating wall-paper till I felt creepy.

The faint figure behind seemed to shake the pattern, just as if she wanted to get out.

I got up softly and went to feel and see if the paper *did* move, and when I came back John was awake.

'What is it, little girl?' he said. 'Don't go walking about like that – you'll get cold.'

I thought it was a good time to talk, so I told him that I really was not gaining here, and that I wished he would take me away.

'Why darling!' said he, 'our lease will be up in three weeks, and I can't see how to leave before.'

'The repairs are not done at home, and I cannot possibly leave town just now. Of course if you were in any danger, I could and would, but you really are better, dear, whether you can see it or not. I am a doctor, dear, and I know. You are gaining flesh and color, your appetite is better, I feel really much easier about you.'

'I don't weigh a bit more,' said I, 'nor as much; and my appetite may be better in the evening when you are here, but it is worse in the morning when you are away!'

'Bless her little heart!' said he with a big hug, 'she shall be as sick as she pleases! But now let's improve the shining hours by going to sleep, and talk about it in the morning!'

'And you won't go away?' I asked gloomily.

'Why, how can I, dear? It is only three weeks more and then we will take a nice little trip of a few days while Jennie is getting the house ready. Really dear you are better!'

'Better in body perhaps – ' I began, and stopped short, for he sat up straight and looked at me with such a stern, reproachful look that I could not say another word.

'My darling,' said he, 'I beg of you, for my sake and for our child's sake, as well as for your own, that you will never for one instant let the idea enter your mind! There is nothing so dangerous, so fascinating, to a temperament like yours. It is a false and foolish fancy. Can you not trust me as a physician when I tell you so?'

So of course I said no more on that score, and we went to sleep before long. He thought I was asleep first, but I wasn't, and lay there for hours trying to decide whether that front pattern and the back pattern really did move together or separately.

On a pattern like this, by daylight, there is a lack of sequence, a defiance of law, that is a constant irritant to a normal mind.

The color is hideous enough, and unreliable enough, and infuriating enough, but the pattern is torturing.

You think you have mastered it, but just as you get well underway in following, it turns a back-somersault and there you are. It slaps you in the face, knocks you down, and tramples upon you. It is like a bad dream.

The outside pattern is a florid arabesque, reminding one of a fungus. If you can imagine a toadstool in joints, an interminable string of toadstools, budding and sprouting in endless convolutions – why, that is something like it.

That is, sometimes!

There is one marked peculiarity about this paper, a thing nobody seems to notice but myself, and that is that it changes as the light changes.

When the sun shoots in through the east window – I always watch for that first long, straight ray – it changes so quickly that I never can quite believe it.

That is why I watch it always.

By moonlight – the moon shines in all night when there is a moon – I wouldn't know it was the same paper.

At night in any kind of light, in twilight, candle light, lamplight, and worst of all by moonlight, it becomes bars! The outside pattern I mean, and the woman behind it is as plain as can be.

I didn't realize for a long time what the thing was that showed behind that dim sub-pattern, but now I am quite sure it is a woman.

By daylight she is subdued, quiet. I fancy it is the pattern that keeps her so still. It is so puzzling. It keeps me quiet by the hour.

I lie down ever so much now. John says it is good for me, and to sleep all I can.

Indeed he started the habit by making me lie down for an hour after each meal.

It is a very bad habit I am convinced, for you see I don't sleep.

And that cultivates deceit, for I don't tell them I'm awake – O no!

The fact is I am getting a little afraid of John.

He seems very queer sometimes, and even Jennie has an inexplicable look.

It strikes me occasionally, just as a scientific hypothesis, – that perhaps it is the paper!

I have watched John when he did not know I was looking, and come into the room suddenly on the most innocent excuses, and I've caught him several times *looking at the paper!* And Jennie too. I caught Jennie with her hand on it once.

She didn't know I was in the room, and when I asked her in a quiet, a very quiet voice, with the most restrained manner possible, what she was doing with the paper – she turned around as if she had been caught stealing, and looked quite angry – asked me why I should frighten her so!

Then she said that the paper stained everything it touched, that she had found yellow smooches on all my clothes and John's, and she wished we would be more careful!

Did not that sound innocent? But I know she was studying that pattern, and I am determined that nobody shall find it out but myself!

Life is very much more exciting now than it used to be. You see I have something more to expect, to look forward to, to watch. I really do eat better, and am more quiet than I was.

John is so pleased to see me improve! He laughed a little the other day, and said I seemed to be flourishing in spite of my wall-paper.

I turned it off with a laugh. I had no intention of telling him it was *because* of the wall-paper – he would make fun of me. He might even want to take me away.

I don't want to leave now until I have found it out. There is a week more, and I think that will be enough.

I'm feeling ever so much better! I don't sleep much at night, for it is so interesting to watch developments; but I sleep a good deal in the daytime.

In the daytime it is tiresome and perplexing.

There are always new shoots on the fungus, and new shades of yellow all over it. I cannot keep count of them, though I have tried conscientiously.

It is the strangest yellow, that wall-paper! It makes me think of all the yellow things I ever saw – not beautiful ones like buttercups, but old foul, bad yellow things.

But there is something else about the paper – the smell! I noticed it the moment we came into the room, but with so much air and sun it was not bad. Now we have had a week of fog and rain, and whether the windows are open or not, the smell is here.

It creeps all over the house.

I find it hovering in the dining-room, skulking in the parlor, hiding in the hall, lying in wait for me on the stairs.

It gets into my hair.

Even when I go to ride, if I turn my head suddenly and surprise it – there is that smell!

Such a peculiar odor, too! I have spent hours in trying to analyze it, to find what it smelled like.

It is not bad – at first, and very gentle, but quite the subtlest, most enduring odor I ever met.

In this damp weather it is awful, I wake up in the night and find it hanging over me.

It used to disturb me at first. I thought seriously of burning the house – to reach the smell.

But now I am used to it. The only thing I can think of that it is like is the *color* of the paper! A yellow smell.

There is a very funny mark on this wall, low down, near the mopboard. A streak that runs round the room. It goes behind every piece of furniture, except the bed, a long, straight, even *smooch,* as if it had been rubbed over and over.

I wonder how it was done and who did it, and what they did it for. Round and round and round – round and round and round – it makes me dizzy!

I really have discovered something at last.

Through watching so much at night, when it changes so, I have finally found out.

The front pattern *does* move – and no wonder! The woman behind shakes it!

Sometimes I think there are a great many women behind, and sometimes only one, and she crawls around fast, and her crawling shakes it all over.

Then in the very bright spots she keeps still, and in the very shady spots she just takes hold of the bars and shakes them hard.

And she is all the time trying to climb through. But nobody could climb through that pattern – it strangles so; I think that is why it has so many heads.

They get through, and then the pattern strangles them off and turns them upside down, and makes their eyes white!

If those heads were covered or taken off it would not be half so bad.

I think that woman gets out in the daytime!

And I'll tell you why – privately – I've seen her!

I can see her out of every one of my windows!

It is the same woman, I know, for she is always creeping, and most women do not creep by daylight.

I see her on that long road under the trees, creeping along, and when a carriage comes she hides under the blackberry vines.

I don't blame her a bit. It must be very humiliating to be caught creeping by daylight!

I always lock the door when I creep by daylight. I can't do it at night, for I know John would suspect something at once.

And John is so queer now, that I don't want to irritate him. I wish he would take another room! Besides, I don't want anybody to get that woman out at night but myself.

I often wonder if I could see her out of all the windows at once.

But, turn as fast as I can, I can only see out of one at one time.

And though I always see her, she *may* be able to creep faster than I can turn!

I have watched her sometimes away off in the open country, creeping as fast as a cloud shadow in a high wind.

If only that top pattern could be gotten off from the under one! I mean to try it, little by little.

I have found out another funny thing, but I shan't tell it this time! It does not do to trust people too much.

There are only two more days to get this paper off, and I believe John is beginning to notice. I don't like the look in his eyes.

And I heard him ask Jennie a lot of professional questions about me. She had a very good report to give.

She said I slept a good deal in the daytime.

John knows I don't sleep very well at night, for all I'm so quiet!

He asked me all sorts of questions, too, and pretended to be very loving and kind.

As if I couldn't see through him!

Still, I don't wonder he acts so, sleeping under this paper for three months.

It only interests me, but I feel sure John and Jennie are secretly affected by it.

Hurrah! This is the last day, but it is enough. John to stay in town over night, and won't be out until this evening.

Jennie wanted to sleep with me – the sly thing! but I told her I should undoubtedly rest better for a night all alone.

That was clever, for really I wasn't alone a bit! As soon as it was moonlight and that poor thing began to crawl and shake the pattern, I got up and ran to help her.

I pulled and she shook, I shook and she pulled, and before morning we had peeled off yards of that paper.

A strip about as high as my head and half around the room.

And then when the sun came and that awful pattern began to laugh at me, I declared I would finish it to-day!

We go away to-morrow, and they are moving all my furniture down again to leave things as they were before.

Jennie looked at the wall in amazement, but I told her merrily that I did it out of pure spite at the vicious thing.

She laughed and said she wouldn't mind doing it herself, but I must not get tired.

How she betrayed herself that time!

But I am here, and no person touches this paper but me, – not *alive!*

She tried to get me out of the room – it was too patent! But I said it was so quiet and empty and clean now that I believed I would lie down again and sleep all I could; and not to wake me even for dinner – I would call when I woke.

So now she is gone, and the servants are gone, and the things are gone, and there is nothing left but that great bedstead nailed down, with the canvas mattress we found on it.

We shall sleep downstairs to-night, and take the boat home to-morrow.

I quite enjoy the room, now it is bare again.

How those children did tear about here!

This bedstead is fairly gnawed!

But I must get to work.

I have locked the door and thrown the key down into the front path.

I don't want to go out, and I don't want to have anybody come in, till John comes.

I want to astonish him.

I've got a rope up here that even Jennie did not find. If that woman does get out, and tries to get away, I can tie her!

But I forgot I could not reach far without anything to stand on!

This bed will *not* move!

I tried to lift and push it until I was lame, and then I got so angry I bit off a little piece at one corner – but it hurt my teeth.

Then I peeled off all the paper I could reach standing on the floor. It sticks horribly and the pattern just enjoys it! All those strangled heads and bulbous eyes and waddling fungus growths just shriek with derision!

I am getting angry enough to do something desperate. To jump out of the window would be admirable exercise, but the bars are too strong even to try.

Besides I wouldn't do it. Of course not. I know well enough that a step like that is improper and might be misconstrued.

I don't like to *look* out of the windows even – there are so many of those creeping women, and they creep so fast.

I wonder if they all come out of that wall-paper as I did?

But I am securely fastened now by my well-hidden rope – you don't get *me* out in the road there!

I suppose I shall have to get back behind the pattern when it comes night, and that is hard!

It is so pleasant to be out in this great room and creep around as I please!

I don't want to go outside. I won't, even if Jennie asks me to.

For outside you have to creep on the ground, and everything is green instead of yellow.

But here I can creep smoothly on the floor, and my shoulder just fits in that long smooch around the wall, so I cannot lose my way.

Why there's John at the door!

It is no use, young man, you can't open it!

How he does call and pound!

Now he's crying for an axe.

It would be a shame to break down that beautiful door!

'John dear!' said I in the gentlest voice, 'the key is down by the front steps, under a plantain leaf!'

That silenced him for a few moments.

Then he said – very quietly indeed, 'Open the door, my darling!'

'I can't,' said I. 'The key is down by the front door under a plantain leaf!'

And then I said it again, several times, very gently and slowly, and said it so often that he had to go and see, and he got it of course, and came in. He stopped short by the door.

'What is the matter?' he cried. 'For God's sake, what are you doing!'

I kept on creeping just the same, but I looked at him over my shoulder.

'I've got out at last,' said I, 'in spite of you and Jane. And I've pulled off most of the paper, so you can't put me back!'

Now why should that man have fainted? But he did, and right across my path by the wall, so that I had to creep over him every time!

Trifles

by Susan Glaspell

From: Barlow, J. E. (ed.) (1985) *Plays by American Women: The Early Years,* Applause Books.

Characters

GEORGE HENDERSON, County Attorney

HENRY PETERS, Sheriff

LEWIS HALE, a neighboring farmer

MRS PETERS

MRS HALE **The setting**

The kitchen in the now abandoned farmhouse of JOHN WRIGHT.

Scene: The kitchen in the now abandoned farmhouse of JOHN WRIGHT, a gloomy kitchen, and left without having been put in order – unwashed pans under the sink, a loaf of bread outside the breadbox, a dish towel on the table – other signs of incompleted work. At the rear the outer door opens and the SHERIFF comes in followed by the COUNTY ATTORNEY and HALE. The SHERIFF and HALE are men in middle life, the COUNTY ATTORNEY is a young man; all are much bundled up and go at once to the stove. They are followed by the two women – the SHERIFF'S wife first; she is a slight wiry woman, a thin nervous face. MRS HALE is larger and would ordinarily be called more comfortable looking, but she is disturbed now and looks fearfully about as she enters. The women have come in slowly, and stand close together near the door.

COUNTY ATTORNEY *(Rubbing his hands)* This feels good. Come up to the fire, ladies.

MRS PETERS *(After taking a step forward)* I'm not – cold.

SHERIFF *(Unbuttoning his overcoat and stepping away from the stove as if to mark the beginning of official business)* Now, Mr Hale, before we move things about, you explain to Mr Henderson just what you saw when you came here yesterday morning.

COUNTY ATTORNEY By the way, has anything been moved? Are things just as you left them yesterday?

SHERIFF *(Looking about)* It's just the same. When it dropped below zero last night I thought I'd better send Frank out this morning to make a fire for us – no use getting pneumonia with a big case on, but I told him not to touch anything except the stove – and you know Frank.

COUNTY ATTORNEY Somebody should have been left here yesterday.

SHERIFF Oh – yesterday. When I had to send Frank to Morris Center for that man who went crazy – I want you to know I had my hands full yesterday, I knew you could get back from Omaha by today and as long as I went over everything here myself –

COUNTY ATTORNEY Well, Mr Hale, tell just what happened when you came here yesterday morning.

HALE Harry and I had started to town with a load of potatoes. We came along the road from my place and as I got here I said, 'I'm going to see if I

360

can't get John Wright to go in with me on a party telephone.' I spoke to Wright about it once before and he put me off, saying folks talked too much anyway, and all he asked was peace and quiet – I guess you know about how much he talked himself; but I thought maybe if I went to the house and talked about it before his wife, though I said to Harry that I didn't know as what his wife wanted made much difference to John –

COUNTY ATTORNEY Let's talk about that later, Mr Hale. I do want to talk about that, but tell now just what happened when you got to the house.

HALE I didn't hear or see anything; I knocked at the door, and still it was all quiet inside. I knew they must be up, it was past eight o'clock. So I knocked again, and I thought I heard somebody say, 'Come in.' I wasn't sure, I'm not sure yet, but I opened the door – this door *(Indicating the door by which the two women are still standing)* and there in that rocker – *(Pointing to it)* sat Mrs Wright.

(They all look at the rocker.)

COUNTY ATTORNEY What – was she doing?

HALE She was rockin' back and forth. She had her apron in her hand and was kind of – pleating it.

COUNTY ATTORNEY And how did she – look?

HALE Well, she looked queer.

COUNTY ATTORNEY How do you mean – queer?

HALE Well, as if she didn't know what she was going to do next. And kind of done up.

COUNTY ATTORNEY How did she seem to feel about your coming?

HALE Why, I don't think she minded – one way or other. She didn't pay much attention. I said, 'How do, Mrs Wright, it's cold, ain't it?' And she said, 'Is it?' – and went on kind of pleating at her apron. Well, I was surprised; she didn't ask me to come up to the stove, or to set down, but just sat there, not even looking at me, so I said, 'I want to see John.' And then she – laughed. I guess you would call it a laugh. I thought of Harry and the team outside, so I said a little sharp 'Can't I see John?' 'No,' she says, kind o' dull like. 'Ain't he home?' says I. 'Yes,' says she, 'he's home.' 'Then why can't I see him?' I asked her, out of patience. ''Cause he's dead,' says she. '*Dead*' says I. She just nodded her head, not getting a bit excited, but rockin' back and forth. 'Why – where is he?' says I, not knowing what to say. She just pointed upstairs – like that *(Himself pointing to the room above)*. I got up, with the idea of going up there. I walked from there to here – then I says, 'Why, what did he die of?' 'He died of a rope round his neck,' says she, and just went on pleating at her apron. Well, I went out and called Harry. I thought I might – need help. We went upstairs and there he was lyin' –

COUNTY ATTORNEY I think I'd rather have you go into that upstairs, where you can point it all out. Just go on now with the rest of the story.

HALE Well, my first thought was to get that rope off. It looked . . .*(Stops, his face twitches)* . . . but Harry, he went up to him, and he said, 'No, he's dead all right, and we'd better not touch anything.' So we went back down stairs. She was still sitting that same way. 'Has anybody been notified?' I asked. 'No,' says she, unconcerned. 'Who did this, Mrs Wright?' said Harry. He said is businesslike – and she stopped pleatin' of her apron. 'I don't know,' she says. 'You don't *know*?' says Harry. 'No,' says she. 'Weren't you sleepin' in the bed with him?' said Harry. 'Yes,' says she, 'but I was on the inside.'

'Somebody slipped a rope round his neck and strangled him and you didn't wake up?' says Harry. 'I didn't wake up,' she said after him. We must 'a looked as if we didn't see how that could be, for after a minute she said, 'I sleep sound.' Harry was going to ask her more questions but I said maybe we ought to let her tell her story first to the coroner, or the sheriff, so Harry went fast as he could to Rivers' place, where there's a telephone.

COUNTY ATTORNEY And what did Mrs Wright do when she knew that you had gone for the coroner?

HALE She moved from that chair to this one over here (*Pointing to a small chair in the corner*) and just sat there with her hands held together and looking down. I got a feeling that I ought to make some conversation, so I said I had come in to see if John wanted to put in a telephone, and at that she started to laugh, and then she stopped and looked at me – scared. (*The* COUNTY ATTORNEY, *who has had his notebook out, makes a note.*) I dunno, maybe it wasn't scared. I wouldn't like to say it was. Soon Harry got back, and then Dr. Lloyd came, and you, Mr Peters, and so I guess that's all I know that you don't.

COUNTY ATTORNEY (*Looking around*) I guess we'll go upstairs first – and then out to the barn and around there. (*To the* SHERIFF) You're convinced that there was nothing important here – nothing that would point to any motive.

SHERIFF Nothing here but kitchen things.

(*The* COUNTY ATTORNEY, *after again looking around the kitchen, opens the door of a cupboard closet. He gets up on a chair and looks on a shelf. Pulls his hand away, sticky.*)

COUNTY ATTORNEY Here's a nice mess.

(*The women draw nearer.*)

MRS PETERS (*To the other woman*) Oh, her fruit; it did freeze. (*To the* COUNTY ATTORNEY) She worried about that when it turned cold. She said the fire'd go out and her jars would break.

SHERIFF Well, can you beat the women! Held for murder and worryin' about her preserves.

COUNTY ATTORNEY I guess before we're through she may have something more serious than preserves to worry about.

HALE Well, women are used to worrying over trifles.

(*The two women move a little closer together.*)

COUNTY ATTORNEY (*With the gallantry of a young politician*) And yet, for all their worries, what would we do without the ladies? (*The women do not unbend. He goes to the sink, takes a dipperful of water from the pail and pouring it into a basin, washes his hands. Starts to wipe them on the roller towel, turns it for a cleaner place*) Dirty towels! (*Kicks his foot against the pans under the sink*) Not much of a housekeeper, would you say, ladies?

MRS HALE (*Stiffly*) There's a great deal of work to be done on a farm.

COUNTY ATTORNEY To be sure. And yet (*With a little bow to her*) I know there are some Dickson county farmhouses which do not have such roller towels. (*He gives it a pull to expose its full-length again.*)

MRS HALE Those towels get dirty awful quick. Men's hands aren't always as clean as they might be.

COUNTY ATTORNEY Ah, loyal to your sex, I see. But you and Mrs Wright were neighbors. I suppose you were friends, too.

MRS HALE *(Shaking her head)* I've not seen much of her of late years. I've not been in this house – it's more than a year.

COUNTY ATTORNEY And why was that? You didn't like her?

MRS HALE I liked her all well enough. Farmers' wives have their hands full, Mr Henderson. And then –

COUNTY ATTORNEY Yes – ?

MRS HALE *(Looking about)* It never seemed a very cheerful place.

COUNTY ATTORNEY No – it's not cheerful. I shouldn't say she had the homemaking instinct.

MRS HALE Well, I don't know as Wright had, either.

COUNTY ATTORNEY You mean that they didn't get on very well?

MRS HALE No, I don't mean anything. But I don't think a place'd by any cheerfuller for John Wright's being in it.

COUNTY ATTORNEY I'd like to talk more of that a little later. I want to get the lay of things upstairs now. *(He goes to the left, where three steps lead to a stair door.)*

SHERIFF I suppose anything Mrs Peters does'll be all right. She was to take in some clothes for her, you know, and a few little things. We left in such a hurry yesterday.

COUNTY ATTORNEY Yes, but I would like to see what you take, Mrs Peters, and keep an eye out for anything that might be of use to us.

MRS PETERS Yes, Mr Henderson.

(The women listen to the men's steps on the stairs, then look about the kitchen.)

MRS HALE I'd hate to have men coming into my kitchen, snooping around and criticising. *(She arranges the pans under the sink which the* COUNTY ATTORNEY *had shoved out of place.)*

MRS PETERS Of course it's no more than their duty.

MRS HALE Duty's all right, but I guess that deputy sheriff that came out to make the fire might have got a little of this on. *(Gives the roller towel a pull)* Wish I'd thought of that sooner. Seems mean to talk about her for not having things slicked up when she had to come away in such a hurry.

MRS PETERS *(Who has gone to a small table in the left rear corner of the room, and lifted one end of a towel that covers a pan)* She had bread set. *(Stands still)*

MRS HALE *(Eyes fixed on a loaf of bread beside the breadbox, which is on a low shelf at the other side of the room. Moves slowly toward it)* She was going to put this in there. *(Picks up loaf, then abruptly drops it. In a manner of returning to familiar things)* It's a shame about her fruit. I wonder if it's all gone. *(Gets up on the chair and looks)* I think there's some here that's all right, Mrs Peters. Yes – here; *(Holding it toward the window)* this is cherries, too. *(Looking again)* I declare I believe that's the only one. *(Gets down, bottle in her hand. Goes to the sink and wipes it off on the outside)* She'll feel awful bad after all her hard work in the hot weather. I remember the afternoon I put up my cherries last summer. *(She puts the bottle on the big kitchen table, enter of the room. With a sigh, is about to sit down in the rocking-chair. Before she is seated realizes what chair it is; with*

363

a slow look at it, steps back. The chair which she has touched rocks back and forth.)

MRS PETERS Well, I must get those things from the front room closet. *(She goes to the door at the right, but after looking into the other room, steps back.)* You coming with me, Mrs Hale? You could help me carry them.

(They go in the other room; reappear, MRS PETERS carrying a dress and skirt, MRS HALE following with a pair of shoes.)

MRS PETERS My, it's cold in there. *(She puts the clothes on the big table, and hurries to the stove.)*

MRS HALE *(Examining the skirt)* Wright was close. I think maybe that's why she kept so much to herself. She didn't even belong to the Ladies Aid. I suppose she felt she couldn't do her part and then you don't enjoy things when you feel shabby. She used to wear pretty clothes and be lively, when she was Minnie Foster, one of the town girls singing in the choir. But that – oh, that was thirty years ago. This all you was to take in?

MRS PETERS She said she wanted an apron. Funny thing to want, for there isn't much to get you dirty in jail, goodness knows. But I suppose just to make her feel more natural. She said they was in the top drawer in this cupboard. Yes, here. And then her little shawl that always hung behind the door. *(Opens stair door and looks)* Yes, here it is. *(Quickly shuts door leading upstairs)*

MRS HALE *(Abruptly moving toward her)* Mrs Peters?

MRS PETERS Yes, Mrs Hale?

MRS HALE Do you think she did it?

MRS PETERS *(In a frightened voice)* Oh, I don't know.

MRS HALE Well, I don't think she did. Asking for an apron and her little shawl. Worrying about her fruit.

MRS PETERS *(Starts to speak, glances up, where footsteps are heard in the room above. In a low voice)* Mr Peters says it looks bad for her. Mr Henderson is awful sarcastic in a speech and he'll make fun of her sayin' she didn't wake up.

MRS HALE Well, I guess John Wright didn't wake when they was slipping that rope under his neck.

MRS PETERS No, it's strange. It must have been done awful crafty and still. They say it was such a – funny way to kill a man, rigging it all up like that.

MRS HALE That's just what Mr Hale said. There was a gun in the house. He says that's what he can't understand.

MRS PETERS Mr Henderson said coming out that what was needed for the case was a motive; something to show anger, or – sudden feeling.

MRS HALE *(Who is standing by the table)* Well, I don't see any signs of anger around here. *(She puts her hand on the dish towel which lies on the table, stands looking down at table, one half of which is clean, the other half messy.)* It's wiped to here. *(Makes a move as if to finish work, then turns and looks at loaf of bread outside the breadbox. Drops towel. In that voice of coming back to familiar things)* Wonder how they are finding things upstairs. I hope she had it a little more red-up up there. You know, it seems kind of *sneaking*. Locking her up in town and then coming out here and trying to get her own house to turn against her!

MRS PETERS But Mrs Hale, the law is the law.

MRS HALE I s'pose 'tis *(Unbuttoning her coat)* Better loosen up your things, Mrs Peters. You won't feel them when you go out.

(MRS PETERS takes off her fur tippet, goes to hang it on hook at back of room, stands looking at the under part of the small corner table.)

MRS PETERS She was piecing a guilt. *(She brings the large sewing basket and they look at the bright pieces.)*

MRS HALE It's log cabin pattern. Pretty, isn't it? I wonder if she was goin' to quilt it or just knot it?

(Footsteps have been heard coming down the stairs. The SHERIFF enters followed by HALE and the COUNTY ATTORNEY.)

SHERIFF They wonder if she was going to quilt it or just knot it!

(The men laugh; the women look abashed.)

COUNTY ATTORNEY *(Rubbing his hands over the stove)* Frank's fire didn't do much up there, did it? Well, let's go out to the barn and get that cleared up.

(The men go outside.)

MRS HALE *(Resentfully)* I don't know as there's anything so strange, our takin' up our time with little things while we're waiting for them to get the evidence. *(She sits down at the big table smoothing out a block with decision.)* I don't see as it's anything to laugh about.

MRS PETERS *(Apologetically)* Of course they've got awful important things on their minds. *(Pulls up a chair and joins MRS HALE at the table)*

MRS HALE *(Examining another block)* Mrs Peters, look at this one. Here, this is the one she was working on, and look at the sewing! All the rest of it has been so nice and even. And look at this! It's all over the place! Why, it looks as if she didn't know what she was about!

(After she has said this they look at each other, then start to glance back at the door. After an instant MRS HALE has pulled at a knot and ripped the sewing.)

MRS PETERS Oh, what are you doing, Mrs Hale?

MRS HALE *(Mildly)* Just pulling out a stitch or two that's not sewed very good. *(Threading a needle)* Bad sewing always made me fidgety.

MRS PETERS *(Nervously)* I don't think we ought to touch things.

MRS HALE I'll just finish up this end. *(Suddenly stopping and leaning forward)* Mrs Peters?

MRS PETERS Yes, Mrs Hale?

MRS HALE What do you suppose she was so nervous about?

MRS PETERS Oh – I don't know. I don't know as she was nervous. I sometimes sew awful queer when I'm just tired. *(MRS HALE starts to say something, looks at MRS PETERS, then goes on sewing.)* Well, I must get these things wrapped up. They may be through sooner than we think. *(Putting apron and other things together)* I wonder where I can find a piece of paper, and string.

MRS HALE In that cupboard, maybe.

MRS PETERS *(Looking in cupboard)* Why, here's a bird-cage. *(Holds it up)* Did she have a bird, Mrs Hale?

MRS HALE Why, I don't know whether she did nor not – I've not been here for so long. There was a man around last year selling canaries cheap, but I don't know as she took one; maybe she did. She used to sing real pretty herself.

MRS PETERS *(Glancing around)* Seems funny to think of a bird here. But she must have had one, or why would she have a cage? I wonder what happened to it.

MRS HALE I s'pose maybe the cat got it.

MRS PETERS No, she didn't have a cat. She's got that feeling some people have about cats – being afraid of them. My cat got in her room and she was real upset and asked me to take it out.

MRS HALE My sister Bessie was like that. Queer, ain't it?

MRS PETERS *(Examining the cage)* Why, look at this door. It's broke. One hinge is pulled apart.

MRS HALE *(Looking too)* Looks as if someone must have been rough with it.

MRS PETERS Why, yes. *(She brings the cage forward and puts it on the table.)*

MRS HALE I wish if they're going to find any evidence they'd be about it. I don't like this place.

MRS PETERS But I'm awful glad you came with me, Mrs Hale. It would be lonesome for me sitting here alone.

MRS HALE It would, wouldn't it? *(Dropping her sewing)* But I tell you what I do wish, Mrs Peters. I wish I had come over sometimes when *she* was here. I – *(Looking around the room)* – wish I had.

MRS PETERS But of course you were awful busy, Mrs Hale – Your house and your children.

MRS HALE I could've come. I stayed away because it weren't cheerful – and that's why I ought to have come. I – I've never liked this place. Maybe because it's down in a hollow and you don't see the road. I dunno what it is, but it's a lonesome place and always was. I wish I had come over to see Minnie Foster sometimes. I can see now – *(Shakes her head)*

MRS PETERS Well, you mustn't reproach yourself, Mrs Hale. Somehow we just don't see how it is with other folks until – something comes up.

MRS HALE Not having children makes less work – but it makes a quiet house, and Wright out to work all day, and no company when he did come in. Did you know John Wright, Mrs Peters?

MRS PETERS Not to know him; I've seen him in town. They say he was a good man.

MRS HALE Yes – good; he didn't drink, and kept his word as well as most, I guess, and paid his debts. But he was a hard man, Mrs Peters. Just to pass the time of day with him – *(Shivers)* Like a raw wind that gets to the bone. *(Pauses, her eye falling on the cage)* I should think she would 'a wanted a bird. But what do you suppose went with it?

MRS PETERS I don't know, unless it got sick and died. *(She reaches over and swings the broken door, swings it again. Both women watch it.)*

MRS HALE You weren't raised round here, were you? *(MRS PETERS shakes her head.)* You didn't know – her?

MRS PETERS Not till they brought her yesterday.

MRS HALE She – come to think of it, she was kind of like a bird herself – real sweet and pretty, but kind of timid and – fluttery. How – she – did – change. *(Silence; then as if struck by a happy thought and relieved to get back to every day things)* Tell you what, Mrs Peters, why don't you take the quilt in with you? It might take up her mind.

MRS PETERS Why, I think that's a real nice idea, Mrs Hale. There couldn't possibly be any objection to it, could there? Now, just what would I take? I wonder if her patches are in here – and her things.

(They look in the sewing basket.)

MRS HALE Here's some red. I expect this has got sewing things in it. *(Brings out a fancy box)* What a pretty box. Looks like something somebody would give you. Maybe her scissors are in here. *(Opens box. Suddenly puts her hand to her nose)* Why – (MRS PETERS *bends nearer, then turns her face away.)* There's something wrapped up in this piece of silk.

MRS PETERS Why, this isn't her scissors.

MRS HALE *(Lifting the silk)* Oh, Mrs Peters – its – (MRS PETERS *bends closer.)*

MRS PETERS It's the bird.

MRS HALE *(Jumping up)* But, Mrs Peters – look at it! Its neck! Look at its neck! It's all – other side to.

MRS PETERS Somebody – wrung – its – neck.

(Their eyes meet. A look of growing comprehension, of horror. Steps are heard outside. MRS HALE slips box under quilt pieces, and sinks into her chair. Enter SHERIFF and COUNTY ATTORNEY. MRS PETERS rises.)

COUNTY ATTORNEY *(As one turning from serious things to little pleasantries)* Well, ladies, have you decided whether she was going to quilt it or knot it?

MRS PETERS We think she was going to – knot it.

COUNTY ATTORNEY Well, that's interesting, I'm sure. *(Seeing the birdcage)* Has the bird flown?

MRS HALE *(Putting more quilt pieces over the box)* We think the – cat got it.

COUNTY ATTORNEY *(Preoccupied)* Is there a cat?

(MRS HALE glances in a quick covert way at MRS PETERS.)

MRS PETERS Well, not now. They're superstitious, you know. They leave.

COUNTY ATTORNEY *(To SHERIFF PETERS, continuing an interrupted conversation)* No sign at all of anyone having come from the outside. Their own rope. Now let's go up again and go over it piece by piece. *(They start upstairs.)* It would have to have been someone who knew just the –

(MRS PETERS sits down. The two women sit there not looking at one another, but as if peering into something and at the same time holding back. When they talk now it is in the manner of feeling their way over strange ground, as if afraid of what they are saying, but as if they can not help saying it.)

MRS HALE She liked the bird. She was going to bury it in that pretty box.

MRS PETERS *(In a whisper)* When I was a girl – my kitten – there was a boy took a hatchet, and before my eyes – and before I could get there – *(Covers her face an instant)* If they hadn't held me back I would have – *(Catches herself, looks upstairs where steps are heard, falters weakly)* – hurt him.

MRS HALE *(With a slow look around her)* I wonder how it would seem never to have had any children around. *(Pause)* No, Wright wouldn't like the bird – a thing that sang. She used to sing. He killed that, too.

MRS PETERS *(Moving uneasily)* We don't know who killed the bird.

MRS HALE I knew John Wright.

MRS PETERS It was an awful thing was done in this house that night, Mrs Hale. Killing a man while he slept, slipping a rope around his neck that choked the life out of him.

MRS HALE His neck. Choked the life out of him. *(Her hand goes out and rests on the birdcage.)*

MRS PETERS *(With rising voice)* We don't know who killed him. We don't know.

MRS HALE *(Her own feeling not interrupted)* If there'd been years and years of nothing, then a bird to sing to you, it would be awful – still, after the bird was still.

MRS PETERS *(Something within her speaking)* I know what stillness is. When we homesteaded in Dakota, and my first baby died – after he was two years old, and me with no other then –

MRS HALE *(Moving)* How soon do you suppose they'll be through, looking for the evidence?

MRS PETERS I know what stillness is. *(Pulling herself back)* The law has got to punish crime, Mrs Hale.

MRS HALE *(Not as if answering that)* I wish you'd seen Minnie Foster when she wore a white dress with blue ribbons and stood up there in the choir and sang. *(A look around the room)* Oh, I *wish* I'd come over here once in a while! That was a crime! That was a crime! Who's going to punish that?

MRS PETERS *(Looking upstairs)* We mustn't – take on.

MRS HALE I might have known she needed help! I know how things can be – for women. I tell you, it's queer, Mrs Peters. We live close together and we live far apart. We all go through the same things – it's all just a different kind of the same thing. *(Brushes her eyes; noticing the bottle of fruit, reaches out for it)* If I was you I wouldn't tell her her fruit was gone. Tell her it *ain't*. She – she may never know whether it was broke or not.

MRS PETERS *(Takes the bottle, looks about for something to wrap it in; takes petticoat from the clothes brought from the other room, very nervously begins winding this around the bottle. In a false voice)* My, it's a good thing the men couldn't hear us. Wouldn't they just laugh! Getting all stirred up over a little thing like a – dead canary. As if that could have anything to do with – with – wouldn't they *laugh!*

(The men are heard coming down stairs.)

MRS HALE *(Under her breath)* Maybe they would – maybe they wouldn't.

COUNTY ATTORNEY No, Peters, it's all perfectly clear except a reason for doing it. But you know juries when it comes to women. If there was some definite thing. Something to show – something to make a story about – a thing that would connect up with this strange way of doing it –

(The women's eyes meet for an instant. Enter HALE from outer door.)

HALE Well, I've got the team around. Pretty cold out there.

COUNTY ATTORNEY I'm going to stay here a while by myself. *(To the SHERIFF)* You can send Frank out for me, can't you? I want to go over everything. I'm not satisfied that we can't do better.

SHERIFF Do you want to see what Mrs Peters is going to take in?

(The COUNTY ATTORNEY goes to the table, picks up the apron, laughs.)

COUNTY ATTORNEY Oh, I guess they're not very dangerous things the ladies have picked out. *(Moves a few things about, disturbing the quilt pieces which cover the box. Steps back)* No, Mrs Peters doesn't need supervising. For that matter, a sheriff's wife is married to the law. Ever think of it that way, Mrs Peters?

MRS PETERS Not – just that way.

SHERIFF *(Chuckling)* Married to the law. *(Moves toward the other room)* I just want you to come in here a minute, George. We ought to take a look at these windows.

COUNTY ATTORNEY *(Scoffingly)* Oh windows!

SHERIFF We'll be right out, Mr Hale.

(HALE goes outside. The SHERIFF follows the COIUNTY ATTORNEY into the other room. Then MRS HALE rises, hands tight together, looking intensely at MRS PETERS, whose eyes make a slow turn, finally meeting MRS HALE's. A moment MRS HALE holds her, then her own eyes point the way to where the box is concealed. Suddenly MRS PETERS throws back quilt pieces and tries to put the box in the bag she is wearing. It is too big. She opens box, starts to take bird out, cannot touch it, goes to pieces, stands there helpless. Sound of a knob turning in the other room. MRS HALE snatches the box and puts it in the pocket of her big coat. Enter COUNTY ATTORNEY and SHERIFF.)

COUNTY ATTORNEY *(Facetiously)* Well, Henry, at least we found out that she was not going to quilt it. She was going to – what is it you call it, ladies?

MRS HALE *(Her hand against her pocket)* We call it – knot it, Mr Henderson.

CURTAIN

A Jury of her Peers

by Susan Glaspell

From: O'Brien, E.J. (ed.) (1917) *The Best Short Stories of 1917*, Small Maynard and Co.

When Martha Hale opened the storm-door and got a cut of the north wind, she ran back for her big woolen scarf. As she hurriedly wound that round her head her eye made a scandalized sweep of her kitchen. It was no ordinary thing that called her away – it was probably farther from ordinary than anything that had ever happened in Dickson County. But what her eye took in was that her kitchen was in no shape for leaving: her bread all ready for mixing, half the flour sifted and half unsifted.

She hated to see things half done: but she had been at that when the team from town stopped to get Mr Hale, and then the sheriff came running in to say his wife wished Mrs Hale would come too – adding, with a grin, that he guessed she was getting scarey and wanted another woman along. So she had dropped everything right where it was.

'Martha!' now came her husband's impatient voice. 'Don't keep folks waiting out here in the cold.'

She again opened the storm-door, and this time joined the three men and the one woman waiting for her in the big two-seated buggy.

After she had the robes tucked around her she took another look at the woman who sat beside her on the back seat. She had met Mrs Peters the year before at the county fair, and the thing she remembered about her was that she didn't seem like a sheriff's wife. She was small and thin and didn't have a strong voice. Mrs Gorman, sheriff's wife before Gorman went out and Peters came in, had a voice that somehow seemed to be backing up the law with every word. But if Mrs Peters didn't look like a sheriff's wife, Peters made it up in looking like a sheriff. He was to a dot the kind of man who could get himself elected sheriff – a heavy man with a big voice, who was particularly genial with the law-abiding, as if to make it plain that he knew the difference between criminals and non-criminals. And right there it came into Mrs Hale's mind, with a stab, that this man who was so pleasant and lively with all of them was going to the Wrights' now as a sheriff.

'The country's not very pleasant this time of year,' Mrs Peters at last ventured, as if she felt they ought to be talking as well as the men.

Mrs Hale scarcely finished her reply, for they had gone up a little hill and could see the Wright place now, and seeing it did not make her feel like talking. It looked very lonesome this cold March morning. It had always been a lonesome-looking place. It was down in a hollow, and the poplar trees around it were lonesome-looking trees. The men were looking at it and talking about what had happened. The county attorney was bending to one side of the buggy, and kept looking steadily at the place as they drew up to it.

'I'm glad you came with me,' Mrs Peters said nervously, as the two women were about to follow the men in through the kitchen door.

Even after she had her foot on the door-step, her hand on the knob, Martha Hale had a moment of feeling she could not cross that threshold. And the reason it seemed she couldn't cross it now was simply because she hadn't crossed it before. Time and time again it had been in her mind, 'I ought to go over and see Minnie Foster' – she still thought of her as Minnie Foster, though for twenty years she had been Mrs Wright. And then there was always something to do and Minnie Foster would go from her mind. But *now* she could come.

The men went over to the stove. The women stood close together by the door. Young Henderson, the county attorney, turned around and said, 'Come up to the fire, ladies.'

Mrs Peters took a step forward, then stopped. 'I'm not – cold,' she said.

And so the two women stood by the door, at first not even so much as looking around the kitchen.

The men talked for a minute about what a good thing it was the sheriff had sent his deputy out that morning to make a fire for them, and then Sheriff Peters stepped back from the stove, unbuttoned his outer coat, and leaned his hands on the kitchen table in a way that seemed to mark the beginning of official business. 'Now, Mr Hale,' he said in a sort of semi-official voice, 'before we move things about, you tell Mr Henderson just what it was you saw when you came here yesterday morning.'

The county attorney was looking around the kitchen.

'By the way,' he said, 'has anything been moved?' He turned to the sheriff. 'Are things just as you left them yesterday?'

Peters looked from cupboard to sink; from that to a small worn rocker a little to one side of the kitchen table.

'It's just the same.'

'Somebody should have been left here yesterday,' said the county attorney.

'Oh – yesterday,' returned the sheriff, with a little gesture as of yesterday having been more than he could bear to think of. 'When I had to send Frank to Morris Center for that man who went crazy – let me tell you, I had my hands full *yesterday*. I knew you could get back from Omaha by to-day, George, and as long as I went over everything here myself –'

'Well, Mr Hale,' said the county attorney, in a way of letting what was past and gone go, 'tell just what happened when you came here yesterday morning.'

Mrs Hale, still leaning against the door, had that sinking feeling of the mother whose child is about to speak a piece. Lewis often wandered along and got things mixed up in a story. She hoped he would tell this straight and plain, and not say unnecessary things that would just make things harder for Minnie Foster. He didn't begin at once, and she noticed that he looked queer – as if standing in that kitchen and having to tell what he had seen there yesterday morning made him almost sick.

'Yes, Mr Hale?' the county attorney reminded.

'Harry and I had started to town with a load of potatoes,' Mrs Hale's husband began.

Harry was Mrs Hale's oldest boy. He wasn't with them now, for the very good reason that those potatoes never got to town yesterday and he was taking them this morning, so he hadn't been home when the sheriff stopped to say he wanted Mr Hale to come over to the Wright place and tell the county attorney his story there, where he could point it all out. With all Mrs Hale's other emotions came the fear now that maybe Harry wasn't dressed warm enough – they hadn't any of them realized how that north wind did bite.

'We come along this road,' Hale was going on, with a motion of his hand to the road over which they had just come, 'and as we got in sight of the house I says to Harry, "I'm goin' to see if I can't get John Wright to take a telephone." You see,' he explained to Henderson, 'unless I can get somebody to go in with me they won't come out this branch road except for a price I can't pay. I'd spoke to Wright about it once before; but he put me off, saying folks talked too much anyway, and all he asked was peace and quiet – guess you know about how much he talked himself. But I thought maybe if I went to the house and talked about it before his wife, and said all the women-folks liked the telephones, and that in this lonesome stretch of road it would be a good thing – well, I said to Harry that that was what I was going to say – though I said at the same time that I didn't know as what his wife wanted made much difference to John –'

Now, there he was! – saying things he didn't need to say. Mrs Hale tried to catch her husband's eye, but fortunately the county attorney interrupted with:

'Let's talk about that a little later, Mr Hale. I do want to talk about that, but I'm anxious now to get along to just what happened when you got here.'

When he began this time, it was very deliberately and carefully:

'I didn't see or hear anything. I knocked at the door. And still it was all quiet inside. I knew they must be up – it was past eight o'clock. So I knocked again, louder, and I thought I heard somebody say, "Come in." I wasn't sure – I'm not sure yet. But I opened the door – this door,' jerking a hand toward the door by which the two women stood, 'and there, in that rocker' – pointing to it – 'sat Mrs Wright.'

Every one in the kitchen looked at the rocker. It came into Mrs Hale's mind that that rocker didn't look in the least like Minnie Foster – the Minnie Foster of twenty years before. It was a dingy red, with wooden rungs up the back; and the middle rung was gone, and the chair sagged to one side.

'How did she – look?' the county attorney was inquiring.

'Well,' said Hale, 'she looked – queer.'

'How do you mean – queer?'

As he asked it he took out a note-book and pencil. Mrs Hale did not like the sight of that pencil. She kept her eye fixed on her husband, as if to keep him from saying unnecessary things that would go into that notebook and make trouble.

Hale did speak guardedly, as if the pencil had affected him too.

'Well, as if she didn't know what she was going to do next. And kind of – done up.'

'How did she seem to feel about your coming?'

'Why, I don't think she minded – one way or other. She didn't pay much attention. I said, "Ho' do, Mrs Wright? It's cold, ain't it?" And she said, "Is it?" – and went on pleatin' at her apron.

'Well, I was surprised. She didn't ask me to come up to the stove, or to sit down, but just set there, not even lookin' at me. And so I said: "I want to see John."

'And then she – laughed. I guess you would call it a laugh.

'I thought of Harry and the team outside, so I said, a little sharp, "Can I see John?" "No" says she – kind of dull like. "Ain't he home?" says I. Then she looked at me. "Yes," says she, "he's home." "Then why can't I see him?" I asked her, out of patience with her now. "'Cause he's dead," says she, just as quiet and dull – and fell to pleatin' her apron. "Dead?" says I, like you do when you can't take in what you've heard.

'She just nodded her head, not getting a bit excited, but rockin' back and forth.

'"Why – where is he?" says I, not knowing *what* to say.

'She just pointed upstairs – like this' – point to the room above.

'I got up, with the idea of going up there myself. By this time I – didn't know what to do. I walked from there to here; then I says: "Why, what did he die of?"

"He died of a rope round his neck," says she; and just went on pleatin' at her apron.'

Hale stopped speaking, and stood staring at the rocker, as if he were still seeing the woman who had sat there the morning before. Nobody spoke; it was as if every one were seeing the woman who had sat there the morning before.

'And what did you do then?' the county attorney at last broke the silence.

'I went out and called Harry. I thought I might – need help. I got Harry in, and we went upstairs.' His voice fell almost to a whisper. 'There he was – lying over the –'

'I think I'd rather have you go into that upstairs.' the county attorney interrupted, 'where you can point it all out. Just go on now with the rest of the story.'

'Well, my first thought was to get that rope off. It looked –'

He stopped, his face twitching.

'But Harry, he went up to him, and he said, "No, he's dead all right, and we'd better not touch anything." So we went downstairs.

'She was still sitting that same way. "Has anybody been notified?" I asked. "No," says she, unconcerned.

'"Who did this, Mrs Wright?" said Harry. He said it businesslike, and she stopped pleatin' at her apron. "I don't know," she says. "You don't *know*?" says Harry. "Weren't you sleepin' in the bed with him?" "Yes", says she, "but I was on the inside." "Somebody slipped a rope round his neck and strangled him, and you didn't wake up?" says Harry. "I didn't wake up," she said after him.

'We may have looked as if we didn't see how that could be, for after a minute she said, "I sleep sound."

'Harry was going to ask her more questions, but I said maybe that weren't our business; maybe we ought to let her tell her story first to the coroner or the sheriff. So Harry went fast as he could over to High Road – the Rivers' place, where there's a telephone.'

'And what did she do when she knew you had gone for the coroner?' The attorney got his pencil in his hand all ready for writing.

'She moved from that chair to this one over here' – Hale pointed to a small chair to the corner – 'and just sat there with her hands held together and looking down. I got a feeling that I ought to make some conversation, so I said I had come in to see if John wanted to put in a telephone; and at that she started to laugh, and then she stopped and looked at me – scared.'

At sound of a moving pencil the man who was telling the story looked up.

'I dunno – maybe it wasn't scared,' he hastened; 'I wouldn't like to say it was. Soon Harry got back, and then Dr Lloyd came, and you, Mr Peters, and so I guess that's all I know that you don't.'

He said that last with relief, and moved a little, as if relaxing. Every one moved a little. The county attorney walked toward the stair door.

'I guess we'll go upstairs first – then out to the barn and around there.'

He paused and looked around the kitchen.

'You're convinced there was nothing important here?' he asked the sheriff. 'Nothing that would – point to any motive?'

The sheriff too looked all around, as if to re-convince himself.

'Nothing here but kitchen things,' he said, with a little laugh for the insignificance of kitchen things.

The county attorney was looking at the cupboard – a peculiar, ungainly structure, half closet and half cupboard, the upper part of it being built in the wall, and the lower part just the old-fashioned kitchen cupboard. As if its queerness attracted him, he got a chair and opened the upper part and looked in. After a moment he drew his hand away sticky.

'Here's a nice mess,' he said resentfully.

The two women had drawn nearer, and now the sheriff's wife spoke.

'Oh – her fruit,' she said, looking to Mrs Hale for sympathetic understanding. She turned back to the county attorney and explained: 'She worried about that when it turned so cold last night. She said the fire would go out and her jars might burst.'

Mrs Peters' husband broke into a laugh.

'Well, can you beat the women! Held for murder, and worrying about her preserves!'

The young attorney set his lips.

'I guess before we're through with her she may have something more serious than preserves to worry about.'

'Oh, well,' said Mrs Hale's husband, with good-natured superiority, 'women are used to worrying over trifles.'

The two women moved a little closer together. Neither of them spoke. The county attorney seemed suddenly to remember his manners – and think of his future.

'And yet,' said he, with the gallantry of a young politician, 'for all their worries, what would we do without the ladies?'

The women did not speak, did not unbend. He went to the sink and began washing his hands. He turned to wipe them on the roller towel – whirled it for a cleaner place.

'Dirty towels! Not much of a housekeeper, would you say, ladies?'

He kicked his foot against some dirty pans under the sink.

'There's a great deal of work to be done on a farm,' said Mrs Hale stiffly.

'To be sure. And yet' – with a little bow to her – 'I know there are some Dickson County farm-houses that do not have such roller towels.' He gave it a pull to expose its full length again.

'Those towels get dirty awful quick. Men's hands aren't always as clean as they might be.'

'Ah, loyal to your sex, I see,' he laughed. He stopped and gave her a keen look. 'But you and Mrs Wright were neighbors. I suppose you were friends, too.'

Martha Hale shook her head.

'I've seen little enough of her of late years. I've not been in this house – it's more than a year.'

'And why was that? You didn't like her?'

'I liked her well enough,' she replied with spirit. 'Farmers' wives have their hands full, Mr Henderson. And then –' She looked around the kitchen.

'Yes?' he encouraged.

'It never seemed a very cheerful place,' said she, more to herself than to him.

'No,' he agreed; 'I don't think any one would call it cheerful. I shouldn't say she had the home-making instinct.'

'Well, I don't know as Wright had, either,' she muttered.

'You mean they didn't get on very well?' he was quick to ask.

'No; I don't mean anything,' she answered, with decision. As she turned a little away from him, she added: 'But I don't think a place would be any the cheerfuler for John Wright's bein' in it.'

'I'd like to talk to you about that a little later, Mrs Hale,' he said. 'I'm anxious to get the lay of things upstairs now.'

He moved toward the stair door, followed by the two men.

'I suppose anything Mrs Peters does'll be all right?' the sheriff inquired. 'She was to take in some clothes for her, you know – and a few little things. We left in such a hurry yesterday.'

The county attorney looked at the two women whom they were leaving alone there among the kitchen things.

'Yes – Mrs Peters,' he said, his glance resting on the woman who was not Mrs Peters, the big farmer woman who stood behind the sheriff's wife. 'Of course Mrs Peters is one of us,' he said, in a manner of entrusting responsibility. 'And keep your eye out, Mrs Peters, for anything that might be of use. No telling; you women might come upon a clue to the motive – and that's the thing we need.'

Mr Hale rubbed his face after the fashion of a show man getting ready for a pleasantry.

'But would the women know a clue if they did come upon it?' he said; and, having delivered himself of this, he followed the others through the stair door.

The women stood motionless and silent, listening to the footsteps, first upon the stairs, then in the room above them.

Then, as if releasing herself from something strange, Mrs Hale began to arrange the dirty pans under the sink, which the county attorney's disdainful push of the foot had deranged.

'I'd hate to have men comin' into my kitchen,' she said testily – 'snoopin' round and criticizin'.'

'Of course it's no more than their duty,' said the sheriff's wife, in her manner of timid acquiescence.

'Duty's all right,' replied Mrs Hale bluffly; 'but I guess that deputy sheriff that come out to make the fire might have got a little of this on.' She gave the roller towel a pull. 'Wish I'd thought of that sooner! Seems mean to talk about her for not having things slicked up, when she had to come away in such a hurry.'

She looked around the kitchen. Certainly it was not 'slicked up.' Her eye was held by a bucket of sugar on a low shelf. The cover was off the wooden bucket, and beside it was a paper bag – half full.

Mrs Hale moved toward it.

'She was putting this in there,' she said to herself – slowly.

She thought of the flour in her kitchen at home – half sifted, half not sifted. She had been interrupted, and had left things half done. What had interrupted Minnie Foster? Why had that work been left half done? She made a move as if to finish it, – unfinished things always bothered her, – and then she glanced around and saw that Mrs Peters was watching her – and she didn't want Mrs Peters to get that feeling she had got of work begun and then – for some reason – not finished.

'It's a shame about her fruit,' she said, and walked toward the cupboard that the county attorney had opened, and got on the chair, murmuring: 'I wonder if it's all gone.'

It was a sorry enough looking sight but 'Here's one that's all right,' she said at last. She held it toward the light. 'This is cherries, too.' She looked again. 'I declare I believe that's the only one.'

With a sigh, she got down from the chair, went to the sink, and wiped off the bottle.

'She'll feel awful bad, after all her hard work in the hot weather. I remember the afternoon I put up my cherries last summer.'

She set the bottle on the table, and, with another sigh, started to sit down in the rocker. But she did not sit down. Something kept her from sitting down in that chair. She straightened – stepped back, and, half turned away, stood looking at it, seeing the woman who had sat there 'pleatin' at her apron'.

The thin voice of the sheriff's wife broke in upon her: 'I must be getting those things from the front room closet.' She opened the door into the other room, started in, stepped back. 'You coming with me, Mrs Hale?' she asked nervously. 'You – you could help me get them.'

They were soon back – the stark coldness of that shut-up room was not a thing to linger in.

'My!' said Mrs Peters, dropping the things on the table and hurrying to the stove.

Mrs Hale stood examining the clothes the woman who was being detained in town had said she wanted.

'Wright was close!' she exclaimed, holding up a shabby black skirt that bore the marks of much making over. 'I think maybe that's why she kept so much to herself. I s'pose she felt she couldn't do her part; and then, you don't enjoy things when you feel shabby. She used to wear pretty clothes and be lively – when she was Minnie Foster, one of the town girls, singing in the choir. But that – oh, that was twenty years ago.'

With a carefulness in which there was something tender, she folded the shabby clothes and piled them at one corner of the table. She looked up at Mrs Peters, and there was something in the other woman's look that irritated her.

'She don't care,' she said to herself. 'Much difference it makes to her whether Minnie Foster had pretty clothes when she was a girl.'

Then she looked again, and she wasn't so sure; in fact, she hadn't at any time been perfectly sure about Mrs Peters. She had that shrinking manner, and yet her eyes looked as if they could see a long way into things.

'This all you was to take in?' asked Mrs Hale.

'No,' said the sheriff's wife; 'she said she wanted an apron. Funny thing to want,' she ventured in her nervous little way, 'for there's not much to get you dirty in jail, goodness knows. But I suppose just to make her feel more natural. If you're used to wearing an apron – . She said they were in the bottom drawer of this cupboard. Yes – here they are. And then her little shawl that always hung on the stair door.'

She took the small gray shawl from behind the door leading upstairs, and stood a minute looking at it.

Suddenly Mrs Hale took a quick step toward the other woman.

'Mrs Peters!'

'Yes, Mrs Hale?'

'Do you think she – did it?'

A frightened look blurred the other thing in Mrs Peters' eyes.

'Oh, I don't know,' she said, in a voice that seemed to shrink away from the subject.

'Well, I don't think she did,' affirmed Mrs Hale stoutly. 'Asking for an apron, and her little shawl. Worryin' about her fruit.'

'Mr Peters says – .' Footsteps were heard in the room above; she stopped, looked up, then went on in a lowered voice: 'Mr Peters says – it looks bad for her. Mr Henderson is awful sarcastic in a speech, and he's going to make fun of her saying she didn't – wake up.'

For a moment Mrs Hale had no answer. Then, 'Well, I guess John Wright didn't wake up – when they was slippin' that rope under his neck,' she muttered.

'No, it's *strange*,' breathed Mrs Peters. 'They think it was such a – funny way to kill a man.'

She began to laugh; at sound of the laugh, abruptly stopped.

'That's just what Mr Hale said,' said Mrs Hale, in a resolutely natural voice. 'There was a gun in the house, He says that's what he can't understand.'

'Mr Henderson said, coming out, that what was needed for the case was a motive. Something to show anger – or sudden feeling.'

'Well, I don't see any signs of anger around here,' said Mrs Hale. 'I don' – '

She stopped. It was as if her mind tripped on something. Her eye was caught by a dish-towel in the middle of the kitchen table. Slowly she moved toward the table. One half of it was wiped clean, the other half messy. Her eyes made a slow, almost unwilling turn to the bucket of sugar and the half empty bag beside it. Things begun – and not finished.

After a moment she stepped back, and said, in that manner of releasing herself:

'Wonder how they're finding things upstairs? I hope she had it a little more red up up there. You know,' – she paused, and feeling gathered, –'it seems kind of *sneaking*: locking her up in town and coming out here to get her own house to turn against her!'

'But, Mrs Hale,' said the sheriff's wife, 'the law is the law.'

'I s'pose 'tis,' answered Mrs Hale shortly.

She turned to the stove, saying something about that fire not being much to brag of. She worked with it a minute, and when she straightened up she said aggressively:

'The law is the law – and a bad stove is a bad stove. How'd you like to cook on this?' – pointing with the poker to the broken lining. She opened the oven door and started to express her opinion of the oven; but she was swept into her own thoughts, thinking of what it would mean, year after year, to have that stove to wrestle with. The thought of Minnie Foster trying to bake in that oven – and the thought of her never going over to see Minnie Foster – .

She was startled by hearing Mrs Peters say: 'A person gets discouraged – and loses heart.'

The sheriff's wife had looked from the stove to the sink – to the pail of water which had been carried in from outside. The two women stood there silent, above them the footsteps of the men who were looking for evidence against the woman who had worked in that kitchen. That look of seeing into things, of seeing through a thing to something else, was in the eyes of the sheriff's wife now. When Mrs Hale next spoke to her, it was gently:

'Better loosen up your things, Mrs Peters. We'll not feel them when we go out.'

Mrs Peters went to the back of the room to hang up the fur tippet she was wearing. A moment later she exclaimed, 'Why, she was piecing a quilt,' and held up a large sewing basket piled high with quilt pieces.

Mrs Hale spread some of the blocks out on the table.

'It's log-cabin pattern,' she said, putting several of them together. 'Pretty, isn't it?'

They were so engaged with the quilt that they did not hear the footsteps on the stairs. Just as the stair door opened Mrs Hale was saying:

'Do you suppose she was going to quilt it or just knot it?'

The sheriff threw up his hands.

'They wonder whether she was going to quilt it or just knot it!'

There was a laugh for the ways of women, a warming of hands over the stove, and then the county attorney said briskly:

'Well, let's go right out to the barn and get that cleared up.'

'I don't see as there's anything so strange,' Mrs Hale said resentfully, after the outside door had closed on the three men – 'our taking up our time with little things while we're waiting for them to get the evidence. I don't see as it's anything to laugh about.'

'Of course they've got awful important things on their minds,' said the sheriff's wife apologetically.

They returned to an inspection of the block for the quilt. Mrs Hale was looking at the fine, even sewing, and preoccupied with thoughts of the woman who had done that sewing, when she heard the sheriff's wife say, in a queer tone:

'Why, look at this one.'

She turned to take the block held out to her.

'The sewing,' said Mrs Peters, in a troubled way. 'All the rest of them have been so nice and even – but – this one. Why, it looks as if she didn't know what she was about!'

Their eyes met – something flashed to life, passed between them; then, as if with an effort, they seemed to pull away from each other. A moment Mrs Hale sat there, her hands folded over that sewing which was so unlike all the rest of the sewing. Then she had pulled a knot and drawn the threads.

'Oh, what are you doing, Mrs Hale?' asked the sheriff's wife, startled.

'Just pulling out a stitch or two that's not sewed very good,' said Mrs Hale mildly.

'I don't think we ought to touch things,' Mrs Peters said, a little helplessly.

'I'll just finish up this end,' answered Mrs Hale, still in that mild, matter-of-fact fashion.

She threaded a needle and started to replace bad sewing with good. For a little while she sewed in silence. Then, in that thin, timid voice, she heard:

'Mrs Hale!'

'Yes, Mrs Peters?'

'What do you suppose she was so – nervous about?'

'Oh, *I* don't know,' said Mrs Hale, as if dismissing a thing not important enough to spend much time on. 'I don't know as she was – nervous. I sew awful queer sometimes when I'm just tired.'

She cut a thread, and out of the corner of her eye looked up at Mrs Peters. The small, lean face of the sheriff's wife seemed to have tightened up. Her eyes had that look of peering into something. But next moment she moved, and said in her thin, indecisive way:

'Well, I must get those clothes wrapped. They may be through sooner than we think. I wonder where I could find a piece of paper – and string.'

'In that cupboard, maybe,' suggested Mrs Hale, after a glance around.

One piece of the crazy sewing remained unripped. Mrs Peters' back turned, Martha Hale now scrutinized that piece, compared it with the dainty, accurate sewing of the other blocks. The difference was startling. Holding this block made her feel queer, as if the distracted thoughts of the woman who had perhaps turned to it to try and quiet herself were communicating themselves to her.

Mrs Peters' voice roused her.

'Here's a bird-cage,' she said. 'Did she have a bird, Mrs Hale?'

'Why, I don't know whether she did nor not.' She turned to look at the cage Mrs Peter was holding up. 'I've not been here in so long.' She sighed. 'There was a man round last year selling canaries cheap – but I don't know as she took one. Maybe she did. She used to sing real pretty herself.'

Mrs Peters looked around the kitchen.

'Seems kind of funny to think of a bird here.' She half laughed – an attempt to put up a barrier. 'But she must have had one – or why would she have a cage? I wonder what happened to it.'

'I suppose maybe the cat got it,' suggested Mrs Hale, resuming her sewing.

'No; she didn't have a cat. She's got that feeling some people have about cats – being afraid of them. When they brought her to our house yesterday, my cat got in the room, and she was real upset and asked me to take it out.'

'My sister Bessie was like that,' laughed Mrs Hale.

The sheriff's wife did not reply. The silence made Mrs Hale turn round. Mrs Peters was examining the bird-cage.

'Look at this door,' she said slowly. 'It's broke. One hinge has been pulled apart.'

Mrs Hale came nearer.

'Looks as if some one must have been – rough with it.'

Again their eyes met – startled, questioning, apprehensive. For a moment neither spoke nor stirred. Then Mrs Hale, turning away, said brusquely:

'If they're going to find any evidence, I wish they'd be about it. I don't like this place.'

'But I'm awful glad you came with me, Mrs Hale.' Mrs Peters put the bird-cage on the table and sat down. 'It would be lonesome for me – sitting here alone.'

'Yes, it would, wouldn't it?' agreed Mrs Hale, a certain determined naturalness in her voice. She had picked up the sewing, but now it dropped in her lap, and she murmured in a different voice: 'But I tell you what I *do* wish, Mrs Peters. I wish I had come over sometimes when she was here. I wish – I had.'

'But of course you were awful busy, Mrs Hale. Your house – and your children.'

'I could've come,' retorted Mrs Hale shortly. 'I stayed away because it weren't cheerful – and that's why I ought to have come. I' – she looked around – 'I've never liked this place. Maybe cause it's down in a hollow and you don't see the road. I don't know what it is, but it's a lonesome place, and always was. I wish I had come over to see Minnie Foster sometimes. I can see now –' She did not put it into words.

'Well, you mustn't reproach yourself,' counseled Mrs Peters. 'Somehow, we just don't see how it is with other folks till – something comes up.'

'Not having children makes less work,' mused Mrs Hale, after a silence, 'but it makes a quiet house – and Wright out to work all day – and no company when he did come in. Did you know John Wright, Mrs Peters?'

'Not to know him. I've seen him in town. They say he was a good man.'

'Yes – good,' conceded John Wright's neighbor grimly. 'He didn't drink, and kept his word as well as most, I guess, and paid his debts. But he was a hard man, Mrs Peters. Just to pass the time of day with him – .' She stopped, shivered a little. 'Like a raw wind that gets to the bone.' Her eye fell upon the cage on the table before her, and she added, almost bitterly: 'I should think she would've wanted a bird!'

Suddenly she learned forward, looking intently at the cage. 'But what do you s'pose went wrong with it?'

'I don't know,' returned Mrs Peters; 'unless it got sick and died.'

But after she said it she reached over and swung the broken door. Both women watched it as if somehow held by it.

'You didn't know – her?' Mrs Hale asked, a gentler note in her voice.

'Not till they brought her yesterday,' said the sheriff's wife.

'She – come to think of it, she was kind of like a bird herself. Real sweet and pretty, but kind of timid and – fluttery. How – she – did – change.'

That held her for a long time. Finally, as if struck with a happy thought and relieved to get back to everyday things, she exclaimed:

'Tell you what, Mrs Peters, why don't you take the quilt in with you? It might take up her mind.'

'Why, I think that's a real nice idea, Mrs Hale,' agreed the sheriff's wife, as if she too were glad to come into the atmosphere of a simple kindness. 'There couldn't possibly be any objection to that, could there? Now, just what will I take? I wonder if her patches are in here – and her things.'

They turned to the sewing basket.

'Here's some red,' said Mrs Hale, bringing out a roll of cloth. Underneath that was a box. 'Here, maybe her scissors are in here – and her things.' She held it up. 'What a pretty box! I'll warrant that was something she had a long time ago – when she was a girl.'

She held it in her hand a moment; then, with a little sigh, opened it.

Instantly her hand went to her nose.

'Why –!'

Mrs Peters drew nearer – then turned away.

'There's something wrapped up in this piece of silk,' faltered Mrs Hale.

'This isn't her scissors,' said Mrs Peters, in a shrinking voice.

Her hand not steady, Mrs Hale raised the piece of silk. 'Oh, Mrs Peters!' she cried. 'It's –'

Mrs Peters bent closer.

'It's the bird,' she whispered.

'But, Mrs Peters!' cried Mrs Hale. '*Look* at it! Its *neck* – look at its neck! It's all – other side *to*.'

She held the box away from her.

The sheriff's wife again bent closer.

'Somebody wrung its neck,' said she, in a voice that was slow and deep.

And then again the eyes of the two women met – this time clung together in a look of dawning comprehension, of growing horror. Mrs Peters looked from the dead bird to the broken door of the cage. Again their eyes met. And just then there was a sound at the outside door.

Mrs Hale slipped the box under the quilt pieces in the basket, and sank into the chair before it. Mrs Peters stood holding to the table. The county attorney and the sheriff came in from outside.

'Well, ladies,' said the county attorney, as one turning from serious things to little pleasantries, 'have you decided whether she was going to quilt it or knot it?'

'We think,' began the sheriff's wife in a flurried voice, 'that she was going to – knot it.'

He was too preoccupied to notice the change that came in her voice on that last.

'Well, that's very interesting, I'm sure,' he said tolerantly. He caught sight of the bird-cage. 'Has the bird flown?'

'We think the cat got it,' said Mrs Hale in a voice curiously even.

He was walking up and down, as if thinking something out.

'Is there a cat?' he asked absently.

Mrs Hale shot a look up at the Sheriff's wife.

'Well, not *now*,' said Mrs Peters. 'They're superstitious, you know; they leave.'

She sank into her chair.

The county attorney did not heed her. 'No sign at all of any one having come in from the outside,' he said to Peters, in the manner of continuing an interrupted conversation. 'Their own rope. Now let's go upstairs again and go over it, piece by piece. It would have to have been some one who knew just the –'

The stair door closed behind them and their voices were lost.

The two women sat motionless, not looking at each other, but as if peering into something and at the same time holding back. When they spoke now it was as if they were afraid of what they were saying, but as if they could not help saying it.

'She liked the bird,' said Martha Hale, low and slowly. 'She was going to bury it in that pretty box.'

'When I was a girl,' said Mrs Peters, under her breath, 'my kitten – there was a boy took a hatchet, and before my eyes – before I could get there –' She covered her face an instant. 'If they hadn't held me back I would have' – she caught herself, looked upstairs where footsteps were heard, and finished weakly – 'hurt him.'

Then they sat without speaking or moving.

'I wonder how it would seem,' Mrs Hale at last began, as if feeling her way over strange ground – 'never to have had any children around?' Her eyes made a slow sweep of the kitchen, as if seeing what that kitchen had meant through all the years. 'No, Wright wouldn't like the bird,' she said after that – 'a thing that sang. She used to sing. He killed that too.' Her voice tightened.

Mrs Peters moved uneasily.

'Of course we don't know who killed the bird.'

'I knew John Wright,' was Mrs Hale's answer.

'It was an awful thing was done in this house that night, Mrs Hale,' said the sheriff's wife. 'Killing a man while he slept – slipping a thing round his neck that choked the life out of him.'

Mrs Hale's hand went out to the bird-cage.

'His neck. Choked the life out of him.'

'We don't *know* who killed him,' whispered Mrs Peters wildly. 'We don't *know.*'

Mrs Hale had not moved. 'If there had been years and years of – nothing, then a bird to sing to you, it would be awful – still – after the bird was still.'

It was as if something within her not herself had spoken, and it found in Mrs Peters something she did not know as herself.

'I know what stillness is,' she said, in a queer, monotonous voice. 'When we homesteaded in Dakota, and my first baby died – after he was two years old – and me with no other then –'

Mrs Hale stirred.

'How soon do you suppose they'll be through looking for the evidence?'

'I know what stillness is,' repeated Mrs Peters, in just that same way. Then she too pulled back. 'The law has got to punish crime, Mrs Hale,' she said in her tight little way.

'I wish you'd seen Minnie Foster,' was the answer, 'when she wore a white dress with blue ribbons, and stood up there in the choir and sang.'

The picture of that girl, the fact that she had lived neighbor to that girl for twenty years, and had let her die for lack of life, was suddenly more than she could bear.

'Oh, I *wish* I'd come over here once in a while!' she cried. 'That was a crime! That was a crime! Who's going to punish that?'

'We mustn't take on,' said Mrs Peters, with a frightened look toward the stairs.

'I might 'a' *known* she needed help! I tell you, it's *queer*, Mrs Peters. We live close together, and we live far apart. We all go through the same things – it's all just a different kind of the same thing! If it weren't – why do you and I *understand?* Why do we *know* – what we know this minute?'

She dashed her hand across her eyes. Then, seeing the jar of fruit on the table, she reached for it and choked out:

'If I was you I wouldn't *tell* her her fruit was gone! Tell her it *ain't.* Tell her it's all right – all of it. Here – take this in to prove it to her! She – she may never know whether it was broke or not.'

She turned away.

Mrs Peters reached out for the bottle of fruit as if she were glad to take it – as if touching a familiar thing, having something to do, could keep her from something else. She got up, looked about for something to wrap the fruit in, took a petticoat from the pile of clothes she had brought from the front room, and nervously started winding that round the bottle.

'My! she began, in a high, false voice, 'it's a good thing the men couldn't hear us! Getting all stirred up over a little thing like a – dead canary.' She hurried over that. 'As if that could have anything to do with – with – My, wouldn't they *laugh?*

Footsteps were heard on the stairs.

'Maybe they would,' muttered Mrs Hale – 'maybe they wouldn't.'

'No, Peters,' said the county attorney incisively; 'it's all perfectly clear, except the reason for doing it. But you know juries when it comes to women. If there was some definite thing – something to show. Something to make a story about. A thing that would connect up with this clumsy way of doing it.'

In a covert way Mrs Hale looked at Mrs Peters. Mrs Peters was looking at her. Quickly they looked away from each other. The outer door opened and Mr Hale came in.

'I've got the team round now,' he said. 'Pretty cold out there.'

'I'm going to stay here awhile by myself,' the county attorney suddenly announced. 'You can send Frank out for me, can't you?' he asked the sheriff. 'I want to go over everything. I'm not satisfied we can't do better.'

Again, for one brief moment, the two women's eyes found one another.

The sheriff came up to the table.

'Did you want to see what Mrs Peters was going to take in?'

The county attorney picked up the apron. He laughed.

'Oh, I guess they're not very dangerous things the ladies have picked out.'

Mrs Hale's hand was on the sewing basket in which the box was concealed. She felt that she ought to take her hand off the basket. She did not seem able to. He picked up one of the quilt blocks which she had piled on to cover the box. Her eyes felt like fire. She had a feeling that if he took up the basket she would snatch it from him.

But he did not take it up. With another little laugh, he turned away, saying:

'No; Mrs Peters doesn't need supervising. For that matter, a sheriff's wife is married to the law. Ever think of it that way, Mrs Peters?'

Mrs Peters was standing beside the table. Mrs Hale shot a look up at her; but she could not see her face. Mrs Peters had turned away. When she spoke, her voice was muffled.

'Not – just that way,' she said.

'Married to the law"' chuckled Mrs Peters' husband. He moved toward the door into the front room, and said to the county attorney:

'I just want you to come in here a minute, George. We ought to take a look at these windows.'

'Oh – windows,' said the county attorney scoffingly.

'We'll be right out, Mr Hale,' said the sheriff to the farmer, who was still waiting by the door.

Hale went to look after the horses. The sheriff followed the county attorney into the other room. Again – for one final moment – the two women were alone in that kitchen.

Martha Hale sprang up, her hands tight together, looking at that other woman, with whom it rested. At first she could not see her eyes, for the sheriff's wife had not turned back since she turned away at that suggestion of being married to the law. But now Mrs Hale made her turn back. Her eyes made her turn back. Slowly, unwillingly, Mrs Peters turned her head until her eyes met the eyes of the other woman. There was a moment when they held each other in a steady, burning look in which there was no evasion nor flinching. Then Martha Hale's eyes pointed the way to the basket in which was hidden the thing that would make certain the conviction of the other woman – that woman who was not there and yet who had been there with them all through that hour.

For a moment Mrs Peters did not move. And then she did it. With a rush forward, she threw back the quilt pieces, got the box, tried to put it in her handbag. It was too big. Desperately she opened it, started to take the bird out. But there she broke – she could not touch the bird. She stood there helpless, foolish.

There was the sound of a knob turning in the inner door. Martha Hale snatched the box from the sheriff's wife, and got it in the pocket of her big coat just as the sheriff and the county attorney came back into the kitchen.

'Well, Henry,' said the county attorney facetiously, 'at least we found out that she was not going to quilt it. She was going to – what is it you call it, ladies?'

Mrs Hale's hand was against the pocket of her coat.

'We call it – knot it, Mr Henderson.'

Bibliography

Abrams, M.H. (1981) *A Glossary of Literary Terms*, Holt, Rinehart and Winston.

Alcott, L.M. (1991 edn) *Moods* ed. and intro. S. Elbert, Rutgers University Press.

Alkalay-Gut, K. (Winter 1984) '"A Jury of her Peers ": the importance of trifles', *Studies in Short Fiction*, 21.1, pp.1–9.

Angelou, M. (1993) 'Voices of respect' in *Wouldn't Take Nothing for My Journey Now*, Random House.

Aston, E. and Savona, G. (1993) *Theatre as Sign System*, Routledge.

Atwood, M. (1991) 'True Trash' in *Wilderness Tips*, Bloomsbury.

Baker, H.A. (1991) *Workings of the Spirit: The Poetics of Afro-American Women's Writing*, The University of Chicago Press.

Bargainnier, E.F. (ed.) (1981) *Ten Women of Mystery*, Bowling Green State University Press.

Barlow, J.E. (ed.) (1985) *Plays by American Women: The Early Years*, Applause Books.

Barrett, M. (ed.) (1993) *Virginia Woolf: On Women and Writing: Her Essays, Assessments and Arguments*, The Women's Press.

Barthelme, G., Paley, G. and Percy, W. (Winter 1976) 'A Symposium on Fiction', *Shenandoah*, 27.2, pp.3–31.

Batey, M. (1980) *Alice's Adventures in Oxford*, Pitkin Pictorials.

Battersby, C. (1989) *Gender and Genius,* The Women's Press.

Ben-Zvi, L. (May 1992) '"Murder, She Wrote": the genesis of Susan Glaspell's *Trifles*', *Theatre Journal,* 44, pp.141–62.

Bigsby, C.W.E. (1980) 'The Second Black Renaissance: essays in black literature ' in *Contributions in Afro–American and African Studies*, No.50, The Greenwood Press.

Blain, V., Clements, P. and Grundy, I. (eds) (1990) *The Feminist Companion to Literature in English*, Yale University Press.

Boddy, K. 'An Interview with Susan Minot', unpublished, London, 13 February 1990.

Boireau, N. (1996) *Drama On Drama*, MacMillan.

Bonner, F. (ed.) (1992) *Imagining Women: Cultural Representations and Gender*, Polity Press.

Brabazon, J. (1981) *Dorothy L. Sayers: A Biography*, Charles Scribner's Sons.

Brantley, B. (June 28, 1994) 'Why Oz is a state of mind in gay life and drag shows', *The New York Times*, p.C19.

Braxton, J.M. and McLaughlin, A.N. (eds) (1990) *Wild Women in the Whirlwind: Afro-American Culture and the Contemporary Literary Renaissance*, Rutgers University Press.

Brewster, Y. (ed.) (1987, 1989) *Black Plays*, 2 vols, Methuen.

Brontë, C. (1973 edn) *Jane Eyre*, Oxford University Press; first published under the pseudonym Currer Bell in 1847.

Broun, H. (14 November 1916) 'Best bill seen at the comedy', *New York Tribune*, p.7.

Busby, M. (1981) *Daughters of Africa*, Random House.

Byatt, A.S. (1991) *Possession: A Romance*, Vintage Books.

Byrd, R.P. (1990) 'Spirituality in the novels of Alice Walker: models, healing, and transformation, or when the spirit moves so do we', in J.M. Braxton and A.N. McLaughlin (eds) *Wild Women in the Whirlwind*, pp.363ff.

Carlson, M. (1993) *Deathtraps: The Post-Modern Comedy Thriller*, Indiana University Press.

Carroll, L. (1977 edn) *Alice's Adventures in Wonderland* and *Through the Looking-Glass* in *Lewis Carroll: Complete Works*, with the original illustrations by Sir John Tenniel, Nonesuch Press.

Carter, A. (ed.) (1986) *Wayward Girls and Wicked Women,* Virago.

Cheney, E.D.L. (ed.) (1889) *L.M. Alcott: Her Life, Letters and Journals,* Roberts Brothers; held by the Berg Collection of the New York Public Library.

Cheney, E.D.L. (1890) *Nora's Return: A Sequel to 'The Doll's House' of Henry Ibsen,* Lee and Shepard.

Cherland, M. (1994) *Girls Reading Gender: Fiction and the Construction of Identity,* Taylor and Francis.

Cherry, D. and Pollock, G. (June 1984) 'Woman as sign in Pre-Raphaelite literature: a study of the representation of Elizabeth Siddall', *Art History,* vol.7 no.2.

Churchill, C. (1991) *Top Girls,* with commentary and notes by Bill Naismith, Methuen; *Top Girls* was first published in 1982.

Churchill, C. (1995) in interview with Lizbeth Goodman, see *Approaching* Top Girls BBC/Open University video.

Cima, G. G. (1993) *Performing Women: Female Characters, Male Playwrights and the Modern Stage,* Cornell University Press.

Cixous, H. (1975) 'The laugh of the Medusa', in E. Marks and I. de Courtrivron (eds.) (1981) *New French Feminisms: An Anthology,* Harvester.

Cixous, H. and .Clément, C. (1983) *The Newly Born Woman;* translated by Betsy Wing, introduction by Sandra Gilbert, University of Minnesota Press; and 1986 edn Manchester University Press; first published as *La Jeune Née* in 1975.

Costello, B. (1991) *Elizabeth Bishop: Questions of Mastery,* Harvard University Press.

Daniels, S. (1991) *Masterpieces,* Methuen.

Davis, A. (1984) *Women, Culture and Politics,* Random House.

Davis, A. (1981) *Women, Race and Class,* Random House.

Digby, J. (1993) 'Transformations in *The Color Purple* in P. Reynolds (ed.) *Novel Images: Literature in Performance,* Routledge.

Douglas, A. (1983) Introduction to *Little Women,* NAL.

Durkin, K. (1985) *Television, Sex Roles and Children: A Developmental Social Psychological Analysis,* The Open University Press.

Dymkowski, C. (March 1988) 'On the edge: the plays of Susan Glaspell', *Modern Drama,* 31.1, pp.91–105.

Egan, M. (ed.) (1972) *Ibsen: The Critical Heritage,* Routledge.

Fell, A. (ed.) (1992) *Serious Hysterics,* Serpent's Tail.

Felman, S. (1975) 'Women and madness: the critical phallacy', *Diacritics* 5, pp.2–10.

Felsi, R. (1989) *Beyond Feminine Aesthetics: Feminist Literature and Social Change* Harvard University Press.

Ferguson, M.A. (ed.) (1973) *Images of Women in Literature,* Houghton Mifflin.

Ferris, L. (ed.) (1993) *Crossing the Stage,* Routledge.

Fetterley, J. (1986) 'Reading about reading: "A Jury of her Peers", "The Murders in the Rue Morgue" and "The Yellow Wallpaper"', in E.A. Flynn and P.P. Schweickart (eds) *Gendered Reading: Essays on Readers, Texts and Contexts,* The Johns Hopkins University Press, pp.147–164.

Findlay, D. (1995), interview with Lizbeth Goodman, see *Approaching* Top Girls, Open University/BBC video.

Fitzgerald, F.S. (1960 edn) *The Last Tycoon,* Penguin; first published in 1941.

Frame, J. (1984) *An Angel at my Table,* Hutchinson.

Gainor, J.E. (1996) *The Plays of Susan Glaspell: A Contextual Study,* The University of Michigan Press.

Garber, S. (1992) *Vested Interests,* Routledge

Gardner, V. and Rutherford, S. (1992) *The New Woman and Her Sisters: Feminism and Theatre 1850–1914,* Harvester Wheatsheaf.

George, K. (ed.) (1993) *Six Plays by Black and Asian Women Writers*, Aurora Metro Press.

Gilbert, S. and Gubar, S. (1978) *The Madwoman in the Attic: The Woman Writer and the Nineteenth-Century Literary Imagination*, Yale University Press.

Gilbert, S. and Gubar, S. (eds) (1985) *Norton Anthology of Literature by Women*, Norton

Gilman, C.P. (1987 edn) *The Living of Charlotte Perkins Gilman*, Ayer; first published in 1935.

Gilman, C.P. (1994 edn) *Women and Economics: A Study of the Economic Relations Between Women and Men*, Prometheus Books; first published in 1898.

Glaspell, S. (1927) *The Road to the Temple*, Frederick A. Stokes.

Goldensohn, L. (1992) *Elizabeth Bishop: The Biography of a Poetry*, Columbia University Press.

Goodman, L. (1996) *Feminist Stages: Interviews with Women in Contemporary Theatre*, Harwood Academic Press.

Goodman, L. (1996) 'Overlapping dialogue in overlapping media', in Rabillard (ed.) *Caryl Churchill*, forthcoming publication.

Goodman, L. (1993) *Contemporary Feminist Theatres*, Routledge.

Goodman, L. (1997) *Mythic Women/Real Women*, Faber and Faber.

Gordimer, N. (1968) 'South Africa', International Symposium on the Short Story, *Kenyon Review* 30, pp.457–61.

Grauerholz, E. and Pescosolido, B. (March 1989) 'Gender representation in children's literature', *Gender and Society*, pp.113–125.

Green, J. (1989), *The Realist Novel*, The Women's Press.

Grewal, S. (1988) *Charting the Journey: Writings by Black and Third World Women*, Sheba Feminist Publishers.

Griffiths, V. (1986) *Using Gender to Get at Drama*, Studies in Sexual Politics Series, no. 9 (series ed. L. Stanley and S. Scott), University of Manchester Press.

Griffiths, V. (1990) 'Using drama to get at gender' in L. Stanley (ed.) *Feminist Praxis,* Routledge.

Gubar, S. and Hedin, A. (December 1981) 'A jury of our peers: teaching and learning in the Indiana Women's Prison', *College English*, 43.8 pp.779–89.

Hare, D. (1988) *The Secret Rapture,* Faber and Faber.

Hedges, E. (1973) Afterword to C.P. Gilman, *The Yellow Wallpaper*, Virago.

Heilbrun, C. (1988) *Writing a Woman's Life*, Ballantine Books.

Higonnet, M. (1986) '"Speaking silences" – women's suicides', in S. Suleiman (ed.) *The Female Body in Western Culture*, Harvard University Press.

Hirsch M. and Fox Keller, E. 'Mary Childers and bell hooks: A conversation about race and class' in Hirsch and Fox Keller (eds.) (1990) *Conflicts in Feminism*, Routledge, pp.60–81.

Hornblow, A. (Jan. 1917) 'Mr. Hornblow goes to the play', *The Theatre*, 21.

Horvitz, S. (1983) 'My Lady of Shalott', *Journal of Pre-Raphaelite Studies*, 3, pp. 64–8.

Hulse, M., Kennedy, D. and Morley, D. (1993) *The New Poetry,* Bloodaxe Books.

Hyam, (1990) *Empire and Sexuality: The British Experience*, Manchester University Press.

Ibsen, H. (1992 edn) *A Doll's House*, anonymous undated English translation from around 1900, Dover Publications.

Ibsen, H. (1981 edn) *Four Major Plays*, translated by J.W. McFarlane and J. Arup, Oxford University Press.

Ishiguru, K. (1989) *The Remains of the Day,* Faber and Faber.

Jacobus, M. (Spring 1981) review article in *Signs*, p.517.

Jacobus, M. (1992) 'An unnecessary maze of sign-reading' in C. Golden (ed.) *The Casebook on The Yellow Wallpaper*, The Feminist Press; first published in M. Jacobus (ed.) (1986) *Reading Woman*, Columbia University Press.

Jacobus, M. (1979) *Women and Madness*, Croom Helm.

Jones, A.R. (1985) 'Writing the body: toward an understanding of *l'écriture féminine* in E. Showalter (ed.) *The New Feminist Criticism: Essays on Women, Literature and Theory*, Pantheon.

Joseph G.I. and Lewis, J. (1981) *Common Differences: Conflicts in Black and White Feminist Perspectives*, Anchor Press/Doubleday.

Joyce, J. (1971 edn) *Chamber Music*, Cape; first published in 1907.

Kaplan, C. (1986) 'Keeping the color in *The Color Purple*', in *Sea Changes: Essays on Culture and Feminism*, Verso.

Kiernan, R.F. (1983) *American Writing Since 1984: A Critical Survey*, Fredrick Ungar Publishing Co.

King, W. and Milner, R. (1972) *Black Drama Anthology*, Columbia University Press

Koedt, A., Lavine E. and Rapone, A. (eds.) (1973) 'A feminist look at children's books', *Radical Feminism*, Quadrangle Books, pp. 94–106.

Kolodny, A. (1985) 'A map for rereading: gender and the interpretation of literary texts' in Showalter (ed.) *The New Feminist Criticisms: Essays on Women, Literature and Theory*, Pantheon Books, pp.46–62.

Ladies of Shalott: A Victorian Masterpiece and its Contexts (exh. cat.) (1985), Brown University Department of Art.

Lanser, S. (Fall 1989) 'Feminist criticism, "The Yellow Wallpaper" and the politics of color in America', *Feminist Studies*, 15, no.3, pp.420–22.

Lawrence, D. H. (1950) *St. Mawr*, Penguin; first published in 1925.

Le Guin, U. (1968) *The Earthsea Trilogy*, Parnassus Press.

Leighton, A. (1992) *Victorian Women Poets*, Harvester Wheatsheaf.

Leonard, T. (1990) *Radical Renfrew: Poetry from the French Revolution to the First World War by Poets Born or Sometime Residentin the County of Renfrewshire*, Polygon.

Lorde, A. (1984) *Sister Outsider*, The Crossing Press.

Manville, L. (1995) interview with Lizbeth Goodman, see *Approaching* Top Girls, Open University/BBC video.

Marks, E. and de Courtrivron, I. (eds) (1981) *New French Feminisms: An Anthology*, Harvester.

Marks, E. and de Courtivron, I. (1981) 'The Laugh of the Medusa' in Marks and de Courtivron (eds) *New French Feminisms*, Harvester.

Martin, R. B. (1969) *Tennyson: The Unquiet Heart*, Clarendon Press.

McDowell, D.E. (1993) 'It's not safe. Not safe at all': sexuality in Nella Larsen's *Passing* in E. Halperin (ed.) *The Lesbian and Gay Studies Reader*, Routledge, pp.616–27.

Merrin, J. (1990) *An Enabling Humility: Marianne Moore, Elizabeth Bishop and the Uses of Tradition*, Rutgers University Press.

Meyer, M. (1992) *Ibsen*, Cardinal Books.

Miles, R. (1987) *The Female Form: Women Writers and the Conquest of the Novel*, Routledge.

Millier, B.C. (1993) *Elizabeth Bishop: Life and the Memory of It*, University of California Press.

Mitchell, J. (1984) *Women: The Longest Revolution: On Feminism, Literature and Psychoanalysis*, Pantheon Books.

Morris, M. (1988) 'Feminism, reading, postmodernism' in Morris (ed.) *The Pirate's Fiancé: Feminism, reading, postmodernism*, Verso.

Morrison, T. (1992) *Playing in the Dark: Whiteness and the Literary Imagination*, Harvard University Press.

Murray, I. (1985) Introduction to *Original Prints: New Writing from Scottish Women*, Polygon.

Naismith, B. (1991) *Commentary and Notes to Caryl Churchill's* Top Girls, Methuen Student Edition.

Noe, M. (1983) *Susan Glaspell: Voices from the Heartland*, Western Illinois University Press.

O'Connor, F. (1963) *The Lonely Voice: A Study of the Short Story*, Harper and Row.

Okri, B. (1991) *The Famished Road*, Cape.

Olsen, T. (1965) *Silences*, Dell.

Omnibus (1986) 'Alice Walker and *The Color Purple*', BBC television, Executive Producers Leslie Megahey and Alan Yentob; Director, Samira Osmain.

Ormond, L. (1993) *Alfred Tennyson: A Literary Life*, Macmillan

Paley, G. (1987) *Later the Same Day*, Harmondsworth.

Paley, G. (Winter 1986) 'Of poetry and women and the world', *TriQuarterly, no.* 65, pp.247–53.

Paley, G. (1980) 'Debts', in *Enormous Changes at the Last Minute*, Virago.

Paretsky, S. (ed.) (1992) *A Woman's Eye*, Virago.

Parker, R.D. (1988) *The Poetry of Elizabeth Bishop*, University of Illinois Press.

Plath, S. (1981 edn) 'The Bull of Bendylaw' in *Collected Poems*, Faber and Faber.

Pratt, M.L. (June 1981) 'The short story: the long and the short of it', *Poetics*, vol.10, nos2–3, pp.175–91.

Pre-Raphaelite Illustrations from Moxon's Tennyson (1978) (exh. cat.), Academy Editions.

Rahn, B.J. (1988) 'Seeley Regester: America's first detective novelist', in B.A. Rader and H.G. Zettler (eds) *The Sleuth and the Scholar: Origins, Evolution, and Current Trends in Detective Fiction*, Greenwood Press, pp.47–61.

Reddy, M.T. (1988) *Sisters in Crime: Feminism and the Crime Novel*, Continuum.

Rhys, J. (1968 edn) *Wide Sargasso Sea*, Penguin; first published in 1966.

Ricks, C. (1969) *The Poems of Tennyson*, Longman

Rose, S. (1991) *The Haunting of Sylvia Plath*, Virago.

Rothstein, (10 November 1986) 'Interview with Alice Munro', *New York Times*.

Rushin K. (1993) *The Black Back–Ups*, Firebrand Books.

Sewall, R.B. (1979) *The Life of Emily Dickinson*, Faber.

Sharp, L. (1995) interview with L. Goodman, Open University/BBC video *Top Girls*.

Shaw, B. (1972 edn) *Pygmalion*, in *Collected Plays*, vol. iv; first performed privately in London, 1902, and publicly in Birmingham, 1925.

Shockley, A.A. (1988) *Afro-American Women Writers 1746–1933: An Anthology and Critical Guide*, G.K. Hall and Co.

Showalter, E. (1986) 'Piecing and writing' in Miller (ed.) *The Poetics of Gender*, Columbia University Press, pp.222–47.

Showalter, E. (1991) *Sister's Choice: Tradition and Change in American Women's Writing*, Oxford University Press.

Showalter, E. (1987) *The Female Malady: Women, Madness, and English Culture, 1830–1980*, Virago.

Showalter, E. (1985) 'Representing Ophelia: women, madness, and the responsibilities of feminist criticism' in P. Parker and G. Hartman (eds.) *Shakespeare and the Question of Theory*, Methuen, pp. 77–94.

Showalter, E. 'Piecing and Quilting', in Showalter, E. (ed.) (1988) *Alternative Alcott*, Rutgers University Press.

Smith, B. (ed.) (1993) *Home Girls: A Black Feminist Anthology*, Kitchen Table/Women of Color Press.

Spender, D. and Hayman C. (eds) (1985) *How the Vote Was Won and Other Suffragette Plays*, Methuen.

Spender, D. (1986) *Mothers of the Novel*, Pandora Press.

Spivak, G.C. (Autumn 1985) 'Three women's texts and a critique of Imperialism', *Critical Inquiry*, 12, pp. 243–61.

Sprinchorn, E. (1980) 'Ibsen and the actors' in Durbach (ed.) *Ibsen and the Theatre*, Macmillan.

Stafford-Clark, M. (1995) interview with Lizbeth Goodman for the Open University/BBC video *Top Girls* .

Stanton, M. (1990) *Sandor Ferenczi: Reconsidering Active Intervention*, Free Association Books.

Stasio, M. 'A sweep through the subgenres' in B.A. Rader and H.G. Zettler (eds) *The Sleuth and the Scholar: Origins, Evolution, and Current Trends in Detective Fiction*, Greenwood Press, pp.69–75.

Stein, K.F. (1981) 'The women's world of Glaspell's *Trifles*' in H.K. Chinoy and L.W. Jenkins (eds) *Women in American Theatre*, Crown Publishers, pp.251–54.

Stern, M. (ed.) (1975) *Behind a Mask and Other Thrillers by Louisa May Alcott*, Quill.

Stern, M. (ed.) (1975 and 1984) *The Hidden Louisa May Alcott*, Avenel Books; first published in two volumes).

Stern, M., Myerson, J. and Shealy, D. (1989) *The Journals of Louisa May Alcott*, Little, Brown and Company.

Stimpson, C. (1990) 'Black Culture/White Teacher' in Stimpson (ed.) *Where the Meanings Are: Feminism and Cultural Spaces*, Routledge; the essay was first published 1970.

Stowell, S. (1992) *A Stage of Their Own: Feminist Playwrights of the Suffrage Era*, Manchester University Press.

Street, D. (ed.) (1983) *Children's Novels and the Movies*, Frederick Ungar Publishing.

Sweeney, S.E. (1990) 'Locked rooms: detective fiction, narrative theory, and self-reflexivity' in R.G. Walker and J.M. Frazer (eds) *The Cunning Craft: Original Essays on detective Fiction and Contemporary Literary Theory*, Western Illinois University Press, pp.1–14.

Todd, J. (1988) *Feminist Literary History*, Polity Press.

Tomalin, C. (1988) *Katherine Mansfield: A Secret Life*, Penguin.

Törnqvist, Egil (1995) *Ibsen: A Doll's House*, Cambridge University Press.

Travisano, T.J. (1989) *Elizabeth Bishop: Her Artistic Development*, University of Virginia Press

Tripp, D. (1986) *Children and Television*, Polity Press.

Tuttle, L. (ed.) (1987) *The Encyclopedia of Feminism*, Arrow Books.

Velissariou, A. (1993) 'Mental illness and the problem of female identity in Ibsen' in Redmond (ed.) *Themes in Drama*, vol. 15: *Madness in Drama*, Cambridge University Press.

Walder, D. (ed.) (1996) *The Realist Novel*, Routledge in association with The Open University.

Walker, A. (1983) *The Color Purple*, The Women's Press.

Walker, A. (1984) 'Saving the life that is your own', in *In Search of our Mother's Gardens: Womanist Prose*; the essay was written in 1976.

Walker, A., *In Search of our Mother's Gardens: Womanist Prose*, The Women's Press, 1984.

Waugh, P. (1995) *Harvest of the Sixties: English Literature and its Background: 1960 to 1990*, Oxford University Press.

Wertenbaker, T. (1991) *Three Birds Alighting on a Field*, The Royal Court Theatre Script series, published in association with Faber and Faber.

Williams, L.R. 'Feminist reproduction and matrilineal thought', in I. Armstrong (ed.) (1992) *New Feminist Discourses*, Routledge.

Willis, S. (1990) 'Alice Walker's women' in *Specifying: Black Women Writing the American Experience*, Routledge.

Wisker, G. (1993) *Black Women's Writing*, Macmillan.

Wolf, N. (1991) *The Beauty Myth, How Images of Beauty are Used Against Women*, Vintage Books.

Woolf, V. (1977 edn) *A Room of One's Own*, Panther; first published in 1929 by Harcourt Brace Jovanovich.

Woolf, V. (1992 edn) 'Women novelists' in *A Woman's Essays*, Harmondsworth: first published in the *Times Literary Supplement*, 17 October 1918.

Woolf, V. (19 May 1923), review article, *Times Literary Supplement*.

Woolf, V. (1991 edn) *Nurse Lugton's Curtain*, illustrated by Julie Vivas, Gulliver Books.

Wright, E. (ed.) (1992) *Feminism and Psychoanalysis*, Blackwell.

Wright, R. (1964) 'The literature of the negro in the United States' in *White Man Listen,* Garden City.

Audio and video material produced in association with this book

Gender and Poetry (1995) BBC/Open University audio cassette. Presented by Lizbeth Goodman with interviews by Angus Calder, produced by Mags Noble.

Behind a Mask: Women's Writing and Women's Lives (1995) BBC/Open University television programme. Presented by Lizbeth Goodman, produced by Mags Noble.

Gender and Drama (1995) BBC/Open University audio cassette, including a performance of Susan Glaspell's *Trifles*. Presented by Lizbeth Goodman, produced by Mags Noble.

A Doll's House (1995) BBC/Open University audio cassettes (2), produced by Jenny Bardwell.

A Doll's House (1995) BBC/Open University video, with scenes directed by Tony Coe and extracts from David Thacker's production. Presented by Lizbeth Goodman and Richard Allen, produced by Mags Noble.

Approaching Top Girls (1995) BBC/Open University video, including Max Stafford-Clark's 1991 televised production. Introduction and interviews presented by Lizbeth Goodman, produced by Mags Noble.

Acknowledgements

Grateful acknowledgement is made to the following sources for permission to re-produce material in this book:

Plath, S. 'The Bull of Bendylaw' from *The Colossus and Other Poems* by Sylvia Plath, Faber and Faber Ltd, copyright © 1962 by Sylvia Plath. Reprinted by permission of Alfred A. Knopf Inc. and Faber and Faber Ltd; Joyce, J. (1907) 'Chamber Music' from *Chamber Music*, 9th impression, 1964, Jonathan Cape with acknowledgement to the Estate of James Joyce; Byatt, A.S. (1991), 'The Fairy Melusine' from *Possession: A Romance*, Chatto & Windus. Reprinted by permission of Peters Fraser and Dunlop Group Ltd.; *Alternative Alcott*, Elaine Showalter (ed.), copyright © 1988 by Rutgers, The State University. Reprinted by permission of Rutgers University Press; Gilman, C.P. 1899, *The Yellow Wallpaper*, Small, Maynard, Boston, in *The Yellow Wallpaper* with afterword by Elaine R. Hedges, Copyright © 1973 by The Feminist Press; Gilbert, S.M. and Gubar, S. 1979, 'The Yellow Wallpaper' in *The Madwoman in the Attic*, Yale University Press; the extract from 'Writing *The Color Purple*' is from *In Search of Our Mothers' Gardens* by Alice Walker, first published by the Women's Press Ltd, 1984, 34 Great Sutton Street, London EC1V 0DX, by permission of David Higham Associates Ltd, and from 'Writing *The Color Purple*' in *In Search of Our Mothers' Gardens: Womanist Prose*, copyright © 1982 by Alice Walker, reprinted by permission of Harcourt Brace & Company; Digby, J. 1993, 'From Walker to Spielberg: Transformations of *The Color Purple*' from Reynolds, P. 1993, *Novel Images: Literature in Performance*, Routledge; the poem 'Dear Alice' is from *In Search of Our Mothers' Gardens* by Alice Walker, first published by the Women's Press Ltd, 1984, 34 Great Sutton Street, London EC1V 0DX, by permission of David Higham Associates Ltd; extract from 'Writing *The Color Purple*' from *In Search of Our Mothers' Gardens: Womanist Prose*, copyright © 1982 by Alice Walker, reprinted by permission of Harcourt Brace & Company; Glaspell, S. 1917, 'A Jury of Her Peers', from O'Brien, E.J. (ed.) 1917, *The Best Short Stories of 1917*, Small, Maynard and Company; Glaspell, S., 1916, *Trifles: A Play in one Act* from Barlow, J.E. (ed.) 1985, *Plays by American Women: The Early Years*, Applause Theatre Book Publishers; Gardner, V., 1992, 'Introduction' from Gardner, V. and Rutherford, S. (eds) 1992, *The New Woman and her Sisters: Feminism and Theatre 1850–1914*, Prentice Hall and University of Michigan Press; 'The Gentleman of Shalott' from *The Complete Poems 1927–1979* by Elizabeth Bishop. Copyright © 1979, 1983 by Alice Helen Methfessel. Reprinted by permission of Farrar, Straus & Giroux, Inc.; 'The Reincarnation of Captain Cook' from *The Animals in That Country* by Margaret Atwood. Copyright © Oxford University Press Canada 1968. Reprinted by permission of Oxford University Press Canada; Plath, S. 'The Colossus' from *The Colossus and Other Poems* by Sylvia Plath, Faber and Faber Ltd, copyright © 1962 by Sylvia Plath. Reprinted by permission of Alfred A. Knopf Inc. and Faber and Faber Ltd; Plath, S. 'Lady Lazarus' from *Ariel* by Sylvia Plath, Faber and Faber Ltd, copyright © 1981 by Sylvia Plath. Reprinted by permission of Faber and Faber Ltd; de Souza, E., 'Autobiographical' from *Ways of Belonging*, Polygon; Adcock, F. (1983), 'Against Coupling' from *Fleur Adcock's Selected Poems*, Oxford University Press; Boland, E. (1990), 'Hanging Curtains with an Abstract Pattern in a Child's Room' from *Outside History*, Carcanet Press Limited; Duffy, C. A. (1993) 'Sleeping' from *Mean Time* by Carol Ann Duffy, Anvill Press Poetry; the poem 'Reflection' by Menna Elfyn is from *In the Gold of Flesh: Poems of Birth and Motherhood* edited by Rosemary Palmeira, first published by The Women's Press Ltd, 1990, 34 Great Sutton Street, London EC1V 0DX; Kay, J. (1991), 'The Telling Part'. Reprinted by permission of Bloodaxe Books Ltd from *The Adoption Papers* by Jackie Kay (Bloodaxe Books,

1991); Nichols, G. (1989) 'Wherever I Hang' from *Lazy Thoughts of a Lazy Woman*, Virago; Rushin, K. (1993), 'The Bridge Poem' from *The Black Back-Ups*, Firebrand Books, Ithaca, New York. Copyright © 1993 by Kate Rushin; Rich, A. (1972) 'Dialogue' from *Making for the Open: The Chatto Book of Post-Feminist Poetry 1964–1984* Chatto & Windus; 'Sojourner Truth, 1797–1883, USA' adapted to poetry by Erlene Stetson, from *Ain't I A Woman: Women's Poetry from Around the World*, Linthwaite, F. (ed.) 1988 Peter Bedrick Books; Feinstein, E. (1977), 'Anniversary' from *Selected Poems* 1994 Carcanet Press Limited; ni Dhomnaill, N. (1990), 'Ce'st na Teangan' translated by Muldoon, P., from *New Poetry* The Gallery Press; Gilman, C. P. 1899, *The Yellow Wallpaper*, Small, Maynard, Boston, in *The Yellow Wallpaper (with afterward)* by Elaine R. Hedges, Copyright © 1973 by The Feminist Press; Woolf, V. 1944, 'The New Dress' from *A Haunted House and Other Short Stories* copyright 1944 and renewed by Harcourt Brace and Company, reprinted by permission of the publisher and by permission of The Hogarth Press, Random House UK Ltd; Kincaid, J. 1984, 'Girl' from *At the Bottom of the River*, Farrar, Straus & Giroux Inc.

Research for this book was supported by an Honorary Visiting Scholarship awarded to Lizbeth Goodman for the Literature and Gender Project, by the Schlesinger Library for the History of Women in America, 1994–1995; thanks to Eva Mosley, Diane Hamer, Wendy Thomas and the rest of the Schlesinger Staff. Thanks are also due to the following institutions: Lesley Morris at the Houghton Library, Harvard University; Maria Powers, Jan Baranchuck, and the staff of Orchard House; The Emily Dickinson Homestead, Amherst, Massachussetts; the family in Wellesley, Massachusetts whose hospitality shall not be forgotten; Karen Kukil and Barbara Blumenthal of the Mortimer Rare Books Room, Plath and Woolf archives, at Neilson Library, Smith College; Holly Hall and Kevin Day at the Department of Special Collections, Olin Library, Washington University, St. Louis; Stephen Crook, Frank Mattison and Liz Smith at the Berg Collection, the New York Public Library; The Photos and Prints Archives of the Schomburg Center for Black Culture, Harlem, New York; The Museum of American Folkart, New York; Connie Cullen at the Hudson River Museum, Yonkers, New York; The Tisch School of Arts, New York University; The Department of Theatre, Cornell University; The Royal Court Theatre, London; Max Stafford-Clark and Out of Joint Productions, London; Syvita, resident in 1994 of Sylvia Plath's former bedroom at Whitstead, Newnham College, Cambridge; Peter Sparkes, Domestic Bursar at Girton College, Cambridge.

Index

397

Printed in the USA/Agawam, MA
February 11, 2010